VERITAS

Also by Ariel Sabar

My Father's Paradise: A Son's Search for His Family's Past

"... not to me. My mother gave me life ...
... " The disciples said to Jesus, "...
... deny. Mary is (not?) worthy of it ...
... " Jesus said to them, "My wife ...
... she is able to be my disciple ...
... Let wicked people swell up ...
... As for me, I dwell with her in order to ...
... an image ...

... my mother
... three
... [*undecipherable*]
... forth ...
... [*undecipherable*]
... [*undecipherable*]

VERITAS

A HARVARD PROFESSOR,

A CON MAN

AND THE GOSPEL OF JESUS'S WIFE

Ariel Sabar

DOUBLEDAY *NEW YORK*

All rights reserved. Published in the United States by Doubleday,
a division of Penguin Random House LLC, New York, and distributed in Canada
by Penguin Random House Canada Limited, Toronto. Simultaneously published
in Great Britain by Scribe UK, London.

www.doubleday.com

DOUBLEDAY and the portrayal of an anchor with a dolphin
are registered trademarks of Penguin Random House LLC.

Front-of-jacket photograph © Denis Tangney Jr / iStock / Getty Images Plus
Jacket design by John Fontana

Library of Congress Cataloging-in-Publication Data
Names: Sabar, Ariel, author.
Title: Veritas: a Harvard professor, a con man and the Gospel of Jesus's Wife /
by Ariel Sabar.
Description: First edition. | New York City: Doubleday,
a division of Penguin Random House LLC, [2019] |
Includes bibliographical references and index.
Identifiers: LCCN 2019029679 (print) | LCCN 2019029680 (ebook) |
ISBN 9780385542586 (hardcover) | ISBN 9780385542593 (ebook)
Subjects: LCSH: King, Karen L., 1954– |
Jesus Christ—Words—Extra-canonical parallels. | Gospel of Jesus's Wife—Manuscripts
(Papyri)—Forgeries. | Coptic manuscripts (Papyri)—Forgeries. | Forgery of antiquities. |
Forgery of manuscripts.
Classification: LCC BS2970 .S235 2019 (print) |
LCC BS2970 (ebook) | DDC 229/.8—dc23
LC record available at https://lccn.loc.gov/2019029679
LC ebook record available at https://lccn.loc.gov/2019029680

MANUFACTURED IN THE UNITED STATES OF AMERICA

1   3   5   7   9   10   8   6   4   2

First Edition

We search after truth. We see but in part.

—THOMAS HOLLIS,
BENEFACTOR OF HARVARD'S HOLLIS CHAIR OF DIVINITY, 1720

CONTENTS

PROLOGUE

Rome

On September 18, 2012, a group of international scholars gathered in a building across from the Vatican for an obscure academic conference on Egypt's earliest Christians. The weeklong program looked much like those of years past, with highly specialized lectures on Egyptian linguistics, monastery libraries and the wills of abbots. But at 7:00 that evening, the conference lost any semblance of the ordinary. A senior Harvard University professor rose to the lectern to make an astonishing announcement, one that a select group of journalists was at that very moment transmitting across the globe: she had discovered an ancient scrap of papyrus with the power to convulse the Roman Catholic Church.

The professor, a fifty-eight-year-old historian named Karen King, was a well-known and deeply respected figure in the field of biblical studies. Harvard had recently promoted her to its Hollis Professorship of Divinity, the oldest endowed chair in America and one of the most prestigious posts in the study of Christianity. She was familiar to the public, too, as a best-selling author and TV commentator on the first centuries of the faith.

But the events of September 2012 would put her in a brighter—and crueler—spotlight than any she had known before. In a room overlooking the dome of St. Peter's Basilica, King told the audience of elite scholars that she had already given her discovery a name.

"I dubbed it—just simply for reference purposes—'The Gospel of Jesus's Wife.'"

NINE MONTHS EARLIER, a middle-aged Florida man settled into a window seat in the first row of a midday Delta Air Lines flight to Boston's

Logan International Airport. In his luggage were four tattered scraps of papyrus, one of them small enough to fit in the palm of his hand.

When he arrived at Harvard Divinity School, Karen King gave him a tour of its Gothic grounds. A highlight, for the man, was a row of windows on the top floor of the theological library. The stained glass depicted a goblet-bearing woman, Cupid aiming an arrow, and a half-naked Jesus beneath riven skies—a peculiar patchwork of symbols from heraldry, classical myth and Christianity. He asked King's permission to take photographs of inscriptions that loped across the tarot-like panels. "She didn't quite know what it meant," he thought. But he had a flair for language puzzles, and he took the liberty of reading some of it to her. The medieval German blackletter, an extravagant script, could confound the eye; but the words themselves were banal, just the names of the windows' prosperous donors—husbands and wives, now long departed, from some towns near the Swiss-German border. He also answered her questions on a technical point of Middle Egyptian grammar.

He liked the feeling of knowing things she didn't.

"I tremendously enjoyed my meeting with her," the man would reflect later. "I feel that over the years we've almost become friends."

ACT 1

DISCOVERY

Do not be ignorant of me.
For I am the first and the last.
I am the honored one and the scorned one.
I am the whore and the holy one.
I am the wife and the virgin.
... I am control and the uncontrollable.
I am the union and the dissolution.

—The Thunder, Perfect Mind

SOLICITATIONS

D r. Karen Leigh King had reached the summit of her field as a dazzling interpreter of condemned scripture. On her bookshelves at Harvard Divinity School were ancient texts as mysterious as they were startling. Among them were the Sophia of Jesus Christ, the Secret Revelation of John and the Gospel of Judas. The Gospel of Mary—as in Magdalene—was a favorite. So was The Thunder, Perfect Mind, a poem voiced by a female god whose paradoxical self-affirmations King found "incredibly inclusive."

Such writings were nowhere to be found in the church-sanctioned collection of sacred literature commonly known as the New Testament. Early bishops had rejected them as heresies and sought their eradication. For hundreds of years, no one knew what became of them. But in the late 1800s, fragments of papyrus bearing traces of these lost scriptures began turning up at archaeological sites and antiquities shops across Egypt. The story they told about the earliest centuries of Christianity would force historians to reexamine almost everything they thought they knew about the world's predominant faith. The more pieces of papyrus the deserts disgorged, the more the official history of Christianity—"the master story," as King called it—began to look like a lie.

To King, these newly unearthed texts were the missing pieces of a Bible that might have been, had history taken a different course. In the suppressed writings of ancient believers she saw a Christianity more open-armed and less taken with violence than the one passed down by the long line of powerful popes and Sunday sermonizers. "We are only beginning to construct the pieces of a fuller and more accurate narrative of Christian beginnings," she declared. "The dry desert of Egyptian Africa has yielded a feast for the nourishment of the mind and perhaps for the spirit as well."

When colleagues published a book celebrating her scholarship, they titled it *Re-Making the World*. "In a quiet voice," they wrote, "she has changed the face of early Christian studies."

AS AN EMINENT HARVARD HISTORIAN of banished gospels, King could pack a college lecture hall nearly anywhere in the world. But students weren't the only ones who sought her instruction. Her work at the fringes of faith drew notice from mystics, conspiracists and mediums, some of whom regarded her as a bearer of secret knowledge. One email correspondent sent her a code he said unlocked the mysteries of the Bible. Another asked for the key to the seemingly random order of Jesus's sayings in the apocryphal Gospel of Thomas. "Some woman offered me 'True facts about Mary Magdalene,' because, she told me, 'I am Mary Magdalene,'" King recalled. "I get a lot of that kind of stuff."

To many orthodox and evangelical believers, the gospels King studied were no less blasphemous now than they had been to the Church Fathers: they were delusions wrought by the devil, detours from the one true way. And this explained the other genre of email King had to contend with—the dark stream of threats and hate. Some messages were so toxic that King quarantined them in a folder she labeled "Poison."

"Repent," people had urged her, "while there's still time."

JULY 9, 2010, WAS A FRIDAY at the end of a long Boston heat wave. At a little before noon, King, who worked at home in the summers, received an email that Harvard Divinity School's spam filters had labeled "SUS-PECT." King didn't recognize the sender. But the subject line—"Coptic gnostic gospels in my collection"—suggested someone more credible than the "kooky" strangers who sometimes emailed. The scriptures King wrote about, which dated from the second to fourth century A.D., were sometimes called Gnostic, because of their view that salvation came not from the death and resurrection of Jesus but from personal knowledge, or *gnosis*, of the divine. Coptic, meanwhile, was the language of Egypt's earliest Christians and of some of the oldest surviving copies of the gospels. Most of the known Gnostic manuscripts were discovered between the 1890s and the 1940s, and many had long since been cataloged and conserved in libraries and museums in Egypt, Germany and the United Kingdom. Were a set of previously unknown gospels to come to light now, it would electrify biblical studies. The field had so few texts for so many scholars that every discovery occasioned a kind of stir—along with sometimes jealous fights for access.

The sender introduced himself as a manuscript collector. He told King he had about fifteen fragments of Coptic papyrus, one of which had recently rekindled his curiosity. "Unfortunately I don't read Coptic," he wrote. But he had an English translation. It "points," he wrote, "towards a gnostic gospel, in which Jesus and a disciple had an argument about Mary.

"Since I read some of your publications you [*sic*] name came to my mind," he continued. "If you are interested in having a closer look, I gladly email photos."

King replied that she was very interested.

Five hours later, the man emailed images of a dozen papyrus fragments. He called her attention to two. Coptic Papyrus 01-11 was a piece of the Gospel of John he believed dated to the third century A.D. The other—Coptic Papyrus 02-11—was the text about Mary he'd mentioned in his first email. He now called it "an unknown Gospel." A metal ruler, pictured along its bottom edge, showed it to be about three-by-one-and-a-half inches, nearly the dimensions of a business card. Its front side, or recto, was covered with eight lines of thickly stroked Coptic handwriting. Every line was incomplete, a sign that the scrap had probably broken off, or been cut, from the middle of some larger page.

King recognized some of the surviving words. The first line, for instance, recalled a verse from the Gospel of Thomas. Other phrases smacked of the Gospel of Mary, a second-century text that depicted Mary Magdalene as superior, in Jesus's eyes, to the male apostles. It happened that King was the world's foremost expert on the Gospel of Mary; her research on it, as a young scholar in California, had first brought her to Harvard's attention in the 1990s. In books and lectures, King had used the text to dispel what she saw as one of the most pernicious falsehoods in the history of Christianity: the portrayal of Mary Magdalene as a repentant prostitute—a slander, sanctioned by popes, whose true purpose, King believed, was to keep Christian women from power as the fledgling Church courted the patronage of patriarchal Rome.

The parallels between these familiar texts and the collector's "unknown Gospel" were remarkable. But what riveted King was the one line lacking any known precedent: "*peje Iēsous nau ta-hime*" was Coptic for "Jesus said to them, 'My wife.'"

The phrase was so extraordinary that King didn't quite believe it. But the surrounding words seemed to leave little doubt. Just before Jesus speaks, the disciples pose a question about the worthiness of a woman named Mariam, or Mary. "My wife...," Jesus replies, "...she is able to be my disciple.../...Let wicked people swell up.../...As for me, I dwell with her in order to..."

It was a portrait of Jesus—married, living with his wife Mary Magdalene, cursing her detractors—unlike any known to history.

FOR MORE THAN FIFTEEN CENTURIES, Christian authorities had equated sex—and, in turn, women—with sin. For centuries, preachers and theologians taught believers to feel shame and revulsion at the most human of yearnings. If evidence existed that Jesus married and chose his wife as a disciple—or even just that some early Christians believed he did—it would bring unprecedented scrutiny to how and why this vilification of sex prevailed. The celibacy of clergy and the exclusion of women from the priesthood were predicated, in no small part, on the presumption of Jesus's bachelorhood and on his choice of only male apostles. If a group of early Christians saw Mary Magdalene as Jesus's wife, it might explain why the Church went to such lengths to recast her as a prostitute—a tearful outcast who washes Jesus's feet with perfumed hair after repenting her sins.

King had spent much of her career questioning the completeness of the Church's "data," as she pointedly called it. Modern discoveries like the Gospel of Thomas and the Gospel of Mary—and now perhaps this text, too—showed just how effective the Church Fathers had been at skewing the data by literally burying the beliefs of Christians they didn't like. Indeed, the sands of Egypt might have swallowed these forbidden scriptures forever, were it not for the territorial ambitions of a twenty-eight-year-old French general.

STRANGE TEACHINGS

On July 1, 1798, Napoleon Bonaparte landed in the Egyptian port of Alexandria with forty thousand soldiers and dreams of empire. Fresh from his victories in Italy, he lusted for greater glory—a spectacular conquest that would simultaneously thwart British trade with North Africa and slake what some have called his "Oriental complex."

"I saw the way to achieve all my dreams," he said of Egypt. "I would found a religion, I saw myself marching on the way to Asia, mounted on an elephant, a turban on my head, and in my hand a new Koran that I would have composed to suit my needs." He aimed to exploit "the realm of all history for my own profit."

The expedition was, for Napoleon, a rare military fiasco. Under the cover of an August night in 1799, he slipped onto a frigate back to Europe, leaving Egypt to chaos and his soldiers to privation and mutiny. Napoleon could claim for his misadventure just one triumph: it had opened the land of the Pharaohs to the exploits of Western scholars. Along with arms, ships and soldiers, Napoleon had ferried with him from France some 170 intellectuals, or savants—some of the most luminous scientists, artists and engineers of his day. The savants returned with drawings of Egyptian wonders, from the tombs at Luxor to the zodiac at Dendera. A company of French soldiers expanding a fort near the town of Rosetta, meanwhile, uncovered a slab of polished granite engraved with three parallel blocks of text: one in Egyptian hieroglyphs; one in Greek; and one in demotic, a precursor to Coptic. The slab would become known as the Rosetta Stone. The French scholar Jean-François Champollion used its side-by-side translations to crack the code of hieroglyphics, opening the writings of the ancient Egyptians to the modern world. The savants published their extraordinary finds in a set of twenty-three volumes, *Description de l'Égypte,* that effectively established the field of Egyptology and lofted Europe into the throes of "Egyptomania."

Egypt was soon awash with Western merchants, diplomats, spies and adventurers, along with a cavalcade of antiquities hunters and dealers, who discovered what the French scholar Hélène Cuvigny called "an archaeological El Dorado." The lust for exotica from a grand civilization was so unquenchable that deals were struck in which neither buyer nor seller knew exactly what was trading hands. Warnings about price gouging and forgery were sounded as early as the 1830s. Occasionally, though, a buyer got very lucky.

ON A JANUARY DAY IN 1896, a German scholar named Carl Reinhardt strolled into an antiquities shop in Cairo. A dealer took out a codex, or book, of Coptic papyri and claimed that a *fellah,* a peasant, had found it wrapped in feathers and stuffed in a wall niche in the city of Akhmim, three hundred miles south of Cairo. Neither the dealer nor Reinhardt could decipher its contents, but Reinhardt paid the man and carried the codex back to Berlin, depositing it in the city's illustrious Egyptian Museum. By the summer, a young German Coptologist named Carl Schmidt had sat down to try to make sense of it. Schmidt called the handwriting "of uncommon refinement" and dated its style to the fifth century A.D. But it wasn't until he reached the end pages—where ancient scribes left titles—that he saw the breathtaking words:

The Gospel
according to
Mary

If looks didn't deceive, it was the first known gospel written in the name of a woman.

In a central scene, the risen Jesus tells the disciples to go out and "preach the good news." Yet when Jesus departs, the disciples weep, fearful of coming to the same gruesome end as the Savior. "If they did not spare him," they ask, "how will they spare us?"

A woman named Mary, who appears to be Mary Magdalene, stands up to fire their courage. "Do not weep and be distressed nor let your hearts be irresolute," she says. "For his grace will be with you all and will shelter you."

"Sister," the apostle Peter replies, "we know that the Savior loved you more than all other women. Tell us the words of the Savior that you remember, the things you know that we don't because we haven't heard them."

"I will teach you about what is hidden from you," Mary says, then gently mocks the men's cowardice. She says that when she found Jesus in a vision, he answered, "How wonderful you are for not wavering at seeing me!"

But Jesus's revelation to her—about the soul's ascent, past dark powers, to a place of silence—arouses suspicion in Peter's brother, Andrew, who complains that he doubts Mary's "strange ideas."

Peter, for his part, throws a jealous fit over Jesus's preference for Mary. "Did he, then, speak with a woman in private without our knowing about it?" he asks. "Are we to turn around and listen to her? Did he choose her over us?"

"My brother, Peter, what are you imagining?" Mary asks, weeping. "Do you think that I have thought up these things by myself in my heart or that I am telling lies about the Savior?"

The disciple Levi puts an end to the quarrel, calling Peter temperamental and telling the others to be ashamed. He reminds the men that only the Savior decides who can announce the good news. "For if the Savior made her worthy," Levi says of Mary, "who are you then for your part to reject her? Assuredly the Savior's knowledge of her is completely reliable. That is why he loved her more than us." The gospel ends with the chastened disciples going out into the world to preach.

It was a striking reversal of expectation. In the tradition familiar to modern believers, Peter is "the rock" upon which Jesus founds the Church, and Mary Magdalene, a reformed prostitute. Here, Peter is a hothead, and Mary, the rock, the only person steady enough to succeed Jesus as counselor to the disciples. To doubt her, as Levi suggests, was to doubt the Savior himself.

UNTIL THE DAY IN 1896 when Reinhardt acquired the codex, almost everything scholars knew about texts like the Gospel of Mary came from the fulminations of second-century heresy hunters. Epiphanius, a bishop from Cyprus, called his diatribe *The Medicine Chest*, comparing Gnostic interpretations of Jesus's teachings to a sickness on the Christian body. The Gnostics were "deluded people" who "forge nonsensical books," having "grown from [their teachers] like fruit from a dunghill," he wrote. These "despicable, erring" believers "assault us like a swarm of insects, infecting us with diseases, smelly eruptions, and sores."

Irenaeus, the bishop of Lyon, took a different tack, accusing the Gnostics of preening narcissism. "They proclaim themselves as being 'perfect,' so that no one can be compared to them," he writes in *Against Heresies*. "They assert that they themselves know more than all others, and ... are free in every respect to act as they please, having no one to fear in anything." Among other outrages, Irenaeus said, the Gnostics "boast that they possess more Gospels than there really are." Gnosticism's favor among women was a particular irritant; its teachers, Irenaeus wrote, "deceived many silly women, and defiled them."

Through this fog of venom, it was hard for modern scholars to get a true picture of the Gnostic texts. It was as if, say, every copy of James Joyce's *Ulysses* had been destroyed and all a prospective reader could go on—to see if it was any good—were the reviews of critics who hated it. The one certainty was that these second-century bishops succeeded in elevating their model of Christianity to orthodoxy while demoting their rivals' to heresy. The Roman Catholic Church eventually sainted Epiphanius and Irenaeus, honoring them as "Church Fathers." The Gnostic gospels they raged against, meanwhile, vanished from places of worship. If anyone in antiquity recorded the means of destruction—whether it was by burning, burial or neglect—their accounts don't survive.

The discovery of the Gospel of Mary—along with three other lost texts tucked in the same codex—was a breakthrough of incalculable proportions. Silenced groups of early Christians were at last speaking in their own words, their voices creaky from long burial but muzzled no more. "We are thus for the first time," wrote Carl Schmidt's colleague Adolf von Harnack, "able to check the Gnostic system, as the Church Fathers presented it, against the original."

Karen King was fresh out of graduate school in the mid-1980s when senior scholars asked her to introduce the Gospel of Mary in a new edition of *The Nag Hammadi Library in English*. The book was the definitive collection of the most important set of Gnostic gospels. (The cliffs near Nag Hammadi, Egypt, were the site, in 1945, of the largest single discovery.) In a previous edition of the book, a pair of distinguished male scholars had between them eked out just two paragraphs. King's introduction, her first published words on the Gospel of Mary, spanned two pages. It was clear, even then, that she saw prior interpretations as severely wanting. The Gospel of Mary, she argued, was nothing less than a "head-on" attack on "orthodox positions that deny the validity of esoteric revelation and reject the authority of women to teach."

As King saw it, debates over women's spiritual authority were as contentious in the ancient world as they were in her own time. The Catholic catechism barred women's ordination because "the Lord Jesus chose men to form the college of the twelve apostles, and the apostles did the same when they chose collaborators to succeed them." The New Testament was even more proscriptive. "I do not permit a woman to teach or to exercise authority over a man; rather, she is to remain quiet," the apostle Paul writes in his First Epistle to Timothy. Paul says that women will be saved by childbearing, so long as they maintain "self-control." If women have questions, he writes in his First Epistle to the Corinthians, "let them ask their husbands at home. For it is shameful for a woman to speak in church."

The Gospel of Mary told a decidedly different story, and King would spend years mining its fragmentary pages for clues to its origins and meaning. She presented her findings in a breakthrough 2003 book, *The Gospel of Mary of Magdala: Jesus and the First Woman Apostle*. The Gospel of Mary, she argued,

> presents a radical interpretation of Jesus' teachings as a path to inner spiritual knowledge; it rejects his suffering and death as the path to eternal life; it exposes the erroneous view that Mary of Magdala was a prostitute for what it is—a piece of theological fiction; it presents the most straightforward and convincing argument in any early Christian writing for the legitimacy of women's leadership; it offers a sharp critique of illegitimate power and a utopian vision of spiritual perfection; it challenges our rather romantic views about the harmony and unanimity of the first Christians; and it asks us to rethink the basis for church authority. All written in the name of a woman.

The Gospel of Mary, in other words, challenged almost everything modern Christians took for granted about their faith, from the meaning of Jesus's death to the basis of the Church's legitimacy. It was no accident that the longest chapter in King's book bore the magisterial title "The History of Christianity." As a young scholar in the 1980s, King had seen the Gospel of Mary through a pinhole, as a critique of the leadership of Peter and Andrew. The longer she sat with its pages, however, the more they opened up to her. She saw them now as the other side of a rancorous debate over gender in the early church—a fight that took place *before* men monopolized control, a fight that might well have gone the other way. King argued that Mary was a contemporary of some of the twenty-seven books that would make the New Testament, and not—as most scholars believed—a late second-century reaction to them. It was a daringly original argument. No one had interpreted Mary this way, King wrote, "until now."

KING'S TRAILBLAZING INSTINCTS traced in part to her childhood amid the soaring mountains of southwest Montana. She'd grown up riding horses and trailing cattle in a valley ringed by abandoned gold and silver mines with names like Smuggler, Paymaster and Lucky Strike. The road through Sheridan—a no-stoplight, seven-hundred-person town an hour's drive south of Butte—is still known as the Vigilante Trail, after the citizens' committee that brought frontier justice to the masked highwaymen who terrorized prospectors during Montana's nineteenth-century gold rush.

"She was someone who loved to go up in the Rockies on a horse and camp for days," recalled Robert Berchman, a graduate school classmate at Brown University. "The idea of striking out on your own and achieving your goals—whether it was trekking through grizzly country for three days and coming out alive—that was part of Karen's character." Asked who the "grizzlies" were in his metaphor, Berchman said, "Anyone sitting in the audience who was listening to your paper and was going to come after you."

"I was raised to think that emotions were irrational," Karen King once said. Montana had "a very cowboy ethic," and part of it was, "Show no vulnerability."

THE BEST-KNOWN PRIVATE COLLECTORS of biblical manuscripts were early twentieth-century business tycoons: Alfred Chester Beatty was a mining magnate known as the King of Copper; Charles Lang Freer, a railroad baron; J. Pierpont Morgan, a Wall Street financier. They had the riches to compete with a syndicate of European universities and museums, known as "the papyrus cartel," for the most exhilarating finds. The hunt for ancient copies of the Bible reaped American-style publicity, with colorful details that evoked the era's stereotypes about the exotic East. "Words of Christ, Lost 1,300 Years," declared a banner headline in a 1908 issue of a Chicago newspaper. "Charles L. Freer Tells the Story of His Great Find in Egypt's Sands: How a Moslem Arab Who Made the Wonderful Find Let Him into the Secret and How the Purchase Was Completed After Secret Conferences and Tedious Negotiations—Manuscript Is More Valuable than the One Held Sacred in British Museum."

The twenty-first century produced a new breed of collector: wealthy evangelical Christians. Robert Van Kampen, a multimillionaire investment banker, and Steve Green, the billionaire president of the Hobby Lobby craft store chain, stockpiled large caches of Christian manuscripts in hopes of proving the Bible's God-given inerrancy across the ages.

As best as King could tell, her email correspondent belonged to neither camp. "A complete stranger," King said of him in August 2012, when I began reporting a story on the papyrus for *Smithsonian*. (The magazine, published by the Smithsonian Institution, had learned of her discovery a few weeks before her announcement in Rome.) I had hoped to interview the collector for my article or to at least learn more about his background. But King couldn't oblige. The man, she said, did not want to be identified.

Her colleagues were naturally curious about the fragment's origins, but King was by no means the first scholar to defer to a private collector's wishes. Though the world of manuscript collecting had its publicity seekers, it also had its more reclusive habitués—hobbyists with smaller budgets, more idiosyncratic tastes and no interest in press. There was no single "type" among these amateur collectors, according to the Christian manuscript scholar Brent Nongbri, but at least a few were people, often with some academic training, who savored the idea of owning "a little bit of the past."

Where this man lived, what he did for a living, his nationality— King wasn't free to say. But she had no reason to suspect he was hiding anything. In her very first email to him, she had asked about the papyrus's provenance, or ownership history. Knowing where an antiquity came from—and whose hands it had passed through—helped scholars determine whether it was legally obtained and genuinely ancient. The man responded within a few hours: he had purchased his papyri from a German American man in the 1990s; the German American, in turn, had acquired them in communist East Germany in the 1960s. Where the papyri were before the 1960s the collector didn't seem to know. But few papyri, even those in museums, could be traced with any certainty to the patch of desert where some *fellah* first plucked them from the sand. And the stories of discovery that Egyptian antiquities dealers retailed to Western buyers in the early twentieth century? Scholars are now of a mind that most were tall tales, hatched by dealers to deter customers from bypassing middlemen and going straight to the source. What mattered in the eyes of the law and academic ethics was that antiquities were in Western hands before new international restrictions in the 1970s on the export of cultural artifacts from their lands of origin. To judge by the collector's paperwork, the papyri were in Germany no later than the early 1960s, which put King well in the clear.

A CHALLENGE FOR HISTORIANS of antiquity wasn't just how few ancient manuscripts survived but how little remained of those that did. Papyrus was a brittle medium, made from the flattened, sun-dried stalks of a flowering sedge native to the Nile. For a codex to stay intact for hundreds of years, even in a climate as arid as Egypt's, would be extraordinary. Oxygen, insects and the ravages of time visited slow but inexorable destruction. Most papyri in collections today were so decrepit that they looked less like the pages of a book than like continents on a map, with rugged coastlines, odd peninsulas and plunging straits. Scholars needed to draw on deep wells of learning to propose restorations of missing text. The itch to get creative—not just by filling gaps, but by "correcting" the surrounding text in ways that make a manuscript more exciting—can grow so strong that the late American papyrologist Herbert Youtie coined a dictum. Known as *Lex Youtie,* Latin for "Youtie's Rule," it advises, "*Iuxta lacunam ne mutaveris,*" or, roughly, "Next to a hole, thou shalt not edit."

The papyri that called to King were often Christianity's most damaged and cryptic—the ones whose holes, or lacunae, posed the knottiest tests of intellect and erudition. For her doctoral dissertation at Brown, she deciphered a Nag Hammadi text called *Allogenes,* or "The Stranger." It survived in a single Coptic manuscript so mangled that many scholars saw it as too fragmentary to properly interpret. King wrested from its incomplete pages a universal story of a soul's alienation and redemption. The protagonist, an anonymous figure called the Stranger, "represents every person who is not at home in the world," King wrote.

The full text of the Gospel of Mary was no less elusive. Ten of its nineteen pages—including the first six and middle four—were missing. The surviving nine were strewn with archipelagoes of lacunae. But enough remained for King to summon what she called a "Christianity lost for almost fifteen hundred years." When someone at a public lecture asked whether she thought of herself as a "treasure hunter"—an Indiana Jones who scoured the outback for talismans—King demurred. "The metaphor that probably comes closer," she said, is "puzzle figure-outer, a solver of mysteries."

THE GAPPED ENGLISH TRANSLATION in the collector's July 2010 email to King was itself a kind of riddle:

> me not. For my mother she gave to me the
> ( ) The disciples said to Jesus this ( )
> ( ) abdicate, Mary be worthy of you (not)
> ( ) Jesus said this to them: My wife (and)
> ( ) she can become a disciple to me and
> No man who is wicked, is he? SIC!
> I exist within her, because ( )
> ( ) a ( )

The "SIC!" signaled that someone had found an error in the sixth line, but whether the fault lay in the translation or in the original Coptic was unclear. If the rest of the translation was accurate, however, the collector's hunch looked right: the papyrus appeared to concern a dispute between Jesus and the disciples over someone named "Mary."

But which Mary? The name belonged to nearly a quarter of the Jewish women in Palestine between 330 B.C. and A.D. 200, according to the Israeli historian Tal Ilan. In the New Testament, the ratio was more lopsided still: six of the sixteen named women were Marys, and at least two of them, Jesus's mother and Mary Magdalene, were close to Jesus. To narrow the field, one needed texts showing *fights* over a Mary, and these occurred in just one place: the Gnostic gospels. No fewer than three Gnostic texts depicted conflicts over a woman by that name, and in each case that woman was Mary Magdalene. Among them, only the Gospel of Mary portrayed an all-out row over Magdalene, but Jesus isn't present for it. Not in the surviving pages. Could the quarrel at the end have had a prologue? Could the collector's papyrus be a piece of it?

King had long believed that Mary's lost pages would one day surface, and for a simple reason: the codex that Carl Reinhardt purchased in Cairo a century earlier was in reasonably good shape. One theory was that its missing pages had simply decomposed over the preceding 1,500 years. But another struck King as more likely: modern antiquities dealers, she believed, had probably sold the pages piecemeal, in a misguided effort to maximize profits. "These missing leaves of the Gospel of Mary probably still are extant," King told a Northern California audience in October 2003, during a four-hour seminar on the gospel, one of several she led for the public in those years.

"Maybe they're sitting in somebody's drawer somewhere," she said, nodding at the audience. "And they may not even know what they have."

HOW COULD THE COLLECTOR have missed the translation's most striking line? Why had his first email pointed to "an argument about Mary," rather than the showstopping "Jesus said this to them: My wife"? It didn't matter. The fragment distilled all the themes King found most compelling in the Gospel of Mary, then went them one better. Its twist—about Mary Magdalene as Jesus's wife *and* disciple—redeemed the wrongly maligned Magdalene twice over; challenged Church teachings on priestly celibacy and women's leadership; and filled one of the biggest holes in gospel accounts of Jesus's life. It was the missing link between texts King had spent decades writing and talking about. She made up her mind before so much as translating the fragment herself: Coptic Papyrus 02-11 was a modern forgery.

THE HARVARD IMPRIMATUR

For as long as Christians have found God in the written word, the written word has given forgers the power to play God. No doubt some pretenders had the holiest of intentions, like the anonymous second-century author who wrote 3 Corinthians in the name of the apostle Paul. Later fakes, like the Donation of Constantine, were naked power grabs. The Roman emperor's "inviolable gift" of political supremacy to the Church shaped centuries of history before an Italian literary critic studying its crude Latin in the sixteenth century unmasked it as a medieval forgery.

In the mid-nineteenth century, a Greek manuscript dealer named Constantine Simonides announced the discovery of a Gospel of Matthew that purported to be written "at the dictation" of Matthew himself just fifteen years after Jesus's ascension. That would make it a century older than any surviving gospel manuscript and the only one all but autographed by a living apostle. Almost as surprising as its supposed date was an odd word change in the otherwise familiar text: Jesus declares it harder for a rich man to enter heaven than for a "cable"—rather than a "camel"—to pass through the eye of a needle. Simonides, whose counterfeits fooled scholars across Europe, appeared to be acting in this instance on patriotic impulse. Amid an outpouring of national pride following Greek independence from the Ottoman Empire, he sought to bolster the case for Greek—rather than Hebrew, with its camel-driving patriarchs—as the New Testament's original tongue. (Simonides was briefly jailed, then faked his own death.)

More recently, Hershel Shanks, the editor of the popular magazine *Biblical Archaeology Review*, staged a press conference at a Washington, D.C., hotel in 2002 to unveil an ancient limestone ossuary, or burial box, inscribed in Aramaic with the words "James, son of

Joseph, brother of Jesus." The "James Ossuary," as it became known, made international news as the first archaeological proof of Jesus's earthly existence. "WORLD EXCLUSIVE!" crowed the magazine's cover. "Evidence of Jesus Written in Stone." Except that it wasn't. Leaving aside the ubiquity of the names James, Joseph and Jesus in the first century, technical experts deemed the words "brother of Jesus" a modern forger's addition.

Jesus speaking of a wife was exciting, to be sure. But King had been around long enough to be wary of artifacts that looked too good to be true. "Okay, Jesus married? I thought, 'Yeah, yeah, yeah,'" she said. "Just the *idea* of it, you know?" But something else unnerved her, too. "The name of Harvard University carries a weight, and so one wants to be very careful about how one uses that kind of influence and prestige," she said. "I was highly suspicious that the Harvard imprimatur was being asked to be put on something that then would be worth a lot of money."

She didn't relay these thoughts to the collector; there was no need. She closed his email and moved on.

THREE WEEKS LATER, in late July 2010, King traveled to the former East Berlin for the annual meeting of the Studiorum Novi Testamenti Societas, an august international society of New Testament scholars. The presidential address, titled "The Female Body as Social Space in 1 Timothy," was of special interest to King. Delivered by the Yale scholar Adela Yarbro Collins, it suggested that women in ancient Christianity faced a double bind. The early Christian leader Marcion appointed female and male leaders but ordered his followers to renounce marriage and sex. The apostle Paul's First Epistle to Timothy, meanwhile, encouraged women to marry and have children but barred them from speaking, teaching or leading. Without saying so explicitly, Collins zeroed in on an abiding conundrum: Why couldn't early Christian women be wives, mothers *and* preachers? Why did even more egalitarian leaders, like Marcion, force them to choose?

Or did they? The timing was uncanny, but the stranger's papyrus had conjured a third way, one in which women had the sanction of Jesus himself to both marry and lead. Odder still, the collector sent King another email, unbidden, on the very day of Collins's lecture, when King might have been seen as particularly receptive to more examples of bias in the "data" on which the Church based its teachings. "Since I haven't heard from you," he wrote, "I want to make sure that you received my email and the enclosed photos."

Was the collector, or someone he knew, in the auditorium during Collins's talk? King waited for the conference to end, then sent a curt reply, saying she was busy. When she finally emailed him again, almost a year later, it was to send him away. "I made some initial attempts at the material you sent, but without real success," she wrote, on June 25, 2011. "It is a disappointment to me as well, but perhaps you have found someone who can offer more help." She was being polite. "I didn't believe it was authentic," she explained later, "and told him I wasn't interested."

Rebuffed, the collector could have taken his papyrus to world-renowned professors at any number of other universities. But he didn't. He came back at King, pinning hope on a scholar who hadn't meant to give him any. His reasons could only be guessed at. Perhaps it was King's expression of "disappointment." Perhaps it was the simple fact that after a year's silence she'd bothered to write at all.

"I understand your frustration," he wrote to her the next day, saying that he, too, had struggled to make sense of his papyri, having consulted "several people" in the last couple of years, including a Coptic priest. His email included new photos, this time of modern documents. One was a typed letter from a Berlin professor who had looked at the fragments in 1982, when the German American had owned them. The other was a note in handwritten German—unsigned and undated, but possibly from the same professor—that called one of the papyri "the sole example of a text in which Jesus uses direct speech with reference to having a wife," and "evidence for a possible marriage." In an apparent effort to make sure King understood the German, the collector reiterated, in English, that "the professor back then saw a possible husband-wife connection of Jesus and Mary Magdalene."

"My problem right now is this," the collector continued:

A European manuscript dealer has offered a considerable amount for this fragment. It's almost too good to be true. Since these Coptic fragments typically don't see that high, I assume that with this one the value is in the content. I had several people look at it in the past couple of years. We finally came up with a transcript and a tanlation[*sic*]-suggestion, which seems to make sense.

One situation I want to avoid is a situation whereby this fragment disappears in some archive or private collection for good, if it really is hat [*sic*] we think it is. Before letting this happen I would like to either donate it to a reputable manuscript collection or wait at least until it is published, before I sell it.

I know you are very busy, but if I could please ask you for a little more of your time. Could you please look at the enclosed translation, and tell me your ideas, how I could possibly get this documented and published. I am completely clueless as far as this goes. Does our translation make sense. Does the Gospel make sense?

SOME FIVE YEARS EARLIER, doctors had diagnosed King with olfactory neuroblastoma, a rare cancer of the upper nasal tract and brain. There were questions about whether she would live. Doctors cut open her skull to remove the tumor, but mistakes were made. She underwent seven surgeries, which left her in harrowing pain and altered the appearance of her face.

Before her diagnosis, King had begun to write an opus about Christian conceptions of what it means to be human. She had deliberately sworn off discussion of the body; many of the theorists she read treated the human form less as flesh and bone than as a stage—or "social space," as Collins had put it—on which we "perform" our identities as women or men, black or white, young or old. King's brush with death, however, had brought her face-to-face with the ineluctable physical reality of the body. It "revolutionized my thinking," she wrote in 2006, "although I would be hard-pressed to articulate how very clearly, at least yet." All she knew was that the original focus of her book manuscript "no longer made any sense to me at all." She had lived inside her head for so long that it took being sick to realize that one's body—*her* body— was really there. She left the hospital with an idea for a new book that addressed these epiphanies head-on. Its subject, she decided, would be martyrdom.

In the early centuries of Christianity, when some persecuted believers would sooner burn at the stake than renounce their faith, the theologian Tertullian declared that their willingness to suffer and die before a crowd, in imitation of Christ, would inspire mass conversion. "Kill us, torture us, condemn us, grind us to dust," Tertullian wrote to the rulers of the Roman Empire in A.D. 197. "We conquer in dying.... The oftener we are mown down by you, the more in number we grow."

After the agonies of radiation and surgery, King questioned whether Jesus truly wanted believers to suffer. Should Christians really understand pain—whether from illness or violence—as Christlike? The Roman Catholic Church venerated martyrs with feast days, saint-hoods and hagiography. But when King returned to the Gnostic texts during her convalescence, she found evidence of passivism, quietism and nonviolence in the face of persecution. "There were other [early] Christians who said, 'No, God doesn't want this. God never wanted the death and cruelty and suffering involved in this.'"

Yet for reasons no one seemed to know—possibly the cancer, pos-sibly her perfectionism—King appears never to have completed the manuscript. Despite grants and sabbaticals and notices in mainstream news stories about forthcoming books, she had published no books at all since her illness.

IN THE FALL OF 2011, the collector opened his email to find a message he could hardly have expected. Four months earlier, after ignoring him for almost a year, Karen King had told him she couldn't help. She was too well-mannered to call his papyrus a fake, but from her tone and brevity—and her failure to respond to his threat to sell it—he might have intuited her suspicions.

But there was no mistaking this out-of-the-blue email: she had reconsidered. "I did spend a bit more time on the gospel fragment and was able to make some real progress," she wrote. "I would be very happy to arrange to have a papyrological specialist authenticate and date the fragment, and would myself be interested in publishing it, probably with a colleague from Princeton.

"If authentic, the fragment is of important historical value, as well as public interest," King continued. "As you suggest, publication would ensure that it not be lost into the oblivion of a private archive. I would also be happy to intervene for you with the Harvard University Library collection, where the fragment would be well taken care of, and join one of the ancient fragments of The Gospel of Thomas among other important works."

It must have struck the collector as nothing short of a miracle.

ANNEMARIE LUIJENDIJK is a well-liked figure on the Princeton University campus, where the student newspaper included her in a write-up of "fashion-conscious professors." She wears her long red hair in a chic bun and has a taste for high heels, tortoiseshell glasses and faux animal print. "I'm a very visual person," she told the student newspaper, explaining her attention to stylistic detail. "My scholarly work is also very visual—I work with papyrus."

Luijendijk (pronounced *Lion-dike*) grew up Protestant in a heavily Catholic province of the southern Netherlands. As a child she thought of becoming a minister, in part because of how much she enjoyed talking with ordinary people. But in a theology master's program in Amsterdam, she grew fascinated by the intellectual puzzles of early Christianity and shifted her sights to academia. The lives and languages of ancient believers "opened up worlds for me."

In 1995, at the age of twenty-seven, she found herself in a van with a stick shift on a Harvard Divinity School–led tour of Christian ruins in Greece and Turkey. On a narrow road in the mountains one day, the van's driver—a man who'd left a banking career to study divinity at Harvard—gunned the engine and crossed the center line to overtake a slow-moving truck. Out of nowhere, an onrushing car materialized, forcing him back into his lane. They were milliseconds from a catastrophic head-on collision. Her heart pounding, Luijendijk watched as another woman in the van instructed the former banker to pull over. The woman advised him, with an almost preternatural sangfroid, that she would be taking the wheel. The woman's name, Luijendijk had recently learned, was Karen King, a California college professor on a yearlong Harvard fellowship for scholars studying women and faith.

"She just stood up and drove the stick," Luijendijk recalled admiringly some two decades later. "I really think that's who she is. She likes to control and make sure. You don't walk over her."

When Luijendijk came to Harvard the next year, to pursue a doctorate in theology, King was a finalist for a full-time post on the divinity school faculty. King's "job talk"—the public lecture candidates give—so impressed Luijendijk that she wrote an enthusiastic letter to the search committee. King had it all, in Luijendijk's view: a command of language, history and theory, along with an eye for "implications"— the effects of biblical interpretation on everyday life. King got the job, and Luijendijk asked King to supervise her dissertation, an incisive case study of personal letters exchanged by ancient Christians in the lost Egyptian city of Oxyrhynchus.

In 2006, within months of graduation and with King's backing, Luijendijk landed a coveted faculty job at Princeton. The school's distinguished religion department was home to the scholar Elaine Pagels, a MacArthur Foundation "genius" whose 1979 best seller, *The Gnostic Gospels,* won the National Book Award and introduced the long-lost scriptures to spellbound American readers.

Luijendijk had just submitted her tenure application in the fall of 2011 when an email with a photo arrived from Karen King. Unlike her former adviser, Luijendijk was a papyrologist; King wanted her expert opinion on the papyrus in the photo. Luijendijk didn't yet know it— she'd never seen the papyrus before—but King had already assigned her a role in its launching. Three days earlier, King had written the collector that a "papyrological specialist," a "colleague from Princeton," would not only authenticate and date the fragment but probably publish it with her. If King had perhaps presumed, it wasn't without reason. She knew Luijendijk well, and it was hardly uncommon for scholars to involve former students in their work.

Luijendijk studied the papyrus—what she could see of it in the photo—and found no cause for suspicion. If anything, it was the opposite. Not only was the fragment so damaged that the lines of text were incomplete, but certain of the letters had lost so much ink they were unreadable. "If you were a forger, you wouldn't do that," Luijendijk told me a few months later, while I was reporting my story for *Smithsonian.* You would be loud and clear. You would produce complete sentences in an easy-to-read hand that left no room for misinterpretation. The sentence fragment "Jesus said to them, 'My wife...'" was certainly tantalizing. But it could end in any number of ways. One, at least theoretically, was "Jesus said to them, 'My wife? I've no need for one.'" Another, in step with Christian tradition, might be something like "Jesus said to them, 'My wife is the Church.'" Luijendijk knew how risky it was to presume how a broken line might end. Her master's thesis, which sought to restore lost line endings to a Greek scrap of the Gospel of Thomas, began with an epigraph from the renowned papyrologist E. G. Turner, who urged colleagues to "distinguish between what is certain or given by the text and what is a matter of inference." The abrupt break after "My wife" made King's papyrus a kind of Rorschach test or Mad Lib: interpreters of every stripe could supply their own endings, stirring a tempest of debate perhaps but no sure answers. If a trickster's aim was to goose the Church by yoking Jesus to an actual wife, why allow so many contradictory readings?

The papyrus's small size reminded Luijendijk of the scraps she wrote her dissertation about, the fragments of private letters that archaeologists had found in fifteen-hundred-year-old garbage dumps outside Oxyrhynchus, a provincial capital built by prosperous Greek settlers. Some ancient might have trashed this papyrus, too, Luijendijk thought, either because its ideas fell out of favor or simply because a scribe made a fresh copy when this one wore out. Luijendijk had recently published a paper titled "Sacred Scriptures as Trash: Biblical Papyri from Oxyrhynchus." It argued that Christians might have deliberately torn up holy writings to desacralize them before disposal. "That is exactly the look that we have here," she said of the collector's Coptic Papyrus 02-11. "It is clear if you look at the edges of this papyrus that these are ancient breaks." She had come to see the fragment through the "garbological" lens of her latest scholarship. "It would be impossible to forge," she thought.

To make sure she hadn't overlooked anything, she brought the photo of the papyrus to the Manhattan home of the world's greatest living papyrologist.

WHEN ROGER SHALER BAGNALL was thirteen years old, his mother decided that the local high school was beneath her son. She phoned the history department at nearby Stanford University, and a professor named Don Fehrenbacher told her to send her budding historian over. Fehrenbacher, an authority on Abraham Lincoln, got Roger a Stanford library card and assigned him a stack of books. Every few Saturdays, Roger rode his bike to the professor's house to discuss the readings and receive his next assignment.

At age fifteen, Roger—who with his crew cut, big glasses and dimpled chin looked more boy than adolescent—wrote to the history department chairman at Gettysburg College to ask if he might camp with a friend in the scholar's backyard during the centenary reenactment of the Battle of Gettysburg. The sight of costumed men charging battlefields with powder rifles "was impressive as far as it went," Roger wrote in a diary. But it couldn't compete with the mysteries he was beginning to uncover in a far more distant past. A turning point was the day he pulled *History Begins at Sumer* from his grandparents' bookshelves. In the fourth millennium B.C., in what is now southern Iraq, the Sumerians began etching wedge-shaped characters on tablets of soft clay, inventing cuneiform, the world's first writing system. Scholars of humanity's first written words might be "the narrowest of specialists," the book's author wrote, but they had an "ace in the hole": the power "to satisfy man's universal quest for origins—for 'firsts' in the history of civilization." Roger felt as if he were glimpsing his own destiny.

He graduated first in his high school class of some 430 seniors, at age sixteen. As a classics major at Yale, he fell into the orbit of a charismatic professor named Alan Samuel, a New York–born navy vet who mesmerized students with stories about a ground-shifting innovation in the history of writing. Unlike Sumer's clay tablets, this new material was light and flexible and took easily to pen or brush. It would democratize writing, bringing the written word from the palaces of kings into the homes of ordinary people. It was the forefather of paper; it was how "paper" got its name. Yet for all its importance, it remained a terra incognita, a sprawling graveyard of ancient voices against which scholars had only begun to press their ears.

The earliest known papyrus manuscript dates to about 2900 B.C. But it wasn't until Alexander the Great conquered Egypt in 332 B.C. that demand for papyri boomed. The vast territories under Greek—and soon Roman—rule required heaps of paperwork to administer, and no land produced papyrus like Egypt, where the swamp-dwelling plant flourished in full sun on the banks of the Nile. To turn *Cyperus papyrus* into a writing surface, Egyptians sliced its long triangular stalks into thin strips, moistened them with river water, then pressed a horizontal layer across a vertical one. The plant's natural glues bonded the layers together, and the sheets hardened in the sun.

If the Nile was a sumptuous cradle for papyrus, the desert was a cosseting grave. The parched, nearly lifeless sands sheltered the writings of the ancients from the depredations—insects, rain, air—that crumbled and pulped papyri sent to other parts of the world. Scribes who put pen to papyrus, unlike those who put chisel to rock, harbored no hope of lapidary longevity. Like paper today, papyrus was a throwaway medium. And throw it away Egyptians did, dumping it in rubbish heaps like the one outside Oxyrhynchus or abandoning it to the winds as they left one settlement for another. The irony isn't lost on papyrologists: the manuscripts that desert refugees most cherished—the ones they carried to new homes in the cities—vaporized under wet skies and the trample of urban life, while the ones they forsook in the desert endured. It was no surprise that the first papyrus Roger Bagnall translated and published, in an eminent journal, was a late third-century hardware receipt. "This papyrus contains a virtually complete order for nails," the twenty-one-year-old Bagnall began.

The sense of papyrology as an extravagant waste of intellect had vexed the discipline since its birth in 1788, when a Danish classicist published the first modern edition of an ancient papyrus. "The excitement aroused by the text before it was published," remarked one scholar, "matched the lack of interest subsequently shown, when it turned out to be a list of forced labourers on the dykes." Similar anticlimax met the manuscript hunters who set upon the Roman resort town of Herculaneum, which Mount Vesuvius had entombed beneath ninety feet of volcanic ash in A.D. 79. The town's so-called Villa dei Papiri was the only large library to survive intact from antiquity. Hopes swelled for lost works by the likes of Sophocles and Aristotle. What were found, instead, were the musings of a minor Greek philosopher named Philodemus, whom one nineteenth-century scholar labeled "an obscure verbose, inauthentic Epicurean from Cicero's time." The condescension heaped on papyri often extended to the specialists who saw the medium as worth their time. "Outside Italy," a Dutch classicist said in 1843, "one would look in vain for bigger nitwits."

The prejudice persisted well into Bagnall's undergraduate years at Yale. A new classics chairman had no sooner been recruited from Harvard than led a putsch of the papyrologists, archaeologists and other technical specialists who made Yale's classics department a force in the study of antiquity. Classics, for the new chairman, was the literature of great writers, not the receipts of nail smiths. Alan Samuel, Bagnall's mentor, was among the professors effectively forced out. The chairman soon came after the teenage Bagnall, too, firing him from his work-study job in the department's slide library.

To escape the chairman's clutches, Bagnall dropped his classics major and won appointment as "Scholar of the House," a prestigious Yale-wide program that excused exceptional students from class for independent projects. (Bagnall had by then piled up a trophy chest of undergraduate prizes in Greek and Latin.) He struck back at the new chairman the next year, with a review in the student-published *Yale Course Critique* so eviscerating that it was covered in the local newspaper. "Charging that the classics have been 'emasculated,' Bagnall wrote that the department has 'virtually eliminated archaeology,' and that one of the chairman's first acts was 'to deny tenure to one of the best young numismatists in the country,'" *The New Haven Register* reported in April 1968. That the target of his ire was sixty-four years old and still chairman—and Bagnall a twenty-year-old senior with ambitions in the field—offers a sense of the latter's self-assurance. Elevating papyrology to respectability would become his life's mission.

Bagnall joined the classics faculty at Columbia University at age twenty-seven and was dean of the university's Graduate School of Arts and Sciences at forty-two. Unlike many papyrologists before him, who plied narrow paths, Bagnall envisioned the field maximally. Whereas others confined themselves to publishing airless *editiones principes* of individual manuscripts, Bagnall roamed through vast caches of papyri to write sweeping social and economic histories. A seventeen-hundred-year-old order for nails wasn't just an order for nails. It was a window into the economy of the ancient Mediterranean; into the hierarchies among workers on construction projects; into the building materials, technologies and measurement systems of ancient Egypt. Bagnall rapped traditional papyrologists for seeing themselves as little more than the fingerprint dusters of classics programs. If they wanted to liberate the field from its "ghetto," they would need bold new collaborations that shunned "the simplistic form of papyrologist as drudge working with historian as thinker." Bagnall personified those aspirations. On top of writing 239 journal articles and all or part of more than forty books, he ran an archaeological dig in Egypt and beamed the field into the digital age, leading a project to put images of every known papyrus online. The Andrew W. Mellon Foundation awarded him a $1.5 million humanities prize in 2003. Four years later, New York University lured him from Columbia with the directorship of a new, $200 million Institute for the Study of the Ancient World.

Yet for all Bagnall had accomplished, he worried as he neared retirement about how "small and perpetually vulnerable" the field of papyrology remained. His college years—in which a big shot from Harvard had made a mockery of his mentors—were a painful reminder of how easily it could all come undone.

ON THE EVENING OF October 24, 2011, Roger Bagnall and his wife, Whitney, a research librarian, tidied their Upper West Side apartment for the usual suspects. Roughly every other week since the late 1980s—typically on a Monday—the couple hosted an informal workshop in their home for New York–area papyrologists. Young scholars were encouraged to bring slides of papyri they were working on, and Bagnall would preside, guiding the discussion as scholars nibbled on chocolate chip cookies he baked for the occasion. Some eight papyrologists made the pilgrimage to his eighteenth-floor apartment that night. As they settled into his living room, AnneMarie Luijendijk, a regular, handed Bagnall a thumb drive.

"What do you think?" she asked as Coptic Papyrus 02-11 filled the projector screen.

They had known each other since 2001, when Luijendijk wrote to Bagnall to ask if he would serve with Karen King on her dissertation committee. She had concluded her letter with a popular sign-off among the Greek-speaking Christians whose papyri she was studying: "I often pray that you would be well, my master." King followed with a letter of her own. "Your expertise in Egyptian papyrus," she wrote, "is unmatched—certainly by anyone here." Not that Bagnall needed more laurels at this stage in his career, but a professor at Harvard— which had supplied the snooty chairman Bagnall blamed for the gutting of Yale's classics department—was now telling him that he had more talent in his field than anyone at Harvard. Bagnall accepted, and Luijendijk wrote a dissertation that was in many respects a book-length tribute to his scholarly legacy. She quoted, footnoted or referred to him more than a hundred times, an average of about once every three pages. When she mailed Bagnall the finished work for formal evaluation, she included a postcard calling him "my 'papyrological hero.'"

Bagnall had a good first impression of her latest project. The writing surface of Coptic Papyrus 02-11 looked genuinely ancient. "As Justice Stewart said, 'You know it when you see it,'" Bagnall recalled. He was referring to a 1964 Supreme Court case in which Justice Potter Stewart said he could not define "hard-core pornography" but could tell on sight whether a film belonged to the genre. "Anyone who has spent any time in Egypt," Bagnall said, "has seen a lot of fake papyrus, made of banana leaves and all sorts of stuff. The fake stuff has a different texture, different thinness, strips not laid out the same way. The pattern of the fibers look different." One can acquire new, artisanal papyrus, but its blonder hue gives away its modernity. "The stuff that looks as if it's been around for fifteen hundred years probably was."

It might sound like a low bar, but another encouraging sign was that the script on Luijendijk's papyrus was an actual language. The fakes Bagnall had come across over his long career were, to a one, written in a chicken scratch that was neither Greek, Coptic nor any other tongue. Antiquities dealers palmed them off on tourists and other naïfs who could tell neighbors back in Peoria that the precious piece of history in their luggage was a magic spell from the Pharaohs. Mom-and-pop frame shops could spot these trinkets as easily as could scholars. ("I have little to no respect," a framer in Oregon groused in a web forum a few years earlier, "but I understand people who have gone on those kinds of trips and brought back the 'Rosetta Stone of Papyruses' that they bought for $1.25.")

The art world, of course, attracted forgers of virtuosic ability. But there was a crucial difference: lost works by world-renowned artists could fetch huge sums. Between 1994 and 2009, a Chinese artist working out of his garage in Queens, New York, made paintings that rogue dealers passed off as newfound originals by modernist masters like Jackson Pollock, Mark Rothko and Willem de Kooning. The fakes gulled experts, prominent collectors and New York's oldest art gallery, selling for some $80 million. Prices for papyri, by contrast, tend to be commensurate with the medium's reputation as antiquity's scrap paper. There was simply too little financial incentive to entice any but the most penny-ante of forgers. "I don't know of a single verifiable case," Bagnall said, "of somebody producing a papyrus text that purports to be an ancient text that isn't."

The only feature of Coptic Papyrus 02-11 that made him suspicious that night was the handwriting. It had neither the beautifully proportioned refinement of most sacred texts nor the cursive slope of informal, or "documentary," manuscripts, like private letters or business contracts. "We all sort of stared at it, and our first reaction was, 'Wow. This is really ugly,'" Bagnall recalled. "The handwriting is not nice—thick, badly controlled strokes made by somebody who didn't have a very good pen."

The scribe appeared to be attempting a "unimodular" script—a style in which each letter fits snugly inside an imaginary square. But he, or she, didn't quite pull it off: the letters varied in height from three to five millimeters and in width from two to five millimeters. In some cases, a letter's size changed each time it was written. The scribe also appeared to be trying for bilinearity—letters whose strokes stay within a set of upper and lower margins. But this too fails. Strokes strayed senselessly beyond the tops of letters, and lines of text bobbled as they crossed the papyrus. The ink, moreover, was so inconsistently applied that its color varied from a whispery gray to a tarry black. The scholars wondered whether the scribe was aiming for "thick-and-thin" calligraphy, a popular biblical style in which thick vertical strokes alternate with thin horizontal ones. The trouble was that this scribe had only managed the thick, in places to the point of smudging. "The flow of ink was highly irregular," Bagnall thought as he squinted at the slide. "It really looks incompetent."

To some of the papyrologists in Bagnall's apartment, the handwriting suggested a student, or even a child, trying, badly, to copy a text in a foreign alphabet with writing tools he was using for the first time. Student exercises were common enough in antiquity. But the simplest explanation, the scholars realized, was forgery. The creator of Coptic Papyrus 02-11 may have been smarter than any previously known papyrus forger, but not smart enough to fool the experts in Bagnall's apartment that night.

THOUGH WELL INTO HIS SIXTIES, Bagnall retained the air of a whizbang boy wonder. It wasn't just his youthful visage, his floppy hair and the persistence of the childhood nickname Rusty. It was his knack for efficiency. His walking pace left scholars half his age huffing. His books—like his emails—were legendarily brief, dispensing fully articulated thoughts with what could feel like an algorithmically derived minimum of words. Bagnall's home papyrology workshops were often just as brisk, and tonight was no exception. Minutes after raising the specter of forgery, the scholars doubled back. Soon a full reversal was under way: the appalling handwriting, which Bagnall first saw as a tell of forgery, became an obvious mark of authenticity. A forger, the papyrologists decided, would have *known* to have better handwriting. "That is one of the things that tells you it's real," Bagnall decided. "A modern scribe wouldn't do that." It was a variation on Luijendijk's reasoning, about the multiplicity of readings left open by the fragment's unfinished lines. What kind of person would forge something that looked so awful? "If I really wanted to make money with a fake," Bagnall said, "I would produce one with multiple pages in excellent condition written in a nice calligraphic hand on nice, quality papyrus. And some collector besotted with Christian origins would pay me millions for it. This is not that kind of thing." Of the papyrologists in his living room that evening, he said, "we were unanimous in believing, 'Yes, this was okay.' . . . That awkwardness we saw was genuine."

This logic might have been sound, but it was also serpentine: A papyrus that looked like a clumsy fake was apt to be real, because an actual forger would have tried harder. Meanwhile, a papyrus that looked unimpeachably genuine—with complete lines, full pages and historically appropriate handwriting—was probably fake. Could a forger have anticipated just this sort of counterintuitive reasoning? It wasn't impossible. But it felt like a stretch. "You'd have to be really kind of perversely skilled," Bagnall thought. The more he reflected on it, the more he saw a perfectly reasonable explanation for the unusual hand: the scribe's reed pen, known as a calamus, wasn't working well. "Somebody was having a bad pen day," he said. "The pen was blunt. It wasn't holding the ink very well. The letters look much, much more messy and irregular than I think the writer was capable of creating."

Bagnall, in other words, had intuited the scribe's *aptitude* for neater handwriting, even though it was nowhere in evidence in the only sample known to exist.

FIVE MONTHS LATER, on March 12, 2012, Bagnall set aside an hour of his busy afternoon for a meeting with AnneMarie Luijendijk and Karen

King. It was at his office at the Institute for the Study of the Ancient World, which occupies a six-story town house on East Eighty-fourth Street, around the corner from the Metropolitan Museum of Art. The last they had all been in a room together was May 2005, when they celebrated Luijendijk's successful dissertation defense over lunch at the Harvard Faculty Club.

The photo of Coptic Papyrus 02-11 had impressed Bagnall, but he was withholding final judgment until he could see the fragment first-hand. He offered the visitors seats at a conference table, and King, who'd taken the train from Boston, withdrew the Plexiglas-mounted papyrus from her red leather bag. She'd had it since December, when the collector came to Harvard for a handoff. Bagnall set it beneath a magnifying glass and began his examination. The front of the papyrus, its recto, was in relatively good condition, and all but covered in eight lines of text. The verso was worse off. It appeared to have once contained six lines, in a larger script, but most of its top fibers were missing, leaving only three legible Coptic words:

> ...my mother
> ...three
> ...forth...

There was a good deal of ink where the fragment's surface remained intact, and none where the surface wore away, exactly what one would expect in a genuine piece. A forger who acquired a blank scrap of ancient papyrus, then wrote on it, was apt to leave telltale ink dribbles on a fragment's exposed lower layers, layers that wouldn't have been exposed in antiquity. A gifted enough artist could pull it off, Bagnall thought. But the number of people with the manual dexterity and knowledge was vanishingly small. He knew his beloved field well enough to put the census of colleagues with the *character* for it at zero. Papyrologists so prized their goodwill toward one another that the field long ago coined a Latin name for it—*amicitia papyrologorum.* "The world," Bagnall thought, "is not really crawling with crooked papyrologists."

Perhaps not crawling. But all it took was one. If anyone might have known, it was Roger Bagnall. When I examined the personal papers he donated to Columbia University, I discovered how close he had been to a scholar accused of the most successful Christian forgery of the twentieth century.

IN THE WINTER OF 1941, a twenty-six-year-old graduate of Harvard Divinity School rode a donkey from Jerusalem toward an ancient monastery in the desert cliffs above Bethlehem. Morton Smith had come to Mar Saba to study the prayer of its Greek Orthodox monks. He left two months later with what he called "a new understanding of worship as a means of disorientation." The monks' devotions "were unmistakably hypnotic... dazzling the mind and destroying its sense of reality."

Columbia University hired Smith onto its history faculty in 1957, but within a year Smith said he was "ready for a rest." He returned to "the tranquility of Mar Saba," having developed an interest in what he called "manuscript hunting." He was in the monastery's tower library one afternoon, cataloging books, when he claimed to find a letter describing a previously unknown "secret" version of the Gospel of Mark. The letter, attributed to the Church Father Clement of Alexandria, quotes a passage from this secret gospel in which Jesus raises a Lazarus-like youth from the dead, then spiritually initiates him through what appears to be a gay encounter:

> The youth, looking upon [Jesus], loved him and began to
> beseech him that he might be with him.... And after six days
> Jesus told him what to do and in the evening the youth comes
> to him, wearing a linen cloth over his naked body. And he
> remained with him that night, for Jesus taught him the mystery
> of the kingdom of God.

Making text out of subtext, Clement writes that a more explicit phrase—"naked man with naked man"—does *not* appear in Secret Mark, as the recipient of the letter, one Theodore, had thought. The "naked man" line, Clement implies, was added later by a group of "blasphemous and carnal" Gnostics, as one of their "utterly shameless lies." But Clement vouches for the authenticity of a different passage, in which Jesus rejects women.

The discovery landed Smith on the front page of *The New York Times* in 1960, much as Karen King's find would half a century later.

Eminent scholars added the Secret Mark letter to the standard edition of Clement's works. Yet as the years passed, scholars began to suspect that the field had fallen prey to a masterful hoax. The case for forgery is complex and multipronged, ranging from problems with the handwriting to anachronisms—like "remained the night" as a euphemism for sex—that sound more like 1950s America than second-century Egypt. Skeptics noted that Smith, a onetime Episcopal minister who had lost his faith, was a closeted gay man in an era when homophobia ran deep. Smith's personal demons, or simply his sardonic sense of humor, might have driven him to depict a gay Jesus whose followers are saved by sin. Unlike other scholars, Smith promoted the homoerotic reading. The naked boy's initiation, he wrote, represented the "completion of the spiritual union by physical union."

In a 2007 book, the Princeton scholar Peter Jeffery, a MacArthur "genius" grant winner, argues that Smith forged Clement's letter as a tribute to Oscar Wilde, the gay playwright who died, demoralized and destitute, at forty-six after his imprisonment on charges of "gross indecency" with men. Clement's "letter," Jeffery notes, mentions Salome (a title of one of Wilde's plays); "seven veils" (a reference to the Salome of Wilde's play, rather than the Salome who followed Jesus); and "the things not to be uttered," an echo of "the love that dare not speak its name," a phrase coined by Wilde's young lover, Lord Alfred Douglas.

In his best-selling 1973 book for general readers, Smith, who shared Wilde's waggishness, seems to almost wink at the parallels. "Salome, in early Christian literature, was a very shady lady," Smith wrote. The one in Secret Mark "should not be confused with the Herodian princess celebrated by Oscar Wilde. The name was common." Another seeming wink appeared in Smith's preface. "No doubt," he wrote, "if the past, like a motion picture, could be replayed, I should also be shocked to find how much of the story I have already invented." The audacity of the apparent hoax became clearer at the turn of the twenty-first century, when a theologian browsing in a used-book store in Detroit stumbled on a sixty-year-old novel, *The Mystery of Mar Saba,* which had somehow escaped a long line of Smith's critics. The thriller, a work of fiction, tells the story of a Nazi plot to undermine the Christian world by depositing a forgery at the Mar Saba monastery. As in Smith's case, a Western scholar stumbles on the sensational Greek manuscript as he prepares to depart the monastery. "The other two [manuscripts] need not concern us, since they . . . do not invalidate any doctrine of Scripture," the fictional scholar, Sir William Bracebridge, tells his associates. "It is this one, gentlemen, that may change the history of the world." The book was published in 1940, the year before Smith's first visit, and became a best seller, with more than a dozen printings over the next three decades.

Though Smith still has some prominent defenders, many scholars, even those once in his camp, have come to regard Secret Mark as an ingenious ruse: "the most outrageously successful 'inside job' ever perpetrated in the modern field of early Christian studies," writes Jeffery, "at least that we know of."

Yet for all its brilliance, it lacked something obvious. What Smith claimed to discover at Mar Saba wasn't Secret Mark itself. Nor was it a letter in Clement's hand from second-century Alexandria. It was a "tiny scrawl" of Greek handwriting in an eighteenth-century style on the endpapers of a printed seventeenth-century book. At best, this meant that some unknown person three centuries ago had used blank pages in the back of a book to copy some version of a letter penned some fifteen hundred years earlier, about a never-before-seen gospel from a century and a half before that. That Clement wasn't known to have written letters made the find all the more curious. Stranger still, Morton Smith never produced the book he'd claimed to have found. All he had were photographs he said he'd taken on his 1958 visit. (The story called to mind a line from Umberto Eco's postmodern gospel thriller *The Name of the Rose*. "On sober reflection," one narrator says, "I find few reasons for publishing my Italian version of an obscure, neo-Gothic French version of a seventeenth-century Latin edition of a work written in Latin by a German monk toward the end of the fourteenth century.") If Smith were indeed the forger, his use of copies of copies of copies took some of the bloom off his rose. A more skillful con man would have fabricated an ancient document, an *original* that could withstand firsthand scrutiny by both humanities scholars and laboratory scientists. Not even Jeffery, a grudging admirer of Smith's wiles, thought Smith capable of that. "A forged ancient papyrus, he well knew, would be too easily discredited."

SMITH, WHO DIED IN 1991, ordered his executor to destroy all his correspondence. But I discovered that a few letters survived. In 2002, Roger Bagnall had donated his own papers to Columbia's Rare Book and

Manuscript Library. On a visit there, I found a folder labeled "Morton Smith," filled with personal notes Smith wrote to Bagnall when both were Columbia history faculty. Before coming to Columbia in 1974, Bagnall had spent two years as a classics professor at Florida State University, in Tallahassee. In the fall of 1973, in the middle of his stint there, he persuaded the university's library to buy a collection of papyri and ostraca. (Ostraca are pottery shards that the ancients used, like papyri, as an informal writing surface.)

Virtually all of the thirty-two pieces were the letters and records of a Roman army garrison in second-century Egypt. The twenty-first ostracon, however, looked wholly out of place. Composed in a markedly uglier hand, its Greek letters didn't even seem to form actual words. It was hardly unusual for dealers to launder forgeries by sneaking them into genuine collections. This one rated only a glancing mention in Bagnall's 1976 book *The Florida Ostraka*. "One fake is not published here," he wrote. In a handwritten April 1977 note that I found among Bagnall's papers, however, Morton Smith seized on the throwaway line. "I wish you'd published the fake," Smith wrote to Bagnall. "It helps to be shown what they look like." A collection of forgeries, Smith added, "would be both instructive and amusing."

After Bagnall sent him a photograph of the dubious ostracon, Smith said he was "clueless" about what the text might say. Still, he wanted pointers on what had aroused Bagnall's suspicion. "Would anything in the writing or physical appearance have led you to think it a fake," Smith wondered, "or does your opinion depend solely on the fact that the text is incomprehensible?" The papers record only Smith's side of the correspondence, so it was hard to know how Bagnall responded. But it looked very much as if Smith were fishing for insights into how to get a forgery past the likes of Roger Bagnall.

In 2010—the year the anonymous collector contacted Karen King—Bagnall published the ostracon. Writing in the journal *Chronique d'Égypte,* Bagnall said he was wrong three decades earlier when he seconded a colleague's pronouncement of forgery. He was more experienced now and realized that despite "its ungainliness" the handwriting could have come from the second or third century A.D. He and a colleague, Raffaella Cribiore, even managed to tease out the formerly unintelligible Greek text. What emerged was a previously unknown comic speech, by an unnamed author, depicting a ribald threesome.

The anonymous speaker, of uncertain gender, watches a man having sex with a barbarian woman and jealously offers him or herself in the woman's stead. Bagnall and Cribiore published the following translation:

> the crowns...
> Why are you crazily rocking a silent
> barbarian woman without pleasure?
> So that you can talk and laugh
> in front of me? Since I'm willing,
> pal, take whatever you
> need. I'll give (myself) pathically [that is, anally],
> in a way you don't know, by your
> head, and in a strange way, if I
> hand over my limbs to sleep first.
> What are you doing? I don't know why
> you're searching for me.
> Fuck me so that I can feel it.

In documents I obtained through a public records request to Florida State University, Bagnall acknowledged knowing little about where the ostraca had come from. He had acquired them, he said, from a Dutch papyrologist who moonlighted as an antiquities dealer. "He purported to be acting on behalf of a seller"—a Dutch woman whose father had owned them since 1900—"but it would be impossible to say whether that was only a pretense," Bagnall wrote to an FSU librarian in early 2018. A short while later, Bagnall told me that the provenance supplied by the dealer was likely "a complete cover story."

His and Cribiore's 2010 article about the ostracon, which they titled "An Amorous Triangle," makes no mention of Morton Smith's bizarre questions about it three decades earlier. Whatever its origin, Bagnall might well have posthumously granted not one but two of Smith's wishes: he not only published the fake but decided it was real.

IN BAGNALL'S MANHATTAN OFFICE on that March 2012 afternoon, King maintained the composed air of a senior scholar. As excited as she felt, she was keenly aware of "the disappointment factor," as she called it—

the letdown should Bagnall find something amiss. But he didn't, and now that she was on the sidewalk outside, she was buoyant. "We're not taking the subway," she said, when Luijendijk motioned her toward the nearest station. "The fragment gets a cab."

Inside the taxi, the papyrus cocooned in King's red bag, the magnitude of the day's events finally began to sink in. Not only did the éminence grise of American papyrology give his blessing to the Gospel of Jesus's Wife. He had dated it—on the basis of its handwriting—to the fourth century A.D., when Christians were still deciding which sacred texts belonged in the canon. Bagnall felt that a papyrus so singular could fetch a sum comparable to an early fragment of the New Testament. "Certainly in the six figures, maybe more," he said. To one type of buyer, he said, laughing, it might command an even higher ransom: "Some evangelical nut might pay millions in order to destroy it."

King, for her part, seemed in no mood to joke. Her feelings, as the cab approached Penn Station, were closer to reverence. "Let's stop," she said to Luijendijk, "and just notice this moment."

To her childhood schoolmates in Sheridan, Montana, Karen Leigh King seemed almost to have been born an adult. She didn't giggle or gossip with the other girls. She didn't steal into the Tobacco Root Mountains with six-packs for weekend "beer busts." She didn't ride in cars with boys or squander Saturdays on Main Street, where kids cruised the two-block strip with car radios tuned to Salt Lake City's rock 'n' roll stations. The word that classmates used over and over for Karen was "serious." She was the girl who gave the prayer at church after a pastor administered last rites for a fellow student. She was the straight-A perfectionist who chastised school administrators for having too much fun at a "Safety First" assembly. "Is the best method of impressing the seriousness of the situation through magic tricks and bad jokes?" she wrote in an op-ed for the Sheridan High School newspaper. "I think not. The standard assembly at Sheridan High School does little to prepare, educationally, the student for a lifetime of relevant living."

For years, Karen wondered if she'd ever belong. From the time she was in grade school, kids picked on her. There were drag-out squabbles with her older sister, Marie, a social butterfly who dyed her hair blond and was described in the high school newspaper as a "brown eyed beauty" and "great boy watcher" who "dislikes school very much." The one person Karen craved closeness with was her own father, a man whose seriousness and work ethic matched her own. George King kept his pharmacy, the Pick & Pan, open seven days a week and rarely allowed himself a day—or even a night—off. "Two can live as cheap as one," he liked to say, "if one don't eat." An autumn elk-hunting trip in the high country, with half a dozen other Sheridan men, was the only real break he allowed himself. Before turning twelve, Karen completed a hunter safety program, passing both a written exam and a live firing session at the Sheridan Gun Club. But when she told her father she wanted to join his hunts, he swatted her away.

"No hens," he said.

In a place as small as seven-hundred-person Sheridan, either you were part of the group or you were utterly alone. Some days, the land and the mountains felt like the only places that welcomed her. She rode the family horse, Tiger, into the foothills of the snowcapped Tobacco Roots and hiked and biked solo over great distances through boundless grazing lands, until she reached a sense of spiritual union with the universe. Aloneness, she reflected later, was "an opportunity to spend time in the presence of God."

THE METHODIST CHURCH that George and Minnetta King belonged to might have become one more small-town prison for their younger daughter. People strummed guitars during services, Coca-Cola was served for the Eucharist, a stonemason pastor preached in his dungarees. Karen knew as a teenager that this wasn't how she wanted to encounter God. In an act of rebellion that townspeople still talk about, Karen walked out of Bethel United Methodist one day and into the somber pews of the small Episcopal church across the street. Its members were markedly older and "a little bit stuffier," one classmate recalled. It served wine for the Eucharist. There was no youth group. Its pastor, the Reverend John Vickers, was a high school valedictorian who'd left Montana for seminary in Berkeley, California, founded a Christian "healing home" in Helena, and was a visiting chaplain at the Montana State Prison. Vickers raised eyebrows at Sheridan High football games for refusing to put his hand on his heart during the Pledge of Allegiance. Karen was the only minor in his weekly Bible study.

The Methodist church's lack of earnestness, as King called it, was the public explanation for her walkout. But there was another reason, too, one that even her parents didn't know about. At a Methodist summer camp in the woodlands of Montana, Karen had undergone what she called "an evangelical conversion," repenting and accepting Jesus into her heart. The camps were known for their powerful altar calls, and Karen felt a surging sense of purpose as she pledged herself to Christ. But when she returned to Sheridan to share the good news with her

Sunday school teacher, the woman dismissed her pupil's story as delusion. Whatever transformation Karen imagined she underwent would surely pass, the teacher suggested. "That was a very difficult thing for a Sunday school kid to hear," recalled Kathleen Wuelfing, one of Karen's close childhood friends. "It just really diminished her experience." Not even her own family's church, it seemed, had a place for the kind of Christian she wanted to be.

The perniciousness of orthodoxy was a theme that would later consume King's scholarship. This was twentieth-century America, not fourth-century Rome. King was a child searching for a spiritual home, not some heretic leading the faithful astray. But religious authorities—from bishops down to small-town Sunday school functionaries—were still telling believers that they were doing Christianity wrong, still ostracizing the ones who loved Jesus in their own way. "Who gets to say what the right religion is?" King would tell an audience more than three decades later, in a lecture on the Gospel of Mary. "Who gets to say … what it means to be a true Christian?"

KAREN MIGHT HAVE STOPPED worshipping at Bethel United Methodist. But it remained the town's biggest church, and she hadn't lost sight of its usefulness. In her junior year of high school, she persuaded the church's large youth group to host fund-raising dinners and food sales, in hopes of sponsoring an international student through a Christian exchange program. The local newspaper, quoting "spokesman" Karen King, said that an overseas exchange would serve "to stress the idea that Christians cannot afford to have a horizon which is less than all of humanity." The article presented the opportunity as open to all comers—students and host families alike. But it soon became clear that the effort's sole beneficiary would be its spokesperson. "I almost was afraid of her because she was so smart," said her mother, Minnetta King, a college-educated woman who during King's childhood was a housewife and local adviser to the Future Homemakers of America. "She always knew what needed to be done."

Karen's application to the exchange program showed a nearly perfect grasp of its interdenominational aims. "I was raised United Methodist, but I practice ecumenism," she wrote on the application form. To a question about career plans, she answered, "I am to be a missionary."

Asked decades later whether the exchange had beckoned to her as a spiritual journey, she said, "No, it was the romance, the excitement." If anyone had told her, "Go," in those years, she said, she would have been "off, gone!" By that summer, Karen was on a plane to Norway. She would live with a Lutheran minister's family in the western resort town of Voss for the entirety of her senior year, missing her home-town graduation and her shot—all but guaranteed—at being named valedictorian.

"We came back to school in the fall and she wasn't there," recalls Charles "Leslie" Gilman, a friend who was salutatorian of the Sheridan High Class of 1972. That Karen wouldn't care what people thought—that she might even relish the gasps left in her wake—didn't surprise the closer of her acquaintances. "She had her independence," Gilman said, "and strong will."

In Voss, far from the expectations of family and home, King sum-moned the courage to teach a group of awkward Norwegian classmates a favorite song. It had been written in the 1960s, on Chicago's South Side. Now it echoed through a thirteenth-century church amid the fjords of inland Norway.

"We are one in the Spirit," King began, conducting the teenagers in as rousing a rendition as their halting English allowed. "We are one in the Lord."

And we pray that all unity may one day be restored
And they'll know we are Christians by our love, by our love
Yes, they'll know we are Christians by our love.

"She wanted people to hear it," recalled one of her recruits, Kris-toffer Tjelle, who in the early 1970s was a shy farm boy with a small crush on the visiting American. "Christian unity: she was advocating that." It was the first and last time he sang in church, he said, laughing at the memory. Karen was in most ways as reserved as he, but "she was determined when she put her mind to something."

WHEN KAREN KING ARRIVED at the University of Montana in the fall of 1973, the campus newspaper crackled with stories of social unrest. Spiro T. Agnew resigned from the U.S. vice presidency. Students streaked naked across campus with "Impeach Nixon" signs. The black activist Stokely Carmichael told a thousand-strong crowd of UM collegians that it was "the responsibility of white youth in America to fight against capitalism." But King's hottest fires were not the ones fanned at campus political rallies. Her fires were inside. And her first step toward understanding, and mastering, them came almost by accident, when she wandered into Religious Studies 329, a class with a one-word title: "Gnosticism."

AT FIRST GLANCE, the Gnostic texts have much in common with the books of the New Testament. They deploy many of the same characters: Jesus, the twelve apostles, Mother Mary, Mary Magdalene. They grapple with similar themes: sin, salvation, the beginning and end of the world. But when you zoom in, you see a world that is darker and bleaker, a dystopia of ignorance, alienation and corruption. As the Gnostics would have it, most people drift through life in a dream state, blind to the constructed nature of reality and enslaved by the deception. This counterfeit world, in the Gnostic telling, was built by none other than the God of the Hebrew Bible, the Creator in the book of Genesis who summons heaven and earth "in the beginning." To the Gnostics, this God is a demiurgic pretender, a lion-faced serpent who debases the world with evil rulers and unjust laws and dispatches his demons, the archons, on sinister errands. The true Supreme Being dwells above the creator God, in an ineffable realm called "the Fullness" or "the Light." Every human being carries a flicker of the Light—a divine spark—within him or her. But the creator God has jailed the spark within the human body to blind people to "the truth of their freedom." A believer finds salvation by looking within, finding the spark and reuniting it with its "root" in the Light. But only a spiritual elite has the capacity for such depths of introspection. (*Gnosis* is the Greek word for "knowledge.")

Baptism, repentance, confessions of faith—the familiar steps to salvation—were of little use to the Gnostics. Redemption, for them, was not deliverance from sin but triumph over ignorance. In Roman Catholicism, Jesus's death saves; in Gnosticism, Jesus's teachings do. "If you bring forth what is within you, what you bring forth will save you," Jesus says in the Gospel of Thomas, which most scholars date to the second century. "If you do not bring forth what is within you, what you do not bring forth will destroy you."

In the Old Testament, the material world is God's bountiful creation; the human body, God's image. But in Gnostic scripture, both world and body are soul-killing prisons, and this basic premise anchors its theology. If the body plays no part in the divinity of Christians, then martyrdom—as well as human suffering more broadly—does not advance salvation. If Jesus's physical body is nothing more than a straitjacket for his divine spark, then nothing about Jesus that was holy died on the cross and no flesh was resurrected. "The one into whose hands and feet they are driving nails is his fleshly part, the substitute for him," Jesus says in the Second Treatise of the Great Seth, a Nag Hammadi text. "I was laughing at their ignorance."

The prominence of Mary Magdalene and other female figures in the Gnostic gospels is a product of this same outlook. Because gender is an artifact of the body, it is spiritually moot. What authorized people to preach wasn't their gender—or any other accident of flesh—but the clarity of their vision. While the Roman Catholic Church would deem the twelve male apostles the only conduit for Jesus's teachings, the Gnostics believed that physical proximity to the Savior mattered less than spiritual proximity. If you saw Jesus clearly—whether in his time on earth or in a vision afterward—you had as much right as the twelve to serve as a vessel for the Gospel. "You saw the Spirit, you became spirit," says the Gospel of Philip. "You saw Christ, you became Christ." The Gnostics' true God appears in male and female guises, to project its completeness and, perhaps, to tar the hypermasculine God of Genesis as a deformity. In some Gnostic texts, Jesus has a female analogue, Sophia, a goddess of wisdom whose decision to produce offspring without a male partner disrupts divine harmonies and inspires her repentance.

The texts that made it into the New Testament taught respect for political leaders. "Let everyone be subject to the governing authorities," Paul instructs in his Epistle to the Romans, a line that no doubt found favor with Rome's emperors. The Gnostics, by contrast, saw worldly rulers as illegitimate agents of the Creator and his demon archons. There are people "outside our number who call themselves bishops and deacons, as if they have received authority from God," the Savior says in the Apocalypse of Peter. In reality, "these people are waterless canals."

The first centuries A.D. saw Christians argue heatedly about the meaning of Jesus's life and teachings. It was not hard to understand, if only for practical reasons, why a model of the faith that took all comers (even if only men could lead), enforced a chain of command and preached respect for politicians won out over one with a spiritual admissions test, scant organization and a blanket rejection of earthly power.

FEW EARLY CHRISTIANS were more vilified by fellow believers than the Gnostics. Heresy hunters called them arrogant, diseased, insane: they were wolves in sheep's clothing, "evil interpreters" who shrouded their lies in "attractive dress" to make them look "more true than the truth itself." The discovery of the Gospel of Mary and three other texts in Cairo in 1896 gave modern scholars their first real look at what the Gnostic writings actually said. The year 1945 gave them the store: peasants digging for fertilizer on a cliff talus near Nag Hammadi, Egypt, discovered thirteen leather-bound books of papyri inside a buried clay jar. The codices contained forty-six distinct texts, a full forty-one of them previously unknown. The Nag Hammadi library, as it would be called, would do for the study of Christianity what the Dead Sea Scrolls, discovered a year later, did for the study of Judaism. It would throw everything scholars thought they knew into question. "Never before has a single archaeological find so radically altered the state of documentation for a whole field," the pioneering Gnosticism scholar Hans Jonas wrote in 1970, as unpublished copies of the Nag Hammadi scriptures began circulating among scholars. "From great scarcity we were overnight catapulted into great wealth."

Though the Nag Hammadi codices were discovered in 1945, it wasn't until 1972—just as King entered college—that photographs of their pages began to be published. The nearly three-decade delay owed largely to a rivalry among international scholars for Egypt's permission to work with the manuscripts, a cold-blooded clash of egos that required a United Nations intervention to resolve. But the wait had a silver lining: The Gnostic gospels would debut at a moment when the culture was primed to receive them. The early 1970s saw an America disillusioned by the Vietnam War, Watergate and setbacks in the women's and civil rights movements. Old orders were crumbling, yet new ones were failing to replace them as quickly as activists hoped.

Crestfallen, no small number of people turned their idealism inward, trading noisy protest for quiet self-actualization. Movements like EST and the New Age promised inner change—*self-help*—to people who'd soured on political revolution.

Into this era, the Gnostic gospels brought proof that another old order—the Bible itself, one of the oldest and most ordered—was something other than it seemed. The familiar story of Christianity suddenly looked a lot less certain, its claims to pristine origins challenged by the discovery of multiple "Christianities" vying for dominance in the first two centuries A.D. The Gnostic strain—socially estranged, more open to women, less violent, more centered on the self—was an ancient mirror through which the 1970s could see its anxieties reflected. The Gnostics, too, had lived in a time of disillusioning change. Romans were flooding Syria, Egypt and Palestine with pagan idols, colonial armies and Greek-speaking elites, unsettling local cultures, languages and faiths.

The United Nations granted the Nag Hammadi codices to three teams of scholars, responsible, respectively, for translations into German, French and English. It was Karen King's luck that a junior member of the English-language team was a thirty-five-year-old University of Montana professor named John D. Turner, a motorcycle-riding army vet from New Jersey who had written his doctoral dissertation on a Nag Hammadi text called Thomas the Contender.

Gnosticism's dialogue with the 1970s was a big draw for many of the undergraduates in Turner's classes. "The overriding appeal," said Mike Stokan, a UM schoolmate of King's, "was the story that all the Gods you've been taught to believe in are fakes." Because the Nag Hammadi library was so free from prior interpretation, "we all came up with all kinds of weird notions of what these texts were and meant."

"Mind trips," as another classmate put it. "You had to be in Missoula to understand."

For King, the Nag Hammadi writings were more than just an ancient echo of her own era's counterculture. They were a prism through which to investigate—and perhaps redeem—the silent sufferings of her own childhood. Her high school classmates described the town of Sheridan as "Norman Rockwell" and "pretty much Mayberry."

"There was no crime, no drugs," one said. "Everybody cared for everybody." But maybe people saw only its surface, blind to the archons who sucked some children under even as they forced them to pretend everything was okay. Here, in the breathtaking gospels Turner passed around in class, were Christians not unlike King: cerebral, alienated, striving for meaning in a merciless world. King would later describe the Stranger, the protagonist of the text on which she'd written her doctoral dissertation, as a stand-in for "every person who is not at home in the world, who seeks the higher realities, and who may be one of 'those who will be worthy.'"

Turner's students had the singular privilege of studying the English translations in draft form, a few years before they were published. Many felt as chosen as the Gnostics themselves, a sense heightened by a warning stamped on the mimeographed pages: "This material is for private study by assigned individuals only."

"I felt a very intense attraction to some of this work," King recalled. "At the same time I felt this attraction to these texts, I was told that they were heresy. And so I went on to study them because I felt I needed to find out why I was drawn to what was wrong, as a way to understand what was wrong with me. And to figure out how to fix it."

King no sooner finished Turner's class than made a fateful decision: she dropped the premed track she had been on and declared a religious studies major. If she had ever wanted to be a missionary—as she'd written on the exchange program application—the thought quickly passed. "I definitely chose the university over the church to make a commitment to," she said decades later. "I've never done the church route. Just the vows of obedience, just adherence—because that's the lockdown of the capacity to think freely."

Though the Gospel of Mary would consume much of her scholarship, the text that spoke to her spiritual faculties most intimately was The Thunder, Perfect Mind, an incantation of contradictory first-person affirmations that she would never write about, for fear of stripping away the intangibles that so moved her.

I am the honored one and the scorned one.
I am the whore and the holy one.
... I am the barren one
and many are her sons.

... I am shameless; I am ashamed.
I am strength and I am fear.

I am war and peace.
Give heed to me.

... For I am the one who alone exists,
and I have no one who will judge me.
For many are the pleasant forms which exist in numerous sins,
and incontinences,
and disgraceful passions,
and fleeting pleasures,
which [humans] embrace until they become sober
and go up to their resting place.
And they will find me there,
and they will live,
and they will not die again.

"This is my favorite text," King said at Harvard Divinity School many years later, after a numinous recitation that she'd prefaced with a plea "to sort of turn the lights low and ... imagine that I'm in a trance." She understood its speaker to be a woman oracle. A line King cherished was "'Come forward to childhood, and don't neglect it because it is small and little,'" she told the audience. "It's an affirmation of everything in the divine."

IN HER UNDERGRADUATE RELIGION CLASSES at the University of Montana, King won a reputation for testing boundaries. The meanings she extracted from the Nag Hammadi texts were not "in any kind of synchronization" with the ones Turner taught, he recalled. He focused on metaphysics and Coptic language; King, on "social exchange and power." In a different professor's class, on Greek mystery cults, King asked if she could write a paper on Paul's account of the resurrection in I Corinthians—in place of doing the actual assignment. Paul and the New Testament were nowhere on the syllabus, but the professor, Lane McGaughy, relented. "She's always had some sort of burning question that she's trying to answer," McGaughy recalled.

On the occasions when King spoke up in class, it was clear to classmates that "she was working like two levels above you in understanding the material," said Anthony Peter Kelson III, a fellow religious studies major. Her questions "were consciousness raising for the rest of the class."

King graduated with a bachelor's degree in 1976 and landed a nanny job, through chance connections, in the Greenwich Village brownstone of the writer Calvin Trillin and his wife, Alice. Manhattan was her first big-city experience, and in her time off she visited museums, theaters and the opera. She also got to meet the literary lions the Trillins invited to dinner—Alice, an educator, gave King the guests' books to read beforehand—while the Trillins' daughters got to feast on King's lavishly decorated birthday cakes. "Apparently," recalled Trillin, "she had won a medal in cake decorating at the Montana State Fair—a long way from" Harvard.

But the pull of New York life eventually paled. King returned to Sheridan after a year and proposed to her Montana boyfriend, an artist and stonemason named Barry Chandler. They married in August 1977, in a "double ring ceremony" officiated by an Episcopal priest in Sheridan's Methodist church. Then they left for Brown University, which had accepted King into a PhD program in the history of ancient Christianity. In Providence, King persuaded the rector of a prominent Episcopal church to let her and Chandler live rent-free in a top-floor Sunday school classroom, in exchange for Chandler's physical upkeep of the church. (They divorced in 1982.) On campus, meanwhile, King launched a five-year "running battle" with her doctoral adviser, a German scholar who had sought to steer her away from the Gnostic gospels. What King saw as a "profound and sensitive response to human suffering and powerlessness," her adviser wrote off as an "ethically unacceptable fantasy, which rejected the world as a whole in order to eliminate its faults." To his chagrin, she managed to submit at least one paper on a Gnostic subject in almost every course.

Her defiance was a point of pride. Opposition sharpened her, like a strop, the edge of a knife. In college, she chafed at the compliments professors piled on her. "I sincerely feel more at home in adversity than when things are going well—how's that for sincere masochism!" she wrote to Chandler in April 1976, a few weeks before graduation. "There's something about working one's way through trial that forces one to be centered—but in the midst of compliments, endless oportunity [*sic*] (ie choice + decision), new horizons (bright but insecure), etc. it seems one gets scattered to the winds and quiet certitude is far off."

To deepen her studies of Gnosticism, she traveled alone to the most politically perilous of cities: communist East Berlin, a fearful enclave ruled by the Soviets and watched by the Stasi, the secret police infamous for their totalitarian surveillance of ordinary citizens. King, who was then twenty-eight, arrived at the height of the Cold War. In March 1983, a few months into her year-and-a-half stay, President Reagan would denounce the Soviet Union as an "evil empire." The risks she took were greater than she ever publicly disclosed. To fund her eighteen months of overseas dissertation research, King won a grant from the Deutscher Akademischer Austauschdienst, a prestigious and highly competitive exchange program. The rub was that the grant didn't permit study in East Berlin or East Germany. West Germany ran and funded the DAAD; East Germany was then a separate country and an avowed enemy. In the early 1980s, "DAAD scholarships could be used for study and research in West Germany and West Berlin only," said Ulrich Grothus, the exchange program's current deputy secretary-general. "Nobody would have even considered offering DAAD" scholarships for study in the East.

But King gave herself cover to skirt the rules. On paper, her sponsor was Carsten Colpe, a religious historian at the Free University in West Berlin. In reality, she wrote her dissertation under Nag Hammadi scholars at East Berlin's Humboldt University. At least once a week, she would obtain a day visa from East German authorities and cross the border at the Friedrichstrasse checkpoint, known as the Palace of Tears because of the outpourings of emotion as loved ones parted to opposite sides of the border. King, a citizen of capitalist America toting printed materials filled with runic-looking scripts, endured regular inspection by the communist border guards. Some days, they detained her for hours. Often they demanded to see her research notes, and once they strip-searched her.

She visited the East German professors in their cramped apartments and spoke to them in German, one of several languages—including Coptic—she learned in her first years at Brown. Lunch was taken at home, served by the professors' wives with small children underfoot. The study sessions could break off suddenly, when coal trucks arrived and professors helped their families lug briquettes to the cellar. One professor, Hans-Gebhard Bethge, recalled that King always took part, shoveling coal into ten-liter buckets or carrying them by hand in a drudgery that could last hours. "It was very dirty work," he said. "Everything was black afterward."

Bethge and his wife, Hedda, a pastor, lived in a rectory in Mühlenbeck, a city north of East Berlin and off-limits to King under the terms of her travel visa. "She went to us illegally," Bethge recalled. Once guards waved King through the Friedrichstrasse checkpoint, King would take the Number 7 bus to the edge of East Berlin. Bethge would wait near the bus stop in his East German–manufactured Trabant. The road from the city into greater East Germany was patrolled by Stasi officers disguised as traffic cops, but King slipped through because the officers recognized the car as belonging to a couple who traveled the area on church rounds. King and Bethge took the same road every Tuesday for more than a year, Bethge said, but "the guards didn't suspect anything, thinking Karen was just a colleague, friend or family whom I picked up there regularly. You know, she dressed rather unremarkably, in a way that no one would see that she was an American." For deeper camouflage, or perhaps just in camaraderie, she adopted another hallmark of East German identity: she took up cigarettes and smoked them ceaselessly, like many of the scholars she was studying under. When asked what most impressed him about King, Bethge said, "She was highly motivated."

But she wasn't foolish. King, Bethge said, would never have visited Humboldt University itself. As a Westerner with no permission to study there, "she wouldn't have been let in," he said. "People were controlled at the entrance, and without an employee ID card there was no way they would have let her in." That's why she worked with scholars in their apartments, he said. Yet Karl-Wolfgang Tröger, another East Berlin scholar, whom King thanks in her PhD dissertation, recalled running into King multiple times in the library of the Humboldt University theology department. Though Bethge never knew it, his home wasn't the only verboten area King had found her way into.

After the fall of the Berlin Wall, Bethge went to a government archive where citizens can review the intelligence collected on them by the former East German police. Universities and churches, as potential seedbeds of dissent, were particular obsessions of the Stasi. Bethge had worked in the former and lived in the latter—the rectory of his wife's church. The Stasi, he discovered, had indeed compiled a dossier on him. A binder some two hundred pages thick contained reports on his business trips, university personnel matters, photocopies of personal mail, neighbors' assessments of whether he could be trusted to travel to the West. But something about the otherwise detailed intelligence file left him startled: there wasn't a single mention of the young American on a West German scholarship who had illicitly visited their home for more than a year.

OCCIDENTAL COLLEGE, in the chaparral-draped hillsides of northeast Los Angeles, hired King in 1984, straight out of graduate school. The small, liberal arts campus prized inspirational teaching, and King was a standout. Students recalled being awed by her quietly impassioned lectures, which prodded them to reconsider everything they took for granted about Christianity. A favorite exercise involved asking them to find the words "apple" or "sin" in the Genesis story of Adam and Eve; neither is there. The surprise the students felt was proof, King suggested, of how successful ancient theologians had been at passing off doctrine as fact.

"Are the decisions that were made by male bishops under the Roman emperor in the fourth century what we need for a democratic, pluralistic world today?" King once asked. "What happens if we tell the story differently? ... What if the earliest Christians don't model for us a fixed and certain path, but instead call us to emulate their struggles to make Christianity in our day?"

Questions were the lure King used to draw people to her ideas. Questions were invitations; they led people to water, but they didn't make people drink. "It's like the wink and nod," one former student said. King knew her work had powerful ideological dimensions, "but she's not going to say, 'I have irrefutable proof of this.' She'd say, 'Here's some information. You might want to take the research further and draw your own conclusions.' She was very savvy like that." Not a few of her undergraduate lectures at Occidental ended in "a wild ovation," a former student recalled. Another described her as "this big mind coming out of this plain, soft-spoken young woman."

In a 1989 acceptance speech for one of the two teaching prizes Occidental awarded her, King made no effort to hide what she called her "sneakier" tactic. "To those who walk in with their faith firm (whatever that faith is), with their convictions sure, their moral standards in good condition, I try to take away some of that surety, some of that conviction, some of that confidence," she said. "I know of at least one student here who has had nightmares about me; let me assure you that I have had nightmares about you all, too."

The college named her chair of both religious studies and women's studies and quickly acceded to her proposal to convert a prime campus building into a women's center. "Excellent, important, eminently reasonable, well-conceived, and very much deserving of funding," Occidental's president, John Slaughter, wrote in a memo.

The only struggle was her scholarship. "Well-meaning male colleagues advised me to do something a little more central," she once recalled of her time at Occidental. "They said that work on women and heresy would always keep my work at the margins. They said I should work on something like the Gospel of John, something canonical, you know?" But she outmaneuvered them, just as she had her adviser at Brown, her professors at Montana and the Sunday school teacher who belittled her faith.

IN THE LATE 1980S AND EARLY 1990S, King became increasingly sensitive to a modern image problem for the Gnostics: their apparent political apathy. Theologians old and new had called them aloof solipsists fixated on their own spiritual perfection. The divine spark saved regardless of the virtue or venality of one's earthly life, the argument went. So why trouble with charity or politics? Why bother doing good or fighting for change?

King's first articles on the Gnostics, written at Occidental, took square aim at this view. The Gnostics, she argued, weren't self-absorbed peacocks; they were social critics. They yearned to flee their bodies and the world because the societies they lived in were under assault by "illegitimate domination ... injustice, sexual exploitation, war, poverty and wealth, and slavery." Gnostic theology sprang from "life experiences" under Rome's "totalitarian, colonial rule." Beneath the complex metaphors was history.

King imputed to the Gnostics things that they didn't quite say but that she believed they must have meant. "Unseen behind claims to reject the world and escape to heaven," she wrote, "can often be a very socially intact, politically conscious—though alienated and appalled—

human being, a human being striving for dignity under oppression." Eve's disassociation from her body during a gang rape in one Nag Hammadi text is "a sharp and biting critique of male authority, violence, and aggression," King argued. Mary Magdalene's triumph over Peter and Andrew in the Gospel of Mary is a "sharp critique of illegitimate power." In the Secret Revelation of John, the Savior says that the Creator didn't understand "the mystery" of "the Holy Height" when he made Adam the master of Eve. "To my knowledge," King wrote, "this is the strongest condemnation of women's subordination to men to be found in all of the surviving ancient literature."

King believed that the Gnostics sold themselves short when they depicted themselves "as people who don't belong, as prisoners trapped in a body and world where they are powerless and degraded." Instead of the "conquered and colonized" captives described in their own gospels, King argued, they were "powerful, heroic persons of superior awareness and infinite self-worth" whose myths were a veiled indictment of Roman rule. King's aim was to pull the Gnostics back to earth. She was returning them—for scholarly autopsy—to the bodies and world they so longed to escape.

IN 1994, HARVARD DIVINITY SCHOOL offered King a fellowship with its Women's Studies in Religion Program, which brings five outside scholars to campus each fall for a year of teaching and research. King began what would become her 2003 book on the Gospel of Mary and taught a class titled "Marginalized Persons, Marginalized Traditions: Women and Heresy in Early Christianity." On June 2, 1995, just as her fellowship ended, the divinity school placed an ad in *The Chronicle of Higher Education* for an opening that looked custom-tailored for her: a full-time professorship "in the field of New Testament Studies and the history of ancient Christianity, including the study of Gnosticism." Some women faculty asked her to apply.

King's relatively slender publication record wasn't unusual for professors at small colleges like Occidental, which value teaching over research. But it wasn't typical of historians applying to full-time posts at Harvard. King had written some chapters, book reviews and encyclopedia entries. She had edited two anthologies of articles by other scholars. But more than a decade had passed since graduate school, and though trained as a historian, she hadn't written a single book. More-over, she had placed just one article in a scholarly journal, a periodical published by Polebridge Press, a niche outfit, founded in Montana, in which King was a start-up investor and board member.

In May 1996, after interviewing King and a few other candidates, the divinity school advertised the job again, opening it this time to scholars of junior rank. In an unexpected way, the delay helped King. Less than two months after Harvard reposted the job, she put out her first book. It was a revision of her twelve-year-old PhD thesis and was issued by the same Montana press that had published her one journal article.

Harvard's offer came in 1997, and it stunned King as much as it did others in the field. "It *never* occurred to me that I would be a serious candidate," King recalled, drawing out the word "never." "So when I got the call, it was really shocking."

There had been an impasse over other candidates. King might not have published the most, but none of the others had her exper-tise in noncanonical texts *and* her sophistication in feminist theory. King could not only read the recondite Egyptian language of many of the oldest surviving gospels; she was versed in strains of postmodern thought more often found in film studies than in divinity programs, a fluency that lent her readings of ancient texts a voguish edge. No other candidate, in other words, was palatable to both Helmut Koester and Elisabeth Schüssler Fiorenza, Harvard's warring titans of New Testa-ment studies. "It was a very embattled place politically," said Emily Neill, a graduate student representative on the job search committee. "It could have gone the other way easily." In the end, however, "it was very hard to dismiss her in the way that other feminist scholars are eas-ily dismissed. I was pleasantly amazed but shocked that we got Karen King in that position."

"A lot of people went, 'I got four books, and she's only got one,'" her friend Nicola Denzey Lewis, a Gnosticism scholar who earned her PhD under Princeton's Elaine Pagels, said of the backbiting. "She got this fantastic job, and she was in a sense untested, even though she was a senior scholar." Not long after King's hiring, she met Lewis for drinks at a hot chocolate shop near Harvard Square. "If I can think of any mistakes I've made," King told her friend, "it would be not producing more peer-reviewed stuff."

"You didn't make any mistakes," Lewis replied. "You're at Harvard."

FROM HER OFFICE ATOP a crenellated tower at Harvard Divinity School, King turned out books and articles that were masterworks of learned interpretation, readings that made remote spiritual worlds come alive—and feel relevant—to modern readers. A 2003 book, *What Is Gnosticism?,* blasted the assumptions of her own field, arguing that colleagues unwittingly demoted important Christian scriptures by labeling them "Gnostic," a term she hoped to abolish. King wanted people to see gospels like Mary and Philip as every bit the equals of the New Testament, both as portals to the earliest centuries of Christianity and as fodder for modern-day ethics. Her work, she felt, was as vital to the study of Christianity as it was to its *practice.* "What history can do is show that people have to take responsibility for what they activate out of their tradition," she said. "It's not just a given thing one slavishly follows. You have to be accountable."

As a charter member of a California-based project called the Jesus Seminar, King took her scholarship directly to the pews, mounting day-long presentations to paying audiences from Florida to Oregon. The lectures bore thrilling titles—like "Forbidden Scriptures"—and were often filmed for sale on videotape or DVD. The Jesus Seminar sought to topple the wall between ivory tower and church, between reason and faith, and King had become one of its stars. In public lectures, she liked to call the Christian texts she worked with "data," a word that invested her scholarship with an air of scientific detachment. "Some people call this 'revisionist history,'" she told a New York audience. "I call it 'getting it right.'"

But it was a struggle. Tradition—garrisoned by creed, canon and clergy—didn't give way overnight. Nor did the powerful men who remained its gatekeepers, in pulpits as much as in faculty lounges. Like many women of her generation, King felt at times that she had to work twice as hard as her male counterparts to be seen as their peers. As a student, during a break in a two-hour presentation she had prepared for professors, she went to the bathroom, blacked out and suffered a concussion. Rather than postpone the second half of her talk to seek medical attention, she carried on as if nothing had happened. Her footnote-packed writing, the sense she gave colleagues that she never took a day off: these appeared to be no accident. She was making sure that no one could accuse her of cutting corners, that no one could mistake her for some New Age guru peddling self-help on finding your inner goddess.

King was by disposition a soloist, a free climber who would sooner fall and take her lumps than reach for a safety rope. Except that she never fell. She was chair of New Testament Studies within two years of her arrival at Harvard, Winn Professor of Ecclesiastical History within six. In the fall of 2009, at age fifty-five, she made history herself, when the dean of the divinity school named her Harvard's Hollis Professor of Divinity. The post had been established more than half a century before the Declaration of Independence, when Harvard's mission was the education of Puritan ministers for the New England colonies. (Among other perquisites, its holder retains the right, dating to Cambridge's days as a farming village, to graze a cow on Harvard Yard.) Over the preceding 288 years, the Hollis chair had been held by Calvinist Congregationalists, Unitarians, a Quaker and a Baptist. But never before had it been held by a woman. That King had devoted her career to righting history's wrongs against the founding women of Christianity made her elevation to the school's grandest stage all the more resonant. Never far from her mind was another female teacher who had struggled for too long for her rightful place in a world of disbelieving men.

THE COMPLICATION OF MARY

In March 1531, the Duke of Mantua, seeking a gift for a friend, commissioned a painting from the renowned Venetian artist Titian. In the finished masterpiece, a nude Mary Magdalene—eyes glistening with tears, pearlescent jar of ointment at her hip—casts her gaze heavenward with a look of abject surrender. Her hands are clasped across her body, clutching coils of auburn hair as she tries, in vain, to cover her breasts. The Palazzo Pitti, the sumptuous Florence museum where the portrait now hangs, describes its subject as "a penitent prostitute, a woman with a dissolute past [who] is naked due to her resolve to strip herself bare of her past." Almost no artwork better distills the heady mix of sensuality, shame and sorrow that many believers still summon when they think of Mary Magdalene.

The difficulty was that Titian's *Penitent Magdalene*—and the long line of others like it—have no basis in scripture. The New Testament depicts Mary as a woman from the town of Magdala who supports Jesus's work out of her own wealth. She follows him to Jerusalem and observes his crucifixion and burial. When she returns with two other women to anoint his body with spices, they find the tomb's cover moved and the corpse gone. Her most consequential scene appears only in John, the latest of the canonical gospels, after Peter and another disciple flee the empty tomb.

> Now Mary stood outside the tomb crying. As she wept, she bent over to look into the tomb and saw two angels in white, seated where Jesus's body had been, one at the head and the other at the foot. They asked her, "Woman, why are you crying?"
>
> "They have taken my Lord away," she said, "and I don't know where they have put him." At this, she turned around and saw Jesus standing there, but she did not realize that it was Jesus.

He asked her, "Woman, why are you crying? Who is it you are looking for?"

Thinking he was the gardener, she said, "Sir, if you have carried him away, tell me where you have put him, and I will get him."

Jesus said to her, "Mary."

She turned toward him and cried out in Aramaic, "Rabboni!" [which means "Teacher"].

Jesus said, "Do not hold on to me, for I have not yet ascended to the Father. Go instead to my brothers and tell them, 'I am ascending to my Father and your Father, to my God and your God.'"

Mary Magdalene went to the disciples with the news: "I have seen the Lord!" And she told them that he had said these things to her.

That is all. The gospels never call her a prostitute. They never show her repenting for anything. They report, without elaboration, that she was once exorcised of "seven demons," but the phrase is thought to refer to spiritual possession, not sin.

That Mary Magdalene was a problem—as much as a puzzle—is evident as early as Mark, the oldest gospel, which scholars believe was composed around A.D. 70. The version of Mark in most modern Bibles has twelve final verses that are entirely missing from its earliest copies. Scholars believe that scribes added these verses later to align Mark with subsequent developments in Christian theology. The most notable development was the story of Jesus's resurrection, which is wholly absent from the oldest Marks. Less noticed is what those earliest copies say—or don't say—about Mary Magdalene. In the earliest Marks, she is neither a survivor of "seven demons" nor the honored first witness to the resurrection (which isn't depicted). On the contrary, the oldest Marks end with a trembling Mary Magdalene so scared by the sight of the empty tomb that she and two other women flee and say "nothing to anyone."

If the earliest copies of the earliest gospel were the best witness to the earliest traditions, then Mary Magdalene was neither sinner nor saint. She was simply a follower of Jesus who watched the Crucifixion "from afar," brought spices for the body—a custom carried out by many women in that era—then ran, like the men, when the body wasn't there.

No one, it seemed, could leave this earliest of Marys alone. Indeed, whoever added the final lines to Mark seemed bent on complicating her. The very first of its tacked-on verses, Mark 16:9, asserts that the risen Jesus "appeared first to Mary Magdalene, from whom he had cast out seven demons." In a single opening volley, this scribe, whom some scholars prefer to call a forger, had telegraphed the vicious cycle of promotion and demotion that would become Mary's lot.

Mary was sunk to her lowest in A.D. 591, not by her own doing, but by Pope Gregory the Great. In a homily delivered at the Basilica of St. Clemente in Rome, the pontiff declared that Mary Magdalene was one and the same as two other women in the gospels: the unnamed sinner in Luke who anoints Jesus with perfume from an alabaster jar; and Mary of Bethany, in John, who rubs Jesus's feet with perfume after he resurrects her brother Lazarus. Pope Gregory seemed unconcerned that the encounter in Luke takes place near the Sea of Galilee, while the one in John, near Jerusalem. "What did these seven devils signify, if not all the vices?" the pope proclaimed. "It is clear, brothers, that the woman previously used the unguent to perfume her flesh in forbidden acts. What she therefore displayed more scandalously, she was now offering to God in a more praiseworthy manner.... For every delight, therefore, she had had in herself, she now immolated herself. She turned the mass of her crimes to virtues, in order to serve God entirely in penance."

The Church had effectively given women two models of piety, each defined by sexual activity. To one side was the Virgin Mary, a revered woman who had no sex; to the other Mary Magdalene, a prostitute who had too much. Magdalene, as King once put it, "became a model for women to immolate themselves for their crimes of sexuality, vanity and bold speech."

It wasn't until 1969 that the Vatican discreetly disavowed Gregory's composite Magdalene. By then, however, the picture of Magdalene as redeemed harlot had burrowed deep into Western culture. "In the Middle Ages, she was the favored female saint—an Everywoman who sins yet still hopes to attain heaven through repentance," writes the religion scholar Diane Winston. "She was also a model for female mystics who, renouncing sexuality as the reformed Magdalen allegedly did, called her an inspiration. By the Renaissance, Mary Magdalen had become the 'penitential pin-up,' a sensuous female form beloved by artists, whose depictions, over time, increasingly reflect a come-hither sexuality." In eighteenth-century London, Mary lent her name to "Magdalen Houses," Catholic reformatories for prostitutes, unwed mothers and other "fallen" women. By the late twentieth century, a new Magdalene took the stage: the musical *Jesus Christ Superstar* and the film *The Last Temptation of Christ* made her an icon of post-1960s sexual liberation.

Late twentieth-century feminist scholars, meanwhile, began scouring the noncanonical gospels for clues to what they saw as her original role as Jesus's "feminine counterpart" and "chief female disciple." The Gospel of Mary was perhaps the best known of these texts, but another, the Gospel of Philip, offered a still more tantalizing Mary. Philip, which survives in a single copy found at Nag Hammadi, is a scrapbook of cryptic and seemingly disconnected excerpts from otherwise unknown texts. Its most quoted passage appears about a third of the way into its thirty-five pages:

> The companion of the Savior is Mary of Magdala. The Savior loved her more than all the disciples, and he kissed her often on her ——. The other disciples . . . said to him, "Why do you love her more than all of us?" The Savior answered and said to them, "Why don't I love you like her?"

The part of Mary's body Jesus kissed is a mystery: the papyrus has a physical hole immediately after the words "kissed her often on her." But most experts believe the missing word is "mouth." Still, virtually every scholar, including King, saw nothing sexual in Jesus's kissing of Mary or, for that matter, in the gospel's description of her as Jesus's *koinonos*, or "companion." In early Christianity, kisses were exchanged, chastely, as a marker of religious identity and as a sort of sacrament through which people exchanged the spirit. Philip itself says as much, declaring that with a kiss "we receive conception from the grace which is in one another." As for *koinonos*, it was an ambiguous term that could mean anything from participant, co-worker or spouse to business associate, companion in faith, or friend. That Jesus is speaking of a spiritual bond with Magdalene, rather than a romantic one, is under-scored by the oft-ignored remainder of the well-known passage. After famously saying, "Why don't I love you like her?" Jesus continues, "If a blind person and one who can see are both in darkness, they are the same. When the light comes, the one who can see will see the light, and the blind person will stay in darkness." The full quotation suggests that Jesus favors Mary for her ability to see spiritual truths, while the male disciples remain blind even in the light.

The turn of the twenty-first century brought proof that Western culture was ready for yet another Magdalene. In March 2003, a little-known novelist named Dan Brown published a thriller about a fictional Harvard professor who uncovers a centuries-old Catholic plot to conceal evidence of Jesus's marriage to—and daughter with—Mary Magdalene. *The Da Vinci Code* went on to become a wildly successful international best seller.

"You're saying the Christian Church was to be carried on by a *woman*?" one of the book's characters, a Parisian detective named Sophie Neveu, says after a historian shows her the Gospel of Mary.

"That was the plan," the historian replies. "Jesus was the original feminist. He intended for the future of His Church to be in the hands of Mary Magdalene."

The literati turned up their noses at the book's prose. Scholars bristled at its distortions. And conservative Christians cringed, fumed and published refutations. But the book's taut plot and clever word games—along with the idea of a mysteriously lost "sacred feminine"—helped move more than eighty million copies, making it one of the best-selling books in history. Though *The Da Vinci Code* is a work of fiction, Brown and his wife, Blythe Brown, carried out voluminous research. They took notes from the Gnostic gospels, from dictionaries of codes and symbols and from books about the Holy Grail and the Knights Templar. To lend a veneer of history to the plot's depiction of Jesus and Magdalene's marriage, characters quote from both the Gospel of Philip and the Gospel of Mary. Brown wanted readers to puzzle over which parts of *The Da Vinci Code* might be true, a curiosity he stoked with an opening page of historical assertions titled simply "FACT."

In one scene, a historian named Sir Leigh Teabing shows the kiss passage in Philip to Neveu, the sleuth.

"It says nothing of marriage," Neveu says.

"*Au contraire*," Teabing replies. "As any Aramaic scholar will tell you, the word *companion*, in those days, literally meant *spouse*."

That the language is Coptic, not Aramaic, and that "spouse" was not the word's literal meaning go without mention. But where Mary Magdalene was concerned, facts seldom got in the way of a good story.

WHEN KAREN KING ANNOUNCED the Gospel of Jesus's Wife in Rome in September 2012, she sought to distance herself from *The Da Vinci Code*. "Dr. King said she wants nothing to do with the code or its author," *The New York Times* reported. That might have come as news to people who had known her in the *Code*'s heyday.

King's 2003 book *The Gospel of Mary of Magdala: Jesus and the First Woman Apostle* was in some sense self-published. Like the 1996 revision of her doctoral dissertation, it was issued by Polebridge Press, which she helped found and lead. As with other academic books—even those from better-known presses—sales projections would have been modest. But King's book was exquisitely timed: Polebridge published it in November 2003, at the height of the *Da Vinci* craze. *Publishers Weekly*, the venerable industry magazine, could all but foresee the result. "The unexpected popularity of the novel *The Da Vinci Code* has boosted sales of various religion books that deal with the Gnostic gospels," it said in a prepublication review of King's book. "The Da Vinci effect may well work its esoteric magic here, even though this is clearly not a book for the dilettante."

A Polebridge editor insisted that the timing was "just coincidental." But the publisher seemed more than prepared to seize the moment. It took the unusual step of hiring a publicist of mass-market books and set up a special website, still online, that touts King as "a national source for background on *The Da Vinci Code*."

King's book was reviewed in *The New York Times* and sold more than ten thousand copies in its first month, and eventually another sixty-five thousand, an impressive number for any book, let alone an academic one. But more important than the "Da Vinci effect" on sales was the soapbox it gave King to disseminate her most treasured ideas. Interview requests about *The Da Vinci Code* poured in from radio stations, magazines and newspapers across the world. She appeared in cover stories about the book in *Time, Newsweek* and *U.S. News & World Report* and became a regular on *Code*-themed TV specials, on ABC's *Primetime*, NBC's *Dateline* and *CNN Presents*. Hosted by the likes of Elizabeth Vargas, Stone Phillips and Sigourney Weaver, some featured interviews with both King and Dan Brown. King took calls from reporters for "a year and a half, two years," she said, "really as long as the press was interested."

Turnout at her public talks swelled. In Houston, more than four hundred people jammed into an Episcopal cathedral on a rainy Sunday night in 2004 for one on Mary Magdalene. "I see just a huge hunger and a fantastic interest for this material that really wasn't there 10 or 15 years ago," King told *Publishers Weekly* at the time. Her involvement with the *Da Vinci* franchise went beyond what even close colleagues knew of it. Though she appears never to have publicly spoken of it, the end credits of the 2006 movie adaptation, starring Tom Hanks, list Karen King as a "consultant."

King's 2003 book on the Gospel of Mary didn't mention *The Da Vinci Code*. But she praised Brown's book in the media for raising important questions about early Christianity. Of the many scholars interviewed about it, King was perhaps the least critical of the book's interweaving of fact and fiction—even when asked for her professional opinion as a historian. On a 2004 MSNBC program about separating its truths from its falsehoods, the host, Deborah Norville, asked King, "As a professor of ecclesiastical history, what bothers you about this book, if anything?"

The answer didn't seem like the one Norville expected. "Well," King said, "I actually think that one of the services *The Da Vinci Code* has done is precisely to let us see the enormous diversity of early Christianity, that we have a lot of voices, that the meaning of the death and resurrection of Jesus, the meaning of his teachings, questions about the roles of women, questions about the nature of the church and authority, were all being hotly debated in the early church." King spoke at such length about how a fast-paced fictional thriller had broadened people's view of Christian history that Norville had to cut in: "Let me stop you there."

Then Norville posed the same question to Harold Attridge, the dean of Yale Divinity School and himself a Harvard graduate and Nag Hammadi editor. "Well, I think the most disturbing thing about the book," Attridge began, echoing the view of most scholars, "is the ways in which there are facts embedded in it that are taken totally out of context and they're given a spin that distorts them I think quite dramatically."

There was no historical evidence of a married Jesus, King was always careful to say. But she found a kind of common cause with Dan Brown. That the Church Fathers demonize Mary Magdalene in *The Da Vinci Code* because of her marriage to Jesus—and in King's book, because of her spiritual leadership—was not a distinction King harped on. She appeared to regard the *Code*'s ends as more important than its means; the historical questions it inspired mattered more than the fictional plot that inspired them. She told a Los Angeles newspaper that she understood why the *Code* was "touching so many people."

"It has to do with people really being suspicious," she said. "If Magdalene is not a prostitute, then what else is the truth?" *The Harvard Crimson* reported that "King deals with many of the same ideas as Da Vinci Code ... in the sense that she asks people to rethink their conceptions of Christianity."

"People are looking for a different kind of religious understanding," King said. Brown's book was "lead[ing] people to ask questions," like "What else haven't we been told?"

"Oh, it was a *huge* teaching moment," she had told me in 2012, when, a few weeks before King announced her new discovery, I had asked about *The Da Vinci Code*. "You know, like, people are actually asking this question about the history of early Christianity and about the texts and materials we worked on."

For King, the *Da Vinci* effect was farther-reaching than any book reviewer had foreseen. It helped turn a scholar whose intellectual passions had been confined to classrooms, academic tracts and the occasional church into a best-selling author with live audiences of hundreds and a television viewership of millions. Yet it put King in a curious bind: On the one hand, *The Da Vinci Code* was just the latest of more than fifteen hundred years of fictions about Mary Magdalene—and fictions about Magdalene were precisely what King had devoted her career to dispelling. On the other hand, this particular fiction—of Magdalene as Jesus's wife—had given King a platform bigger than any she had ever known.

IN THE LATE SPRING OF 2012, Hannah Veale, a twenty-nine-year-old English television producer with long blond hair and a master's in modern languages from Oxford, had just wrapped a National Geographic Channel documentary called *Jesus: Rise to Power*. So she wasn't surprised when Blink Films, a London production house she freelanced for, asked her to be associate producer on yet another documentary on early Christianity. Blink had just signed a deal with the Smithsonian Channel for a series called *Treasures Decoded*. Each episode would focus on a different mysterious artifact: the Vinland Map, Richard III's bones, a miniature golden raft associated with the lost city of El Dorado. The series, according to its promotional literature, would dispatch "a team of investigators around the globe, using modern science and technology" to bring fresh insight to ancient relics.

Days after getting the green light from Smithsonian, Blink Films lost confidence in one of the artifacts it planned to showcase: a set of rusted lead tablets from Jordan with an embossed image of Jesus and a supposedly contemporaneous account of his last years. Blink executives decided there were too many questions about the tablets' authenticity, but they remained keen on a Christian-themed episode, and the clock was ticking toward a fall delivery date.

Veale had interviewed Karen King for the National Geographic documentary and found her an engaging interlocutor on a range of Christian subjects. When Blink asked Veale to find a replacement for "The Jesus Tablets" episode, she remembered King. "If anyone knows about any new developments in this area—papyrus, scriptures, gospels, all this kind of thing—she'd be the one," Veale thought. Veale hadn't thought that King herself would be the subject of a *Treasures Decoded* episode. She just hoped that as a well-connected scholar, King might point her in some interesting direction—perhaps toward a colleague working on "some kind of obscure text that we would have to sort of create a story out of."

"Well, it's interesting that you called, actually," King said, from the other side of the Atlantic, when Veale phoned on June 25, 2012. "Because you just caught me at a quite exciting moment. I've been given this papyrus…"

King described it, and "I'm thinking, I've hit the jackpot," Veale recalled, laughing. "The way she said it wasn't at all like, 'Oh my God, you won't believe it.' It was almost kind of like, 'Yes, you might be interested to know…' She was very, very, very calm and measured." So measured that as soon as Veale hung up she emailed her boss, the producer-director Andy Webb, to ask whether King's find was as major a deal as Veale suspected it was. Webb was as stunned by the discovery as he was by the stature of the scholar behind it. If this had been a lecturer at some no-name college in the boonies, Webb would have had his doubts. But Karen King? Of Harvard Divinity School? "It doesn't get much more senior a pukka," Webb remembered thinking, using British-Hindi slang for "the genuine article."

"It was absolutely key to the credibility of the story," Webb said. "I was absolutely gobsmacked."

Veale called King back. Keeping her cool, so as not to scare King off, Veale said the papyrus might make an interesting subject for a *Treasures Decoded* episode. How would King feel about their bringing video cameras to Harvard?

"I didn't have to do much convincing, I suppose," Veale recalled. "She didn't seem cautious about it at all. She was just, 'Yup, absolutely, yeah, let's make it happen.'" Best of all, King appeared to have spoken to no other media.

On July 3, 2012, a series producer at Blink named Dan Oliver alerted Charles Poe, the senior vice president of production at the Smithsonian Channel. "Do you have a few minutes to talk?" Oliver emailed. "We have had a big / v. exciting / newsworthy breakthrough on one of the stories. It's best if I explain over the phone."

The Smithsonian Channel, founded in 2007 as a joint venture of the Smithsonian Institution and CBS's Showtime Networks, saw at once how big a coup King's discovery would be for the still-young channel, particularly if it got an exclusive. A few months earlier the Smithsonian Institution had coined a new slogan, "Seriously Amazing," to help shake off its musty reputation as "the nation's attic."

King's papyrus "was a shiny new object that was obviously going to be newsworthy," Poe recalled. Channel executives took extraordinary measures to protect the scoop, communicating by phone or face-to-face, instead of by email.

Religion, like politics, is as delicate a subject for the Smithsonian Institution as it would be at a dinner party. Because of its taxpayer subsidy and the twenty-eight million visits people make each year to its free museums and the National Zoo, the institution fiercely guards its reputation as a scrupulous and impartial purveyor of knowledge. Unlike most cable outlets, the Smithsonian Channel can't air a new program until it has been scrutinized by a review panel at institution headquarters in Washington, D.C. Smithsonian curators and other subject-matter experts vet each program for both factual accuracy and alignment with the Smithsonian brand. The Smithsonian Networks Review Committee doesn't typically weigh in until the channel has produced a rough cut. But an ancient manuscript referring to Jesus's wife was a minefield. David Royle, the channel's executive vice president, considered the subject so sensitive that he paid a quiet visit to Smithsonian headquarters before a single frame was shot. If the Smithsonian Institution saw the topic as a nonstarter, there was no point in Blink Films' going forward. Royle, a former National Geographic Channel executive who has led programming at the Smithsonian Channel since its inception, recalled finding support "even from among people who are often very skeptical" of such discoveries. The reason was simple: "This story was originating from Harvard, the oldest chair of religion in America. So it came with great credibility."

A MONTH LATER, on a sweltering afternoon in late July, Hannah Veale and Andy Webb arrived at Harvard Divinity School. For reasons Veale never understood, King insisted that Harvard University's press office not be informed of the documentary. That suited the filmmakers fine. Webb, an Emmy-nominated documentary maker who had gotten his start at the BBC, feared that a press office might try to talk King out of going public so soon. Unfettered access to a Harvard professor unveiling an iconoclastic discovery—one that had not been so much as peer-reviewed—could leave both scholar and school perilously exposed. (A source close to Harvard's press office later confirmed Webb's hunch: Harvard faculty have free rein to talk to the media, but "if Karen had consulted us, we would have said, 'Don't do it.'")

Webb and Veale climbed the stairs to King's monkish office on the fifth floor of Andover Hall. They had reserved the next day for shooting and wanted to square away a few points of housekeeping ahead of time. A key one was what to call the fragment. Its anonymous owner, of course, had given it the plain-vanilla title Coptic Papyrus 02-11—or "Copt-pap. 02-11," as he abbreviated it, likely as part of some personal cataloging system. The filmmakers, in their discussions with King, had been referring to it simply as "the papyrus." For script writing, Webb felt it would be helpful to know if King had given it any kind of formal, technical or scholarly name.

"Well," King replied, "I'm thinking of calling it 'The Gospel of Jesus's Wife.'"

The challenge for documentary makers, in presenting academic work, was always to strike the right balance between engaging ordinary viewers and keeping faith with the nuance of careful scholarship. Webb had interviewed enough scholars over the years to expect the usual impenetrable nomenclature. *This,* he never expected. "If Karen had decided to call it Artifact 957/A, then that would have been fine," he said. "So to be given, as it were, the license to call this little tiny fragment 'The Gospel of Jesus's Wife'...it sort of put the headline on the story that even as a journalist and filmmaker I would never have dared to apply myself." Webb could go to his superiors now with "this extremely vivid and illustrative form of words that we could then use with the full sanction of somebody like Karen.

"The headline was being written for us."

In media interviews in Rome two months later, King took every opportunity to warn that the fragment was not historical proof that Jesus had a wife. The papyrus was written too late, she insisted, to serve as biography. It meant only that some Christians living more than a century after Jesus's death believed he was married, probably to affirm a theology that deemed wives and mothers capable of discipleship—and sexuality compatible with holiness. "In talking to the press," she would gravely tell reporters in Rome, "a big part of my task is to throw cold water on sensationalism."

Webb was as interested in ratings as anyone in the media business. So a part of him was grateful King had come up with "The Gospel of Jesus's Wife," a hook ready-made for Hollywood. But privately, he couldn't help but wonder: If King really saw her job as minimizing confusion and sensationalism, why had she picked a title that all but guaranteed it?

KAREN KING WAS LOOKING into Webb and Veale's cameras in a stained-glass, multi-faith chapel in Andover Hall, but she might have been speaking to the Vatican. The Church likes to claim that Jesus was a celibate bachelor, but in truth the Gospels say nothing about his marital status. "Not a word," King said. This "pregnant" silence allowed Church leaders to fill the void for their own ends. They called Jesus wifeless and Mary Magdalene a prostitute. Then they turned that "story" into a weapon, to force celibacy on priests and exclude women from power.

"But as soon as you have a powerful set of texts and a powerful counter story," King told the cameras, "it becomes much, much more difficult to take those same kinds of positions." If ever there were a powerful counter story, the Gospel of Jesus's Wife was it. King believed she could date it to the second century, the same period in which a Church Father, Clement of Alexandria, made the first-ever assertion that Jesus was celibate. That is, she could give the first known portrayal of a *married* Jesus the same authority as the first known portrayal of a wifeless one.

It was a somewhat complicated case. For one, Coptic didn't emerge as a written language until the third century. For another, Roger Bagnall had dated the Coptic handwriting to the fourth century. Yet if the Gospel of Jesus's Wife were first composed in the fourth century, critics might dismiss it as a potshot at the settled tradition of a celibate Jesus, a kind of fourth-century *Da Vinci Code*. King, however, saw a way around these obstacles. Many Coptic gospels were translations of Greek originals, so why shouldn't this be, too? She arrived at the second-century date by the same method she had used to assign an unusually early date to the Gospel of Mary. Her premise was that authors of ancient texts were "in conversation" with one another, even if they didn't specifically say so. Would Clement and other Church Fathers start saying that Jesus was celibate in the second century simply because they considered it self-evident? Or were they in a stealthy debate with other second-century Christians who claimed Jesus had a wife? King believed it was the latter. "By the time Christians are making overt claims that Jesus was celibate," King contended, "they must be in some ways arguing against a tradition that says he was married."

The Church Fathers never mention such a debate. Nor do they cite the idea of a married Jesus on any of their long lists of known heresies. But because ancient texts were "in conversation" with one another and because Clement wrote his in the late second century, King argued, the Gospel of Jesus's Wife—or rather, the hypothesized Greek original, which a Coptic scribe later translated—was "highly likely" to have been written then, too. For the first time in history, she said, we were hearing the other side of a second-century debate over whether Christians should marry and have sexual intercourse. At the upcoming meeting of scholars in Rome, and in interviews with the media, she planned to state plainly that the fragment did not constitute historical proof of Jesus's marriage. But that didn't make it historically meaningless. As evidence of a silenced tradition, "it puts into greater question the assumption that Jesus *wasn't* married, which has equally no evidence," she said. "This means that the whole Catholic claim of a celibate priesthood based on Jesus's celibacy has no historical foundation. They always say, 'This is the tradition; this is the tradition.' Now we see that this alternative tradition has been silenced."

Biblical scholars were notoriously disputatious, and King expected fierce debates over her interpretation. So little of this text survived that differences of opinion were inevitable. But liberal or conservative, atheist or orthodox, everyone would have to reckon with the line at its very center. The phrase "Jesus said to them, 'My wife,'" spoke "a new word" into the historical silence about Jesus's marital status, King told the documentary makers' cameras. "A word that lets one think possibly that Jesus was married, that marriage was a good thing, that marriage might indeed have the capacity to bring about a spiritual union of people, that it could be conceived of not as simply a concession, but... as something that is fully worthy of the spiritual life.

"A word," King continued, "that in fact had been marginalized and lost and perhaps purposefully erased from the tradition. A word that allows us to recapture the pleasures of sexuality, the joyfulness and the beauties of human intimate relations.

"What it leads us to do," she said of the tiny papyrus fragment, "is to completely re-evaluate the way in which Christianity looks at sexuality and at marriage."

A BRILLIANT JEWEL

In the Egyptian city of Alexandria around A.D. 206, a twenty-year-old Bible teacher named Origen felt unease at the sight of women in his classroom. The prospect of sexual arousal—his own—could jeopardize his standing as a man of irreproachable Christian faith. So he castrated himself. Any pain he might have felt was offset by the inspiration he found in the Gospel of Matthew, in which Jesus describes people who "have made themselves eunuchs for the sake of the kingdom of heaven." At first, Demetrius, the Christian bishop of Alexandria, was in awe at Origen's "daring" act of devotion. But when Origen's fame as a theologian threatened to overshadow his own, Demetrius turned on him, informing "bishops throughout the world" of Origen's "most foolish" deed. Even Eusebius, Origen's ancient biographer, seemed torn. On the one hand, his subject's emasculation "gave the highest proof of faith and continence." On the other, it "evidenced an immature and youthful mind" that had taken Matthew 19:12 "in too literal and extreme a sense."

Only after bishops ordained him a priest—"worthy in the highest degree of the honor"—did Origen seem to admit his misreading. Preaching in the coastal city of Caesarea, Origen said that Jesus's saying about self-made eunuchs was probably just a metaphor. Scalpels, he urged, should be traded for Scripture—the "sharp-cutting Word." Through sexual renunciation, holy men could just as easily sever their souls from the polluting urges of the flesh. But not even Origen could stop the cutting. The Council of Nicaea is famous for issuing the creed that still anchors the orthodox faith. Less known was its first order of business. "If any one in sound health has castrated himself," said its first canon, "then it is good that such a one, if enrolled among the clergy, should cease [his ministry]."

The muddle over how to make one's body Christlike might have been avoided had the Gospels simply described Jesus's marital status. They are matter-of-fact about other details in his earthly life: He gets dressed. He eats. He sleeps. He turns water into wine at a wedding in Cana. But never mentioned is whether Jesus had a wedding of his own. The New Testament speaks of eunuchs and virgins, of lust and fornication, of husbands and wives, of divorce and remarriage. But there is no just-the-facts account of where Jesus falls on that continuum.

To make the case for Jesus as a wifeless virgin, that is, one can't *quote* from the Bible; one must *argue* from it. The logic tends to be inductive and, at bottom, speculative. Mother Mary was a virgin when the Holy Spirit impregnated her, goes one argument, so Jesus *must* have been untainted by sexual desire. Jesus asked followers to break with—and even "hate"—their biological families, goes another, so what example would he set if he'd had a wife of his own? But the arguments didn't end there. The New Testament calls the Church or holy Jerusalem Christ's spiritual bride, so he couldn't have also had a human wife. On Judgment Day, according to Matthew, Jesus will usher the resurrected into a heaven where people "will neither marry nor be given in marriage"; it stands to reason, some have said, that Jesus would forswear marriage in his earthly life in preparation for the next. In Matthew 19:12—the verse on self-made eunuchs that Origen read too literally—Jesus says, "He who is able to accept this, let him accept it." Jesus, therefore, must have been a voluntary "eunuch" himself. "It would be absurd," contends the scholar Birger Pearson, "to think that Jesus placed this challenge before others without accepting it for himself."

Scholars with the opposing view use a similar logic. The God of the Hebrew Bible blesses sex and marriage; he commands his people to "be fruitful and multiply" and tells men of their duty to sexually satisfy their wives. Because Jesus was a Jew, the failure of Gospel writers to note so radical a break from custom could mean just one thing: Jesus was married, like every other Jewish rabbi of his time. Indeed, Jewish marriage was so much the norm that the Gospels rarely mention it for anyone. If not for a scene in which Jesus heals a woman described as Peter's mother-in-law, we might never have known that Peter was married. Then there's the simple fact that Jesus praises marriage as the merging of two people into "one flesh" that no man should "put asunder." How, then, could he have deemed marriage beneath him? One needn't look past 1 Corinthians to see the apostles traveling with their wives. If Jesus didn't see their marriages as disqualifying, how strong could his objections be? Perhaps most dispositively, the apostle Paul admits that the superiority of celibacy is his opinion alone, not Jesus's. "Now concerning virgins," Paul says in 1 Corinthians. "I have no commandment from the Lord, yet I give my judgment."

So if the tradition of certainty about Jesus's celibacy didn't come from the Gospels, where did it come from? The answers can again be found in the Origen story. The self-made eunuch's mentor and predecessor at the Catechetical School of Alexandria was an equally luminous theologian named Clement of Alexandria—the same Clement, incidentally, in whose name an apparently modern forger wrote a letter about Jesus's homoerotic encounter in Secret Mark. In a trilogy of authentic texts called the *Stromata,* or *Miscellanies,* Clement writes in the late second century of some unnamed group of Christians "who say outright that marriage is fornication and teach that it was introduced by the devil. They proudly say that they are imitating the Lord who neither married nor had any possession in this world, boasting that they understand the gospel better than anyone else."

To judge from the surviving manuscripts, it is the first time in history that anyone says anything definite about whether Jesus was married. And it comes not in a gospel but in a thirdhand report written hundreds of miles from the Galilee well over a century after Jesus's death. Clement casually affirms that Jesus was single but rejects the group's claim that marriage is evil. Jesus's celibacy wasn't meant to be copied, Clement insisted. "They do not know the reason why the Lord did not marry. In the first place he had his own bride, the Church; and in the next place he was no ordinary man that he should also be in need of some helpmeet after the flesh. Nor was it necessary for him to beget children since he abides eternally and was born the only Son of God."

Around the same time as Clement makes his report, a theologian in Carthage—more than a thousand miles from the Galilee—makes a similar case. Jesus, says the theologian Tertullian, is not just "*innuptus in totum,*" totally unwed, but "*spado en carne,*" impotent in the flesh. Tertullian invokes Jesus's celibacy as an honorable choice for the spiritually adept. But prohibiting marriage—as some second-century believers advocated—went too far. Matrimony, Tertullian felt, was the best defense for ordinary Christians against sinful desire.

Another two centuries would pass, however, before Christian suspicion of sex would anneal into its most lasting—and, some say, most virulent—form. No one was more responsible for this shift than a man born to a Christian mother and pagan father in a small city in inland Algeria.

AUGUSTINE WAS SIXTEEN years old and at a public bath in A.D. 370 when his father noticed signs, on the boy's nude body, of "*inquieta adulescentia*"—a "restless" sexual maturity that scholars believe was either pubic hair or an unintentional erection. Rejoicing at the prospect of one day having grandchildren, Augustine's father raced home to tell his wife, Monica, who in her Christian piety was "startled with an holy fear and trembling." So Augustine recounts in his *Confessions.* "For she wished," he continued, "and I remember in private with great anxiety warned me, 'not to commit fornication.'" Her advice didn't take. At university in Carthage, Augustine embarked on a series of affairs with women—and possibly men. "I was in the habit of polluting the shared channel of friendship with putrid rutting, and clouding its pale purity with a lust from hell." He fathered a child with an unmarried woman and later took a mistress while engaged to yet another woman. Racked by a libido that seemed to have a mind of its own, Augustine, by then a rhetoric professor, repaired to a church in Milan where he found himself transformed by the sermons of Ambrose, the city's celibate bishop. "Shortly thereafter," writes one historian, "he broke off his engagement to marry, resigned his professorship, vowed himself to perpetual chastity, and determined to return to Africa and found a monastic community." Named bishop of the maritime city of Hippo, in his homeland of Algeria, Augustine exploited his gifts as a master rhetorician to pull off a decisive rewriting of the Adam and Eve story.

In the book of Genesis, God punishes the first couple's disobedience by condemning them and their offspring—humanity—to lives of hardship and death. Augustine argued, against centuries of tradition, that God's actual punishment was something else: ungovernable lust. Before they ate from the Tree of Knowledge, he contended, Adam and Eve had complete dominion over their organs of reproduction. Sex was as deliberate and passionless as a "handshake." But after Adam and Eve defied God and succumbed to the serpent, Augustine claimed,

God took vengeance in kind—by endowing the first couple with sex organs that rebelled against *them*. The penis, and presumably its female counterpart—Augustine was most focused on the male organ—became the only body part that humans could not control through the executive function of the will. It stirred when we didn't want it to, and, too often, it didn't stir when we did. That's why Adam and Eve's first act after tasting the forbidden fruit was to drape fig leaves over their *pudenda*, their shameful parts. God was so implacable that he spared no human the wages of the couple's sin. He did so, Augustine maintained, by implanting the curse of defiant sex organs in Adam's semen, so that every child born of semen hence was tainted at conception by mutinous lust. Augustine's doctrine would become known as original sin. In a clever stroke of logic, it excluded one person: Jesus, whose progenitor, the Holy Spirit, impregnated the Virgin Mary by other means.

A by-product of Augustine's doctrine was the demonization of women. Just as Eve introduced sin to the world by seducing Adam, so has every other woman borne the seeds of man's destruction. Whether wife or mother, Augustine wrote, "it is still Eve (the temptress) that we must beware of in any woman." He warned Christian men to love their spouses as Jesus "loves his enemy": "Love in her what is characteristic of a human being . . . hate what belongs to her as a wife." The Holy See canonized Augustine and named him a "Doctor of the Church," an honorific reserved for saints whose teachings are judged timeless. His rewrite of the Adam and Eve story almost single-handedly yoked sex in the Western imagination with shame and sin. It remains the still-perceptible hum behind debates over abortion, birth control, gay rights and other policy matters in which the specter of sex for pleasure retains the stink of original sin.

IN THE EARLY FOURTH CENTURY, the Council of Elvira, in Spain, became the first provincial body to require priests to renounce sex. But it wasn't until 1123 that priestly celibacy became church-wide law. Pope Callistus II called hundreds of church leaders to Rome for the First Lateran Council. "We absolutely forbid priests, deacons or subdeacons to live with concubines and wives," the council declared in its canons that year. "Marriage contracts between such persons should be made void and the persons ought to undergo penance." The new laws, which incited strenuous protest from clergy, did less to eliminate sex than to drive it underground. Many male clergy continued to have secret wives, concubines, gay lovers, illegitimate children and, in at least one London parish, a special brothel where "only men with a tonsure, the shaven circle representing Christ's crown of thorns, were admitted." The abuse of children by priests, which mushroomed into a global scandal in the twenty-first century, is seen by many critics as the gravest unintended consequence of mandatory celibacy.

A Church crackdown on married priests in the thirteenth century prompted an anonymous poet to lampoon the effort as futile:

Our Lord decreed we should have wives;
Our Pope demurs—and spoils our lives.
. . . .
Priests who lack a girl to cherish
Won't be mindful lest they perish.
They will take whom'er they find
Married, single—never mind!

The Eastern Orthodox Church—which ordains married priests— broke with Roman Catholicism in the eleventh century partly in pro- test of its celibacy policies, as did the Protestants who launched the Reformation five centuries later. Martin Luther, the German Augustine monk who led the Reformation, not only forsook his vow of celibacy but married a former nun. "On our side we have Scripture, the Church Fathers, ancient Church laws and even papal precedent," Luther wrote in 1528. "They have the contrary statements of a few Fathers, recent canons and their own mischief."

The closest the Church came to a reappraisal was the Second Vati- can Council. The meeting of hundreds of bishops, convened by Pope John XXIII in 1962, sought to breathe fresh air into the Church amid the cultural upheavals of the twentieth century. In a major break with his predecessors, Pope John XXIII allowed that priestly celibacy was not divine law. "The Scriptures do not impose it," he told an interviewer in the early 1960s. Rather, it was a doctrine imposed by the Church, changeable with the stroke of a pope's pen. He expressed a surprising measure of compassion for clergy who struggled with its requirements. "The thought of those young priests . . . causes me constant suffering," he said. "For some of them it is martyrdom.... I hear a sort of moan, as if many voices were asking the church for liberation from the burden." But changing the law, he said, "is impossible. Celibacy is a sacrifice, which the church has imposed upon herself—freely, generously and heroically."

His humanism gave celibacy abolitionists hope, but he died in 1963 with the Second Vatican Council still under way. His successor, Pope Paul VI, an Italian lawyer's son, intervened to strike it off the agenda. "Our intention," he said, "is not only to preserve this ancient law as far as possible, but to strengthen its observance." Two years later, in his landmark encyclical *Sacerdotalis caelibatus,* or *Priestly Celibacy,* Paul VI declared that no "modern stirrings of opinion" would "drown out the solemn and age-old voice of the pastors" who had guarded priestly celibacy "as a brilliant jewel" requiring a "truly virile asceticism." The 1960s were just the latest era in which "the practices of a decadent society did not favor the heroic demands of virtue." He had harsh words for the "lamentable" priests begging release from their vows. Sex scandals were a result of priests' individual shortcomings, he said, not of celibacy. He pointed to the "example" of Christ, who he said "remained throughout His whole life in the state of celibacy, which signified His total dedication to the service of God and men." That "Christ's example"—as either celibate *or* married—is found nowhere in the gospels seemed not to matter. What counted was tradition.

In 1969, a secret Vatican study, which was leaked to the Italian press, found a tenfold jump since Vatican II in the number of priests who, wishing to marry, asked and received dispensation from their vows of celibacy, thereby losing their clerical powers. But Paul VI was unmoved. In an audience at St. Peter's Basilica, he fulminated against "a revolutionary mentality" on the loose in the Church.

In 1976, two years before his death, Pope Paul VI headed off a debate over women's ordination with similar dispatch, ordering the Vatican's anti-heresy office to publicize the biblical basis for the all-male priesthood. The office's Croatian prefect, Cardinal Franjo Šeper, issued an official statement. He wrote that Jesus's unusual closeness with women—as well as the often superior faith it inspired in them—was deliberate and courageous. It broke sharply from what he called "the Jewish mentality, which did not accord great value to the testimony of women." Moreover, "in the life of the Church herself, as history shows us, women have played a decisive role and accomplished tasks of outstanding value."

Šeper acknowledged that it was not "immediately obvious" why any of this should bar women from the priesthood. But "this is no surprise, for the questions that the Word of God brings before us go beyond the obvious." As Šeper saw it, Jesus's radical inclusion of women in his inner circle gave weight to what must have been their deliberate *exclusion* from "the Twelve." Put simply, if a proto-feminist like Jesus never chose a female apostle—not even one as perfect as his own virginal mother—then the faithful had to accept it as one of Christ's ineffable mysteries. (Mary Magdalene's absence from Šeper's fifty-four-hundred-word statement is glaring.) The cardinal saluted the gains of modern women in the secular world, but this was the Church. "The priestly office cannot become the goal of social advancement," he wrote. In refusing to ordain women, the Church was bound by "Christ's manner of acting": "Jesus did not entrust the apostolic charge to women."

Pope Paul VI couldn't have been more pleased. "Anyone who substitutes his own spiritual experience, his own feeling of subjective faith, his own personal interpretation of the Word of God certainly produces a novelty, but it is a ruin," he said of the calls for change. "New things cannot be produced in the church by a *break* with tradition.... Novelty, for us, consists essentially in a return to genuine tradition."

Which raised an interesting question: What if someone were to discover a genuine tradition of a married Jesus? And what if that same tradition showed Jesus entrusting the apostolic charge to his own wife? What of celibacy and the all-male priesthood then? Front and center on King's papyrus were two lines so full of firepower they could almost be bullets:

...Jesus said to them, "My wife...
...she is able to be my disciple..."

THE SMITHSONIAN CHANNEL SHOOT, on July 25, 2012, was a kind of Rubicon. It hitched King's reputation—and Harvard's—to the papyrus in ways that could not be easily undone. As the cameras rolled at Harvard Divinity School, no one besides Roger Bagnall and Anne-

Marie Luijendijk had examined the papyrus. King had yet to so much as submit her article to the *Harvard Theological Review,* which meant that not a single journal editor or peer reviewer had seen her analysis of it. Her planned announcement in Rome—and the insights it might yield from a far broader group of scholars—was still two months away. Yet King was already rhapsodizing on film about her discovery's sweeping historical significance, for a documentary not scheduled to air for another three months.

The very morning after the shoot, the papyrus's owner—whom King informed of the documentary—wrote that he needed money. He would donate the Wife fragment to Harvard, he said, but wanted the university to shield him from journalists and purchase the rest of his collection, which included a Coptic fragment of the Gospel of John. "I kind of feel that this is eventually going to get out, and everybody will start hounding me," he wrote to King on July 26. "Honestly, I don't feel like dealing with the DaVinci-crowd at all.... I wouldn't mind donating it to Harvard, so it's on your back, and you can fight off reporters.

"Unfortunately," he added, "I am not extremely wealthy, like most other players in that field, so I can't just walk away from it all." As a price benchmark, the owner mentioned a third-century vellum scrap of Paul's Epistle to the Romans that had sold at Sotheby's that month for some $490,000, nearly double the auction house's initial estimate. The buyer was the Green family, the evangelical billionaires who own the Hobby Lobby craft store chain and who were stockpiling ancient manuscripts for a Bible museum they planned to open near the National Mall in Washington, D.C. The Romans fragment "sold for almost half a million last week in London," the collector wrote to King, "so, after nothing really moved in this area for the past 20 years, we have an amount as a measuring scale at least for canonical fragments." The implication was that Harvard pay a similar sum for his John fragment.

If the timing of the request—or the price tag—gave King pause, she didn't let on. Rather, on the afternoon of the same day, she sent the collector her unreserved gratitude. "I am stunned and overwhelmed by your generous proposal," she wrote. "I'll take your proposal to my 'powers that be' asap and see what they have to say. I hope they fully appreciate your offer."

She emailed with good news the next day. "I did contact my Dean yesterday and got the go-ahead to pursue your plan—indeed there was a lot of excitement and hope that we could make this work." In an apparent response to the collector's request that she "fight off reporters" on his behalf, King wrote that she and Luijendijk were "happy to take the heat!!"

Another threshold had been crossed. "My Dean" appeared to refer to David Hempton, a Christian historian who'd won the leadership post just four weeks earlier. King had served on the search committee that recommended Hempton to Harvard's president, Drew Faust. In just two days, the reputations of Harvard's Hollis Professor of Divinity, its new divinity school dean and possibly even Harvard's president had become entangled with the fate of the papyrus.

In mid-August, a pair of Smithsonian Channel executives visited King at Harvard to make sure her confidence in the manuscript hadn't wavered since the shoot. If she had developed doubts—which sometimes happens—they wanted to know. They were giving her an out, at least as far as the documentary was concerned. But when they arrived, King sought only to fan their interest.

"Would you like to see the fragment?" David Royle, the executive vice president of Smithsonian Networks, recalled her asking as they sat in her office. When Royle and his colleague Charles Poe said they did, she took it out of a desk drawer and made clear that they were in a charmed circle. "She said to us that she had not shared it with the dean of the Divinity School, that we were in a tiny handful of people that were going to see this.... That just raised the excitement level that much more.... There was no commentary about 'I didn't mean to say this,' or 'I want to qualify what I told your film crew,' or 'Can we do some more filming?' "

Royle set an October 2012 airdate for the hour-long documentary and told editors at *Smithsonian,* the magazine of the Smithsonian Institution, that King was also willing to be interviewed for a print story. Time was scarce. The magazine wanted a major feature that would be ready to publish on September 18, the day King planned to announce the discovery in Rome. An editor called me at home in late August and asked if I could drop everything to take on the story. I booked one of the next planes to Boston.

KING HAD AGREED to meet for dinner, on September 4, 2012, at Bergamot, a restaurant a few blocks from the divinity school. Our reservations were for 5:30 p.m.

King arrived at 5:45 and apologized. "There was a crisis," she said.

The *Harvard Theological Review* had sent King's article—along with photographs of the fragment—to outside peer reviewers. One thought the papyrus looked "okay," King told me. But another—whose review had arrived just that afternoon—flagged a host of troubling problems, from errors in the Coptic grammar to oddities in the appearance of the ink. The reviewer suspected that the fragment was a forgery.

"My first response was shock," King told me, once we'd sat down. "My second reaction was, 'Well, let's get this settled. Ahead of time.'"

THE CONFERENCE IN ROME was now just two weeks away, and the journal, she said, had planned to publish her big paper the following month. I asked what level of certainty she needed, on the question of authenticity, to proceed with her presentation in Rome. "Is it 100 percent? Is it 95 percent?"

"One hundred percent doesn't exist, but, boy, high—I mean, way, way, way, way high," she replied, with a laugh that suggested she was not messing around. "Fifty-fifty doesn't count, and seventy-thirty doesn't count. I mean, 'No, no, *uh-uh, uh-uh.*'" Some of the world's most prestigious institutions—the British Museum, the Metropolitan Museum of Art, the Louvre—had been hoodwinked by hoaxes. "I have zero interest in publishing anything that's a forgery. Period." As she later told *The Boston Globe*, "If it's a forgery, it's a career breaker."

With stakes so high, I was interested in the steps she planned to take to reach the level of confidence she said she needed. I knew that she was a historian, not a scientist or papyrologist. She would have to rely, to some degree, on others' expertise for certain key assessments. With one anonymous peer reviewer in favor and one against, King was still—by this measure at least—at no better than fifty-fifty. Had there been another supportive peer review?

There was a third review, King said. It had come in earlier. But "it just doesn't count," she told me. "I mean the person just didn't do what would be needed."

I learned later that this reviewer, too, had deemed the papyrus a likely fake. I would also discover that the two unfavorable reviews had so unnerved the co-editors of the *Harvard Theological Review* that they effectively rejected King's article. "Given the worries of two of the

three reviewers (especially #3), we are reluctant to go ahead with publication at this time," Kevin Madigan and Jon Levenson had written to
King at 3:56 p.m., less than two hours before my dinner interview with
her. "We are as surprised and disappointed by this unforeseen turn of
events as you and would very much prefer to be sending a message of
acceptance right now."

SIX YEARS EARLIER, the National Geographic Society had announced
the discovery of the Gospel of Judas, a seventeen-hundred-year-old
codex that made international news for casting the New Testament
villain in a new light. Rather than being Jesus's betrayer, the text suggested, Judas Iscariot was his close friend and favorite disciple. To help
make the case for authenticity, the society had subjected the papyrus to
radiocarbon dating, ink analysis, electron microscopy, micro X-ray dif-
fraction and other laboratory tests. Scientific analysis might well yield
similar assurances about King's papyrus, and perhaps break the impasse
among the peer reviewers, whose opinions now ran two to one against
authenticity. It was true that Roger Bagnall and AnneMarie Luijendijk
had identified no signs of forgery. But King had sought them out, and
the trio's relationships were entwined: Luijendijk was King's former
student and was now under tenure review, an intensely stressful period
in which Princeton would be well within its rights to contact King
for her opinion. Luijendijk's doctoral thesis, meanwhile, was a kind of
paean to the scholarship of Roger Bagnall, who in turn had sat on her
dissertation committee and hosted her overnight at his family's apartment during her research trips to New York.

At the *Harvard Theological Review,* by contrast, peer reviews are
double-blind; the author doesn't know the reviewer's identity, and the
reviewer doesn't know the author's. The two-way anonymity is thought
to foster candid exchange, free from fear or favor. As stewards of one of
the field's marquee journals, the *Review*'s co-editors would almost certainly have chosen referees with world-renowned expertise in Coptic
Christian papyri.

Yet King saw no need for scientific testing. Chemical tests were
"not usually done and not relevant," she told me. Carbon dating was too
imprecise, she insisted, and multispectral analysis—an imaging technique that can help identify erased or overwritten text—"wasn't going

to show anything." A determined forger could acquire a blank scrap of centuries-old papyrus (even on eBay, where fragments are routinely auctioned) and make ink from ancient recipes. Scientists would be none the wiser.

Yet what if a forger hadn't been so careful? What if they had used ink whose chemicals weren't manufactured until, say, 1928, or if radiocarbon tests dated the papyrus to the eighteenth century A.D., or, stranger still, to 400 B.C.? Wouldn't King want to know before contacting the media? Wouldn't she want the information before going public across from the Vatican, where scrutiny of her find—and her motives—was apt to be especially fierce? Lab tests could take a few weeks, but there was no shortage of other opportunities for King to announce her find. Her field's next big conference, the annual gathering of the Society of Biblical Literature, in Chicago, was just two months after the one in Rome.

THE NEXT DAY, I climbed a narrow set of stairs to her office, a garret-like space atop Founders' Tower, a Gothic column in Andover Hall whose parapet was engraved with the faces of Matthew, Mark, Luke and John.

"So here it is," King said when I entered. The papyrus was there on her desk, next to an open can of Diet Dr Pepper. The fragment was the color of honey, its edges notched and frayed. When King lifted it to one of her trefoiled windows, sunlight pricked through holes where the reeds had worn thin. "It's in pretty good shape," she mused. "I'm not going to look this good after sixteen hundred years." On a wall beside the window hung a modern illustration, in medieval style, of a hooded Mary Magdalene coolly announcing the resurrection to eleven lost-looking male apostles.

At about 12:50 p.m., as our meeting concluded, something on her computer caught her eye—an email from Roger Bagnall. "That was a fast response!" she said.

That afternoon, some twenty minutes before I arrived, King had forwarded him the three anonymous reviews, including the one that triggered the previous night's crisis. "Deeply in need of your advice and help," she had written.

Bagnall replied, with characteristic speed, in under half an hour. He was unconvinced by some of the objections but urged her to find "any parallels" for the "non-standard" Coptic that had unsettled the reviewer. He also suggested she enlist a senior expert on Coptic script "to make a proper case [for the handwriting]—which is probably necessary." He quipped, "I'm glad at least that referee 3 doesn't think that you're Morton Smith redivivus!"

"Ahh, yeah, okay!" King said, clearly buoyed by his reply. "Go, Roger!"

"Okay, just a little thanks," she said as she typed out a reply. "Have to thank your people."

The General Curia of the Order of Saint Augustine stands on the sloping grounds of a former Renaissance villa, across a narrow street from St. Peter's Square. No major Catholic order has its headquarters closer to the Vatican. On a high-backed throne at the foot of its cobblestoned driveway sits a life-size statue of its patron, the theologian most responsible for Christianity's tortured view of sex. The rugged Augustine, in ornate miter and long robe, appears at first to be keeping watch over all who pass. But on closer inspection, the eyes, beneath heavy lids, are empty sockets. Propped in his lap, like a shield, is his book *De civitate Dei—The City of God*—his response to pagans who accused Christianity of precipitating the fall of Rome.

After the Second Vatican Council, the Augustinians, an eight-hundred-year-old mendicant order, resolved to move forward by looking back. The friars built a school that awarded priests advanced degrees in the "sacred science" of patristics, the branch of theology devoted to the lives and writings of Church Fathers like Origen, Clement of Alexandria and, of course, Augustine. The school was wedged onto the order's small lot beside the Vatican and inaugurated in 1970 by Pope Paul VI, who had recently defended the celibate, all-male priesthood against a reformist crusade. The Institutum Patristicum Augustinianum became the first stand-alone institute of patristics in the world. "It caught like a raging fire because it was the only one," Cardinal Prospero Grech, one of the Augustinianum's founders, said when I reached him by phone in Rome. I asked why, at a time of reform and renewal, the Church would be eager for a backward-looking institution. "Because the whole Catholic teaching is with reference to the first century," Grech said. He had just published a book called *"What Was from the Beginning."* It was a response to scholars, like Karen King, who argued that "there was initially a variety of Christianities," out of which one splinter, Catholicism, prevailed. The idea of "it's from the beginning" is the touchstone of orthodoxy, Grech told me. The Augustinianum was needed, in times of change, "to retain the backbone of the faith."

ALBERTO CAMPLANI, a historian of Coptic Christianity at Rome's Sapienza University, couldn't have been more grateful when the Augustinian fathers offered him the use, *gratis*, of the classrooms at its patristics institute. An amenable and fast-talking Milanese who wears his glasses low on his nose, Camplani, who was fifty-one, had spent three years organizing the Tenth International Congress of Coptic Studies. Figuring out where to hold the scholarly conference was always a challenge. The quadrennial gathering brought together the world's foremost specialists in Coptic language and culture. More than three hundred of them were set to descend on Rome in September 2012 to present their latest research in more than two hundred papers. Though attendees paid a small fee, the conference subsisted on donations from outside benefactors. The Vatican not only agreed to make the Augustinianum available; it also staged a special exhibit, in the Vatican Apostolic Library, of its own invaluable Coptic scriptures. The Vatican's in-kind donations were worth nearly half the costs not covered by attendance fees, but they weren't wholly altruistic. Many early copies of the canonical gospels survive in Coptic, and the Church has an interest in promoting their study. In addition, since the Second Vatican Council, a growing ecumenism had fueled bridge building with Copts and other orthodox Christians who had long ago broken with the Western church. The Coptic conference usually drew a couple of dozen learned Coptic priests from Egypt, whose long black robes stood out against the secular scholars' leather jackets, khaki and tweed.

For Camplani, the hardest part of planning the conference was less the fund-raising than "stupid problems that took a lot of time": the logistics of coffee breaks and projector rentals, the coordination of travel grants, the scheduling conflicts. With hundreds of scholars arriving from twenty-seven countries, none of those things were simple. Atop all that, Camplani and his Italian colleagues had to evaluate scholars' proposals, rejecting some outright and asking others for revisions. When Harvard's Karen King submitted her proposal, it was so short and cryptic that Camplani had to ask her to rewrite it. It was an awkward request to make of so prominent a scholar. But as conference organizer, Camplani had to know what people intended to talk about.

On June 25, 2012, the same day she disclosed her discovery to the Smithsonian Channel filmmakers, King emailed Camplani what she termed a "somewhat more informative abstract."

> The paper will present a previously unpublished papyrus.... It contains dialogue between Jesus and his disciples concerning family and discipleship. The paper will discuss the possible significance of the fragment's contents.

This was a bit clearer, Camplani thought, but its proposed title—"A New Coptic Gospel Fragment"—remained ambiguous. Was it the "Coptic Gospel" that was "new" or just the "fragment" on which it had been copied? Did the dialogue between Jesus and his disciples concern *Jesus's* family or just the idea of family? Camplani didn't press. He had been scheduled to give a paper on his own discovery—a copy of the Canons of St. Basil that Polish archaeologists had recently found in a hermit's rubbish heap—on the same evening as King's. But he saw no reason to change the time, either for fear of competition or out of intense curiosity. Because the conference met just once every four years, papers on ho-hum finds of one sort or another were relatively routine. Aside from King's somewhat vague abstract, there was nothing to suggest that the Tenth International Congress of Coptic Studies would be any different from the nine that had preceded it.

FROM A CROWDED DEPARTURES LOUNGE at Washington Dulles International Airport, I emailed a draft of my story to my editor at *Smithsonian*. It was September 15, 2012. The magazine planned to post the piece—based on interviews with King at Harvard and with Bagnall and Luijendijk by phone—on its website three days later, the minute King announced her discovery at the conference. While the editors set to work on an edit and fact-check, I boarded a red-eye to Rome's Leonardo da Vinci Airport. The magazine planned to publish a fuller story in its next print issue and wanted me in the room when King presented her find to colleagues.

I caught up with her at 9:00 a.m. on September 18, in the Aula Magna, a brightly lit, wood-paneled auditorium on the Augustinianum's first floor. When I sat down, her second husband, Norman Cluley, a retired engineering professor, stood up and waved goodbye—apparently preferring the sights of Rome to a day of lectures on Coptic. He'd be back for her big talk, which wasn't until 7:00 that night.

"How goes the battle with technology?" I asked King. In an email three days earlier, she had mentioned that her laptop suddenly stopped working on her flight to Rome.

"The battle with technology was lost," she said. Her prepared remarks were on the laptop, she said, as were the photos of the papyrus that she planned to show colleagues. (The papyrus itself remained at Harvard.) Not only would she have to rewrite her talk from memory, she said. She'd have no images to show during her big presentation.

THE WALLS OF THE Augustinianum's Room 2 were hung with faded maps of the Roman Empire, vast territories stretching from "Britannia" and "Galatia" to "Africa Proconsularis" and "Aegyptus." As King entered the room, she remembered that the academic booksellers downstairs were offering half-price discounts to customers who claimed their orders early. "Sweetie," she said, turning to her husband, "will you remind me to pick up a book I ordered?"

King's talk was the last of the evening. Shortly before the appointed time, she passed out copies of her translation and took her place behind the lectern. Looking out over some three dozen of the world's leading Coptic scholars, she acknowledged that anonymous peer reviewers had raised "substantive questions" about "whether this text might indeed be a forgery." One of the reviewers, for all she knew, could well be in the room, she said. But she minimized their concerns. Roger Bagnall had already "judged the fragment to be authentic," she said, and the *Harvard Theological Review,* "after some significant hesitation, has now decided to go ahead with publication." In any case, she said, papyrology and linguistics—from which the forgery suspicions sprang—were not her forte. "My focus, as those of you who know my work [are aware], is primarily in interpretation and the significance of this fragment, and I want to spend most of the time today talking about that."

LINE 1: "... *not [to] me. My mother gave me li[fe]* ..."

The papyrus's first words matched a snippet of the Gospel of Thomas, a noncanonical list of 114 "secret sayings" that Jesus was said to have disclosed to someone named Thomas the Twin. The words belonged to a famous saying, with parallels in Matthew and Luke, in which Jesus redefines family, urging his disciples to replace ties of blood with bonds of faith. To find a sort of topic sentence in a scrap this small was unquestionably helpful. It identified the theme as "family and discipleship," King told the audience, which "of course is a widespread topic in early Christian literature."

The second line set the scene:

LINE 2: ..." *The disciples said to Jesus, "*...

For readers of the gospels, the scene was exceedingly familiar: Jesus and his disciples in conversation.

The next appeared to introduce conflict:

LINE 3 (FIRST ALTERNATIVE): ... *deny. Mary is worthy of it*...
LINE 3 (SECOND ALTERNATIVE): ... *deny. Mary is not worthy of it*...

Whether Mary was being called "worthy" or "not worthy" of something—and whether Mary's worthiness or unworthiness was the thing being denied—were hard to say, in part because of a stray letter at the end of the line. But the existence of at least one argumentative word—"deny"—sufficed to establish the nature of the conversation: There was a dispute. Something about Mary's worth had inspired controversy.

The easiest inference was that the Mary at issue was Jesus's mother; the papyrus's first line—"My mother gave me life"—all but said so. But the fourth line led King in a different direction.

LINE 4: ...." *Jesus said to them, "My wife*...

And the next seemed to braid all the preceding lines together.

LINE 5: ... *she is able to be my disciple*...

The New Testament describes various people as worthy—or unworthy—of a great many things: blessings, acts of healing, worker's pay, a wedding invitation, discipleship, resurrection, a visit from Jesus, the unlacing of sandals, the right to call a man one's father. So when Line 3 calls Mary worthy (or unworthy) of "it," the "it" could theoretically be any one of those things or something else altogether. In a similar vein, the "she" at the start of Line 5 could be "my mother" in Line 1; "Mary" in Line 3; "my wife" in Line 4; or some other woman entirely. Too much adjoining text was missing to say with certainty.

But for King, there was at least one known text that looped nearly all these strands into a bow: the Gospel of Mary, which portrayed Mary Magdalene as the flash point in a debate over discipleship. Even if the papyrus wasn't one of the Gospel of Mary's lost pieces, it could well concern the same, or at least a similar, argument. In the article she had submitted to the *Harvard Theological Review,* King drove readers toward these conclusions by a sort of compounding speculation. Unless Jesus had married his mother—an absurd idea—wouldn't the "Mary" in Line 3 have to be the same woman as "my wife" in Line 4? And wouldn't "my wife" have to be the same woman as the "she" in Line 5? If each of these premises was true, then it wasn't hard to see that the "it" that Mary was called worthy (or unworthy) of in Line 3 had to be Line 5's "to be my disciple." If that supposition were true, King wrote, then it was "highly likely that this Mary would have been understood to be Mary of Magdala, given the existence of early Christian traditions which identified a close relationship between Jesus and Mary, and some which questioned Mary's worthiness."

In the next line, Jesus might have gone so far as to curse Mary's doubters:

LINE 6: ... *Let wicked people swell up* ...

In the final two, King argued, Jesus explained his marriage's larger, symbolic significance:

LINE 7: ... *As for me, I dwell with her in order to* ...
LINE 8: .... *an image* ...

In Gnostic texts like the Gospel of Philip, an "image" was sometimes used to mean an earthly copy, or counterpart, of some aspect of the divine. If the word meant the same thing here, then the union of Jesus and Mary Magdalene in earthly wedlock prefigured the unification of every believer's divine spark with its angelic twin in the Light. Jesus was teaching not just "correct sexual relations," King argued, but "the nature of salvation."

This ingenious connecting of dots was precisely how she had made her name in biblical studies. Her style of argument might not have been every religion scholar's cup of tea. "I used to tell my students that 'maybe,' 'maybe,' 'maybe,' 'maybe' does not mean 'surely,'" one told me. Yet King's conjectures were informed by years of scholarship, and she alchemized them into a case for a thoroughgoing Gospel of Jesus's Wife, a hypothetical codex originally written in Greek within 170 years of Jesus's death and spanning some untold number of pages, then copied two centuries later into Coptic, from which only the present, minuscule fragment survived. Some thirty Coptic words on eight discontinuous lines—in the middle of a random page of unknown size—were all King needed to summon a powerful narrative: Jesus's male followers challenge Mary Magdalene's qualifications for disciple-ship, but Jesus sets them straight, calling her "my disciple" and "my wife," wishing ill on her critics, and teaching the spiritual meaning of marriage. From thirty words on eight disconnected lines King had extracted a fully realized story, with setting, conflict and resolution—beginning, middle and end.

"Even a tiny fragment of papyrus can offer surprises with the potential to significantly enrich" history, King said as she concluded her twenty-six-minute presentation. "I await very eagerly your response."

THE FIRST QUESTION CAME from Einar Thomassen, a religion profes-sor at Norway's University of Bergen. "Thank you, Karen, this is truly sensational," he said, to nervous laughter from the room. A tall and distinguished-looking metalworker's son, Thomassen was a friend of King's and an expert on the Gospel of Philip. He was well known for his view that Philip treats Jesus's baptism as both literal and symbolic—a physical cleansing that for Jesus's followers also became a spiritual cleansing. In her talk, King had sought to extend Thomassen's theory to Jesus's wedding, portraying it as both a real act and a symbol—"an image"—of the fusion of a believer's inner divinity with its angelic twin in the higher realm.

Thomassen wasn't entirely convinced. Though the Gospel of

Philip portrayed Jesus and Mary Magdalene as spiritually close, he didn't see it as portraying an earthly marriage. Nor did he see the word choices in King's papyrus as in keeping with the theology of Philip. One of the most obvious problems was the unusual word on which the entire fragment pivoted. Coptic had two words for "wife," and they were of almost identical spelling. The far more common, *shime* (pronounced *seh-HEE-meh*), was also a generic word for "woman." To figure out whether it meant "wife" or "woman," a scholar had to look at what was being said around it. Coptic copies of 1 Corinthians 7:4, for instance, read, "The *shime* does not have authority over her own body but yields it to her husband." There the scribe clearly means "wife." By contrast, 1 Corinthians 11:8 states, "It was from man that *shime* was taken." Here it means "woman."

But in 1900, a distinguished British Egyptologist observed that a far rarer word—*hime* (pronounced *HEE-meh*)—permits no such uncertainty. *Hime* "means 'wife' not 'woman' in all passages in which I can trace it," the Egyptologist declared in a 1900 article. The odd thing, though, was that *hime* wasn't much used. When Coptic scribes translated the word "wife" from the Old Testament, they favored *shime* over *hime* by a ratio of nearly three to one. In the New Testament, the ratio was almost six to one. Found nowhere in any known text from antiquity—religious, documentary or otherwise—is the specific Coptic phrase *ta-hime*—"my wife." Of the half a dozen times "my wife" turns up in early Christian manuscripts in Coptic, scribes used *ta-shime*—literally "my woman"—every single time.

Whether some rule of syntax treated *hime* differently from *shime* is unknown; ancient Copts didn't leave behind grammar books. What is clear is that *ta-hime* (pronounced *tah-HEE-meh*) appears in exactly one known Coptic text: the tiny fragment that a stranger had given Karen King.

> ...*peje Iēsous nau ta-hime*...
> ...Jesus said to them, "My wife..."

The papyrus would thus be noteworthy not just for its content but for its singular use of language. Had an ancient scribe used *ta-shime* instead of *ta-hime*, no scholar would have translated "Jesus said to them, 'My wife...'" differently. No one would think that Jesus, in referring to "my woman," was speaking of, say, a girlfriend. But *ta-hime* took no chances. It doubled down. It was an unprecedented, belt-and-suspenders locution. Most important, it lifted the curse of ambiguity that plagued the word *koinonos,* or "companion," whose mistranslation as "spouse" by *The Da Vinci Code* made the novel's claims an easy target for scholars. Had the Gospel of Philip called Mary Magdalene the *hime* of Jesus instead of his *koinonos,* there would have been no doubt of the gospel's meaning and no doubt about *The Da Vinci Code*'s interpretation. But it didn't.

The problem, for Thomassen, the Norwegian scholar, was that the Gospel of Philip delighted in double entendre. If the same community of believers composed something like the Gospel of Jesus's Wife—as King suggested—he wasn't convinced they would choose a word for "wife" that was so, well, single entendre. "I think maybe *ta-hime* is a bit strong," he said, to another ripple of laughter from the audience. "It's very concrete a word to describe that special relationship."

What word would he have expected? King cut in.

"Maybe a word like 'partner' or something like that would be more suitable here."

King's conceptual leaps, Thomassen suddenly seemed to notice, rested on facts that weren't entirely in evidence. "The text doesn't actually *say* that Mary is that partner," Thomassen said. "But it is something that people supply in the text," he said, diplomatically alluding to King's guesswork.

Another expert on the Gospel of Philip, a Finnish professor at the University of Helsinki, also spoke up, saying he struggled to see a historical context for King's reading. King had argued that the Gnostic teacher Valentinus, whose ideas inform the Gospel of Philip, might have also inspired the Gospel of Jesus's Wife. But the Finnish professor reminded King that Valentinus had called Jesus "continent" in "all things," a man so self-contained that "he ate and drank in a special way without excreting his solids." It would be hard to square such descriptions with a married, sexually active Jesus. "We don't have any evidence," he told King.

Madeleine Scopello, a Sorbonne-educated expert in Gnosticism who served as the session's moderator, was the first of several scholars to suggest that the papyrus could just as well be part of a well-known tradition of Coptic homilies about the Virgin Mary. To lend biblical license to the Coptic Orthodox Church's many feasts, anonymous monks in the fifth to seventh centuries wrote dialogues in the voices of one or another of the apostles. Their aim was to fill the Bible's blanks, like the death of Jesus's mother, an event, known as Dormition, that the Gospels themselves don't record. A number of these homilies con-flate the Virgin Mary and Mary Magdalene, describing the former as a Magdala-born woman who was the first witness to Jesus's resurrection. At least one such homily, another scholar noted, has Jesus kissing his mother on the mouth.

King pushed back. "But the *wife* bit is a little *not* Dormition."

"But we don't know exactly what that word ["wife"] refers to," said Alin Suciu, a Romanian scholar of Coptic manuscripts at the Göttingen Academy of Sciences and Humanities, in Germany.

King, with a flash of pique, replied, "Just that Jesus says, '*My wife...*' Other than that, we know nothing."

"It can be *anything*," Suciu replied. The line broke off before iden-tifying the wife.

In many ways, Suciu was right. The New Testament was replete with images of the Church, or Jerusalem, as Jesus's bride. Both Mark and Luke, for instance, compare Jesus to a bridegroom who refuses to let wedding guests fast. The Gospel of John, meanwhile, likens him to a bridegroom whose voice delights wedding attendants. In Ephesians, Paul compares Jesus's relationship to the Church to that of husband to wife and urges husbands to love their wives as Christ loved the Church. The book of Revelation, meanwhile, calls Jerusalem "the wife of the Lamb," the Lamb being Jesus. These examples are so well attested that theologians group them under the rubric "Bride of Christ," a subject of countless books, papal letters and hundreds of years of Christian tradi-tion. In view of that history, "she is able to be my disciple" and "I dwell with her" could be symbolic references to the Church, rather than to a specific woman. King's fifty-two-page draft article, which Harvard had posted online as her talk got under way, made no mention of the Bride of Christ tradition, not even as a footnoted aside.

The question-and-answer period had barely begun, and some half a dozen hands were still in the air. But King sounded eager to leave. "We have to be out of here by eight o'clock," she said, "or they lock us in."

Doing a slow burn in the back of the room was Wolf-Peter Funk, a scholar at the Université Laval in Quebec and one of the world's senior authorities on the Nag Hammadi library. Funk, who is German, was part of the East Berlin translation team that King studied with while working on her PhD. Her dissertation names him as one of the scholars to whom a "profound debt of gratitude…is beyond repayment." Earlier in the day, Funk had been scheduled to moderate a session on Coptic linguistics, only to realize that he had left his papers in his hotel room. When a cab arrived outside the Augustinianum to whisk him back to the hotel, Funk tripped while sprinting down the cobblestoned driveway. The fall, near the Augustine statue, left a bloody gash on his head.

As he stood up now in the back of the classroom, Funk, whose bandaged cranium seemed the outward manifestation of his reputation for surliness, said, "I'm dissatisfied." How could scholars be expected to comment on a major new papyrus without seeing it? "You haven't shown us a picture," he said, his voice rising. "Why aren't you—"

"The reason you're not being shown a picture," King interjected, "is that my computer *died* on the plane on the way here."

A commotion erupted. Funk looked furious. This was a major announcement, and all King had for her audience was a word-processor printout with her transcription and translation? For scholars of Coptic, a manuscript's physical appearance was paramount. The handwriting style, the look of a papyrus, the ink application—all of it was critical to assessing a manuscript's place in history and its authenticity.

AnneMarie Luijendijk, who was in the room, had high-quality images of the papyrus on her own laptop. Harvard University had multiple images on its servers. Three days had passed since King said her computer had crashed; why she neither copied the photos from her colleague nor had her employer email them to the conference was a mystery. Because King called the papyrus a "gospel," Funk wanted to compare the handwriting with the elegant calligraphy on other gospel papyri. "Is this a book script?" he asked.

King didn't give a direct reply, but said she would be interested in everyone's views on the handwriting once they had a chance to see it. "Yeah, I can't wait to hear—"

"I just got on the web!" a scholar broke in excitedly.

"It's on the web!" another cried, finding the images either on Harvard's website or in one of the just-posted news stories.

A hubbub ensued as scholars jockeyed for position behind colleagues who had brought iPads or laptops. The clamor reached a high enough pitch that the moderator banged a book against the table, like a judge gaveling a court to order. "Some silence, please!" she shouted.

From what Funk could see on a neighbor's laptop, the fragment's ugly, ill-proportioned hand was anything but book script. "The question of genre," he said, wearing an anguished look. "Nothing, nothing, nothing proves that this is part of a real literary gospel."

"Not with anything this size," King conceded. "That's right, that's right."

The talk ended at 7:37 p.m., with twenty-three minutes to spare before the Augustinianum shut its doors. While colleagues lingered in the room to discuss the discovery, King and her husband strode out the door.

A SHOCKING DISCOVERY that gored Catholic tradition. Unveiled by a Harvard professor on a street—Via Paolo VI—named for the pope who championed celibacy against the onslaughts of Vatican II. Inside the walls of a priestly order dedicated to the Church Father who turned Christians against sex.

What had begun as an obscure scholarly conference had taken on the aspect of a Hollywood thriller. Was the Gospel of Jesus's Wife some kind of elaborate payback? Anyone alert to the layers of symbolism might be forgiven for thinking so. I followed King out the door and asked what she made of her colleagues' reactions.

"It was substantive and thoughtful," she said. "They proposed alternatives: 'This could be this; this could be that.' This is exactly what we do." King and her husband briskly descended a marble staircase toward the cobblestoned driveway. "This will have long legs," she said as I tried to keep up. "It may well be discussed for a long time. You can quote me on this—'This is the first word, not the last.'"

ON THE FAINTLY LIT STREETS OUTSIDE, Karen King moved quickly toward a nearby research institute, where a phone had been set aside for an international conference call with the media. Far away, in Cambridge, news trucks converged on Harvard Divinity School, which had just posted a two-and-a-half-minute sizzle reel to the university's YouTube channel, for TV stations and websites to use in place of an interview with King. Word of the discovery spread across the world, and public reaction was swift, divided and strong.

"Being married myself, I always wished Jesus really was married," a woman identifying herself as Lisa M. wrote in the comments beneath one article. "He gives me someone to look at as a role model." A Florida woman who described herself as a lapsed Catholic said, "Jesus was all about unconditional love. I could live with the extension of him loving a woman." A Phoenicia from Texas, for her part, hoped the fragment would "help to end the religious discrimination against women and gays and lesbians."

A "mary" in Pennsylvania, however, bristled at the idea of taking cues from any ancient text. "Am I the only person who feels a little angry that my worth and place depends on what other people believe to have happened 2000 years ago?"

Some wondered what history had to do with religious belief, which was by definition the acceptance of things unseen: "That's what 'faith' is." Others saw the historical record as important, but questioned the evidentiary value of anything so small and incomplete. "We have 27 documents that were written within 65 years of Jesus' death that say nothing of a wife," a John Smith wrote beneath a *New York Times* story. "Along comes this that was written 300 years later. Which is more reliable? It's a no-brainer."

Still others sniffed a political agenda. "The next scrap of parchment likely will say Jesus was homosexual—as soon as they can learn to forge 'gay' in ancient Coptic," wrote a Doug in Orlando, Florida. "And the owner of the earth-shattering parchment chooses to remain anonymous! You don't have to believe in Jesus to suspect this is all contrived nonsense!"

The coolest heads counseled both sides against a rush to judgment. "Reading the comments...I can't help but marvel why people are so opposed to the idea that Jesus was married and thought women worthy disciples," one reader remarked. "One doesn't...have to leap on the Dan Brown bandwagon, one needs only to say, interesting, see how it goes."

Strangers swamped King's email in-box, and while threats and hate abounded, she took heart from the many people who felt moved. Catholic women were "the biggest fan group," she reported. "They love this idea." One had written to King to say, "Now I talk with my daughter. It's going to be okay for her to be a woman."

"It made me weep," King said. "This is what was so interesting to me: we have this imagination in our heads that, 'Oh, Catholics are going to be upset by a married Jesus, because then the hierarchy and everything is going to come crumbling down.' In the reactions that I got to this fragment, to the suggestion that Jesus was married, almost all of it came from Protestants. I was thinking, 'That's really interesting.'

"The question for me is, 'Why then would that be the one issue that a Protestant would not take up?' What's at stake? What's hanging on this unmarried Jesus issue that isn't even about the priesthood? It may not even be about celibacy."

OVER DINNER THAT NIGHT at trattorias and pizzerias around Rome, scholars struggled to make sense of what they had just seen. They held Karen King, Roger Bagnall and AnneMarie Luijendijk in the highest regard. But something felt off. "We all thought it was weird that the sides were broken so cleanly; we'd never seen a fragment like that," recalls Nicola Denzey Lewis, the Gnosticism scholar and friend of King's. Indeed, the scrap was an almost perfect rectangle. The odds of so squared off a geometry were as slim in a papyrus missing all its textual margins as they might be in a shard of glass from the middle of a smashed window. The top was clean and virtually straight, while the sides were frayed. The bottom, meanwhile, was a snaggle of saw-toothed serrations. If a dealer had, say, purposely resected a rectangle from the middle of a page, why the wildly different cuts? The location of the edges was of no small importance; if the fragment was meant as a window onto the past, the edges were the window's frame, its view-finder. They encouraged the eye to begin in one place and to end in another. So it was odd, Lewis thought, that the line about Jesus's wife was right in the middle, where it couldn't be missed. It looked less like a random piece from a larger page than like a blank scrap that someone with an eye for framing had later written on. "If this is authentic," Lewis thought, "it's the weirdest thing."

The gravest doubts that night came from scholars highly special-ized in ancient Coptic manuscripts. They could conjure no parallel for the script, which one said "looked like twenty-first-century hand-writing." Experts on Coptic papyri were reluctant to endorse Bagnall's "bad pen day" hypothesis. The chunky letters—a few with forks and hairline streaks—looked very much as if they had been applied by a paintbrush. The trouble, historically, was that Egyptian scribes stopped using brushes more than two centuries before Christ. By the fourth century A.D., using a brush, rather than a reed pen, to write on papyrus would be like riding a horse on an interstate highway: not impossible, but not likely, either.

On computer screens in their hotels that night, professors of Coptic began noticing unusual features in the text—missing characters, an impossible double conjugation that one linguist termed a "grammatical monstrosity." Some wondered why King had failed to consult a senior Coptic papyrologist beforehand. As towering a figure as Bagnall was in papyrology, his specialty was Greek documentary texts like personal letters, contracts and receipts, not Coptic scripture.

KING'S ANNOUNCEMENT BLINDSIDED CAMPLANI. Only his wife and secretary were supposed to have his cell number, but it had somehow slipped out, and by early the next morning it was ringing and ringing. Most journalists and camera crews didn't bother to call; they simply showed up at the Augustinianum, buttonholing gray-haired women in hopes that one might prove to be King and contenting themselves, in her absence, with any sentient scholar. Inside the building, Camplani was confronted by a young, black-robed friar, Rocco Ronzani, who served as the Augustinianum's vice president. Ronzani taught classes on Pope Gregory the Great, the sixth-century pontiff whose sermons had seared Magdalene's harlot persona into Western consciousness. Ronzani had read the overnight news stories with displeasure; he suspected that Camplani knew of King's announcement in advance and perhaps deliberately concealed it. "He was not so happy," Camplani recalled. "He was concerned there could be a problem between the Augustinian fathers and the Holy See." The friars, Camplani thought, might now throw the whole lot of them out of doors.

Meanwhile, another headache was developing. The Coptic Orthodox Church was in an interregnum. Pope Shenouda III of Alexandria, whose episcopate had lasted forty years, had died in March 2012, and the church had yet to elect a successor. A few Coptic priests worried that their presence at the conference could hurt the bishops whose papal candidacies they were backing. One priest in attendance, Father Bigoul el-Suriany, a distinguished librarian at the Deir al-Surian Monastery in Egypt, told me that Copts also feared reprisals from extremists back home. Islamist suicide bombers had demolished Coptic churches in Egypt, killing scores of Christians. El-Suriany was afraid that radical Muslims would exploit news of the discovery to undermine the New Testament and incite further animus against Egyptian Christians. "The Muslims will use this to say the Bible is not the truth," he said. "If we are in the West, we can handle such things" by setting them in a scholarly context. "But we are in the Middle East. When you are handling such things in an atmosphere which is already inflamed, you have to be cautious."

Hany Takla, a Copt who teaches at UCLA and runs a Coptic library and museum in Los Angeles, was so concerned that he placed a statement in the conference's official minutes that the fragment "belongs to the genre of Gnostic texts, which the early Church of Alexandria has rejected decisively."

When I returned to the Augustinianum that afternoon, the halls buzzed with talk of King. "I heard she was on CNN," a woman in the lobby said to some colleagues. "I heard her email in-box is just exploding." The Augustinian fathers were desperate to corral the roving journalists. "*Sciocchezzuole, sciocco*"—foolish, nonsense—one young friar muttered, after a reporter asked for his thoughts on King's discovery. A friar suggested to Camplani that King meet with all the reporters at once, if only to make them go away. The Augustinians would be happy to provide a conference room.

Camplani searched the building for King. "I said I could stop the journalists if she was tired. I could tell the Augustinianum not to let them enter," he recalled. "She said, 'No, it's okay.' She was tired, but she was also eager" to speak with the press.

I had been the only journalist in the room when King gave her paper the evening before. I wasn't any longer. At about 4:40 p.m., I filed into a fourth-floor conference room with nearly a dozen other reporters. Among them were major Italian newspapers, German public radio and CBS News. King, in a plum-colored blouse, floral scarf, and rimless oval glasses, sat beneath a cross at the head of a long wood-veneer table.

Marco Ansaldo, a sharply dressed Vatican correspondent for the Italian newspaper *La Repubblica,* led with a question that can't have been far from the minds of his readers. "You announced it here in Rome," he said, "just in front of the Vatican."

"It was an accident really," King insisted. "It has no larger symbolic meaning."

Allen Pizzey, the Rome correspondent for CBS, pressed. "Why choose to release it here next to the Vatican?"

"I didn't choose to release it here," she said. Discoveries were often announced at the Coptic Congress, and this year it happened to be in Rome.

She had to realize, Ansaldo continued, that the fragment could open up "big questions" about the legitimacy of canon law. Had she heard from the Vatican?

"I assume this is a venerable institution," King said. "They will respond as they wish in their time.... But if the question is—'Will this raise a lot of discussion?'—in the United States there already is much discussion. About issues of marriage within the Catholic Church, about the celibate priesthood, and also, of course ... about same-sex marriage. In my own church, the Episcopal Church"—whose consecration of an openly gay bishop in 2003 split the denomination—"there are lots of issues about ordination."

"How it will be used is a concern to me," King said of her papyrus. "My own faith, and the faith of other Christians, is best built on good history. That is my task: to do careful, good history." She rapped her fingertips against the table for emphasis.

Was she concerned that people would denounce her as a provocateur, as they had proponents of the Shroud of Turin, which had been exposed as a medieval hoax?

"I'm sure the reaction to me personally will cover the entire breadth of the reaction to this fragment," she said. "My interest is in my integrity as a historian."

"Dan Brown," Ansaldo said. He surmised, correctly, that no other prompt was needed.

"Dan Brown wrote a novel that claims Jesus was married to Mary Magdalene," King said. "There will be people who say, 'It's a fake.' They will criticize me. This surely has already happened. But again, as a historian, what we want to do is the best job we can with the little historical data we have."

KAREN KING HAD STAGED a media coup with just a little help, and only in the final stretch, from Harvard University's publicists. Before taking the fragment public, she had hooked the Smithsonian Channel on a documentary and invited journalists for *The New York Times, The Boston Globe* and *Smithsonian* magazine to Harvard for advance interviews. She ensured that the news media and the public would see photos of the discovery before the scholars at her photo-free presentation in Rome. She helped set up a Gospel of Jesus's Wife website, filmed a YouTube news release and took to the phones after her talk at the Augustinianum for a conference call with reporters. The next day, King kept the momentum going with an unscheduled news conference with a gaggle of international press.

The portrait that emerged in the first news cycle was of a scholar in full command of the media. The Gospel of Jesus's Wife was "big news" and "getting a lot of attention," she said at the news conference inside the Augustinianum. But she warned reporters against crediting her for the hoopla. "In talking to the press, a big part of my task is to throw cold water on sensationalism and let the good history have a say."

King had correctly forecast the need to distance herself from a certain kind of coverage: the tabloids and clickbait sites that would inevitably mischaracterize the scrap as biographical proof that Jesus was married. But she failed to grasp something essential about the more responsible news organizations: they were not there to do her bidding and move on. Their duty was to the truth and, if the truth was murky at first, their job was to keep seeking it. When reporters showed up at the Augustinianum on September 19, they didn't go home after interviewing King. They sought out other scholars, many of whom voiced reservations about King's reading of the text, her belief in its authenticity, or both. Within twenty-four hours, the news stories took a dark turn. Headlines like "A Faded Piece of Papyrus Refers to Jesus' Wife" and "Was Jesus Married?" gave way to "Doubts over Harvard Claim of 'Jesus' Wife' Papyrus" and "Is It a Fraud?" The *Times,* the *Globe* and *Smithsonian,* the publications to which King granted interviews before the announcement, wasted little time publishing follow-up pieces with quotations from skeptics.

King's secular colleagues—people as interested in "good history" as she was—had raised the specter of mischief even faster than the

Holy See. The Vatican newspaper, *L'Osservatore Romano*, waited a full nine days before dismissing the papyrus as an "inept forgery" whose text King had misconstrued all the same. "The completely improbable interpretation of the Gnostic phenomenon, with a twisted bias to match a modern ideology, is far removed from the history of Christianity and from the figure of Jesus," wrote the newspaper's editor in chief, who suspected that the real aim was "the sale both of this fragment and of other manuscripts by a private person to a prestigious institution."

King had hoped the fragment would occasion earnest discussion in classrooms and churches across the world. Instead, it became fodder for late-night comedy. "What is the rule on wedding gifts?" Stephen Colbert, a devout Catholic, said on his Comedy Central show. "You have two thousand years, right?"

"Jesus was married? That is some pure, uncut, sitcom bait," Jon Stewart cracked on *The Daily Show*. Turning to another camera and affecting an announcer's voice, he said, "He can raise the dead, but heaven help him when he forgets to put down the toilet seat." Stewart marveled at how anything could be read into a sentence that breaks off after the words "My wife."

"That's your proof?" he said incredulously. "Well, let me see if I can fill that sentence out for you: Jesus said, 'My wife ... *If I ever find one.* We will really have to like Thai food.' Or how about this? 'My wife'— question mark—'No. I'm not married.'"

The Smithsonian Channel, meanwhile, announced an indefinite postponement of its documentary amid the questions about authenticity. Also stepping back was AnneMarie Luijendijk. She was scheduled to give a paper on the fragment at the Society of Biblical Literature's annual conference in Chicago that November but canceled after the announcement in Rome.

A more public rebuke came from the historian Elaine Pagels, the most celebrated figure in Gnostic studies. She and King were friends; they had cowritten a best-selling book on the Gospel of Judas just a few years before. But when I called Pagels for my *Smithsonian* article in late September 2012, she pointedly questioned King's decision to call the Wife papyrus a "gospel." The word "gospel," she told me, implies a text professing to chronicle real events in Jesus's life. The Wife papyrus could just as easily be a "dialogue text," in which followers describe often symbolic visions from Jesus. Or it could belong to a genre of ancient writing that some specialists liken to fan fiction.

"When you call it 'The Gospel of Jesus's Wife,' I just think, 'What are you talking about?'" Pagels said. "At least 99 percent of this text is missing," she went on. "Calling it a gospel, I'm sorry, I don't understand that except to make it sound more, well—what's the word?—important. It's much more sensational than what we can infer." In Pagels's view, King had read things into it that simply weren't there. "I don't think this piece says anything about Mary Magdalene." She wasn't even sure Jesus was the speaker. All told, she said dryly, "I guess my enthusiasm is not as great as hers."

The next domino to teeter was King's article for the *Harvard Theological Review*. King had told me in early September that the esteemed journal was set to publish the piece in its October 2012 issue, an extraordinarily quick turnaround for an article she first submitted just two months before. The unfavorable peer reviews gave the editors pause, she said at her presentation in Rome, but the journal was "quite satisfied" with her revisions and "has now decided to go ahead with publication."

The journal told me that almost none of those things were true. It had hoped to publish King's article in its January 2013 issue; "however, everything is now on hold until we are able, with Professor King's help and by scientific dating, to establish the authenticity of the text," Kevin Madigan, a Harvard scholar of medieval Christianity who co-edited the journal, emailed me on September 23, 2012, when I asked about it for my *Smithsonian* article. Acceptance was "conditional" on "further verification from Coptological papyrologists and grammarians"—an apparent reference to skills that Roger Bagnall did not count among his strong suits.

The editors weren't just reading the headlines from Rome; they were receiving alarmed emails from scholars. A Brown University Egyptologist named Leo Depuydt, who didn't attend the Coptic conference but saw images of the papyrus online, wrote the editors of a "colossal double blunder" in the papyrus's grammar. Features of the error, he thought, hinted at a present-day European grappling with ancient Coptic. The perpetrator was less likely "a very incompetent ancient scribe," Depuydt emailed, than "a modern author who might have benefited from one more semester of Coptic."

Depuydt also noticed that *ta-hime*, "my wife"—particularly the *ta*, or "my"—was conspicuously darker than most of the other words on the papyrus, as if deliberately to catch the eye. "Using bold letters for emphasis to my knowledge never occurs in ancient Coptic literary manuscripts," Depuydt wrote. "I am unable to escape the impression that there is something almost hilarious about [it]. How could this not have been designed to some extent to convey a certain comic effect? ... something like: '**My** wife. Get it? **MY** wife. You heard that right.' The papyrus fragment seems ripe for a Monty Python sketch.... If the forger had used italics in addition, one might be in danger of losing one's composure." (Interestingly, Roger Bagnall had spotted the same peculiarity. "It's really about as clear a passage as you get in the whole papyrus," he observed in a segment of his Smithsonian Channel interview that wound up on the cutting-room floor.)

For his dissertation at Yale, Depuydt—a tall, stringy-haired man who grew up on a farm in Flanders—cataloged the Coptic manuscripts in the Pierpont Morgan collection in Manhattan. But he remembers his Yale days as fondly for his prescient doubts about a bizarre demotic translation of the Gospel of Thomas. Demotic was the language that served as the bridge, on the Rosetta Stone, between hieroglyphics and Greek. It was spoken by Egyptians before Coptic and, most scholars thought, before Christianity. A demotic Thomas would be revolutionary. As a transcription began to quietly circulate among scholars, Depuydt alerted colleagues to what he called a "fatal blunder" in demotic grammar that he believed no native writer would make. In 1991, the Oxford University journal *Discussions in Egyptology* published the demotic Thomas anyway, to its lasting regret. The tip-off came just as the issue began shipping to subscribers. A British scholar had written up the find for the *Financial Times*, but his daughter soon noticed something funny about the name of the self-described American Egyptologist who claimed to have discovered it: "Batson D. Sealing," she told her father, sounded a lot like "bats on the ceiling." Sealing had left forwarding addresses at academic departments in Montana and Iowa, but when the British scholar contacted them, they said they'd never heard of such a person. *Discussions in Egyptology* had not only published an article by an Egyptologist who didn't exist; it failed to notice that the sources in his footnotes were just as phantasmic. The journal's editor abruptly recalled the entire issue and sent out a replacement, minus the Sealing article. Among demotic scholars, the original is now something of a collector's item. Remembering the debacle, Depuydt cautioned the *Harvard Theological Review* against a rush to publish. "The danger of making a fool of oneself is real."

Madigan, the journal's co-editor, replied quickly and with gratitude. "We are very mindful, and somewhat anxious, about the possibility of making fools of ourselves."

KING HAD ALWAYS DONE her best work in the midst of storms. Adversity centered her. It felt like home. "How's that for sincere masochism,"
she'd once said of the craving. A week after the announcement in Rome,
King told *The Boston Globe* that she wasn't troubled by the absence of
support from people in her own field. "Scholars are by nature cautious."
Their prudence was appropriate, she said, because most had not examined the papyrus firsthand. "We'll be talking about this for a very long
time," she said, "and I think the public will, as well."

But the forces set loose by the Gospel of Jesus's Wife were greater
than anything King had previously encountered. In the days before
her announcement, she seemed to sense that a kind of honeymoon—in
which the papyrus was hers alone to contemplate—was nearing an end.
"I'm already missing the long, quiet days pouring [*sic*] over the fragment and its possibilities," she wrote to the collector on August 24.

His reply bordered on sarcasm. "'... *but I'm already missing the long,
quiet days* ...,'" he typed, quoting the key words of her wistful comment
within a pair of ellipses, a format that mirrored her translation of the
Wife fragment's amputated lines.

"Well," he remarked, "you make the bed you lie in. LOL."

ACT 2

DOUBT

"Proof," I said, "is always a relative thing.
It's an overwhelming balance of probabilities.
And that's a matter of how they strike you."

—Raymond Chandler, *Farewell, My Lovely*

T hat Andrew Bernhard had eclectic interests was no secret to his office mates at a Portland, Oregon, vocational college. Before he'd taken a job there—analyzing spreadsheets of student data as a regulatory compliance officer—he'd worked as a software marketer, renewable energy grant evaluator, writing instructor and real estate broker. At thirty-six, he had the same rangy frame that had made him a high school tennis ace with a hundred-mile-per-hour serve. What few people at Bernhard's day jobs knew was that he was also an Oxford-trained scholar who had published a book on the noncanonical gospels before he turned thirty.

Bernhard was on a morning break at the vocational school on September 18, 2012, when he saw a *New York Times* piece on a fascinating papyrus discovery. He quickly sent an email to the editors of a new book of noncanonical scriptures, to which he had already contributed a first-ever English translation of a fifth-century hagiography called the Life and Martyrdom of John the Baptist. "Are you guys going to include the newly discovered 'Gospel of Jesus' Wife'?" he asked. "If you are, might I get a crack at it?" It would be thrilling, he thought, to produce his own translation of this remarkable new text, one squired into the world by no less a figure than Dr. Karen King, a scholar whose books he owned and admired.

As a teenager, Bernhard had rebelled against his liberal, Presbyterian parents by turning himself, almost overnight, into a Bible-thumping fundamentalist. His father and two older siblings all had Princeton degrees and traditional careers in science and law. Bernhard wanted his own identity, and in the progressive, enlightened Portland of the 1990s there was perhaps no faster way to get one than to become a creationist who regarded the Bible as literal truth. The transformation was so sudden that his parents wondered if he'd joined a cult or was taking drugs. "We're Christians, not morons," they told him. "We can believe in God *and* evolution."

But Bernhard would have none of it. He cleaved to his New King James Bible and found, in verses like Luke's "Love your enemies," signposts for surviving the social anxieties of high school. In college, at Willamette University, an hour's drive south of Portland, he wanted little more than to read the New Testament in its original Greek. He wanted to face the gospels as written, before translators and theologians applied their inevitable spin. But after joining a campus evangelical group, something inside him began to crack. His new friends, people as passionate about scripture as he, weren't just drawing personal inspiration from the Bible. They were using it to police other people. An "accountability group" had gone so far as to split up student couples whose relationships looked bound for immodesty. "It was like *1984*," Bernhard recalled, "but with a focus on sexual sins." When they accused one of his favorite professors of heresy for asking students to think more critically about ideas like the resurrection, Bernhard wondered what he had gotten himself into.

"I am done with Christianity completely," he scrawled in his diary, before breaking with the evangelical group and suffering a nervous breakdown. He took leave the fall of his junior year and went home to his parents, agonizing over how his quest for independence could have wound up in so claustrophobic a place.

He returned to campus that spring, a loner. In the lyrics of bands like Nirvana and Live, he began to discover a "punk rock" ethos of radical freedom that went hand in hand with personal integrity. From that point forward, he told himself, he would hold his theological inquiries to the same benchmark. His studies, originally devoted to the texts of the New Testament, began drifting toward those outside it. Less known and less interpreted, they felt freer from the calcifications of dogma. For his senior thesis, he translated seven Greek gospels outside the canon, celebrating them in much the same way as had Karen King. "Their recovery," he wrote, "has opened up innumerable new avenues for research and theological reflection." When he graduated, in 1999, after winning back-to-back scholarships as the school's top religion student, he bought the domain gospels.net and began posting his translations online. His professors pleaded with him to pursue a PhD. But

a life in academia, he feared, would seethe with the sorts of ideological battles that had contributed to his nervous break. To write books
and articles—which was all he wanted—he felt that a master's degree
would more than suffice. He was accepted at Oxford University, where
he studied Coptic and ensconced himself in the school's renowned
papyrus collections. He'd soon gathered enough material to write the
world's most expansive English-language collection of noncanonical
Greek gospel fragments. He kept his introduction to each fragment
colorless and brief, so that readers could encounter the texts on their
own terms. His manuscript, prosaically titled *Other Early Christian Gospels*, sold to a distinguished academic press and was published, to strong
reviews from major scholars, in 2006, when Bernhard was just twenty-
nine years old.

THREE DAYS AFTER reading news of King's discovery, Bernhard stumbled on a blog post that gave him pause. Its author, a British New Testament scholar named Francis Watson, had noticed that the Gospel of
Jesus's Wife bore a curious likeness to the Gospel of Thomas. "Likeness" wasn't even the right word. The Wife papyrus, Watson contended,
was a "patchwork" of Coptic phrases cut from Thomas and then re-
arranged to say something new, like a ransom note spelled with letters
snipped from different magazines. The only original words in the entire
fragment, Watson argued, were "my wife."

Bernhard reproached himself for how quickly he'd presumed
the papyrus's authenticity. In his excitement over the famous scholars behind the discovery, he'd forgotten the code of independence to
which he had sworn himself. He wasn't sure Watson was right. But
before pitching any more editors on his own translation, he felt he
needed to step back. It turned out he was in a good position to test
Watson's theory. He had just started work on a new book—this one
on noncanonical Coptic gospels—and had recently typed every line
of Thomas into a Microsoft Word file. This had taken some time but
was not especially difficult; only one complete ancient copy, from Nag
Hammadi, survives, and it had been published numerous times. Without relying on Watson's post, Bernhard called up his Thomas file and
began dropping strings of Coptic letters from the Wife papyrus into the
search box.

Within moments, he saw that the entire first line could be wrought by selectively deleting words from Saying 101 of the Gospel of Thomas.

[Jesus said]...~~"And whoever does not love his father and his mother in~~ ~~my way, he can be a disciple~~ not to me. My mother, ~~for.....~~ ~~but my true~~ [mother] gave me life.

The second line of the Wife papyrus—*"the disciples said to Jesus"*—was also a distinctly Thomasine expression. It appears nowhere in the New Testament, but three times in the Gospel of Thomas.

The papyrus's fifth line scavenged another passage from Thomas:

~~Whoever does not hate his father and his mother in my way~~, he is able to be my disciple ~~not~~.

The Wife papyrus had a "she" instead of a "he," but a first-year Coptic student would know that a swap of just one letter (a *sigma*) for another (a *fai*) would flip the pronoun from male to female. Similar patterns held for all but one of the lines: the sixth. And as Bernhard saw it, that line posed a serious problem for Watson's "patchwork" hypothesis. The easiest way to translate its convolutions was

Never does man who is wicked always does bring.

Coptic specialists had variously called it a "grammatical monstrosity," a "horrendous syntactic mash," or, simply, "Frankenstein." The Gospel of Thomas itself was grammatically sound. If the Wife papyrus was an otherwise intelligible cut and paste of Thomas, why was this one line such a disaster? Watson argued that a forger had simply blundered. The hoped-for version of Line 6, he guessed, was some version of "an evil man brings forth," a fragment from Saying 45 in the Gospel of Thomas. Were a forger inclined to deepen his work's resonance, a line of this sort—about the state of one's soul as destiny—would have fit well in a debate over the qualifications for discipleship.

King, who teaches Coptic at Harvard, had somehow failed to spot most of the text's grammatical irregularities. "I am truly embarrassed not to have addressed the grammtical [*sic*]/lexical isses [*sic*] with more care," she had written to Bagnall on September 5, 2012, the day after the third peer reviewer had brought them to her editors' attention. For help, King wrote to a friend, Ariel Shisha-Halevy, an eminent linguist renowned for his minority view that too little is known about Coptic to call any irregularity a mistake. Shisha-Halevy is so skeptical of certainties in Coptic that during King's talk in Rome he said he wasn't even sure that *hime*—the key word in Line 4—meant "wife."

"No one knows actually," he had said, raising eyebrows among the other specialists in the room. When even one of King's critics said, "That's a married wife, that's for sure," Shisha-Halevy replied, "It must be shown by a study." King never quoted Shisha-Halevy on that view. But she publicized a different opinion of his in her revised article and in conversations with reporters: the text's "noteworthy" grammatical features, he'd told King in a September 7 email, "do not warrant condemning it as forgery." If most Coptologists were inclined to give Line 6 an F for grammar, King could thus assign it an A for ingenuity. What others had called mistakes or, worse, "monstrosities," King now deemed "interesting features" and an "as-yet only partially understood phenomenon."

Coptic, like other ancient languages, was composed in *scriptio continua,* with no spaces or punctuation between words. Scholars encountering such texts sixteen hundred years later had to decide whether, say, "madamimadam" meant "Madam, I'm Adam" or "Mad am I, Madam!"—or "Mad? Am I mad?" with the final "am" perhaps the first letters of the next word. In damaged texts missing all their margins, *scriptio continua* was like a word search puzzle; scholars had unusual freedom to decide where one word ended and the next began. And this was key, King felt, to explaining what most Coptologists saw as Line 6's impossible double conjugation. If you transposed the "Never does" into a different Coptic dialect, it could mean "Let." And if you left out the line's last two letters, the "always does" morphed into an extremely rare Coptic word for "swell." It took a few tries, but King found an error-free way to parse the text. Line 6 didn't say, "Never does man who is wicked always does bring." It said,

Let wicked people swell up.

If King was right, it was an incisive piece of last-minute detective work. But if she was wrong and a modern forger had simply bungled "an evil man brings forth," her inventive reading must have struck the forger as the most merciful of pardons.

On September 24, Bernhard published a short article on his website concluding that "there is not yet any basis for accusations of forgery or fraud. Just because *GJW* could have been composed using words and phrases exclusively from [the Gospel of Thomas] does NOT mean that it was." Proponents of the patchwork theory, he felt, had made too many assumptions. To make it hang together, they had to accuse the forger of mistakes in Line 6, then fix those mistakes to make the words fit Thomas. If one could pull out a grammatically sound line without such editorial interference, Bernhard thought, then perhaps it was Watson, not King, who had leaped to conclusions.

THREE DAYS LATER, a pair of European scholars posted an image that sent Bernhard back to his notes. It was an enlarged photo of Line 6's third letter from the right—a character whose right side was marred by multiple ink streaks. It had struck experts from the start as a scribal error, or what a child might call an "oopsie." But the nature of the error was unclear. At this higher magnification, however, one could almost make out the original mistake *and* the attempted correction. Coptic, a product of Alexander the Great's conquest of Egypt, is a kind of creole: it is the Egyptian tongue written in the twenty-four letters of the Greek alphabet, complemented by half a dozen Egyptian characters for sounds—like "sh" and "ch"—absent from Greek. To Bernhard, the streaked letter looked like a cross between an *epsilon* and an *iota*. Or rather, it looked as if someone had first written one letter, then tried to write over it with—or cram in—another. The letter looks like no other *epsilon* or *iota* in the entire fragment, a fact King had left out of her September article. When Bernhard saw the magnified image that morning, it took just a few moments to grasp its significance: it was the missing piece in Watson's argument. If a forger had meant to write both the *epsilon* and the *iota*, then the resulting words—"does bring"—were a perfect match for the Gospel of Thomas. Every word except "my wife" could be traced to a single text. But the image did more; it profiled the forger. A highly trained scholar wouldn't need to recycle Thomas to fake a text about Jesus's wife. They would know enough Coptic, and enough early Christian literature, to write something both believable *and* original. But a person with limited Coptic—someone, say, who could read a little but not write—would need a crutch. When Bernhard thought about the crutches available for texts in ancient languages, there was just one obvious kind: an interlinear translation, in which each line of original text is followed by the same line in translation. Interlinears aren't the most common form of translation, but amateur language students sometimes prefer them because they make it easy to link foreign words and phrases, in context, to their English equivalents. Bernhard needed to find a Coptic-to-English interlinear of Thomas. Then he remembered: there was just one. It had been created not by a professional scholar but by an eccentric computer programmer living out his retirement in the suburbs of Detroit.

THE KINGDOM OF GOD PUZZLE

M ike Grondin discovered he was most alert when the world around him was asleep. In the tidy house he shared with his wife, Letty, in Macomb, Michigan, he regularly stayed up until 3:00 a.m., devouring mystery novels, solving sudoku or testing his wits at solitaire. His gray goatee and gruff voice gave him the air of a street-tough uncle. But he was nearing seventy now, and when he wasn't sleeping until noon or padding around the house in slippers, he was on his computer, searching for coded messages in the Gospel of Thomas.

Raised by working-class Catholic parents near Pontiac, Mike Grondin had wanted to become a priest. But the Church's teachings on sex had turned him into an atheist. His doubts culminated in college, at the University of Michigan, but they had started when he was twelve and smitten by a girl in a pink sweater. "I thought, 'Wait a minute, God made us, sex is inherent in us, why should even the thought of it be considered a sin?'" he recalled. "I could never reconcile that, and eventually I decided there was just no evidence for the existence of God."

Drafted by the army in 1968, he was posted to a technology unit at the Pentagon, where he learned the computer programming language Fortran. Writing code suited him for the same reasons as his overnight job squaring receipts against guests' accounts at a Northern Virginia hotel: he took pleasure, he said, in "the resolving of discrepancies." Back at school on the GI Bill, Grondin earned a master's in philosophy but ran out of money before completing a PhD. He spent the rest of his working life in coding jobs in the automotive and medical industries. He slaked his intellect at home, where he devoted hours to solving difficult math and logic problems.

On his forty-fifth birthday, in 1988, his father made a cutting remark about all the time he wasted on brain games. "Well, that's very nice,

Michael, but couldn't you do something that has more significance?" he told his son. Beneath his father's comment, Grondin felt, was lingering resentment over his rejection of Catholicism. "My subconscious was saying, 'He thinks the only important thing is religion—all right, I'll do something in religion.' So I started looking at the gospels." Not looking at the gospels as believers did, he decided, but as a logician might, as "raw data."

He was perusing an academic book on the Gospel of Thomas one day when he came across a question the author raised, in passing, in the appendix: Was the sequence of Jesus's 114 sayings as random as it looked, or did it follow an invisible logic? "I look forward," the author had written, "to the time when someone unambiguously uncovers the secret to Thomas' order."

Grondin had found his gospel puzzle.

HE GAVE HIMSELF to Coptic like a zealot to the faith. He bought an introductory grammar, and after Letty turned in for the evening, he would spend four to five hours in his basement buried in its pages. The book had thirty lessons, and at a pace of a lesson a night he was done, he said, in thirty days. It was, by his own admission, a crash course; scholars take years to master Coptic. But Grondin didn't require mastery. He needed just enough know-how to convert Thomas's Coptic into searchable data, which he could then scour for hidden designs. He tallied the number of letters per line and the number of lines per block of text. He wrote computer programs that scanned for patterns in the frequency of certain words and in the locations of line breaks. He looked for sayings that seemed to mirror each other, then calculated the distance between them. "It's well known that there are doubles in the Gospel of Thomas," Grondin said. "Sayings so similar that you wonder why they put them both in there." The gospel's prologue was the first clue. "These are the secret sayings which the living Jesus spoke," it begins, "and which Didymos Judas Thomas wrote down." The word "Didymos" meant "twin" in Greek, and "Thomas" was "twin" in Aramaic: a twin of Jesus, identified by twin words for "twin."

The research was so consuming that Grondin began showing up late to work in the mornings, to the displeasure of his bosses. He would surreptitiously continue his investigations at the office, using his company's powerful mainframes to mine the data. "There were times when I had to rush over to the printer to make sure nobody else saw what I was printing out." He kept his worksheets in a walk-in storage room in the basement of his house; cardboard boxes overflowed with color-coded numerical tables with penciled-in computations in a neat and minuscule hand.

Over two decades, Grondin had made some intriguing discoveries: Thomas contains five hundred Greek words and names, comprising twenty-four hundred letters. There were other fascinating symmetries in the word and letter counts of certain lines. He had yet to unearth the skeleton key to Thomas's structure, but his research convinced him that its author had concealed puzzles inside, both to please God and to test initiates. "I think there was cash value, as we used to say in my philosophy classes, in the idea that only the elect can understand this," he said. The code breaker's reward was great. In the first of Thomas's 114 sayings, Jesus announces, "Whoever discovers the interpretation of these sayings will not taste death."

"The reader wasn't just supposed to read it," Grondin thought, "he was supposed to interact with it in some way." This interaction, he believed, "might have involved changing things around in the text." The home page of his website quoted Dashiell Hammett's noir mystery novel *The Thin Man*. One character says, "I guess I can put two and two together," to which the other replies, "Sometimes the answer's four, and sometimes it's twenty-two."

IN 1996, GRONDIN STARTED a website to interest people in his theories. He doubted professional scholars would pay it much mind, but hoped that hobbyists like himself might want to help play detective. He downloaded a Coptic font and spent a couple of days typing Thomas into a Microsoft Word document. He preserved all 668 original line breaks from the Nag Hammadi codex, because he thought the location of the breaks might be important. Directly beneath each word—and often beneath the morphemes, or parts, of compound words—he typed an English translation.

He was the first to admit that his translation would neither endear him to Coptic lexicographers nor win style points. Nor would it scan particularly well if read aloud. But those were never his intent. To make his theories intelligible to laypeople, he chose English words that best served their role as uniform data. Grondin didn't care if the meaning of a Coptic word or morpheme changed according to context. Because his statistical analyses required a one-to-one correspondence between Coptic word and English translation, he had to come up with a single English word that straddled the different possible meanings of its Coptic counterpart. For instance, a Coptic word that scholars translated as "am" in some lines and "dwell" in others, Grondin standardized as "exist," to cover both meanings. Where possible, he even chose English words with the same syllable count as their Coptic cousins— the better to reflect his mathematical tack. Though other translations of Thomas contained Coptic and English text on facing pages, no one before Grondin had set an English word directly beneath each Coptic one. Grondin posted the interlinear to his website in 1997, each page a GIF image that had to be individually downloaded.

In November 2002, the Society of Biblical Literature was holding its annual conference in Toronto, five hours by train from Detroit. It was the largest annual gathering of biblical scholars, typically drawing more than ten thousand attendees per day. It might be the perfect place, Grondin thought, to enlist real academics in his hunt for Thomas's secrets. To make his interlinear more user-friendly, he cleaned up the layout, retyped it and converted the individual page images into a single pdf. He packed six printed copies in his luggage and placed each in an envelope with a thirty-one-page "prospectus" he titled "A New Paradigm for Thomas: The Kingdom of God Puzzle."

But he found few takers. America was still reeling from the 9/11 attacks and a set of anthrax-laced letters that had left five people dead and the country on edge. A number of professors at the conference seemed reluctant to accept envelopes from a manifesto-bearing stranger. On the train back to Detroit, Grondin reproved himself for his "delusions of grandeur."

"You think it's so important and that the minute you reveal it to somebody, they will jump all over you," he said. "But no." He let out a rueful laugh. "If you had somebody to interact with, to suggest different things to complement your own, that would keep you going." The truth, he realized, was that most people didn't care.

———

ANDREW BERNHARD HAD NEVER MET Mike Grondin. But they ran in the same circles online. Both were independent researchers. Both had launched websites in the late 1990s. Both were pioneers in bringing the full texts of noncanonical gospels to the web. Bernhard had even joined the Gospel of Thomas group that Grondin hosted on Yahoo; like most of its other members, he was there less out of interest in Grondin's theories than to chat about mainstream Thomas research. Bernhard hadn't much thought of Grondin's interlinear over the years, but as the debate over the authenticity of King's papyrus intensified, he began to regard Grondin's translation as a possible accessory to forgery.

Bernhard was on a morning break on September 27, 2012, when he decided to download Grondin's interlinear. He searched for the two Coptic words—*mareh romah*—that began the Wife fragment's puzzling Line 6. He found them midway through the pdf, in Thomas's Saying 47, as expected. What rattled him was the English directly beneath them. A technical translation of the two Coptic words would be "never does man." But Grondin, in keeping with his data-driven translations, had streamlined: he changed "never does man" to "no man." This was fine for sentences like the actual one in Thomas; "No man drinks old wine" was for all intents the same as the more literal "Never does man drink old wine." But not even Grondin would translate *mareh romah* as "no man" in a sentence where the verb was already conjugated.

Yet what if a visitor to his website didn't know that? What if someone assumed that the Coptic words in Grondin's interlinear were identical to the English ones Grondin had placed beneath them? It would be an easy mistake. His interlinear's tidy formatting—with every Coptic word astride its seeming English translation—gave an illusion of perfect equivalence. And that's when Bernhard saw it. The Wife fragment's Line 6 was a Frankenstein in Coptic, but almost poetry in Grondin's English. "The forger was thinking in English, not Coptic," Bernhard realized. The person, whoever he or she was, had set out to write a simple line, "no man who is wicked brings," which jammed a negation into a well-known saying of Jesus's about a wicked man bringing forth wickedness. But because "no man who is wicked brings" doesn't appear in Thomas, the person had to cobble the words from different places in the interlinear's English—"no man" from one line, "who is wicked" from another, and "brings" from a third. Then he replaced each of the English words with the Coptic above them. The person thought he could make clean swaps of English for Coptic, not realizing that the Coptic words were fused to their neighbors by a grammatical tissue that Grondin didn't always translate.

The phrase "no man who is wicked brings" scans fine in English. But if you used Grondin's interlinear to reverse the English back into Coptic, you got "Never does man who is wicked always does bring." A person who took Grondin's English at face value was safe so long as he uprooted and repotted whole Coptic expressions. This was why the other seven lines had held up. But if someone attempted finer cuts—in order to make a single line from multiple nonadjacent words—he risked creating a monster.

"The one time he tries to do it," Bernhard thought, "he screws up."

That the Wife papyrus was a fragment was perhaps no accident. By creating the impression that it came from a larger manuscript, the forger absolved themselves of having to grammatically link its eight partial lines. Anything larger—never mind a complete gospel—would have left them wholly out of their depth.

BERNHARD HAD NOW GONE Watson one better. He found parallels not so much to the ancient Coptic text of Thomas as to a pdf created in 2002. Both of the grammatical snafus in Line 6 could be explained by a forger's misunderstanding of Grondin's idiosyncratic translations. But these blunders weren't the only—or even the most obvious—signs that the pdf had served as a cheat sheet.

As other scholars had already noted, the Wife papyrus's first line— "...not [to] me. My mother gave me life..."—contained a grammatical error. A one-letter word, *mu*, should have appeared between "gave me" and "life." The word, another variety of grammatical tissue, tells readers that "life" is the direct object while "me," the indirect. Bernhard found the phrase "my true mother gave me life" in his own transcription of Thomas. The *mu* was there. He dashed to his basement bookshelf and opened a volume of photographs of the original Nag Hammadi papyri, including the only surviving Coptic copy of Thomas. The *mu* was there, too.

Then he opened Grondin's pdf: no *mu*.

The Wife papyrus contained the same mistake as the only interlinear translation of Thomas, one that happened to be easily accessible to anyone with an internet connection. Grondin told Bernhard he had never noticed the error. In his rush to convert the text from his website into a pdf handout for the biblical studies conference, he must have accidentally deleted the *mu*. He was adding and deleting spaces to keep the line margins justified. His best guess was that he'd cut the *mu* when he'd meant to cut a space. It was a onetime oversight; Grondin had the *mu* in every version of his interlinear before and since. He had rarely consulted the pdf after his ill-fated trip to Toronto. Still, he kept it up on his website. Some visitors preferred it to the translation's other format—the bundle of GIF images—because the pdf was a single file and therefore easier to download, search and print.

Bernhard's discovery thrilled Grondin as much as it sickened him. For years, the retired computer programmer had dreamed of attracting real religion scholars. Few had taken him very seriously. Still, he took pride in his work ethic and his nose for detail, a vigilance that bordered on perfectionism. Once Bernhard published his discovery, Grondin would at last have the attention of the world's greatest Gnostic scholars. They would all know his name. He'd be famous not for his decades of dogged investigation, he realized, but for a senseless typo.

ANDREW BERNHARD DRAFTED a fifteen-page article and emailed it to Mark Goodacre, a New Testament scholar at Duke University with one of the field's best-read blogs. Goodacre sensed that Bernhard might have a smoking gun; he agreed to publish. Fueled by twenty-four-ounce bottles of Gatorade and the company of Buster, his Australian cattle dog, Bernhard wrote late into the night, polishing and double-checking every detail. He pressed the send button on a final draft at 3:37 a.m. on October 11, 2012. Then he went to bed.

Goodacre had the piece online within an hour. "Just when you might have thought that the story of the Gospel of Jesus' Wife was dying down," he wrote to his blog's readers, "there is another twist in the tale."

The British newspaper *The Guardian* published an article that shot Bernhard's finding across the world. Other papers followed, including the *New York Post* ("Jesus Khrist! Typo in papyrus scroll derails theory of holy wife") and *Der Spiegel*, which spotlighted the "treacherous spelling mistake."

Never far from Bernhard's mind was Secret Mark, seen by many as the greatest Christian hoax of the twentieth century. Debates over its authenticity had scorched biblical studies, turning colleagues against one another and leaving scars that had yet to fully heal. None of it might have happened, Bernhard realized, had scholars moved faster. Morton Smith, perhaps strategically, had waited a decade and a half between disclosing his find and publishing it. By then, the original text had mysteriously vanished. Whether people believed Smith came to hinge more on appraisals of his character and sexual orientation than on the surviving evidence. Some scholars had become so personally invested in Secret Mark's authenticity that they had begun including it in prestigious anthologies and using it to write history. Bernhard wanted answers about the Wife papyrus before the trail went cold and there was only shouting. His article on Goodacre's blog came just twenty-three days after King's announcement. "You've got to move before the evidence is disturbed," Bernhard thought, likening certain kinds of scholarly research to police work. "You don't want somebody visiting the crime scene and rearranging everything."

But Bernhard was a detective without a badge. He had no university affiliation and no PhD. His office was the unfinished basement of his small Portland home, where his jerry-rigged desk jostled for space with a washer-dryer, a snarl of extension cords and piles of dirty laundry. His discovery about the missing *mu* had wound up on some news sites and a blog. But that likely meant little to scholars as established as King and Bagnall. They belonged to a generation in which academic debates unfolded at a genteel pace in quarterly journals and yearly conferences. Blogs like Goodacre's had democratized and quickened these exchanges; they brought researchers of every rank together to vet discoveries fast, before the harm—to scholars, to universities, to the integrity of the historical record—became permanent. Bernhard wondered whether any of the online conversation was reaching the field's elders. "I've never learned to use these media," King told colleagues a couple of years later. "I'm not on Facebook. I am a very rare consumer even of really good blogs." Yet if the Gospel of Jesus's Wife was truly an internet-age forgery—as Bernhard maintained—absenting oneself from the web was perilous. Online documents like Grondin's pdf could as freely facilitate a forgery as help expose one.

But then something unexpected happened. The dates King had

announced for scientific testing came and went with no news. Weeks of silence from Harvard stretched into months. Bernhard came to suspect that King was disowning the fragment, but tiptoeing away slowly, in an understandable desire to save face.

She had already paid a steep price for bearing the Gospel of Jesus's Wife into the public square. Strangers had sent death threats, damnations and what she called "ugly and unprintable" words. Her colleagues had all but abandoned her. Less than two weeks had passed since King's September 18 announcement when *The Chronicle of Higher Education* published "The Lessons of Jesus' Wife," a story that framed the ensuing crash and burn as a cautionary tale of what happens when scholars publicize a major discovery without doing enough homework. Harvard, meanwhile, armed King's office with a panic button. It would eventually move the Wife papyrus from the divinity school to Houghton, its most closely guarded library. Security measures for the fragment surpassed those of every other holding, including the handwritten poems of Emily Dickinson, a Gutenberg Bible and ancient fragments of Plato, Thucydides and Homer.

This was not the way King expected things to go. After the backlash in Rome, a friend recalled, "there was a period when she hated herself and the field." A Harvard affiliation endows a professor with incomparable clout when things are going well. But when things go amiss, it invites withering scrutiny and schadenfreude. "Harvard is like riding a tiger," as one professor there put it. "It's fine if you stay on the back; it's terrible if you slip off."

RIDING A TIGER

On April 10, 2014, after nearly nineteen months of silence, Harvard Divinity School issued an exultant press release: "Testing Indicates 'Gospel of Jesus's Wife' Papyrus Fragment to be Ancient." There was no explanation for the long wait, but the results were in at last. Scientists at Columbia, Harvard and the Massachusetts Institute of Technology had carried out laboratory analyses, and "none of the testing has produced any evidence that the fragment is a modern fabrication or forgery." The *Harvard Theological Review* finally had what it needed to publish. It devoted more than half of its April 2014 issue to King's paper and the supporting scientific reports.

Again King gave exclusives to *The New York Times* and *The Boston Globe*, affording advance access to her scientists and their reports. The news—of an adventurous scholar vindicated by high-level science—spun across the globe.

"Ancient Scroll Mentioning Wife of Jesus Is the Real Deal, Scientists Say," read a UPI headline.

"Tests Prove Gospel of Jesus' Wife Authentic," said the *Washington Examiner*.

"'Jesus Wife' Text No Fake," read the headline in Northern Ireland's *Belfast Telegraph*.

"No Forgery Evidence Seen in 'Gospel of Jesus's Wife' Papyrus," *National Geographic* reported.

Diane Sawyer weighed in from the *ABC World News* anchor desk. "It was once thought to be a fake," she said as a close-up of the papyrus scrolled across the screen. "Tonight [scholars] say carbon testing proves it is an ancient document." The Smithsonian Channel announced that its long-delayed documentary would finally air, and there was talk of displaying the fragment at a Smithsonian museum on the National Mall.

King hoped the science would "dispel all rumors of forgery" so that students and the public could at last discuss the text's broader implications for "family, marriage, sexuality, and so forth," she said in an April 2014 conference call with reporters. The early focus on forgery, she said, had been a "big disappointment."

THOUGH NOT EVERY journalist noted it, the *Harvard Theological Review* had taken the unusual step of publishing a rebuttal of King's article in the same issue. It was written by Leo Depuydt, the Brown University Egyptologist who had privately warned its editors the day after King's Rome announcement that "the danger of making a fool of one-self is real." (Depuydt was among the first to suspect that the demotic Thomas—the early 1990s handiwork of one Batson D. Sealing, a.k.a. Bats on the Ceiling—was a fake.) In his paper, which ran eighteen pages, Depuydt cast himself as the outraged tribune of humanities scholars. He focused on the grammatical snafus and what he, like Andrew Bern-hard and Francis Watson, saw as unmistakable copying from the Gospel of Thomas. A historian of mathematics as well as an Egyptologist, Depuydt calculated that the probability of so many Thomas phrases appearing randomly in a text as brief as the Wife fragment was one in a trillion. The scientific tests might have been able to expose the papyrus as a forgery, Depuydt said, but they could never authenticate. Columbia's ink study, for instance, couldn't say when the ink was made, only that it didn't contain chemicals as newly invented as those in, say, a Bic pen. Making carbon black, the ink type the Columbia scientists identified on the papyrus, was as simple as mixing soot from a candle or fireplace with water and, optionally, gum arabic.

Harvard had touted the scientists' carbon 14 tests as proof that the papyrus material was "ancient." But that depended on how loosely one defined the term. The tested samples had a median date of A.D. 741. That was a far cry from A.D. 350 to A.D. 400, the date confidently assigned by the papyrologist Roger Bagnall. To lay readers who got far enough into the rare news story noting the discrepancy, it might have seemed moot: ancient was ancient. But to historians of Christianity—Ivy or bush league—the difference between the fourth and the eighth centuries was epochal: it was the difference between antiquity and the Middle Ages. In the fourth century, Roman emperors ruled Egypt, the

Christian canon was still forming and some "heretical" gospels were still being copied. By the middle of the eighth century, Rome had fallen, Muslims had conquered Egypt and heretical gospels had been out of circulation for several hundred years. The eighth-century date was in many ways the most important scientific test result. But it wasn't the lifesaver that the Harvard press release, and the ensuing news stories, held it out to be; it was a thorny problem. A scholar would need to carry out a painstaking historical investigation to explain why anyone would be writing, copying or circulating a previously unattested text like the Gospel of Jesus's Wife in Islamic Egypt in the early Middle Ages.

None was to be found in King's twenty-nine-page *Harvard Theological Review* article, which continued to characterize the find as part of "an early Christian debate over whether women who are wives and mothers can be disciples of Jesus." In her final paragraph, which she labeled "Afterword," King suggested that the dating results came too late for her to square with her main argument; the latter's ink had, as it were, already dried. "In January 2014, I concluded this article by stating it would not be the last word on the subject," she wrote. "And now in early March, I received news" of the papyrus's eighth-century origins. The implication was that her draft, as it had stood before the afterword, was already past the point of revision, recall or postponement. The radiocarbon dating was thus like a mail-in ballot that arrived after election day—too late to alter the race and unworthy of too much comment. The Harvard press release, issued well after the lab results were in, drew no attention to the unexpectedness of the eighth-century finding. Like King, it called the papyrus "ancient," when in fact it was medieval—a distinction that an elite divinity school had to know mattered.

A closer look at the *Harvard Theological Review*'s mid-April issue showed no evidence of actual tardiness in the early March test results. The journal published the scientists' dating reports in the same issue as King's piece, and King herself casually cites the eighth-century date in the body of her article, without saying a word about its historical dissonance or the threat it posed to her central thesis. Not until the final sentence of the final paragraph—the "Afterword"—does she gesture at the possibility of a problem. "This date," she wrote, "suggests a new line of inquiry into the context of the fragment's circulation in Egypt of the Islamic period."

KING DIDN'T IGNORE the questions raised by Bernhard, Depuydt and other skeptics, but she didn't find them credible, either. She wrote that she couldn't imagine a con artist capable of getting so many details right and so many other details wrong. How, for instance, could a forger cunning enough to craft a scientifically undetectable fake be so clumsy with Coptic handwriting and grammar? How could anyone astute enough to set the words "my wife" within well-known gospel debates about family and discipleship be so dense as to think an accredited scholar would take it as proof that the historical Jesus was married? "In my judgment," she concluded, "such a combination of bumbling and sophistication seems extremely unlikely."

In a TV interview in April 2014 on Boston's PBS affiliate, King told the host that the scientific case for authenticity was "just about as strong as you're gonna get."

"I'd say you nailed this one pretty well," the host replied.

"Pretty nailed, yeah," King said.

If the papyrus's owner was watching, he no doubt agreed. "I see the possibility of a forgery as non-existent at this point," he'd written to King three months earlier, after she let him in on the lab results and expressed hope that he'd like her article. "Even close to perfect manuscript-forgeries," he said, "can typically be identified within minutes with a simple loupe." He said that tests from labs like MIT's—which yielded "findings on a molecular level here, vibrations of atoms, etc."—were "the ultimate confirmation for me that we've been right all along, confirming again what has been obvious from day one."

ACT 3

PROOFS

The forger confronts a chessboard full of ... corroboratory
and contradictory texts. How is he to move his own new
pieces in such a way as not to expose them to a rapid
checkmate? Two possibilities have consistently presented
themselves. The forger may claim to sweep the board
clean of any pieces but his own. Or he may try to castle,
using genuine pieces to intervene between his own shaky
falsehoods and detection. Often he undertakes both
maneuvers—contradictory though they seem—at once.

—Anthony Grafton,

Forgers and Critics: Creativity and Duplicity in Western Scholarship

In 2009, the billionaire evangelical owners of the Hobby Lobby arts-and-crafts chain went on an antiquities buying spree. The Green family spent millions of dollars at an often heedless clip, acquiring what would soon become the world's largest private collection of biblical artifacts—archaeological proof of what they deemed "the absolute authority and reliability of the Bible." Warehouses at Hobby Lobby's corporate campus in Oklahoma City brimmed with some forty thousand relics. There were Dead Sea Scrolls and ancient biblical papyri. There were cuneiform tablets, Hebrew Torahs and illuminated medieval manuscripts. The collection was destined for a $500 million Museum of the Bible that the Greens dreamed of building at the center of American political power: the National Mall in Washington, D.C. The opulent eight-story building, with high-tech exhibit spaces and a curved glass roof that evokes both a scroll and an ark, would open in November 2017.

The last time Hobby Lobby made headlines was June 2014, when the U.S. Supreme Court ruled that Obamacare's contraception mandate violated the religious freedom of the company's Pentecostal owners. Even before the museum opened, skeptics denounced it as a thinly veiled mission to spoon-feed evangelical doctrine to the public in a setting many would mistake for a Smithsonian institution. In part to blunt such criticisms, the Greens launched a program to fund scholars interested in working with their collection. One of their young stars was a New Testament Coptologist named Christian Askeland. A blunt-spoken Florida native with a recent PhD from the University of Cambridge, Askeland had been hired to help manage the program, then known as the Green Scholars Initiative.

IN SEPTEMBER 2012, as Karen King began her presentation in Rome, Askeland was giving a talk downstairs on Coptic copies of the book of Revelation. Askeland was a comer. The International Association for Coptic Studies, which runs the conference, had presented him that week with its Award for Academic Excellence, for the best PhD dissertation on a Coptic subject in all the preceding four years. Still, he saw himself as a long shot for jobs at secular American universities, where religious studies faculties often looked down on evangelical scholars as irremediably biased. The truth, Askeland believed, was that you could find "fundamentalists" on both left and right. That made it all the more critical for scholars to judge research on its thoroughness and accuracy, not on the faith or politics of the researcher. "It's profiling: 'This is how evangelical Christians are, so they shouldn't be part of the debate,'" Askeland said. "Anytime anyone suggests that a particular scholar might have a bias because of their beliefs, that's the point where you want to turn around and say, 'What are your biases?' The dangerous people are usually the ones pointing the fingers."

Religious studies faculties had more women and minorities than ever before, which was a step forward. But intellectually, Askeland felt, they were monoliths, often blind to their own liberal pieties. As a conservative, he was even more of an odd man out in Coptic studies, a field that tended to attract disaffected Christians drawn to "alternative" gospels. Askeland refused to exile himself. He was famous for the informal dinners he hosted at Japanese restaurants during the annual gathering of the Society of Biblical Literature. While liberal colleagues downed their share of beer and sake at his "Coptic Sushi" outings, the abstemious Askeland got just as punchy debating the latest developments in the field. "He's the only evangelical I know who hangs with this crowd," said Dylan Burns, a ponytailed scholar of Gnosticism who was born to a Jewish mother and Southern Episcopalian father and raised as a Zen Buddhist. "It's pretty ballsy, to be honest."

Askeland's parents were committed Lutherans. But in high school he gravitated toward evangelical classmates and the Southern Baptist Church, where he discovered a Savior more forceful than the "sissy Jesus" he'd been raised with. Askeland claimed to have no theological quibble with the text of the Jesus's Wife papyrus; no one took it as history, and he could square his belief in a divinely inspired Bible with the fact—well established from genuine finds—that early Christians thought lots of different things about Jesus. That said, he was skeptical of scholars who treated lost gospels like Philip and Mary as proto-feminist manifestos. In his reading—and in that of some feminist scholars, too—these gospels promoted female figures like Mary Magdalene for the chief purpose of "smacking down" the wavering men apostles. "This is all about role reversal," Askeland thought. Roman society was deeply patriarchal. Nothing stung worse than being compared unfavorably with a woman. Women might well deserve to be leaders in the modern church, but scholars erred, he felt, when they went searching antiquity for proof. As his dissertation adviser at Cambridge was fond of saying, "Amazing new things in the Gospel I see, some put there by God, some by me."

"The best any of us can do is recognize our biases," Askeland thought. "You want to bring people in from different perspectives so you can check each other." It was a fair point, but Askeland wasn't always its most effective messenger. His unfiltered, confrontational style—and his yen for charged language like "liberal fundamentalists" and "hyperfeminist sensibilities"—often alienated the very people he most wanted, and needed, as allies across the aisle.

ON THE AFTERNOON of April 24, 2014, Askeland was finishing his day at the Institute for New Testament Textual Research, at the University of Münster in Germany. He was on a German government-funded research team working on early Coptic translations of the Bible. Askeland had read the scientific reports on the Wife papyrus in the new issue of the *Harvard Theological Review*. But in his in-box that afternoon he found an interesting email from a colleague: the scientists had produced extended reports—far longer than the summaries in the *Review*—and Harvard had posted them on its special Gospel of Jesus's Wife website. Askeland clicked on a link to a twenty-nine-page ink study and was startled by its photographs. Its authors, scientists at Columbia University, had tested not just the Gospel of Jesus's Wife but another papyrus from the same owner: a fragment of the canonical Gospel of John, the piece that the owner had hoped to sell Harvard, along with the rest of his other papyri, in exchange for his donation of the Wife scrap. (This was the sale the owner had broached in July 2012, the day after the Smithsonian Channel shoot, when he pointed to the half a million dollars a buyer at Sotheby's had just paid for a piece of Romans—a buyer that turned out to be the Green family.)

King had made glancing references to the owner's John fragment as early as September 2012; Harvard had the physical object on loan since that November. But in an echo of her photo-free presentation in Rome, she never released images of the John scrap. With no basis for doubt, most scholars assumed that John was a genuine piece meant to confer legitimacy on the star attraction. But when Askeland stumbled on the first-ever photos—in the extended Columbia ink study—he was beside himself. There are roughly two hundred known copies of John in old Coptic dialects, most of them fragmentary manuscripts. But just two are in Lycopolitan, a rare early dialect in which the letter *alpha* appears in place of the standard dialect's *omicron* and *epsilon*. One Lycopolitan John was a short school exercise; the other, a nearly complete gospel. If Askeland's eyes didn't deceive, this fragment would now be a third. He didn't need a reference book to grasp how big a deal this was. The PhD dissertation he wrote at Cambridge was the world's first definitive study of all the Coptic translations of John. Using tools from linguistics, biblical studies and statistics, Askeland compared the earliest Greek editions with translations, over fifteen centuries, in no fewer than seven Coptic dialects. The dissertation had not only won the academic prize at the conference where King announced the Wife papyrus. De Gruyter—a 260-year-old German publishing house that published luminaries from Goethe to the Brothers Grimm—quickly acquired the manuscript, publishing it as *John's Gospel: The Coptic Translations of its Greek Text*. A discovery of only the third known Lycopolitan John was major scholarly news. To describe it simply as "a fragment of the Gospel of John," as King had in her article, was like identifying a newfound copy of Shakespeare's First Folio as "a Shakespeare book." Did King even realize what she had?

As he looked more closely at the photo, something began to unsettle him. It was the handwriting. He was sure he had seen it somewhere before. It had the same ungainly quirks, he realized, as the script on the Gospel of Jesus's Wife. His head throbbed on the train home. He had been working late that week, and he'd looked forward to a relaxing dinner with his wife, Stephanie, their three children and Stephanie's mother, who was visiting from Florida. Warm plates of lasagna and calzone were waiting on the dinner table when he walked in. But Askeland no sooner opened the front door than dashed upstairs. "The Gospel of Jesus's Wife thing has blown up," he called to Stephanie, apologizing.

Tucked in his home office, he turned on his laptop and began dropping strings of letters from the owner's John fragment into a searchable online database of the Coptic New Testament that he had helped build. The recto, he saw, contained John 5:26–31, in which Jesus claims to be God's son; the verso, John 6:11–14, where he proves it by multiplying loaves and fishes. The brief Lycopolitan school exercise, written in the third or fourth century and now housed in a Dublin library, contained neither of those verses. But the other Lycopolitan John, which covered forty-three papyrus leaves and some 85 percent of the gospel, contained both. A British archaeologist had found it in Egypt in March 1923. It had been wrapped in linen and tied with thread, then stashed in a red jar beneath an ancient graveyard near the village of Qau. The Qau codex, as it became known, dated to the latter half of the fourth century; it was the earliest Coptic copy of John, and quite possibly the earliest surviving John in any language. The first edition of the codex was published in 1924 by a British Egyptologist named Herbert Thompson. Askeland knew Thompson's edition well; for his dissertation, he had gone so far as to double-check it against the original papyri, which he examined under a geological field microscope in the special collections of the Cambridge University Library.

That April evening in Münster, he called up a 152-page pdf of Thompson's book, which had been scanned by a consortium of university libraries. Askeland wanted to see how closely the Lycopolitan of "Harvard John," as he dubbed it, tracked with the Lycopolitan of the Qau codex. For language obsessives like himself, even minute differences were fascinating. But when he compared the texts, he saw that the similarities went considerably beyond dialect. Each and every one of the seventeen line breaks in Harvard John matched a line break in the Qau codex. The front of the papyrus copied the beginnings of lines from the Qau manuscript, and the back, the endings. This was unprecedented. Biblical texts in those days weren't broken into chapter or verse. Moreover, scribes wrote in *scriptio continua*, without spaces between words. The widths and lengths of papyrus leaves varied, and the size of scribes' handwriting was often as different as the person. In *scriptio continua*, lines broke in weird, random places all the time; there was no reason to copy the line breaks of another scribe, and lots of reasons not to. For one, a scribe would want to make the most of the peculiar margins of his particular papyrus, if for no other reason than to avoid the expense of additional pages.

At most, copies of an ancient biblical text might—by mere chance—share two or three line breaks. After that, they would begin to diverge. It was like two runners of different ability in the same race. They started at the same line, but the distance between them grew with every lap. With Harvard John and Qau, however, all seventeen line breaks matched, as if justified by Photoshop or Microsoft Word. Askeland was beside himself. "How stupid could you be?" he thought. "That was a level of foolishness or carelessness."

Harvard John, he realized, was a third-rate forgery. The perpetrator had barely tried to hide it: they copied one line of the Qau codex, then omitted the next, copied another, then omitted the next. *Even if someone were to notice,* Askeland imagined the forger thinking, *no one could call it an* exact *copy. It was just a larger papyrus, whose lines happened to be precisely twice as long.* But the forger had bungled even this cover—by once forgetting to skip a line. When Askeland looked back at Thompson's transcription, he saw why. The second-to-last line in Harvard John was the last line on a page in Thompson's book. When the forger turned the page, he seems to have lost his place. Instead of starting with the second line on the next page of Thompson, the forger started with the first, betraying the ruse as gracelessly as a puppeteer who lets his hand slip into the camera frame.

But those were only the most obvious goofs. Stephen Emmel, a Yale-trained scholar who is one of the world's top codicologists, or experts on ancient bookmaking, quantified the amount of text missing between the verses on the front and the verses on the back. Because the Gospel of John is a known quantity, a fragment with text on both sides allows a skilled codicologist to calculate the page size and page count of the codex it had once been part of. Harvard John measured eight centimeters by ten centimeters, a little larger than a playing card. Had the gospel survived in its entirety, Emmel found, its page size would have been taller or wider than any Greek, Latin or Coptic papyrus codex in history—on any subject. The forger, it seemed, didn't realize that John 6:11–14, in handwriting so large, had no business being on the flip side of John 5:26–31.

Finally, there was the rare Lycopolitan dialect. A knowledgeable forger might have picked it for financial gain. As the dialect of the oldest known copy of John, it would have made the text more attractive to buyers. But there was a hitch: King's radiocarbon tests had dated the papyrus leaf on which the John verses were written to A.D. 718, hundreds of years after Lycopolitan had died off. There is no evidence that anyone copied Lycopolitan after the fourth century A.D. That it should appear on papyrus harvested in the early Islamic era was deeply suspect.

Askeland, who had followed Andrew Bernhard's work on Grondin's interlinear, saw the same MO in Harvard John. A forger was copying from easily accessible online pdfs of Coptic manuscripts, then introducing minute changes, either through carelessness or to cover his tracks, or some combination of both. Just as the Wife scrap replicated typos found in Grondin's interlinear of Thomas—but not in Thomas itself—Harvard John appeared to copy a modern typesetting feature in Thompson's Qau transcription that was not in the Qau codex itself. In both cases, the forger had used papyrus leaves that, while centuries old, were still too young to easily square with their dialect or content.

In early 2017, I contacted Bill Hook, a Vanderbilt Divinity School librarian who oversaw book digitization for the university consortium that scanned Thompson's Qau book for the web. Hook told me that the pdf of Thompson's volume was posted online in January 2003. That was just two months after Grondin's website had posted his pdf interlinear of the Gospel of Thomas.

The time and manner of both suspected fakes were coming into sharper focus. To obtain source material, all the perpetrator required was an internet connection, which would mark a milestone in the digital democratization of antiquities fraud. If the online pdfs were their building blocks, the forgeries had to have been produced between November 2002, when Grondin uploaded his interlinear, and July 2010, when the collector contacted King. The collector, by his own account, was the papyri's sole owner over that eight-year period.

CHRISTIAN ASKELAND COULD have taken his scoop straight to a major newspaper. Instead, he chose to announce it on a little-known blog for scholars who see the Bible as divine revelation. Contributors to the site, *Evangelical Textual Criticism,* hail from respected universities. But to post articles, they must submit a statement of doctrinal commitment to the Thirty-nine Articles, the Westminster Confession or another traditional pledge of evangelical faith.

It was a curious venue for a man who claimed to be deeply sensitive to the distrust his conservativism bred in other scholars. He knew the Jesus's Wife papyrus had by now become a battleground for larger ideological wars within biblical studies. A year before Askeland was hired, Steve Green, the president of Hobby Lobby, all but made antipathy to King's interpretation a prerequisite for funding by the Green Scholars Initiative. "If you want to say that this piece of [papyrus] says that Jesus had a wife then I don't have use for you because you are making that up, it is not what it says," Green declared in March 2013 in a speech to the Council for National Policy, a Washington group whose members include some of the country's most powerful social conservatives. "But if you are going to give me the facts, I don't care what stripe you are from." Green, however, made clear that some facts suited his story of the Bible better than others. Of the strategy behind his antiquities collecting, he said, "We are storytellers first, and ... we're buyers of items to tell the story. We pass on more than we buy because it doesn't fit what we are trying to tell."

What Green didn't mention was that his buying spree was already under federal investigation. Hobby Lobby would eventually pay $3 million and forfeit thousands of ancient Iraqi artifacts to settle civil claims by the U.S. Justice Department that the company helped smuggle Iraqi relics into the United States in 2010 and 2011. Israeli authorities, meanwhile, arrested five Palestinian dealers who allegedly sold the Greens some $22 million in smuggled antiquities. The police said the dealers doctored invoices, in exchange for kickbacks, to help an unnamed American claim large tax breaks on the purchases. "We should have exercised more oversight and carefully questioned how the acquisitions were handled," Steve Green said in a statement after the scandal broke. Federal prosecutors said that Hobby Lobby had ignored a series of red flags, including warnings from a hired expert that the artifacts—thousands of cuneiform tablets and clay bullae—might have been looted from archaeological sites. Before long, humanities scholars and lab scientists unmasked a number of the Greens' Dead Sea Scroll fragments as fakes. The Museum of the Bible next accused one of its well-paid consultants—a major Oxford classicist—of fraud. Museum officials alleged that the scholar sold Hobby Lobby canonical gospel fragments that were stolen from Oxford's papyrus collections and falsely dated to the first century A.D. In their thirst for manuscripts that told a particular story about early Christianity, the Greens had made themselves easy marks.

The founder of *Evangelical Textual Criticism*, the University of Cambridge scholar Peter Williams, conceded that Askeland took a short-term hit for his decision to post his discovery on a blog for confessional scholars. But there was a long-term upside: greater academic credibility for scholars who happen to be evangelical. For Askeland to uncover truths about the John fragment that eluded a place like Harvard was "sort of a reversal of who's actually holding the torch of knowledge," said Williams, who was Askeland's PhD adviser and directs Tyndale House, a prominent biblical research institute.

When his blog post went live, however, Askeland discovered that the biggest target on his back was something other than his evangelical faith.

ASKELAND INSISTS IT WAS nothing more than a harmless play on the intertwining themes of Jesus's family and unsightly forgeries. But "Jesus Had an Ugly Sister-in-Law" as the title for an evangelical blog post aimed at a high-ranking female divinity professor? Many scholars saw it as crossing a line. "The use of an ugly woman as a metaphor for a sloppy, forged, worthless text" could teach people "a great deal about issues of gender in modern scholarship," Eva Mroczek, then a Judaic studies scholar at Indiana University, wrote in a widely circulated article that accused Askeland of "sexist language." Though "Ugly Sister-in-Law" referred to the Gospel of John forgery, Mroczek argued that it doubled as a knock on King as a woman. Biblical studies remains a predominantly male fiefdom; women make up just a quarter of the members of the Society of Biblical Literature, a share that has stayed stubbornly flat in recent years. Debates, conference panels and publications were almost invariably dominated by men. Trailblazers like King deserved better than seeing a manuscript in their care likened to an unattractive woman. "Metaphors matter," Mroczek wrote. Askeland's motif—"a long and illustrious tradition" in which "Cinderella's ugly stepsisters are the obvious example"—"perpetuates old ideas that have marginalized and shamed women." She linked Askeland, and by extension his forgery findings, to the Greens' "strong evangelical agenda." Though Mroczek didn't cite it, Askeland had given another incendiary title—"Was Mrs. Jesus Pimped?"—to a September 2012 post that took King to task for "hyping a fragment whose origins and significance are so uncertain."

Askeland deleted the word "ugly" from the headline, changing it to "Jesus Had a Sister-in-Law." But it was too little, too late. The word "ugly" remained in the post's URL, and his efforts at damage control— he purged the blog's comments section of sexism accusations—found him in still hotter water. Several scholars warned him that his academic career was over. Commentators on the right, meanwhile, saw a case of identity politics run amok. "The stance seems to be that any scholar—no matter how impressive the credentials or carefully supported the argument—who dares to assert forgery with respect to the Jesus' Wife fragment is a misogynist with an 'agenda' for raising the claim," Charlotte Allen, a reporter for *The Weekly Standard,* wrote in the opinion pages of the *Los Angeles Times.* "Because, you see, King is a woman, and you can't criticize a woman, ever. And that goes double if you, as a scholar, also happen to be an evangelical Christian."

Andrew Bernhard was no evangelical, but King had privately questioned his politics, too. In September 2011, a year before her announcement in Rome, Bernhard and King had met, for the first time, at a public lecture she gave in Oregon. Afterward, Bernhard asked her to sign his well-thumbed copy of her Gospel of Mary book. He then gave her his own book on Greek fragments of the noncanonical gospels.

"Where is the Gospel of Mary?" King asked as she flipped through the pages. His book lacked translations of two small Greek scraps with a few of the gospel's lines. (The bulk of Mary is preserved in a Coptic text.) Bernhard explained that he had limited the book to noncanonical Greek fragments about the earthly, adult life of Jesus. For reasons of space, he had to exclude postresurrection texts like the Gospel of Mary and pre-adult ones like those dealing with Jesus's infancy.

"It seems like the girls always get left out," King replied.

WHEN MAINSTREAM NEWS OUTLETS finally caught wind of Askeland's discovery, the ugly-sister imbroglio interested them less than his scholarly findings. "It's never a good sign for a text of doubtful authenticity to be found in the company of a sure forgery," a pair of scholars wrote on CNN's *Belief Blog,* referring, in turn, to the Wife and John fragments. "Simply put: If one is a forgery, they're both forgeries." Two days later, Askeland's boss at the Green Scholars Initiative published an op-ed in *The Wall Street Journal* headlined "How the 'Jesus' Wife' Hoax Fell Apart."

As it had two years earlier, the Smithsonian Channel found itself overtaken by events. On April 23, it announced that because "scientific results" showed the Wife fragment was "authentically ancient and not a modern fake," it would at last premiere its long-delayed documentary. A day later, Askeland posted his findings about the same collector's John fragment. The channel didn't postpone or reedit the documentary this time. But in a stroke of timing that might well have given fits to some Smithsonian officials, *The New York Times* published its own story on Askeland's discovery on May 5, the day the documentary aired. On page 17 of the country's newspaper of record was a smiling portrait of the young scholar in khakis and blazer, holding a copy of his book on Coptic translations of the Gospel of John.

King's triumphant article in the *Harvard Theological Review*—with scientific tests she hoped would close the forgery debate for good—had survived all of two weeks before Askeland rammed it back open.

BEFORE THE JESUS'S WIFE CONTROVERSY, Andrew Bernhard had never heard of Christian Askeland. He was fairly certain that Askeland had likewise never heard of him. Both had turned thirty-six in 2012. Both were Americans with advanced degrees from Britain's best universities. But their politics, their Christianity and their places of residence— Bernhard in Portland, Askeland in Oklahoma City—could hardly be more different. Askeland had met his wife through the same campus ministry whose denunciations of premarital sex precipitated Bernhard's break with Christianity.

Their shared pursuit of the truth about the Gospel of Jesus's Wife, however, had erected a bridge. They began video chatting on Skype, talking about their families and arguing over which of their alma maters—Oxford or Cambridge—was the better school. Though they groused about doing scholarship in basements alongside loads

of laundry, they'd also come to see advantages: life outside academia's high walls afforded freedoms unavailable inside. Bernhard and
Askeland didn't have to worry about what Harvard might think of
them. They didn't have to weigh the professional cost, as many young
scholars do, of challenging powerful gatekeepers who might one day
sit on a hiring or tenure committee.

FRANCIS WATSON, the first scholar to spot the parallels between the
Gospel of Thomas and the Gospel of Jesus's Wife, became editor of the
journal *New Testament Studies* in 2014. Watson regarded the April 2014
issue of the *Harvard Theological Review*—edited by Harvard scholars and
promoted by Harvard publicists—as a wholly inadequate response to
the papyrus's many doubters. King, he felt, had distorted the arguments
of critics and drew unwarranted conclusions from the scientific studies. "Forgeries corrupt—and are intended to corrupt—the scholarly
work of those who may be deceived by them," Watson felt. One reason
that skeptics like Bernhard had been easy for King to ignore, Watson
thought, was that they'd published their findings on blogs or personal
websites. Hot takes scattered across different online forums in multiple
countries over two years were no match for the dreadnought of a single,
peer-reviewed journal bearing the name Harvard. There was a good
chance that within a few decades the blogs would go dark and the only
surviving totem in the scholarly literature would be Harvard's tenden-
tious take in the *Harvard Theological Review*. To level the field, Watson
asked the most incisive critics of the papyrus for formal articles. He
sent their submissions for peer review. Then he published six of them,
in July 2015, in a single issue of *New Testament Studies*. Among them were
back-to-back articles, twenty-one pages apiece, by Andrew Bernhard
and Christian Askeland. Truths hounded in basements might take a
bit longer to find their way into the ivory tower, but they got there
eventually.

KAREN KING RESPONDED to the special issue of *New Testament Studies*, but
not directly and not in a peer-reviewed journal. Her response appeared
in *Biblical Archaeology Review*, the same popular magazine whose editor,
Hershel Shanks, had turned the "James, Brother of Jesus" ossuary into

a media spectacle a decade earlier, only to see experts debunk it as a fraud. "Among the real scholars, [Shanks] is something of a joke," the journalist Nina Burleigh wrote in her book on the James Ossuary, "but they take him seriously insofar as he can deliver their papers to a wide audience." King's contribution to the magazine's September/October 2015 issue wasn't a paper but a reply to a question that a Baltimore rabbi had sent Shanks. The rabbi's family had wondered, over dinner one night, whether Harvard John could have been copied from the Qau codex in antiquity. "If so," the rabbi wrote, "it would not be a forgery."

Scholars had answered this question more than a year earlier. Not only had the Lycopolitan dialect gone extinct a few centuries before the eighth-century papyrus plant on which Harvard John was written, but the number of matching line breaks—seventeen in total—lacked even a close precedent.

King wrote to the magazine to encourage the rabbi. "Your suggestion is a good one," she said. "I am not a specialist in the history of Christianity in Egypt during this period." Though the rabbi wasn't either—his training was in bioethics and the Talmud—King asked him whether the John and Wife fragments could have been products of early Islamic Egypt. "I would be interested in what you and your family have to say," she wrote. "One might imagine that a (poor and error-filled) copy of the Coptic Gospel of John (written in an ancient and no longer used dialect of Coptic) might have been made simply because of the esteem and holy power that Christians ascribed to Scripture." Without naming him, King questioned Stephen Emmel's claim that a complete page of Harvard John would cover a sheet of papyrus bigger than any known to history. That was true, King hinted, only if the codex contained the *entire* Gospel of John. Maybe it contained just a selection of favorite verses, a kind of greatest hits. And maybe its author chose these passages, rather than all of John, because they "emphasize two points of agreement with Muslim teachings about Jesus: that he was a prophet and raised people from the dead for judgment." Forgery was certainly one theory, she allowed. But it was "important, however difficult, to stay open [to] the enormity of the gaps in our knowledge of both ancient and modern contexts. Your family discussion, Rabbi Reisner, is a great example."

WHEN ANDREW BERNHARD read King's note in the magazine, he was surprised. After Askeland's discovery, a few people had clung, privately, to the possibility that the Wife papyrus was real. But none believed John was. King now signaled that both scraps were still very much in play. King had dismissed Bernhard's case—about Grondin's interlinear—with as much dispatch as she had Askeland's. The existence of Thomas-like phrases in the Wife fragment meant little, she argued, because gospel writers routinely borrowed from one another. The books of Matthew, Mark and Luke were Exhibit A: they remained "theologically distinctive" despite a good deal of overlapping narrative. As for the missing *mu*—the bizarre typo that appears both in Grondin's Thomas and the Wife papyrus—King had recently found a few "rare" examples of the same anomaly in genuinely ancient texts. The flaw in Bernhard's argument, King contended, was that it assumed forgery and then worked backward to prove it. A more basic problem was that his dates didn't work. If a Berlin professor saw the papyrus in the 1980s and the current owner bought it in the 1990s, how could the fragment have plagiarized a pdf that didn't exist until 2002? Bernhard's case, she wrote, requires "proof that the statements and documentation provided by the owner are also false or forged."

Over the preceding three years, scholars and journalists had asked repeatedly for those very documents. The papers—a typewritten 1982 letter and a handwritten note, both possibly from the same Berlin professor—mentioned the John and Wife papyri, but not the current owner. Their release wouldn't have compromised King's promise of anonymity. Why King refused to release them, even to colleagues who offered to vet them confidentially, was hard to fathom.

"She's saying, 'You need to prove these documents are false,'" Bernhard thought. "How am I supposed to do that when I can't see them?"

Then, one day, he had an idea.

BERNHARD STORED ALMOST EVERY NEWS ARTICLE, journal paper and blog post on the Wife papyrus in a set of fastidiously organized binders and accordion folders. It was time to put every one of those words under the microscope again. As he reread a printout of my first *Smithsonian* story, he tripped over the most banal of words. The owner, I wrote, had emailed King an unsigned translation with the phrase "Jesus said this to them: My wife…" In her own, later translation, King revised the line to a simple, "Jesus said to them, 'My wife…'" What stopped Bernhard was the one word King struck—the word "this."

Grondin, he remembered, had used the same word in the same incorrect way in his interlinear. Where English uses quotation marks to show someone speaking, Coptic uses the two-letter word *je*. The word, when signaling a direct quotation, had no English equivalent. Grondin knew it, but for the algorithms of his Kingdom of God Puzzle, he needed an unobtrusive placeholder; he came up with "this."

The matching Coptic errors in the Wife papyrus and Grondin's pdf of Thomas had not concerned King, who viewed them as coincidence. But what if the owner's translation of the Wife fragment and Grondin's translation of Thomas contained identical *English* errors? *That*, Bernhard thought, would be decidedly harder to explain away. Grondin's English idiosyncrasies weren't common mistakes that any novice might make. They were his private code—word choices made for the express use of his arcane intellectual puzzles. This wasn't a fact Grondin prominently advertised. A casual visitor to his website would have no reason to think that Grondin's translations diverged from the dictionary.

In January 2013, Bernhard had asked to inspect the papyrus first-hand at Harvard. ("It's available to everyone immediately now," King had said in her September 2012 presentation in Rome. "Come visit Harvard!") But Bernhard never received a reply. This left him little hope that King would release the owner's full translation. As he reread his news clippings, Bernhard came to suspect that King might be more responsive to a journalist than she was to her own colleagues. He sent a Facebook message to a college friend, Ryan Teague Beckwith, who had become a senior editor for *Time* magazine.

"You need to figure out who would have the motivation to help you," Beckwith responded. *The New York Times*'s religion reporter had scooped *The Boston Globe* on Askeland's discovery, beating the Boston paper on its own turf. The *Globe* might jump at a chance to strike back.

Beckwith sent a group email to a list of fellow Columbia Journalism School graduates. A *Globe* journalist who received it alerted the paper's religion reporter, Lisa Wangsness, who had covered the Wife saga from the start. Wangsness called Bernhard and heard his case for King's disclosing the owner's translation. Then she began work on a larger news story about the limbo the papyrus still found itself in. At Wangsness's request—as Bernhard expected—King released the owner's translation.

Bernhard was on his laptop at his basement desk when he clicked on the link from Wangsness. What he saw next caused him to nearly topple out of his chair. The translation was an interlinear—with a line of English beneath each line of Coptic, just like Grondin's. Moreover, every single line of English bore signs of copying from Grondin. It wasn't just the word "this"—a translation unseen outside Grondin. It was that nearly every error and anomaly in the owner's English translation of the Wife papyrus matched errors and anomalies in Grondin's English translation of Thomas. The copying was so ham-handed in places that the owner's interlinear contained English translations of Coptic words that appeared in Thomas but not in the Gospel of Jesus's Wife.

Most damning, however, was another of Grondin's one-offs. The word *arna,* which Coptic borrows from Greek, appears twice in the Gospel of Thomas. Dictionaries translate it, variously, as "deny," "disown," "refuse," "repudiate" or "renounce." Grondin, however, coined his own translation: "abdicate." It is found in no dictionary. Because of the standardization his algorithms required, he'd wanted a single English verb that could function with or without a direct object.

But why, of all words, "abdicate"? "Where I got it from wasn't any Greek dictionary, but from personal memory of reading about the abdication of an English king," Grondin wrote to me, when I'd asked. "Specifically (as I now recall), the abdication of Edward VIII to marry Wallace [*sic*] Simpson, an American divorcee, in 1936."

Arna, it turned out, was the first word in the Wife fragment's Line 3. King had translated the line, correctly, with the word "deny":

deny. Mary is (not?) worthy of it

The owner's translation signed, sealed and delivered Bernhard's case for forgery. Its Line 3 read,

abdicate, Mary be worthy of you (not)

———

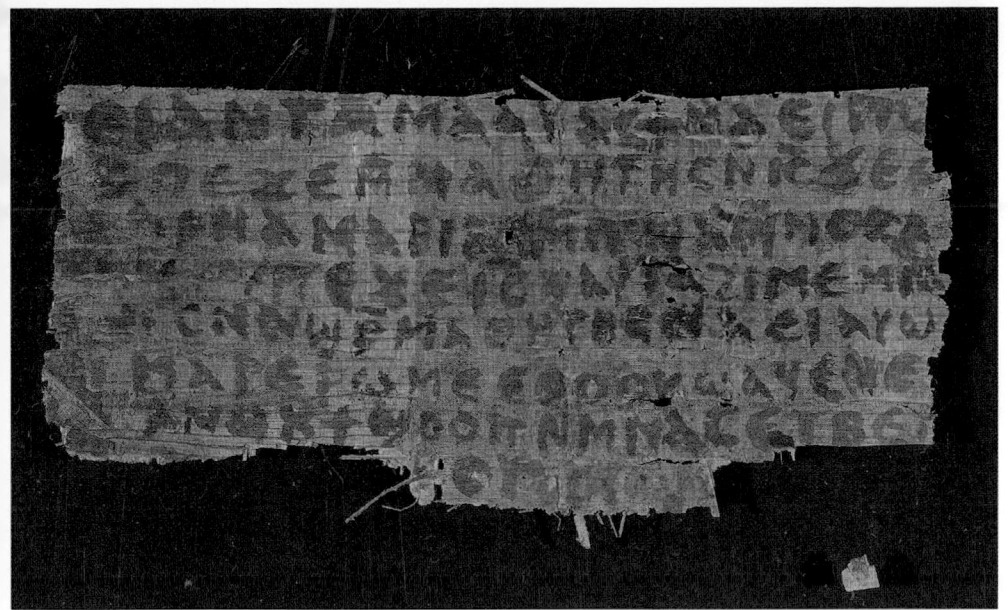

The Gospel of Jesus's Wife, recto. The phrase "Jesus said to them, 'My wife . . . '" appears, in the ancient Egyptian language of Coptic, on the fourth line of the papyrus fragment's front side. The fragment is a little smaller than a business card.

The Gospel of Jesus's Wife, verso. The fragment's back side is so damaged that just a few Coptic words—including "my mother" and "three"—are decipherable.

Professor Karen King holds the Wife papyrus in her office at Harvard Divinity School on September 13, 2012, five days before she announced the find.

Princeton University professor AnneMarie Luijendijk (pictured) earned her doctoral degree under Dr. Karen King at Harvard.

Dr. Roger Bagnall, director of the Institute for the Study of the Ancient World at New York University, is regarded as one of the world's foremost papyrologists. His early views on the Wife papyrus's authenticity were seen as pivotal.

Dr. Karen King addresses the news media outside the Institutum Patristicum Augustinianum, in Rome, at the Tenth International Congress of Coptic Studies, September 19, 2012, the day after announcing a discovery she called "The Gospel of Jesus's Wife."

Class Motto

**The Greatest Pleasure in Life
Is Doing What Others Say You Can't Do.**

Mr. James Corrigan, senior adviser, is in his fifth year on the SHS staff, teaching typing, bookkeeping, secretarial practice, office machines, and clerical office practice. He has a B. S. degree from Western Montana College of Education.

Karen Leigh King

Class secretary 3; Honor Society 1, 2, 3; Girls' State 3; High School Week 3; Social Studies Award 3; F. H. A. 2, 3; Pep Club 1, 2, 3; Small Ensemble 2, 3; Girls' Chorus 1, 2, 3; Drill Team 1, 2; Band 1, 2, 3; Librarian 2; Track 1, 2; District Music Festival 2, 3; State Music Festival 3. Karen spent her last high school year in Norway as an International Christian Youth Exchange Student.

Adviser

ICYE Student

Karen King would have been valedictorian of Sheridan High School's class of 1972, but her senior year abroad disqualified her. The school's yearbook, *The Trailblazer,* which identified her as "ICYE Student"—after the overseas exchange program she took part in—reserved a place of honor for her beneath the class motto, "The Greatest Pleasure in Life Is Doing What Others Say You Can't Do."

4   Friday, November 30, 1984   THE OCCIDENTAL

New faculty member researches old Gnostic religion

by Cynthia Schwab

To many, the term "Gnosticism" might conjure up images of dust-filled rooms with incense burning, ancient priests conducting secret pagan rituals or other esoteric religious phenomena. In actuality there is no clear definition, but Gnosticism may be defined as "a religion which originated during the Roman period and which embodies an attitude of mind that expresses alienation from the world and revolt from the powers that govern it." In simpler terms, the Gnostics were a group of religious sects which sought self-knowledge as a means to overcoming the sense of alienation they felt in the world.

Sound a little confusing? Well, to new religious studies professor Karen King, this strange yet fascinating religious phenomenon has been a subject of on-going interest, on which she recently completed her doctoral dissertation at Brown University.

King attended the University of Montana for her undergraduate work and it was there in the context of her work in religious studies that she first became interested in Gnostic ideas and texts. At Montana, she was first introduced to a particular group of Gnostic texts known as the Nag Hammadi Library and she went on to Brown to continue work with these texts. The Nag Hammadi library is a large group of mainly Gnostic texts which were discovered in 1945 in a cave near the village of Nag Hammadi in Egypt. The texts were found in a large stone jar and are written on papyrus. Among the many texts contained in the Nag Hammadi Library, King has focused most of her attention on one particular text known as *Allogenes*.

Allogenes is a Gnostic text of the Sethian tradition and was originally written in Greek but survives only in this one manuscript in Coptic translation. Coptic is similar to Egyptian Hieroglyphics, only it is written in the Greek alphabet. Nothing is known about the original or translator. It is also not known when it was written or translated, although it was most probably written in Alexandria around the first quarter of the third century and this translation probably dates from the first half of the fourth century.

King's interest in this particular text was sparked by the fact that no one else had ever done anything with it, and she found the philosophical terminology interesting. The purpose behind her thesis was to "contribute to the establishment of a firm textual basis for further study of the Nag Hammadi texts and their relation to the religions and philosophies of Late Antiquity." Further, while working on her doctorate, King also received a grant from the West German government which enabled her to do further research at the University of Berlin where there is a group known as the Coptic Gnostic working group which is the only group of scholars in the world working on these texts. There are no American universities which offer Coptic studies.

The actual text of *Allogenes* is an entirely pagan Gnostic text and draws heavily upon the philosophical terminology then current. The structure of the text is a narrative in the first person. In the text, "Allogenes (whose name in Greek means 'the foreigner') addresses his 'pen Messos' and describes to him a series of revelations and visions given to him and instructs him to proclaim "these five seals of all the books of Allogenes."

"The text focuses upon the character of Allogenes and while he is in no way an historical person, he provides both the message of, and the pattern for, salvation for the race of those who by nature are worthy to be saved. Allogenes is at once the savior and the saved. In the text, salvation is portrayed as the progression from ignorance and fear to the reception of power, rest, stillness and knowledge. This progression from instruction (hearing) to vision through an extrabodily ascent is what leads one to saving gnosis."

Unfortunately, all that is left are the texts and we have no sociological information about the people that practiced Gnosticism or any of their ritual practices if there were any. As King says, "All we have is the texts and no bodies to go with them."

King's work in the religious studies department will include Biblical studies and other works from the Greco-Roman world. Presently King is finishing a book on the *Allogenes* text and she has future plans of writing books on Gnosticism and Neo-Platonism. King is a fine scholar and a welcome addition to the Occidental faculty.

Religious studies professor *Karen King completes her first term at Occidental.*

A bit of real time
on microprocessors

by Mark Thompson

Computers are great for sorting and storing information. The problem is, you can only recover information that you've already stored inside the machine. You can put stuff in the computer's memory by typing it in or having the computer read it off a diskette or a tape. But what if you want the latest information possible? How can your computer communicate with another, especially if it's a different make? The answer: a modem, that will comb the nations electronic data bases for any information you might need. You can also use your credit card number to order merchandise from retailers such as Sears or B. Dalton Books.

And that's just a small part of what's offered. The catch is the price: around $6 an hour after you've used up your free time. OK, you say, I guess I can use some of that stuff. But at that price?

Fortunately, the large information services mentioned above aren't the only places through

After earning her PhD at Brown University in 1984, Karen King was hired onto the religious studies faculty at Occidental College, a liberal arts school in suburban Los Angeles. The college newspaper, *The Occidental,* announced her arrival under the headline "New Faculty Member Researches Old Gnostic Religion." King would become chair of the department.

Working out of his basement in Portland, Oregon, Andrew Bernhard identified features of the Wife papyrus that suggested forgery. To his left is his Australian cattle dog, Buster.

Mike Grondin, a retired computer programmer, in his home office in the Detroit suburb of Macomb, Michigan. His idiosyncratic "interlinear" translation of the Gospel of Thomas contained what scholars believed were clues to the origins of the Wife papyrus.

Dr. Christian Askeland, a Coptic Bible specialist who worked for the billionaire evangelical owners of the Hobby Lobby craft store chain, spotted signs of forgery in another papyrus—a fragment of the Gospel of John—in the same collection as the Gospel of Jesus's Wife.

All seventeen line breaks on the recto (pictured) and verso of the anonymous collector's Gospel of John fragment were identical to those on the earliest surviving Coptic copy of John.

The anonymous owner of the Gospel of Jesus's Wife claimed that the fragment was one of half a dozen papyri he bought from a German American man named Hans-Ulrich Laukamp (pictured).

A typewritten letter, dated July 15, 1982, suggested that a collector named H. U. Laukamp had shown his papyri to Dr. Peter Munro (pictured), an Egyptologist at West Berlin's Free University.

An unsigned, undated note in the files of the Wife papyrus's current owner reported that Dr. Gerhard Fecht (pictured), chairman of the Free University's Egyptology Institute, had declared the fragment "evidence for [Jesus's] possible marriage."

Axel Herzsprung (pictured) and Hans-Ulrich Laukamp became friends as young toolmakers in Germany. In 1995, they founded ACMB Metallbearbeitung GmbH, a Berlin company that made brake components for BMW automobiles.

Mid-1970s. Walter Fritz's mother, Inge Klöck (maiden name, pictured), astride a horse belonging to Willi Götz, a wealthy factory owner in the conservative Catholic town of Bad Wurzach, Germany. Both were married, with children, when they began an affair.

Walter Fritz on a field trip to Italy with Egyptology classmates from the Free University, 1988. In his first years at the school, he had the looks of "a harmless country boy," one classmate recalled.

Walter Fritz (left, second from top) on the steps of the Free University's Egyptology Institute, November 11, 1989. The Berlin Wall had fallen a couple of days earlier, and East German Egyptology students had come to the Free University, in the West, to meet their counterparts. Dr. Christian Loeben (center, top) recalled Fritz's talent for turning himself into the "little darling" of professors he wanted to impress.

Walter Fritz (third from right) outside the Free University's Egyptology Institute, around 1991, after his "country boy" look gave way to slicked-back hair and business attire. Also pictured are classmates Nicola Hensel (far right), Kim Ryholt (second from right, in blue plaid shirt); and Susanne Voss (fourth from right, in white blouse). Professor Karl Jansen-Winkeln (far left) identified his former student in a 2006 photograph that the author discovered in Florida.

Walter Fritz, 27, studierter Altertumswissenschaftler, ist der Nachfolger von Erich Mielke – an dessen Schreibtisch in der einstigen Ost-Berliner Stasi-Zentrale. Als Direktor der Forschungs- und Gedenkstätte der Antistalinistischen Aktion (Astak) hütet er die Kultgegenstände seines Vorgängers: zum Rot-Front-Gruß geballte Holzfäuste, gewebte und gehäkelte Bildnisse vom Übervater des »Konspiratismus«, Feliks Dzierzynski, und als Krönung das lebensgroße Email-Konterfei Mielkes. Neben den Zeugnissen für den schlechten Geschmack der einst

Worte, wettert gegen einen Gesetzentwurf des Gesundheitsministeriums, der ein generelles Rauchverbot an öffentlichen Plätzen, in Zügen und Flugzeugen sowie am Arbeitsplatz verlangt. »Die Ayatollahs der Anti-Tabak-Front gefährden Tausende von Arbeitsplätzen«, sagt Charasse, dessen Ministerium jährlich etwa 8,4 Milliarden Mark Tabaksteuer kassiert.

FOTO: FRANK BUCHE

Hüter im Mielke-Museum: Walter Fritz

In February 1992, the German magazine *Stern* covered Walter Fritz's appointment as director of the new Stasi Museum, located in the former headquarters of East Germany's dreaded secret police.

Portrait of Walter Fritz, Sarasota, Florida, April 2016.

IF THE FORGER and the author of the owner's translation were one and the same, as now seemed certain, they had tried to paint a scene even more dramatic than the one that carried over into Coptic. King saw the "deny" in Line 3 as signifying controversy among the disciples over Mary's worth. But if the forger had taken Grondin's translation at face value, Mary wasn't the only person whose status the disciples were debating. The owner's translation—but not the actual Coptic—suggested a dispute over whether Jesus should relinquish his own divine crown to be with Mary: "The disciples said this to Jesus, '...abdicate, Mary is worthy of you (not).'" When Jesus responds that his wife is able to be his disciple, he is defending not just Mary but himself; he exposes the choice between Christ the King and Jesus the husband—between divine devotion and spousal love—as a false dilemma. The forger's ardor for this particular message appears to have eclipsed any impulse to check Grondin's translation against a dictionary.

A WEEK AFTER her whirlwind trip to Rome, King finally did what Roger Bagnall had encouraged her to do beforehand: she asked a seasoned Coptic papyrologist to examine the Wife fragment. Malcolm Choat, a goateed Australian scholar renowned for his work on Coptic Christian papyri, traveled to Harvard in November 2012. Though he stopped short of labeling the fragment a forgery, he told King he could find no ancient parallel for its handwriting. Three years later, his curiosity piqued by Bernhard's and Askeland's findings, Choat returned to Harvard for a painstaking reinspection of the Wife and John fragments. "I invited myself," he recalled. The divinity school tried to offer him an honorarium for an unrelated talk during his visit. "I said no." He examined the papyri for ten to twelve hours, some ten times longer than had Bagnall. This time Choat spotted traces of ink on lower-level fibers where there shouldn't have been any. And he found no ink on surface fibers where there should have been. The clearest examples were the blank spaces at the end of the Wife fragment's Lines 3 and 6. If the piece were genuine, the letters would have marched all the way to the edge—like blindfolded people off a cliff—because the *scriptio continua* would have extended beyond the place where the fragment happened to break. The spaces suggested a writer who was conscious of a right margin but who shouldn't have been.

A few days later, *The Boston Globe* published the story that had germinated with Bernhard's outreach to the reporter Lisa Wangsness. "For now," Wangsness concluded, after surveying the latest findings, "it is hard to find anyone who will defend the Gospel of Jesus's Wife as authentic." Just one major question remained: *Whodunit?* "In private conversations, speculation is raging: If this is a fake, what was the forger's motive? Was it ideological? Financial? Just a bizarre prank gone wrong?"

A FEW YEARS LATER, while I was out running one night through the streets of Washington, D.C., something about the word "abdicate" left me shaken. I was familiar with the Christian idea of Jesus as king. I had also heard of Edward VIII, who had given up the British crown for a scandalous marriage to a twice-divorced American. But I wondered now if I'd overlooked another possibility. If the forger was someone who relished wordplay—as his knack for remixing gospels suggested—he had perhaps found in Grondin's translation the perfect double entendre. The "king" whose abdication he sought might well have been Karen King.

ACT 4

THE STRANGER

Both read the Bible day and night,
But thou read'st black where I read white.

—William Blake,
"The Everlasting Gospel"

Leamas nourished Fiedler's suspicions
with hints and oblique indications—never
overdone, you understand, never emphasised,
but dropped here and there with perfidious
subtlety.

—John le Carré,
The Spy Who Came In from the Cold

CROSSROADS

After my stories for *Smithsonian* in late 2012, I moved on to new assignments on different subjects for other magazines. Now and then a Google Alert would show up in my email with some new wrinkle in what seemed like a never-ending controversy. But I didn't follow closely.

In the summer of 2015, however, *Smithsonian* dispatched me back into the wilderness of early Christianity. The editor wanted a cover story on the archaeology of what scholars call "Jesus's world." The magazine sent me to Israel's Galilee region, where Jesus is said to have launched his ministry, and asked me to report on the excavations under way there. One of my stops was Migdal, the presumed site of Magdala, the ancient fishing city said to be Mary Magdalene's home. The Legionaries of Christ, a Catholic order, had wanted to build a guesthouse and retreat on a patch of vacant waterfront. Before it could break ground, the Israel Antiquities Authority had to mount a "salvage excavation," a routine dig to ensure that no important ruins lay beneath the proposed building site. IAA archaeologists were about to give the all clear in the summer of 2009 when their picks hit a buried wall that turned out to be the ruins of an early first-century synagogue. The Gospels say that Jesus preached in synagogues "throughout all Galilee." Yet despite decades of excavation, archaeologists had never uncovered one from the time Jesus was said to have lived. The Magdala dig was soon awash in speculation about whether its newly discovered synagogue might be the place where Jesus and Mary Magdalene first met, an encounter the New Testament doesn't record. The discovery prompted the Legionaries to scale back the guesthouse and turn the better part of the twenty-acre property into a public archaeological park.

Father Juan Solana, the silver-haired Mexican priest who acquired the site, told me that his late mother, Amparo—a homemaker who raised thirteen children—had felt close to Mary Magdalene. As a young woman, Amparo had attended a spiritual retreat where a priest led a meditation on the risen Jesus's appearance to Mary. The meditation made Amparo prayerful, and she set out on foot to a nearby chapel. She couldn't stop ruminating on the dramatic scene in the Gospels where solitary woman meets risen Savior. Before arriving at the chapel door, Solana said, his mother heard an otherworldly voice call, "María." She felt stricken, as if the name were her own. "Somehow, with that meditation, she experienced the love of God in her life," Solana said as his assistant poured us coffee in the rectory kitchen. "It really was a decisive turning point." His mother told him the story first when he was a young seminarian and again in a letter before her death. When the chance came to acquire waterfront land where Mary Magdalene was said to have lived, Father Solana leaped—persuading the Vatican and private donors to put up the funds. The site is now home to an institute devoted to "the dignity of women."

Solana told me that archaeologists had yet to find material proof that Jesus or Mary was ever there. But belief was a powerful thing. "We will find evidence," he insisted. "I *dream* to find evidence. A name, an inscription or something that may confirm..." He trailed off.

When I asked if faith needed fact, he said, "We don't need it, because we believe." But facts, proofs—these would unite heaven and earth. "To have scientific, archaeological evidence of Jesus's presence is not a small thing for a Christian," Solana said, thrusting his palms toward the sky. "It will offer historical confirmation, the historical support for our beliefs."

But what if the history he finds contradicts his beliefs?

A smile spread across the priest's lips. "The Catholic Church is not afraid of the truth," he said. "We will keep digging."

AS I EXITED MAGDALA's dusty parking lot onto the highway that rings the Sea of Galilee, I remembered something that had occurred to me after Karen King's presentation in Rome three years earlier. The crossroads of faith and reason was as heady as it was perilous. It was a place where the nebulae of spiritual life met the grit of fact, where the fire of inner yearning encountered the cold indifference of the physical world. When faith went searching for fact, it wandered into a valley of illusion and temptation. Somewhere still in that valley was a figure who had haunted me since my 2012 stories on the Gospel of Jesus's Wife: the invisible stranger who set the entire spectacle in motion. He had materialized out of the ether one day and revealed a new gospel to a specially chosen woman, a leader in a field of doubtful men. The woman, a scholar of uncommon vision, offered the stranger protection, devotion and "our sincerest thanks," then she carried his revelation into the world. Yet the stranger's name remained ineffable, his face seen only by King. His existence hinged not on evidence—King had refused to provide any—but on faith.

The time had come to find and speak his name.

"We'll call him a 'he'" was the only thing Karen King told me in our first interview, in late August 2012.

Was he someone she had known before? I asked.

"A complete stranger," she replied. But he gave her an account of where the Wife and John fragments had come from. He said that in 1963 a German American named H. U. Laukamp had acquired the papyri in Potsdam, a communist East German city that bordered West Berlin. Laukamp, in turn, sold them to the current owner in the 1990s. The owner's supporting documents took some concentration to follow, but it was worth the effort. The first, King said, was a typewritten 1982 letter to Laukamp from a Dr. Peter Munro, an Egyptology professor at the Free University, a prominent school in West Berlin. Laukamp had apparently consulted Munro about the papyri, and Munro had written back that his colleague, a "Prof. Fecht," had identified one of the pieces as a fragment of the Gospel of John.

"Prof. Fecht" appeared to be Gerhard Fecht, an authority on Egyptian language who chaired the Free University's Egyptology Institute and was effectively Munro's boss. Munro's letter doesn't mention the Wife papyrus. But the collector emailed King a scan of a handwritten note, in German, that did. "Professor Fecht believes that the small fragment, approximately 8 cm in size, is the sole example of a text in which Jesus uses direct speech with reference to having a wife," it said. "Fecht is of the opinion that this could be evidence for a possible marriage." This note was neither signed nor dated. But its presence alongside Munro's 1982 letter suggested to King that it was part of the same correspondence. Finally, there was a signed contract, dated November 12, 1999, recording the current owner's purchase of the papyri from Laukamp.

I asked King why neither Fecht nor Munro would have sought to publish, or publicize, so spectacular a discovery. Fecht apparently had no trouble grasping its singularity as "the sole example" of a text portraying a married Jesus.

"People interested in Egyptology tend not to be interested in Christianity," King replied. "They're into Pharaonic stuff. They simply may not have been interested." Neither would Laukamp have necessarily wanted publicity. Many collectors are businesspeople first. This Laukamp, whoever he was, might have decided that a sub-rosa sale would fetch the best price with the least fuss. How much the current owner paid, however, was unclear. The sales price was whited out on the copy the owner gave King.

Documents are generally a valuable form of corroboration. But all three of these—the letter, the note, the contract—came from a single source with a vested interest in the papyri they purported to describe. I'd asked to see the documents while reporting my *Smithsonian* story in 2012, but King declined, saying that she had adequately described their contents in her journal article. I next thought to call Laukamp, Fecht and Munro, to ask whether the documents in their names were actually of their hand. But all three had recently died: Laukamp, in 2002; Fecht, in 2006; and Munro, in 2009.

The date of Munro's letter to Laukamp—July 15, 1982—was also perhaps convenient. The very next year, Egypt toughened its cultural heritage laws, declaring as state property all Egyptian antiquities whose ownership had not been established by 1983. The letter's 1982 date was just early enough to place the papyri in the West prior to the new law. It was just late enough for a letter bearing Munro's name to appear on Free University stationery; 1982 was Munro's first full year as a professor there.

The 1982 date raised other questions, but they felt almost preposterous to consider. While working on my *Smithsonian* story, I had downloaded King's twenty-one-page curriculum vitae from the Harvard Divinity School website. On the second line of its very first page, under the heading "EDUCATION," was the following entry:

1982–83 Freie Universität, West Berlin

King, it seemed, had been at the Free University in the same year that Munro had written his letter to Laukamp. When I asked King what she was doing there, she told me the story of living in Berlin for a couple of years while completing her PhD dissertation. She had not known Fecht. But "Munro's name I knew," she told me. "I think I may have met him."

I tried to focus the picture. King was a visiting graduate student at the Free University in 1982 and 1983, a relatively brief period in a place far from home. Yet in one of those years a professor she meets there writes a letter to a collector, now dead, about the same batch of papyri that a stranger gives her at Harvard nearly three decades later. It could have been coincidence: the universe of Gnostic specialists was small. But Munro didn't study Gnosticism. He was an expert on wooden tomb markers in pre-Christian Egypt. The only link between Munro, Gnostic scholarship and the Wife papyrus was Karen King and the "complete stranger" she declined to identify. The only confirmed link, because of her refusal to name the owner, was King.

The Gnostic text King had traveled to Berlin to study in 1982 came back to me now. It was called "The Stranger," after a protagonist whose deliberate anonymity was "at once an invitation and a mystery to be uncovered," King had written. "The fictive character of the name invites the reader to discover what mystery it hides ... and in so doing, discover one's own true identity."

TO JUDGE BY HER RÉSUMÉ, King had visited Germany no fewer than four times between July 2010, when the owner first emailed her, and the fall of 2015. She spoke German and could have made personal inquiries about Laukamp, Munro or Fecht. But her provenance investigation consisted of little more than a brief online search. "I just sort of googled them," she said of Munro and Fecht. She saw from their lists of publications that neither was a historian of early Christianity and that while Fecht was an expert in Egyptian language, its last phase, Coptic, "was not his strong suit." Yet even this minimal finding should perhaps have raised a red flag. If Fecht's métier was neither Coptic nor Christianity, how had he deciphered a ragged Coptic papyrus missing all its margins and then confidently declared it "the sole example" of Jesus referring to a wife?

Another figure who failed to excite King's curiosity was the fragment's former owner. She had identified him in her draft article as "H. U. Laukamp." When I asked what the "H. U." stood for, she said she didn't know. Did she have any other information about Laukamp? I asked over our September 2012 dinner near the divinity school. I had made a few searches for mentions of such a collector, to no avail. "How do you know that he died in 2002? Was there an obituary?"

"Well, um, the current owner knew him personally," King said. All her information came from the current owner, and she took him at his word.

When I reminded her in her office the next day of my interest in Laukamp's first name, she said she would ask the owner. A week after my Harvard visit, I emailed King another reminder of my interest in the prior owner's full name. King responded to the email but ignored the question. Five days later, she announced the Gospel of Jesus's Wife in Rome, without any ostensible knowledge of the full name or background of the prior owner. Ten days after that—just before my *Smithsonian* article had to be shipped to the printers—I asked King, for the fourth time, what the "H. U." stood for. "I didn't think I had it, but I do!" she wrote, responding this time in under an hour. "Hans-Ulrich." Either she didn't know Laukamp's full name, or she didn't want me asking questions about him before the Wife papyrus went global.

A year and a half later, without doing any more investigation, King declared the fragment's origins all but unknowable. "The lack of information regarding the provenance of the discovery is unfortunate," she lamented in the April 2014 issue of the *Harvard Theological Review,* "since, when known, such information is extremely pertinent." Two days after the article's publication, a Boston TV anchor, seeming to agree with King about the importance of provenance, led with a question that addressed it head-on. "We're very intrigued about this collector," the anchor, Emily Rooney of WGBH, Boston's PBS affiliate, said. Rooney was pointing to the one fact about provenance that King *did* know: the collector's name. "That's something you have kept very secret," Rooney said. "Would that lend more credibility to this if you could say where this originated?"

"Knowing his identity, um, I don't think makes any difference," King replied.

———

WHILE REPORTING MY *Smithsonian* piece in early September 2012, I had asked King for the first emails she exchanged with the collector. I had wanted to see, and show readers, his overture and the ensuing mating dance of scholar and stranger. After multiple requests, King sent me the emails, but only after deleting the collector's name, email address and other identifying details.

In some of the messages, the man comes across as a hapless amateur. He tells King he doesn't read Coptic. He says he's no expert, so can't tell if his papyrus is old or real, or if the translation someone did in the 1980s is any good. He says he is "completely clueless" about how to document and publish an ancient manuscript. After King spots similarities to other noncanonical texts, he suggests they never occurred to him. "Interesting," he writes. "I was not aware of the direct parallels to the Gospels of Mary/Thomas."

In other messages, however, he betrays far more sophistication. He says the translation in his possession "seems to make sense." He identifies the Wife papyrus's dialect as "Sahidic" and its origins as third to fifth century A.D. He notes that papyri can be carbon-dated "using only a few fibers," a sign of familiarity with both manuscript conservation and the sample sizes required for radiocarbon dating. After Roger Bagnall and AnneMarie Luijendijk discuss the idea of the fragment's being an amulet rather than a gospel, the owner quibbles on technical grounds, suggesting that its oddly "symmetrical shape could be due to natural breakage" or "an ignorant previous owner," rather than some ancient amulet maker's deliberate cutting.

Even more bizarre, in retrospect, is his first email to King. The July 2010 message makes no mention of his papyrus's showstopping line— the pretext being he can't read Coptic. Only after King rejects him a year later does he spell out for her what he seemed to hope she'd notice on her own: the text shows "a possible husband-wife connection of Jesus and Mary Magdalene," he says, again revealing a deeper awareness than he first lets on.

The dates in his provenance story were similarly slippery. In one email to King, he says Laukamp acquired the papyri in the 1960s; in another, that Laukamp or his family possessed them "prior to WWII." The date he'd bought them from Laukamp was, alternatively, "the mid-90s" or "the late 90-ies." He committed to a specific year—1997—in one email. But two weeks after the Rome announcement, when he finally emailed King a copy of the sales contract, it bore the date 1999. These inconsistencies weren't so great as to sound an alarm, perhaps, but enough to suggest the possibility of a mind still working out the pros and cons of various dates.

I used a commercial website called US Search to see whether any-one named Hans-Ulrich or Hans U. Laukamp had ever turned up in public records in the United States. In the emails King gave me, the current owner described Laukamp as "German-American." It stood to reason that he'd at some point resided in America. The search returned a single result: A Hans-Ulrich Laukamp had lived with a woman named Helga Laukamp in Venice, Florida, a middle-class Gulf Coast retire-ment community half an hour's drive south of Sarasota. In 1997, the couple had built a house with a swimming pool in a modest neigh-borhood near the intracoastal waterway. By 2002, the Sarasota County clerk had recorded both of their death certificates. Florida property records listed their primary residence as Berlin, Germany.

When I'd first asked King what "H. U." stood for, she said she could probably find out, because the current owner had known Laukamp "personally." I wondered now if the owner was a Venice neighbor. Lau-kamp had "brought [the papyri] over when he immigrated to the USA," the owner told King in one email. The word "over" intimated that the owner was already in the United States. Because the sales contract for the papyri was dated November 1999—two years after the Laukamps built the Venice house—it was a fair bet that both buyer and seller were in America at the time of the sale.

I called the Laukamps' former neighbors in Venice, but none remembered the couple as having close friends there. Nor was there any sense that they were collectors. Then again, the Laukamps were seldom around. "They were nice, but they didn't speak much English and kind of kept to themselves," remembered Karen Lehmann, a real estate agent who still lived next door. "They'd pop in for a month, and then they'd leave." Laukamp sounded more like an occasional visitor than an immigrant.

Neighbors in Germany had scarcely more insight into the papyrus sale. Christa Stremlow was the longtime caretaker of the Laukamps' apartment building, in Berlin's Charlottenburg neighborhood. She had known the couple well. When I asked whether they collected manu-scripts or antiquities, Stremlow let out an incredulous laugh. "*Nein*," she said. Stremlow had lived in the building fifty-five years and had been in the Laukamps' small, simply furnished flat many times. "There wasn't anything like that." The Laukamps had come from the lower rungs of the economic ladder. Helga ironed clothes in a laundry, she said. Hans-Ulrich was a toolmaker from East Germany who never finished high school.

Another neighbor, a prosthetics maker named Matthias Dümke who had visited the Laukamps in Florida, said he had seen no collectibles there either. The couple's only real hobby was tropical travel—they loved the Bahamas, he said. But they never immigrated to the United States. The Venice property was nothing more than a "holiday home."

I told Stremlow that a story had circulated in the United States that Laukamp had sold a batch of papyri to another individual in 1999. Where might such a story—true or not—have originated?

"Maybe it was someone else in his company," she said.

A FEW YEARS BEFORE BUYING the Florida house, Laukamp had elevated his station in life. He had worked for decades as a machinist on a factory floor. But after the fall of the Berlin Wall, he and his brother won a small contract to clean public buses in Potsdam. With the proceeds, Laukamp and an old friend named Axel Herzsprung went into business together. The pair capitalized on their technical training as former toolmakers and made the leap, at middle age, from factory machinists to factory owners. Their new company, ACMB Metallbearbeitung GmbH, won a contract to manufacture hand-brake components for BMW automobiles. ACMB was soon drawing profits of about $250,000 a year.

For Laukamp, it was like stumbling on a hoard of treasure. He was already in his fifties; the time to enjoy life was now. He bought a black Pontiac Firebird and coaxed Axel Herzsprung and his wife, Ingrid, to build a home a few doors down from his and Helga's in Venice, Florida. For the first time in his life, Hans-Ulrich had real money. He bought household furnishings he couldn't afford, burned through credit cards and picked up perhaps too many of his friends' restaurant tabs. If business stayed this good, Laukamp hoped that he and his friend might one day retire right there in Venice.

But those dreams dried up almost as soon as he'd landed in the Sunshine State. Doctors diagnosed both Hans-Ulrich and Helga Laukamp with lung cancer; they had been chain-smokers. Helga died in December 1999, two years after they'd bought the Venice house. She was just fifty-six, and her husband was devastated. Herzsprung gave up on Venice in 2001, and ACMB—the company that was the friends' prize after decades of backbreaking toil—filed for bankruptcy in August 2002. Four months later, Hans-Ulrich was dead. He was fifty-nine.

The Laukamps' Berlin neighbors had described Venice as no more than an occasional getaway, so I was surprised to find that an auto-parts manufacturer calling itself ACMB had filed to incorporate as a Florida business. In Berlin, the initials ACMB had stood for Allgemeine CNC Metallbearbeitung—German for "General CNC Metalworking." (CNC is an acronym for a metal-cutting technique.) In Florida, however, someone had anglicized the name to "American Corporation for Milling and Boreworks," maintaining the German company's initials— ACMB—even though the words they stood for had changed. The American ACMB incorporated on December 23, 1999, a mere four days after Helga Laukamp's death. I didn't know much about the Laukamps' marriage, but it seemed odd for a widower to use the days immediately after his wife's death to found an overseas manufacturing business, one headquartered in a state with no ostensible clients.

When I took a closer look at the Florida incorporation records, I noticed that Laukamp and Herzsprung weren't the company's only officers. There was a third man, someone named Walter Fritz. His was the only signature on the filings, and a year later he struck both Laukamp and Herzsprung from the annual reports, leaving himself as sole director. To judge from public records, this Walter Fritz still lived in Florida. On paper he looked like an unremarkable local: fifty years old, married, RV owner, license to fish and hunt. He lived in a single-story house in the city of North Port, a thirty-minute drive inland from Venice. If Fritz stood out for anything, it was his civic ardor. He wrote eloquent letters to the editor of the *North Port Sun*. He led neighbors in a successful protest against overhead power lines. He was a regular at the 7:15 breakfasts of the North Port Early Bird Kiwanis Club, even if, in online photos, he looked a couple decades younger than the other members.

When city commissioners gathered to hash out North Port's annual budget, Fritz—a tall, square-shouldered man with crew-cut black hair, chiseled features and an unplaceable European accent—

sat through hours of tedious discussion for a chance to harangue the elected leaders about a proposed recession-year property tax hike. "What are we going to do next year, raise taxes again?" he declaimed in one videotaped meeting, leaning aggressively into the lectern. "And the year after again? Until we make the Guinness book? No! We need to pull the plug now." His remarks had the studied cadences—and ready facts and figures—of a practiced politician. But when the commissioners questioned his evidence, Fritz wilted. He morphed from bully to milquetoast with the quickness of a flipped switch. "I think you're right," he allowed, deferentially, when a commissioner noted that most people would see lower tax bills because of depressed real estate values. "That's what it is, indeed."

When I ran Fritz's name through a database of Florida companies, I found that the American Corporation for Milling and Boreworks wasn't his only business interest. Four years earlier, in 1995, he incorporated a company in the city of St. Augustine, on the Atlantic coast, some 250 miles to the northeast. The company was called Nefer Art. The name put me in mind of Nefertiti, the famous Egyptian queen. *Nefer*, it turned out, was the Egyptian word for "beauty." If a business associate of Laukamp's had an affinity for Egyptian art, that person was probably worth talking to, if for no reason than that Egypt was the source of nearly all ancient papyri.

I ran "Walter Fritz" and "Egypt" through some search engines, and one of the hits caught my eye: In 1991, someone named Walter Fritz published a scholarly article in a prestigious German-language journal, *Studien zur Altägyptischen Kultur,* or Studies in ancient Egyptian culture. I found a copy and turned to the contributors' section. It listed this Fritz's affiliation as the Egyptology Institute at Berlin's Free University—the very place that had employed Peter Munro and Gerhard Fecht, the professors who supposedly examined Laukamp's papyri in 1982. Could the article's author and the Florida auto-parts executive possibly be the same man?

I called a few prominent Egyptologists, who told me that the article in *Studien zur Altägyptischen Kultur* remained influential. Its subject was the series of diplomatic letters, on clay tablets, sent by Near East kings to the Pharaohs some thirty-four hundred years ago, when the city of Amarna was Egypt's throne. The article's author had made a close study of one of the tablets, Amarna Letter EA 27, in hopes of deciphering some indistinct text. With the help of infrared photography, tracing paper and a quartz-iodine lamp, he concluded that too little room remained along its worn right edge for the regnal year "12" to fit. The finding helped overturn a prevailing theory that Akhenaton and his father had served jointly as Pharaohs, rather than in succession. The author reinforced his case with fine-grained visual descriptions and hieroglyphics copied from the tablet by hand.

Though the article was now more than two decades old, major scholars continued to cite it as a definitive source. It turned up even in coffee-table books like *Pharaohs of the Sun,* a companion to an important Amarna exhibit at Boston's Museum of Fine Arts. The paper's conclusion held for a simple reason: its author ignored the blustery theoretical debate and went straight to the physical evidence. "Pretty much everyone followed it," Jared Miller, a professor at Ludwig Maximilian University in Munich and an expert on the chronology of the Amarna age, told me when I reached him by phone. "It's referenced in pretty much all the works on the issue, including in mine."

But none of the scholars I spoke to—not even the German journal's former editors—could remember who this Walter Fritz was or what had become of him.

MY FLIGHT LANDED at Tampa International Airport on a humid Wednesday afternoon in November 2015. I drove the interstate south for an hour and a half, then exited onto a road that wound through pine forests tangled with runaway vines. Walter Fritz's house lay in a kind of borderlands where the streets ended and nature took over. To the north spread a vast state park where alligators gather in a watery pit known as Deep Hole.

Most North Porters lived on quarter-acre lots and commuted to service and construction jobs in wealthier Sarasota. But North Port Estates, as Fritz's neighborhood was called, had a minimum lot size of three acres and the sort of resident, as the *Sarasota Herald-Tribune* once put it, who likes "to raise horses, kennel dogs and park a semi-trailer in the front yard without worrying about what the neighbors think." Police activity in the area centered on off-roaders, illicit marijuana "grow houses," and backyard target shooters whose stray bullets had an unfortunate tendency to tear through neighbors' windows. A newcomer complained to the newspaper that the hail of multi-round gun-fire each weekend sounded like "World War III." That a onetime Berlin Egyptologist lived here seemed exceedingly unlikely. Still, I hoped this Walter Fritz could at least tell me something about Laukamp.

When I turned onto Fritz's street, the only part of his house I could see was a gray-shingled roof that narrowed, like a Mayan pyramid, into the drooping slash pines. A metal field gate barred the driveway, which snaked behind a curtain of Virginia creeper and muscadine vine. I could find no intercom or bell, and though I saw no construction, a sign at the entrance said, NO TRESPASSING: THIS IS A DESIGNATED CONSTRUCTION SITE. ANYONE TRESPASSING ON THIS PROPERTY, UPON CONVICTION SHALL BE GUILTY OF A FELONY (STATUTE 810.09 & 810.011). When I raised my camera to snap a photo, a muscular bullmastiff I hadn't noticed before stirred from a bed of pine needles and locked its eyes on mine. It was a house that didn't expect visitors.

Back in my kitchenette at the Venice Beach Villas, I worked my way down a list of possible phone numbers for Fritz. Eventually, one was picked up. The man had a faint European accent.

"Hi, Mr. Fritz?" I said, presuming.

"Yes."

I introduced myself as a journalist working on a story about the Gospel of Jesus's Wife and its former owner, Hans-Ulrich Laukamp. I had first written about the discovery in 2012, I said, as a correspondent for *Smithsonian*.

"You're a writer for *The Onion?*" he said.

"*Smithsonian*," I said, though I was fairly certain he had heard the first time.

When I told him I was in town and wanted to meet, he declined, grew agitated and made clear he wanted to get off the phone. He never studied Egyptology at the Free University, he insisted. He never wrote an article for a German journal, nor did he know any Walter Fritzes who might have. Sure, ACMB's website had listed him as the president of its U.S. branch, and, yes, public records called him a director, but in truth, he said, he was just a local consultant and web engineer. Laukamp and Herzsprung spoke little English, so Fritz filled out some Florida forms to get the company started. That was all.

"Are you a German immigrant?" I asked, wondering how ACMB's German owners might have found him.

"I'm a U.S. citizen," he said, parrying the question. He couldn't even recall how they'd all met. When I asked whether Laukamp collected antiquities, Fritz bristled. "I don't want to comment."

Some people wondered whether Laukamp had ever owned papyri, I said.

"He was interested in a lot of things," Fritz said.

Like what? I said.

"I know he had a beer-mug collection."

Fritz then made what I took to be a cryptic allusion to the debate over the papyrus's authenticity. "There will always be people who say yes and people who say no," he said. "Everybody is up in arms and has an opinion."

When I asked for *his,* he said, "I don't want to comment." He said he didn't even understand the media interest. "There's a lot of speculation, the need for sensation."

Was he the owner of the Gospel of Jesus's Wife? I asked.

"No," he said, his voice shooting up an octave. "Who said that?"

No one, I answered. But he was one of Laukamp's few American acquaintances in a period when Laukamp was said to have sold the papyrus. I just wanted to be sure.

He wasn't the owner, he said. He had no idea who was.

FRITZ HAD REFUSED to give me his email address. So after our phone chat, I wrote a letter introducing myself at greater length and letting him know how to reach me if he changed his mind. Then I drove to the Sarasota branch of the state medical examiner. The Laukamps had died young—and in relatively close succession—so I suspected there might be autopsy reports. The clerk vanished into a warren of file cabinets and came back empty-handed. "No records," she said. When I visited the Sarasota County courthouse later that day, I realized why. Because the county's online system recorded the couple's deaths, I assumed they had died in Florida. But to view the actual death certificates, one had to go to the courthouse. The documents, I saw now, were issued by the German government. Hans-Ulrich and Helga Laukamp had both died in Berlin. This made the timing of ACMB's Florida incorporation, four days after Helga's death, even more mystifying. Would Hans-Ulrich have begun a risky foreign business venture so soon after his wife's passing? Or had Fritz acted on his own initiative while his boss was away?

I got in my car and called the *North Port Sun*. Years earlier, the newspaper had covered Fritz's running battle with a wood-chipping plant that abutted his backyard. "Sometimes the odor is so bad," Fritz told the paper, "that it makes your eyes burn." I asked the reporter who answered the phone if the *Sun* had ever taken his picture. That evening, she emailed me a 2006 photo.

THE 1991 ISSUE OF *Studien zur Altägyptischen Kultur,* the German Egyptology journal, had articles by two authors affiliated with the Free University's Egyptology Institute. One was a Walter Fritz. The other was a Karl Jansen-Winkeln, a sixty-year-old Egyptology professor who appeared still to teach at the university. I sent him an email asking if he recalled a Walter Fritz who had been at the school at the time of the 1991 journal article. "I was hoping you might be able to direct me to whatever institution Mr. Fritz is associated with now," I wrote.

Jansen-Winkeln replied that he did remember someone by that name. Walter Fritz had been a student from about 1988 until around the time the journal article was published. "He left the university without a final examination as far as I remember," Jansen-Winkeln said. "I have never seen him again after 1992 or 1993."

That night, I emailed Jansen-Winkeln the picture from the *North Port Sun*. Did this person in any way resemble the student he'd known two decades earlier?

Jansen-Winkeln's reply was waiting in my in-box the next morning. "The man looks indeed like Walter Fritz," he wrote. It was the first sign that Fritz had lied during our phone call.

Fritz had been working toward a magister artium, the first degree then obtainable in Germany's universities. It was the equivalent of a bachelor's plus a master's in the United States. I wondered why a young and promising student who'd already landed an article in a premier journal would drop out of a program he'd seemed well on his way to completing. I tracked down several people who'd known Fritz at the Free University, but no one had any idea.

"One day he just disappeared," one woman wrote, in a typical reply. "Is he still alive?"

WALTER FRITZ MATERIALIZED in Florida no later than September 30, 1994, when public records show he obtained a state driver's license. He incorporated Nefer Art a year later; its business address was a letter slot—or "Suite," as he called it on state forms—at a Mail Boxes Etc. in a St. Augustine strip mall. Within a few years, Fritz turned up on Florida's other coast, in a rented two-bedroom home, in Venice. His elderly landlady, a German immigrant whose own house abutted the rental, had died in 2011. But her granddaughter, Renee Juntunen, recalled meeting Fritz several times. Despite the four-decade age difference, Fritz and Juntunen's grandmother had become friends, dining at each other's houses and bonding over their shared German heritage, sometimes while Juntunen was visiting. Juntunen, then a flight attendant in her early twenties, recalled Fritz as a contradiction. On the one hand, he appeared to have little money and no source of income. He had moved to the United States, he told his landlady, because "he was looking for a fresh start." On the other, he presented himself as a distinguished artist and connoisseur. His walls, Juntunen remembered, were decorated with fifteen to twenty modern artworks—portraits, mostly—which he'd said were worth "quite a bit of money." He also had an extensive collection of European-looking coins and banknotes, which he stored in plastic-sleeved albums inside large Rubbermaid tubs. He claimed to be either a high-ranking student or possibly a professor at the Ringling College of Art & Design, a respected art school in Sarasota.

When she and her grandmother were at his house one day, Juntunen said, Fritz led Juntunen into the sunroom, which he had turned into his art studio. She was struck by what she saw: a pair of plastic bins overflowing with lumps of charcoal. They weren't for barbecuing, she said, but for his art. He showed her how one could draw on paper with the briquettes, then smudge the lines with a fingertip to create a shaded effect. "His fingers were always dark from the charcoal—he looked like a mechanic," recalled Juntunen, who stayed with her grandmother on days off between flights and now lives with her husband and daughter in the house Fritz had rented. Though Fritz had a few of his own charcoal sketches around the house, Juntunen said she could never understand why he needed so many briquettes. "I always thought, 'What the hell is he doing with all this?'"

In the summer of 2000, her grandmother sent Juntunen's then

boyfriend—now husband—into the house to repair some balky light switches while Fritz was out. John Juntunen still remembers what he saw on the ledge of the sunroom's windows. Old candles had sat burning there for so long that the dripping wax formed "stalactites" along the knee wall. When he remarked to his girlfriend's grandmother that the tenant must have left lit candles out for days, she replied, "I don't know what happens back here." Sometime around 2001, Fritz abruptly cleared out. He left word with Juntunen's grandmother that he was returning to Germany to look after a sick friend.

On January 8, 2001, the same day Fritz signed a government form striking Laukamp and Herzsprung from their directorships of the Florida ACMB, a landowner signed a document deeding Fritz the three acres he now lived on in North Port. Fritz married an American woman that March and hired a contractor to erect a house on the North Port lot. As ACMB's fortunes sank—it declared bankruptcy in Berlin in August 2002—his own appeared to rise.

The prospect of Fritz having been a student or professor at Ringling College—someone who claimed a "big role" there—was ripe with possibility. It would mean that he had training in Egyptology *and* studio art, a formidable pair of talents. I called Ringling to find out when Fritz had taught or studied there. The reply I received from a school official a few days later was starting to fit a pattern. "Neither our registrar or human resources department have found records of a Walter Fritz."

That made his alleged devotion to long-burning candles and large bins of charcoal all the more mysterious. Charcoal is a form of raw carbon, the main ingredient of ancient ink. So is soot, which ancient ink makers turned into lampblack by collecting the black particles from above a burning flame.

NEFER ART—WHATEVER IT WAS—advertised a peculiar miscellany of services. According to its internet site, the company designed websites and photographed children, weddings, industrial tools and erotica. It also offered IT consulting and dealt in antiquities, fine art and "rare prints." Finally, it claimed to document, publish and sell customers' "valuable" art collections. "Our customer database is substantial," the company's website said, "and our discreet and confidential services are perfect for the distinguished collector and seller, who likes to avoid the pushy atmosphere of the big auctions houses."

A page of uncaptioned photographs, titled "Portraits," contained close-ups of girls and boys—who appear to be teenagers—giving the camera sultry looks. Another page, "Gallery Art," included a bust of the Pharaoh Akhenaton; a sculpture of the Virgin Mary cradling the crucified Jesus; well-known paintings of women by Pablo Picasso and Marc Chagall; and a silver coin bearing a relief of a horned Alexander the Great. Other parts of the website, only partially recoverable, were titled "Nefer Art—Fine Antiquities | Egypt | Roman | Greek." One page likened a heart-shaped amulet to "Brooklyn Museum 16.580.31," helpfully citing the accession number of a look-alike in a well-known Egyptian collection. Another described an ancient Egyptian headrest with language that appeared to be cribbed from web pages of the British Museum.

Nefer Art's "About" page was still more puzzling. It consisted of just two images. The first was a sepia-toned photo of "Walt" Fritz, in fedora and fur-collared bomber jacket, leaning rakishly on the handle of an upside-down umbrella; the second, a black-and-white headshot of Helmut Newton, the German fashion photographer famed for his noirish portraits of half-dressed models. There was no explanation for the juxtaposition.

Nefer Art claimed to have a large international clientele of private art collectors, but it was hard to reconcile this impressive-sounding credential with the quality of the web pages themselves. The websites of most professional web designers, photographers and art-world businesses are works of art in their own right, digital galleries of striking images that give prospective clients a taste of an owner's aesthetic. From what I could see of it, Nefer Art's was a hash of poorly edited low-resolution photos, displayed with the blocky inelegance of a student in an introductory design class.

I scoured the site for images of the Jesus's Wife and Gospel of John scraps, with no luck. The closest parallels were two other fragments: a Greek papyrus and an Arabic parchment. I emailed photos of them to a few scholars, who found them comical. The Greek papyrus, which bore a drawing of a nude woman beside a winged phallus, superficially resembled texts from Greco-Roman Egypt known as "magical papyri." But the Greek words made little sense, the scholars said, and the handwriting had the look of modern print. "Perhaps not in Times New Roman," Sofía Torallas Tovar, a papyrologist at the University of

Chicago, observed wryly, "but in a modern typography." The drawing of the female figure, meanwhile, was "in a style unparalleled to my knowledge in an ancient document, but easily found in modern school notebooks." Two experts in ancient Arabic manuscripts, meanwhile, told me that the script on the other fragment was backward, as if someone had photographed it in a mirror.

Though Nefer Art had been in business for two decades, I could find no independent confirmation that it did what its website said. There were no online reviews, no mentions in news articles, no listings in the white or yellow pages of either St. Augustine, Venice or North Port from 1995 through 2015. Well-connected people in St. Augustine's vibrant arts scene told me they had never heard of a Nefer Art or a Walter Fritz. Neither had the national and international dealers and collectors I canvassed, even the ones in Florida. That seemed to leave one of two possibilities: either Walter Fritz was a mediocre photographer and web designer, and an even worse businessman, or Nefer Art's real business was something it didn't advertise.

WHEN IT HAPPENED, it felt almost too easy. I obtained Fritz's email address from a public record and began dropping it, in a variety of formats, into my search bar. Up came a website, who.is, that tracks the ownership history of web domains. On August 26, 2012—more than three weeks before King announced her discovery to the world, when only her inner circle knew of the papyrus and her name for it—Walter Fritz had registered the domain name www.gospelofjesuswife.com. It was the first piece of hard evidence linking Fritz to King. In January 2016, *The Atlantic* magazine put me on a plane to Germany to search for more.

THE LITTLE DARLING AND THE STASI

The taxi ride from Tegel Airport to the heart of Berlin was a blind slog through labyrinths of graffiti-clad apartment blocks, in fog and light snow. On a Sunday afternoon, my interpreter and I showed up unannounced at the apartment of René and Gabriele Ernest, whom the Laukamps had named in a Florida trust as their sole heirs. René Ernest was the stepson of Hans-Ulrich, who had no children of his own. Gabriele was René's wife.

News of Laukamp's alleged association with a papyrus had baffled them, they told me. Laukamp had been born in Nazi-occupied Poland in 1942 and grew up in Potsdam, in communist East Germany. He left school after eighth grade for a career as a *Dreher,* a machinist who used lathes and other tools to shape metal. In March 1961, the eighteen-year-old Laukamp began a daily commute from the Soviet-controlled East to a new job, in democratic West Berlin. Five months later, East Germany sealed the border, ringing West Berlin in the barbed wire, sentry towers and concrete blocks that would soon become the Berlin Wall. Not only was Laukamp out of work, but Soviet propagandists denounced former "cross-border commuters" like him as traitors-in-waiting. Laukamp temporized for just two months before risking his life, in October 1961, in a dangerous bolt to the West. He escaped what immigration officials called his "special plight" by swimming across the Griebnitzsee, a lake separating Potsdam and West Berlin. He came ashore in nothing but his bathing suit. The West Germans gave him clothing, permanent residency and, in May 1962, a special ID designating him an East German refugee.

Laukamp's immigration papers raised questions about a pivotal date in the story told by the current owner of the Wife papyrus. According to the provenance documents the owner gave King, Laukamp had acquired his six Coptic papyri in Potsdam in 1963. That would have been two years *after* Laukamp fled the city. The owner's account thus turned on a dubious scenario: that not long after his defection, Laukamp snuck back into a heavily policed city where he would have been a wanted man, got the papyri, then gambled his life and livelihood again in a second illicit flight to the West. Another problem was that before he went into the auto-parts business with Axel Herzsprung in the mid-1990s, he'd been a toolmaker who didn't collect anything. Not even *Bierkrüge*, the Ernests told me. "He drank beer," René said, laughing, "but he didn't collect beer mugs."

The Laukamps had worked so hard for the little they had, the Ernests said, that they would never have sat on a potentially lucrative manuscript. "If he had ever owned or bought this thing, after his third beer at the pub he would have told everybody about his great coup," Gabriele Ernest said. "And if I knew my father-in-law, he would have immediately tried to make money from it."

I told the Ernests about the 1982 letter the current owner had given King, the one in which Professor Peter Munro tells Laukamp that one of his fragments was the Gospel of John. Could they picture Laukamp consulting a university Egyptologist? The Ernests gave each other a bug-eyed look, then dissolved in fits of laughter. Laukamp had the minimum schooling required by German law, they said. His milieu was the bar down the street—his "second living room," they called it—not some specialized university institute across town.

I asked how Laukamp's signature might have wound up on the current owner's contract for the papyri. Gabriele said that Laukamp was always eager to help people; he brought breakfast to a homeless man in a park where he walked his dog. But he was "simple" and "weak" and "very easily believed things he was told." Too often he put faith in people he didn't entirely know. The Ernsts' concerns about his judgment grew in 2001 and 2002—the final years of his life—when the lung cancer metastasized to his brain.

Did they know anyone by the name of Walter Fritz? I asked.

Gabriele stiffened. She knew this Walter, she said. He was someone Laukamp worked with—one of the people he trusted. "I can easily imagine Walter Fritz saying, 'I need your signature for the company,'" she said. Laukamp "would have signed that without reading everything."

The German trade register listed a man named Peter Biberger as an overseer of ACMB's bankruptcy. My interpreter and I found him in a run-down industrial district on the border between Berlin and Brandenburg. His metal shop made a device that lifted window curtains by remote control. When I asked his opinion of Walter Fritz, he responded wordlessly, moving his forearm in a slither, like a creature swimming through murk. "He was an eel," Biberger said. "You couldn't hold him. He slipped through your fingers."

TWENTY-FIVE YEARS EARLIER, as an Egyptology student at the Free University, Walter Fritz struck classmates as a man who already had it made. On a campus where student fashions ran to grungy jeans, T-shirts and bed head, Fritz slicked back his hair with pomade and stepped out in expensive shoes, dress shirts and blazers. He had two cars—both Mercedeses—and spoke to professors in *Hochdeutsch*, the "high German" of the country's elite. Classmates recalled him as self-assured to the point of arrogance. At coffee breaks in the kitchen of the Art Nouveau villa that housed the Egyptology Institute, Fritz boasted of ties to famous scholars and belittled students he saw as beneath him, often the minute they left the room. His long trench coat, beneath jet-black hair and an ashen face, put one schoolmate in mind of the stock German villains of Hollywood film.

His flashiness stood out at a time of financial unease for many Germans. The Free University exploded in student protests over educational funding in the late 1980s, and the wall's fall in 1989 precipitated a difficult merger of the East and West German economies. Fritz was twenty-two when he enrolled at the university, at least a couple of years older than most of his classmates. Some wondered if he'd had an inheritance or a well-paying former career. Others presumed he was of noble descent. But these were the newest students. The ones who'd been around awhile knew that Fritz's aristocratic bearing was of recent acquisition. When he first set foot on campus, around 1987, one classmate told me, he had the disheveled grooming of "a harmless country boy." He wore high-waisted jeans, white sneakers and a bowl cut that was less Beatles than bumpkin. His natural accent wasn't *Hochdeutsch* but *Schwäbisch*, a singsong that smacked of Swabia, the conservative, rural region of southern Germany whose residents were stereotyped as persnickety pinchpennies. In his first year at the university, on a school-sponsored tour of Italy's Egyptian museums, Fritz turned crimson when he asked female classmates for help buying lingerie for the high school sweetheart he had recently married. He wasn't hitting on them—he was just "a coward," recalled Susanne Voss, now a distinguished Egyptologist. "He told us he would be too shy to go into the store." Voss, finding the request odd, said, "Are you crazy?"

A year or two into his studies, however, Fritz remade himself into a man-about-town with an air of both business executive and boulevardier. "He never explained the change," Andrea Binkowski, another classmate, told me. "It was so unusual." It was almost as if "he was not a student anymore" but "something better."

At the dinner parties he and his wife hosted for fellow students at their apartment in a quiet quarter of West Berlin, Fritz cooked spätzle, a dish from his native southern Germany. He made a show of pressing the noodles by hand. He served white wine he said was from vintners near his hometown—exclusive bottles not available in stores. In another corner of the apartment was a large gun locker, where he appeared to store hunting rifles. At times he identified himself as "Walter von Fritz," using the nobiliary particle "von," by which Germans signal high birth. When I visited Fritz's former Berlin apartment building, one neighbor described him with a single word: "exalted." Another, Norbert Jedamski, had a less charitable view. "He acted like a real snob, with lots of money in his pocket, like he was the inventor of the sun," Jedamski told me, using a German expression. "Everyone else was stupid." Jedamski, a home renovator, served for years as head of the building's residents' association. When he and Fritz clashed over responsibility for a broken window in Fritz's apartment, Fritz bad-mouthed him to neighbors and openly challenged his professional qualifications. "He said, 'You shouldn't pretend you're something that you're not.'"

IN THE LATE 1980s and early 1990s, college was essentially free for Germans, who could study at taxpayer expense without ever having to graduate. Some students enrolled for the easy life. A few were so indifferent that they didn't flip past the first pages of the student catalog before choosing a course of study. Because it began with the German letter *Ä*, Ägyptologie drew more than its share of goldbricks and dilettantes. What many didn't realize was that Egyptology was a notoriously complex subject, requiring mastery of thousands of years of ancient history, as well as a command of art, architecture, archaeology and literature, along with multiple stages of the Egyptian language, from hieroglyphics to Coptic. Students hoping to sail through a few diverting lectures on pyramids and mummies were in for a shock. To top it off, job prospects in the field were close to zero. Within a few months a starting class of twenty Egyptology students could easily dwindle to just four or five. A magister's degree took at least four to five years to complete and required grueling oral exams, a four-hour written test and a lengthy thesis. The Free University might graduate an Egyptology magister's student just once every couple of years.

Many of the professors and former students I reached thought that Walter Fritz had what it took to be one of the survivors. He passed a demanding exam given midway through the program and had his own desk at the Egyptology Institute, an honor reserved for older and more accomplished students. Fritz took a course with Peter Munro, the scholar who ostensibly wrote the 1982 letter to Laukamp, and joined a class trip Munro led to Italy's Egyptian collections. Fritz's then wife told me that she and Fritz had visited Egypt together in his student days, making the rounds at Amarna and the Valley of the Kings. "He had ties to a research center in Cairo, so he could tour places that normal people don't have access to," she said.

Ursula Rößler-Köhler, a visiting professor who taught a class on Egyptian inscriptions, recalled Fritz as "a fresh and energetic student who made vivid contributions to my seminar. I certainly thought he would have graduated."

But Fritz saw himself doing more than merely graduating; he envisioned greatness. He told classmates that two adjoining letters on his license plate—*CT*—matched the academic shorthand for "Coffin Text," a category of Egyptian funerary spells. Fritz said, only half jokingly, that the randomly assigned letters presaged a distinguished future in the field.

Yet Fritz was in most ways a paper tiger. Closer associates, like his friend Christian Loeben, saw the braggadocio as a psychological defense against a deep insecurity. An expert in Egyptian art who studied at the university, Loeben was a regular at Fritz's dinner parties. Fritz, he recalled, harbored an abstract fear that some "terrible mistake" would scuttle his career prospects. Perhaps to guard against it, Fritz made careful studies of the views and motivations of his superiors, so as to stay in their good graces, even if it meant being untrue to himself. "He would wait to see what his counterpart expected," then turn himself into that person's "little darling," Loeben said when we met at the Museum August Kestner, in Hannover, where he holds Munro's former job as curator of Egyptian art. When a professor challenged Fritz's answers in class, for instance, Fritz wouldn't defend himself. "He would just withdraw, adjust," Loeben said. This shape shifting struck some of his teachers as less deferential than calculating. Karl Jansen-Winkeln, the professor who identified Fritz in the *North Port Sun* photo, said, "Fritz was quite eager and interested in Egyptology." He liked to show off his intelligence, but when it came to doing actual scholarship, "he was reluctant to take much effort." Fritz seemed "like a person who wants to sell you something and not like a person who's really interested in research." One subject that particularly tormented him was Coptic—the language of the Gospel of Jesus's Wife. "He was not very good," Jansen-Winkeln said.

AT WEST BERLIN'S EGYPTIAN MUSEUM, home to a legendary limestone bust of Nefertiti and one of the world's largest papyrus collections, Fritz not only worked as a guide for tour groups and schoolchildren but earned money as a student assistant to the museum's staff. A 1991 reference letter from the museum's director listed Fritz's duties as "documentation of objects," "cataloging" and "preparation of publications." Loeben told me he saw Fritz at least once on the restricted top floor, an attic-like workshop for the museum's papyrus conservators. The work there happened in stages. First, the conservators removed papyrus scraps from the tins in which early twentieth-century archaeologists had packed them in Egypt. Then they sorted the pieces into cardboard boxes color coded by discovery location and language. Finally, they photographed, mounted and cataloged them. People who worked or studied at the museum at the time told me that if papyri were filched from the tins or the cardboard boxes before cataloging, they wouldn't be missed. Not just because no one had taken inventory of their contents, but because of their sheer number: the museum had roughly twenty-one thousand fragments, a full half of which had yet to be cataloged.

Visitors known to museum staff had minimal oversight on the top floor. No one looked over their shoulders. There were no surveillance cameras. No one inspected bags on the way out. "Nobody watched me when I was on the fourth floor," Charles Hedrick, an American scholar who studied papyri there in the mid-1990s, told me. "I had free access to anything." The University of Kansas scholar Paul Mirecki, who discovered the Gnostic Gospel of the Savior while toiling in the collection in the late 1980s and early 1990s, said he had "24/7" access to the papyri, having worked unattended overnight. The German scholar Gesine Schenke Robinson remembered seeing "unlisted and unidentified fragments that were sometimes inscribed, sometimes just pieces from the margins, randomly lying in tin boxes almost for the taking.... For an enthusiast, such a treasure trove of unlisted papyrus scraps may have been hard to resist."

The museum's director at the time was the distinguished Egyptologist Dietrich Wildung. I asked whether Fritz, as a student assistant, would have had access to the museum's loose papyri. "It is possible," Wildung told me. "Hundreds of large tin boxes from the Berlin excavations at Elephantine Island (early 20th cent.), full of unregistered papyrus fragments, have been kept there in open shelfs [*sic*]." On Mondays, when the building was open only to researchers, the door to the top floor was not only unlocked but propped open by a doorstop.

In a résumé sent to a government office in Florida in late 2012 or early 2013, Fritz reported an expertise in the arts that included "25 years of collecting manuscripts." That would place the start of his collecting career as either late 1987 or early 1988, his first year as an Egyptology student. No sooner had he entered the Free University's Egyptology program, it seemed, than he had his hands on manuscripts. Nineteen eighty-seven also happened to be Gerhard Fecht's last year at the Free University. Classmates told me that Fritz had certainly studied with Peter Munro, who had written the purported 1982 letter to Laukamp. But they weren't sure whether he'd known Fecht, and whether he knew Fecht was important. Fecht was the Egyptologist whom Munro had supposedly consulted about Laukamp's papyri—the language expert who, in unusually frank terms for a professor, called one of Laukamp's pieces possible "evidence" for Jesus's marriage. If Walter Fritz knew Peter Munro *and* Gerhard Fecht, it would bind him still more tightly to the Gospel of Jesus's Wife.

During one of my trips to Germany, Susanne Voss, the former classmate, said she had something to show me. We were eating lunch in Hannover when she took from her handbag a color snapshot she'd found of Fecht's 1987 retirement party. In the photo, students and faculty are eating and drinking at an L-shaped arrangement of tables in the leafy backyard of the Egyptology Institute. At the near end of the L is Gerhard Fecht, listening to a colleague; at the far end is Peter Munro, stroking his chin. Seated midway between them, at the point where the lines of the L intersect, is a twenty-two-year-old Walter Fritz.

BY ALL ACCOUNTS, Peter Munro had been a brilliant museum director. Foppish and gregarious, an aesthete who penned poetry and tickled a beautiful Debussy from a piano, Munro was as winsome with journalists and corporate donors as he was with museumgoers and visiting school-children. He led the Museum August Kestner, in Hannover, from 1970 to 1981, earning a name for daring excess. The 800,000 deutsche marks he paid for a thirty-three-hundred-year-old indurated limestone bust of Akhenaton was three times the state-sponsored museum's annual acquisitions budget. His signature fashion accessory was a necktie in the official tartan of Clan Munro, a tribute to his Scottish father, a man Munro idolized, despite his father's having deserted the family when Munro was a boy.

As a scholar, Munro was decidedly less distinguished. He had earned the lowest passing mark on his Egyptology PhD at the University of Hamburg and was hired as a professor at the Free University, in 1981, only after two other scholars—Fecht's first choices—turned down the job. It was an important post: never before had a German university employed a full-time Egyptologist specializing in art and archaeology. But over his decade and a half at the Free University, Munro would publish little and attract few graduate students. He was also a suspected malingerer, regularly phoning in sick with migraines on the one day a week he was expected to teach.

Munro whistled as he worked, asked students to report their overnight dreams and did headstands while meditating in his office—clownish antics that made him a frequent butt of student jokes. At Munro's long-running excavation in Saqqara, Egypt, Loeben once spotted him writing on a newly unearthed limestone door. Munro had wanted a clearer view of an ancient inscription, but instead of using tracing paper—as professional practice dictated—Munro wrote with a felt-tip pen on the slab itself. "It was so out of this world," Loeben said, describing Munro's method as, at best, a relic of nineteenth-century archaeology. "You never, ever, ever, ever do that."

It bothered Fritz that a scholar as unexceptional as Munro praised other students more enthusiastically than he did Fritz. When a classmate answered a basic question about Neolithic sites in Egypt, Munro gushed, "You're a genius!"

"Walter would say, 'How can he say that was a good answer? That was a lucky guess and the student is an idiot,'" Ulrike Dubiel, a former classmate and now a lecturer in Egyptian archaeology, said when we met at the Free University. "He was jealous."

Fecht's retirement in 1987 effectively left the institute in the hands of Munro, a second-rate scholar who could do little for the careers of ambitious students like Fritz. The Egyptology chair sat empty until 1990, when the university hired Jürgen Osing, a top-flight scholar of Egyptian language with a reputation as a harsh and exacting teacher. In the whole of Osing's career, I'd heard, just three students managed to complete a doctorate under him. In class, if a question stumped a student, Osing would make everyone wait until the student came up with a satisfactory answer. During the excruciating silence, Osing would mark time by picking up his pen and dropping it from a height so that it clacked against the top of his desk. "We can wait until Christmas," one recalled him saying. Other times, he would shape the chalk dust on his desk into a small pile. When a student flubbed another answer, Osing would sweep the little pile with the back of his hand, launching a cloud of white particles into the air. "He would make you feel like you're nothing," one former student told me. The gesture, another recalled, had a clear symbolism: "You're like the remains of chalk I'm sweeping off my table." Not a few students left his classes in tears. But Fritz was determined to impress.

THE NAME OSING sounded familiar for a reason. In the first footnote of his 1991 journal article, Fritz said that his topic had been discussed by "Herrn Professor J. Osing" in a Free University course in the summer of 1990. That was Osing's first term at the school, and it meant that Fritz jumped at the first chance to study with the new chairman. I found a course catalog for that semester in the university's library: Osing's class had been titled "Problems of History in the New Kingdom," which would have addressed the controversy over whether Akhenaton and his father, Amenhotep III, had ruled jointly or in succession.

Fritz resolved to settle the question. He managed to have the Amarna tablet shuttled from a Near Eastern history museum in Berlin's former East to the Egyptian Museum in the former West; the latter had the technology for a sophisticated study of the slab's eroded inscriptions. "We all knew about the article," recalled Kim Ryholt, a former classmate of Fritz's and now an Egyptology professor at the University of Copenhagen. "He thought he had made an important discovery. He was very proud of it."

If the goal was to publish a paper that stood the test of time, Fritz succeeded brilliantly. Two decades later the article was still cited as authoritative. But if it was to impress Osing, he made a tragic miscalculation. "There was a little problem," Jansen-Winkeln told me. "Many of the conclusions he reached in the paper were what he had heard in Osing's Egyptian-history class." Osing viewed the article as intellectual plagiarism.

"I am grateful," Fritz had written in the article's first footnote, "for [Osing's] encouragement to review the following research question as well as for his invaluable advice." The article, which cited Osing twice more, was by all appearances a deliberate bid for his esteem—a play to become the new chairman's "little darling" by doggedly investigating a research question close to Osing's heart. Instead, it became the "terrible mistake" that Fritz had so assiduously sought to avoid.

PEOPLE HAD WARNED ME that Jürgen Osing was a recluse who hadn't been heard from since his retirement in 2007, which I bore in mind as I rang the bell beside his rusted, cobwebbed front gate in an affluent Berlin suburb. Along a footpath there appeared a diminutive man with disheveled hair, a threadbare sweater and unlaced brown shoes. Professor Osing stared at my translator and me with a look of serene indifference, then returned with a gate key. He led us into his kitchen and poured a bottle of sparkling water into child-size pink cups bearing images of Disney princesses.

It was true, he said. Walter Fritz had upset him. In his class that long-ago summer, Osing had told students that the co-regency debate could be addressed by examining vestigial characters on the Amarna tablet. "The dating depends on the reading," he'd said, "and the reading depends on the traces."

"He took it," Osing said, in English, of Fritz. "He didn't ask me before.... He just went to the museum and got access to the object. I was a bit astonished. I regarded it as my idea, so I should have been consulted and I wasn't. And I should have been, as it was mine." When I asked if Osing had planned to write such a paper himself, he said, "At the time, yes. But after that article, with the photographs, it would have been ridiculous."

Osing deflected when I asked whether Fritz could have continued in Egyptology at the university. "I would not have objected if he had asked Mr. Munro" to take him on. Munro—a scholar whom Osing, like the field's other big shots, saw as many rungs beneath him. Osing told colleagues of his unhappiness but said he never confronted Fritz directly. All he knew was that Fritz disappeared soon after the article was published. "He dropped out without informing any of us about the reasons," Osing said. "I never heard from him again."

MY TRAIL MIGHT HAVE gone cold there if not for a hazy memory: Two of Fritz's acquaintances recalled him resurfacing briefly in the early 1990s as the head of some new museum of modern East German history. One remembered seeing a blurb about his appointment in *Stern,* a major German magazine.

When I got home from Germany, I asked the Library of Congress to pull every copy of *Stern* from 1991 to 1994. In the February 27, 1992, issue, tucked between notices about celebrities like Glenn Close and La Toya Jackson, I found a photograph of Fritz. He was wearing a tie and three-button blazer and standing beside a life-size painting of Erich Mielke, the dreaded chief of the East German secret police. "Walter Fritz, 27, antiquities scholar, is the successor of Erich Mielke—at his desk in the former East Berlin Stasi headquarters," the notice began. He wasn't Mielke's actual successor, the article made clear, but the director of a new museum at Ruschestrasse 103, Haus 1, the Stasi's former command center. "Fritz offers visitors insight into the surveillance methods of the

Stasi, for a five-mark entrance fee. The section 'Caution: Hidden Camera!' showcases devices like birdhouses, watering cans and tree stumps in which cameras were concealed."

When my interpreter called Jörg Drieselmann, the longtime director of the Stasi Museum, he said he remembered Fritz well. In 1990, soon after the fall of the Berlin Wall, East German activists had seized Stasi headquarters to prevent officials from destroying intelligence files. The activists wanted the building preserved as a research center, museum and memorial. Fritz applied for the job of museum director. "Nobody from the group knew him," said Drieselmann, a leader of the activists. But Fritz made a convincing case. "He had come from the Egyptian Museum in West Berlin, so he was experienced in museum work." When asked whether the activists knew that Fritz was little more than a tour guide and gofer, Drieselmann said they might not have probed that deeply. The mere fact that he was a *Wessi*—a West German—made him a "fascination" to the *Ossi* East Berliners who hired him in November 1991.

It rapidly became clear, however, that Fritz knew next to nothing about either museum management or East German history. "Egypt and dead kings—that was by far his favorite subject," recalled Dorit Suárez, a co-worker. According to Drieselmann, who soon became chair of the museum board, Fritz failed to properly maintain records or inform the board of his activities. His chief talent, in Drieselmann's view, was self-promotion—trading on his new title to hobnob with city officials and land his photo in glossy magazines. In March 1992, five months into the job, the museum's board restricted Fritz's powers. Drieselmann said that board members grew concerned about valuables that had gone missing from storage during Fritz's tenure: among other things, a pair of rare medals, known as Golden Party Badges, worn by Nazi elites; secret cameras; a sword given to Erich Mielke by his Soviet comrades; and works by the renowned socialist artist Käthe Kollwitz.

Heinz Kilz, a former Stasi official who led tours at the museum in what he said was penance for his former misdeeds, shared Drieselmann's suspicions. When I found Kilz in the former East German city of Bautzen, still hearty at eighty-three, he said that Fritz had spoken to him about the Kollwitz prints. "I think I may have said I was a fan of Käthe Kollwitz. He said, 'Do you know we actually have stuff by her in the basement?'"

"Yes, I had suspicions that Walter took things, particularly the bird china and the Käthe Kollwitz prints," Kilz said, referring to plates painted with fowl. "In my opinion, he took stuff and it may be more than we know or imagine."

When the board pressed Fritz to account for missing items, he reported what he called "huge differences between [original inventory] lists and what we actually have," according to a transcript of a tape-recorded February 12, 1992, meeting. Fritz said he discovered the discrepancies himself. Rather than blame theft, he suggested that former employees had—in the case of some commemorative coins, for instance—either miscounted or overestimated. "Since I've been here," he insisted, "nothing has gone missing again."

To judge from the transcript, board members were initially inclined to believe him. But three months later, still concerned, they called a meeting to tighten oversight. Fritz failed to appear. The board found his resignation letter on the meeting room table.

BACK IN THE UNITED STATES, I asked Renee Juntunen, the granddaughter of Fritz's former Venice landlady, whether she had ever heard Fritz speak of a Käthe Kollwitz. "That was someone he looked up to," she recalled. "He was always trying to do the same style of artwork as her." (Kollwitz, best known for her haunting black-and-white depictions of everyday suffering, used charcoal in her drawings.) Juntunen remembered Fritz identifying two pieces on his living room wall as Kollwitz's. She said she recalled the name after all these years because of how close it sounded to her German maiden name, Kunkewitz. She also remembered Fritz having a substantial collection of coins, though she had no knowledge of their source.

MY INTERPRETER AND I found Herzsprung Drehteile GmbH, a metal-parts company, in a drab industrial quarter on Berlin's western border. We walked past rows of milling machines to the door of its chief executive, Axel Herzsprung—the toolmaker who'd been Laukamp's friend and business partner in ACMB.

When Fritz and I spoke on the phone two months earlier, he said he couldn't recall how he and Laukamp had met. Herzsprung's memory was clearer. "They met in a sauna," he told me. Sometime between 1992 and 1995, Fritz had struck up a conversation with Laukamp, who was twenty-two years his senior, in the steam room of a Berlin gym. Soon afterward, Laukamp brought Fritz to the office, where Fritz introduced himself, in vague terms, as an antiquities dealer.

How did a stranger in a sauna become a top executive of their auto-parts company? I asked.

"He snuck in," Herzsprung said bitterly. "He was very eloquent. Laukamp was easily influenced—he didn't have a very high IQ—and Fritz was successful in talking his way in." Herzsprung made no effort to hide his animus. "For me, he was the devil on earth," he said. "I was so angry at him that I thought it was better we never meet in the dark somewhere."

Each blamed the other for ACMB's bankruptcy. Fritz, in our brief phone interview, had accused Herzsprung of evading taxes and embezzling huge sums from ACMB to fund a side business. "There was substantial money missing," Fritz had told me. "We're talking probably seven figures."

Herzsprung, for his part, accused Fritz of a Machiavellian scheme to commandeer ACMB by driving a wedge between the old friends and lodging bogus complaints with prosecutors and tax officials. "Until Walter Fritz stepped into my life, Laukamp was a totally ordinary man with a normal life. Then he changed. His behavior changed." Fritz, he said, had a knack for exploiting people's vulnerabilities. "Laukamp was like a puppet. Walter Fritz would pull on the strings, and he'd do whatever Fritz wanted." Herzsprung acknowledged accounting irregularities at ACMB but said that he and Laukamp had benefited equally from them. In the end, he said, the overdue taxes were paid, and neither was charged with a crime.

In Herzsprung's telling, it was Fritz's arrogance that ultimately brought down ACMB. To demonstrate his superior business acumen, Fritz had ordered expensive new machines he boasted would streamline production. But they turned out to be the wrong kind. Fritz might have been a good salesman, Herzsprung said, but he knew nothing about manufacturing. His purchases plunged ACMB into debt, and as the company imploded, Fritz sold the older machines—the ones that had worked fine for years—to a nearby competitor, APG Automotive Parts. Fritz then got himself hired by APG and persuaded BMW to let him take the ACMB contract with him.

A question I still couldn't answer was why ACMB sought a presence in Venice, Florida—a retirement town not known for its industrial base—at a time when the German ACMB was collapsing. Herzsprung identified a single reason: Fritz had met a woman. He had split with his German wife and taken up with a thrice-divorced Floridian. Fritz wanted to manage ACMB remotely, and because Laukamp didn't object, Herzsprung went along—not least because it would keep Fritz out of the Berlin office. Fritz called himself the president of ACMB USA, but ACMB was never big enough to open a real U.S. office, much less any kind of factory.

When Herzsprung saw news reports calling Hans-Ulrich Laukamp the owner of a suspected papyrus forgery, his thoughts turned immediately to Walter Fritz. Laukamp was a perfect fall guy, a simpleton in thrall to the "antiquities dealer" who'd talked his way from steam room to corporate suite. Fritz, he suspected, had turned Laukamp into "a puppet for a fake story." If something went wrong—if the papyrus were exposed as a fraud—Fritz could pin the blame on a childless dead man who couldn't talk back. When I found the owner of APG Automotive at home one evening on a gritty block in Berlin's Spandau neighborhood, he told me that the business had flourished for a few years, thanks in part to Fritz's sales talent and the BMW work he'd brought with him from ACMB. But APG began dissolution proceedings in February 2008, after a former employee broke in to its warehouse and destroyed the machine that made brake parts. "A new machine would have cost a million euros and taken six months to build," said APG's owner, who asked not to be named. "We couldn't make our deliveries to BMW."

Two months later, Fritz put his North Port house up for sale. In February 2010, he listed it again, lowering the asking price by more than a third, from $349,900 to $229,900. On July 8, 2010, the house still unsold, Fritz had an angry letter published in the *North Port Sun,* demanding layoffs at North Port City Hall and 35 percent salary cuts for highly paid city staffers. It was the right thing for the city to do, he argued, in light of the pay cuts and joblessness that people in the business world were facing.

The next day, Karen King received her first email from a man claiming to have an interesting set of Coptic papyrus fragments.

BY EVERY INDICATION, Fritz had the means and opportunity both to forge the Wife papyrus and to shepherd it into the world. He was the missing link between all the players in the provenance story. He was a practiced reader of motivation, a sycophant with a salesman's silver tongue. He traveled to Egypt, had access to ink-making ingredients and a large papyrus collection, and was clever enough to decipher a damaged hieroglyphic text for a scholarly journal. Yet for all his talent and ambition, he was stymied by a language—Coptic—and a professor—Osing—and he quit before earning the most basic of degrees. Such a background could well explain the "combination of bumbling and sophistication" that Karen King had deemed "extremely unlikely" in a forger.

When a Free University classmate saw online images of the Wife papyrus, she found herself unnerved by the script. "I must say, it looks exactly like those texts we were writing at university, when we learned how to write Coptic," Nicola Hensel, who had been a top Egyptology student, told my interpreter. "The letters look so clumsy and untrained; for example, the *mu* really rather looks like a Latin *M*."

But if Fritz did do it, what was his motive? Greed—or simply financial need—inspires many forgers, and by 2010 Fritz's assets and income appeared to have taken a beating. But the facts didn't entirely square with this theory. The owner of the Gospel of Jesus's Wife may have wanted to get rich, but he didn't seem in a hurry. He had agreed to loan the Wife papyrus to Harvard for a decade, even after the university rejected his proposed deal—that the school buy his other papyri in exchange for his donation of the Wife papyrus. This didn't eliminate a financial motive; a seal of approval from Harvard would glamorize the fragment, gild its eventual sales price and clear the way for the production and sale of other fakes with less scrutiny.

But other motivations seemed just as viable. By all accounts, Fritz had seen his Egyptology dreams thwarted. He might well have nursed a grudge against the elite scholars who had failed to appreciate his intellectual gifts—who told him he was mediocre at Coptic and short on original ideas. Not a few forgers have been driven by an impulse to show up the experts. A yearning to settle scores might have intensified at a time when Fritz—beset by joblessness, corporate bankruptcies and an unsellable house—found his life in free fall. Middle age was when many people took stock of chances missed, of what might have been, if only.

At least a few of his university classmates suspected that Jürgen Osing—the ruthless Egyptology chairman—was Fritz's original target.

But something, they felt, must have changed Fritz's mind, something that steered him instead toward Karen King.

Curious about whether Fritz owned any domains besides gospelof jesuswife.com, I ran what is known as a "Reverse Whois" search, which identifies websites registered to a particular name, mailing address, email or phone number. When the results came back, I felt as if I'd tumbled through a trapdoor.

HOTWIFE

Starting in 2003, Walter Fritz had launched a series of pornographic websites that showcased his wife having sex with other men—often more than one at a time. A home page billed her as "America's #1 Slut Wife." The couple advertised the dates of "gangbangs" and asked interested men to email "Walt" a photo and phone number, so he could clear them to attend. (The Fritzes noted their convenient location, "about 2 hours away from Disney.") There was no charge and faces could be obscured, but the men had to agree to Walt's filming. "I just wanted to thank you for a wonderful time during the gangbang on Friday," someone named Doug was quoted as saying on a fan mail page. "Don't get me wrong Walt you are a great guy, but [your wife]...Wow!!!" Fritz's websites belonged to a fetish genre built around fantasies of cuckolded husbands powerless to stop their wives' unslakable lust. The genre is called "hotwife."

"My first husband was incredibly jealous and we were constantly arguing about my (miss-) behavior," Fritz's wife, who went by the porn name Jenny Seemore, said in a 2005 interview on a fetish blog. "When I met Walt he told me that he actually likes women who screw around. That was the perfect match for me and ever since we got married I do what I do best: I fuck as many men as possible." She cast the lifestyle as an emancipation from traditional gender norms. "After all we [were] brought up to be 'good girls' and it takes an awful lot of time to throw all those inhibitions overboard." For Walter Fritz, the fetish played, paradoxically, to a sense of superiority. When a poster on one forum asked, "Why is this such a turn-on?" someone writing under one of Fritz's porn names replied, "Because you know everyone wants your hot wife. Would you like to drive a shitbox car that nobody wants to steal? Probably not."

The couple's main website, which required a paid monthly membership for full access, was no shoestring operation. The site kept meticulous logs of new uploads, and every few days brought another original video, photo series or "erotic book." Its output was prodigious and, by all indications, original. An archived 2014 home page boasted "over 40 HOURS of downloadable movies in 2 formats, 45.000+ photos, 500 eroti[c] stories, 120 books, erotic art, & more."

In an interview on one of their German-language websites, Fritz's wife described herself as the daughter of a U.S. military officer who had been stationed in Berlin when she was a teenager. I filed a public records request for her father's military records and discovered that the man—actually her stepfather—was a Russian-language specialist who had served in air force intelligence and at the National Security Agency. In the mid-1960s and late 1970s, he had been stationed at the Tempelhof airfield in West Berlin, where his stepdaughter—Fritz's future wife—attended the Berlin American High School. Her mother was a retired Florida legislative aide, and her birth father, a Las Vegas hypnotist. She and Fritz appear to have met in 1996, in Florida, where she worked as a licensed cosmetologist at a Macy's. (Laukamp bought the vacation home in Venice, apparently at Fritz's bidding, the very next year.)

Southwest Florida has a vibrant swingers' community. Couples can get to know one another at brick-and-mortar clubs with names like Eyz Wide Shut, Master's Quest and the Woodshed. In one online forum, Fritz's wife mentioned performing with a well-known scenester named Art Hammer, who was featured in a VICE channel TV miniseries on "the lifestyle: the insatiable wives and their cuckolded white husbands obsessed with sex with black men."

"The basic rule of swing is, Ladies rule—they set the terms, they're always in control," Hammer said when I reached him by phone. He met Jenny Seemore when she was looking for performers for her and Fritz's pornographic movies. "I have a gangbang group and she was looking for gangbangs, and my group is well known." Hammer leads the Florida Mandingos, a group of African American performers who engage in sex acts with married white women at swingers' parties while husbands watch. Hammer said that most couples do it exclusively for fun. Fritz and his wife stood out because they sought to monetize it: they were commercial pornographers. "That's how they became very well known," Hammer told me. "People who were not camera shy would perform" in their movies, which would often be filmed at "parties" they hosted. "Jenny had one of the biggest websites—man, oh, man, was it huge," he said. "Everybody knew her."

By contrast, he added, "the true hotwife is very private."

In another departure from convention, "Jenny Seemore" appeared to have become Fritz's hotwife *before* she was his actual one. She launched their Yahoo discussion group, femalebarebackgangbangextreme—an "international Club for women (and their husbands) who love extreme gangbangs"—on January 27, 2001, two months before their wedding. Before Yahoo shut it down in 2004, femalebarebackgangbangextreme had nearly fifty thousand members. "My group has become the biggest group at Yahoo!" she boasted on its home page. In March 2010, a few months before Fritz emailed King images of the Jesus's Wife papyrus, the fetish's leading blog ranked Seemore its fifth most popular hotwife, calling her "this incredible, extreme, married woman from the breeding ground of hotwifedom which is the state of Florida."

"I have nothing but good things to say about them," Hammer told me. "Very open, very warm." Of Fritz, he added, "Walt's a great guy, very down to earth." Hammer said he lost contact with the couple in 2012, when he broke off a content-sharing relationship with their website and moved to a different one, the Swinging Granny, which he said paid better.

On September 25, 2012, a week after King announced the Wife papyrus, Walter Fritz began changing the street addresses to which his porn websites were registered. Gone was the address of his Berlin apartment, which was linked through Florida public records to Nefer Art and his home in North Port. In its place was a nondescript office building on Berlin's Ringstrasse to which he had no other discernible ties. Then, in 2015, as scrutiny of the Jesus's Wife papyrus intensified, all the porn websites went dark.

HUSBANDS OF HOTWIVES are sometimes called cuckolds, or "cucks," and Fritz often played to type, entering the frame after his wife's lovers departed and silently submitting to her insults and sexual demands. But mostly he is behind the camera—seen only in reflection, in the bedroom mirrors, a man with a lens for a face, a cipher who watches and waits. "Call me Wolf," Fritz wrote on a website that showcased his own porn persona. "I am dominant and enjoy using women, but I can switch too. Every good dom needs to know the other side, the side where the true strenght [*sic*] lies." The idea of submission as stronger than dominance could well be his personal code. To become the "little darling" to your betters. To recoil when confronted. To be the wolf in sheep's clothing, the wolf in grandmother's bed. For Walt—or at least for Wolf—this was how servant became master, how tables were turned.

In the mid-1980s, Mark Hofmann, a master con man from Salt Lake City, forged a series of manuscripts that undermined the official history of the Church of Jesus Christ of Latter-day Saints. Hofmann, a disaffected Mormon, used antique paper; mixed ink from sixteenth-century recipes; artificially aged his manuscripts with chemical solutions; and ventriloquized the writing style of the Mormon founder, Joseph Smith. But his success owed as much to his aw-shucks persona as to his technical wizardry. Shy, hesitant and self-effacing—a "scholarly country bumpkin," in the words of one observer—Hofmann buttonholed buyers predisposed, by ideological bent or professional interest, to believe his manuscripts were real. Yet once in the door, he did something counterintuitive: he expressed doubts about his own discoveries. He left buyers and their experts the thrill of unearthing signs of authenticity that he, the amateur, had somehow missed. "Usually he just leaned back quietly and let his delighted victim do the authentication, adding now and then a quiet, 'Do you really think it's genuine?'" recalled Charles Hamilton, at the time the country's leading forgery examiner. Hamilton and another top manuscript examiner had helped expose the sensational Hitler Diaries as fakes just a few years earlier. But Hofmann's forgeries fooled them both, along with experts for the U.S. National Archives and the FBI.

That Hofmann was something other than the "sweet, unobtrusive" scholar he appeared to be became clear on October 15, 1985. At eight that morning, a Mormon bishop who bought one of his fakes reached for an office package containing a nail-packed pipe bomb, which detonated and killed him. A few hours later, the wife of another bishop picked up the newspaper outside her front door. A bomb was wrapped inside it, and she was killed. Hours later, a third explosive—which detectives suspect was meant for another person Hofmann feared would unmask him—blew up in the forger's own car, blowing off the fingertips of his right hand. Hofmann's counterfeits fetched him an estimated $2 million, before the murders landed him a life sentence in a Utah prison. But money was only one motivation. "I won't go so far as to say I wanted to change Mormon history," he told prosecutors. "Let me take that back. Maybe I did. I believed that the documents that I created could have been a part of Mormon history.... The questions I asked myself in deciding on a forgery—one of the questions—was what *could* have been."

Reading about Hofmann put me in mind of the owner of the Wife papyrus, who, in his first emails to King, comes across as a guileless greenhorn. King is an esteemed Harvard professor and feminist scholar, but the owner addresses her as "Mrs." rather than "Dr." or "Professor." He tells her he can't read Coptic. He writes that Peter Munro's 1982 letter is from "the Berlin University," which no educated person would call the Free University. (The German capital is home to several universities, and "the Berlin University" was never a nickname for the Free University.) His emails are strewn with the sorts of typos that a single proofread could catch. Most chilling, however, are his Hofmann-esque flourishes: "I am completely clueless"; "I am not an expert myself"; "I cannot guarantee that this makes any sense"; "You are certainly more qualified/experienced than I am."

His unstinting deference made a favorable impression on King. Pressed by *The Boston Globe* in 2015 on her steadfast refusal to identify him, she said, "The owner supplied the actual papyri. He has said yes to every request made for testing and examination. He has agreed to store these for further analysis at Harvard."

Supplied. Said yes. Agreed. His submission to her every request made King feel duty-bound to honor his one.

BEING A PORNOGRAPHER hardly makes one a forger. Nor does it exclude a person from being a legitimate manuscript collector: adult video is a legal business. But the particulars of Fritz's websites made a case for relevance. A man who produced fantasies about modern wives—and whose own spouse called herself "America's #1 Slut Wife"—might also be drawn to fantasies about ancient wives, particularly if he had once been a student of antiquity. The "About" page of a site billed as "Jenny

Seemore's Personal Website," which featured mostly clothed photos of Fritz's wife, had the look of a manifesto. Its first section, "About Perception and Reality," featured a meditation on the slipperiness of truth and the tricks of subjectivity. "The state of the seen always depends on the perception of the spectator," it said.

> Examples: A child sees a ghost and hides under the bed.
> Someone sees a snake in the driveway, is scared, and runs away.
> At a closer look, the ghost turns out to be a shadow, and the
> snake was just a tree branch. Yet both people were scared, even
> though there was no real threat. So why were they scared?
> Because they perceived reality wrong.

The page goes on to say that the only eternal truth—the one through which all other truths enter the world—is ourselves. "If we were able to find out the nature of our own reality (the part that exists and is immortal), we may have a chance of finding the reality of the world as well. That's why Jesus says: THE KINGDOM OF HEAVEN IS WITHIN YOU! It means: find your own reality within, then you will know it all." It was a variation on a central dictum of Gnosticism: find the divine spark within, and you will know the All.

The page then segues into a series of musings on sexual compulsion, paganism and famous women who were at once empowered and enslaved by their own sexual appetites. The story of Valeria Messalina, the reputedly promiscuous third wife of the Roman emperor Claudius, "who used sex to enforce her power and control politicians," is told in a section labeled "The Perfection of Sluthood." According to the text, the first-century poet Juvenal called Messalina a "whore-empress" who "plied her trade, under the name of 'The Wolf-Girl.'" Posted nearby is "First Fig," the poem by Edna St. Vincent Millay, the early twentieth-century American writer noted for her critiques of monogamy and her many lovers, male and female.

Another section, about "the Grave Dangers of Satyrasis [*sic*]," quotes all 666 words of "Leah Sublime," viewed as one of the most obscene poems in the English language. The poem's author was Aleister Crowley, the English writer and adventurer, who traded his native Christianity for the occult. Crowley became an exalted leader of the Ordo Templi Orientis, a still-active fraternity of Gnostic revivalists founded by Germans at the dawn of the twentieth century. Crowley wrote the order's "Gnostic Mass," along with a system of erotic rites he called "Sex Magick."

WALTER FRITZ MADE ALMOST no effort to distinguish his fantasy persona from his real one. Unlike his wife, he often used his real first name on the couple's porn sites and in web forums. On the "Bio" page of a site he launched the year he contacted King, he wrote, "I am a 45 year old executive, living in S. Florida. Stats: 6'2", 185 lbs., brown hair, slim, no belly, clean cut, and well endowed.... I am college-educated with a technical MA-degree form [sic] a major university, and an associate degree in arts. I speak three languages fluently and read two old languages." The bio moved directly from his academic credentials to his views of women, as if the connection were clear enough to warrant no explanation. "I respect women in daily life and am very cordial and friendly," he wrote, "but when it comes to sex I only see them as a hole, to be used by any man." The through line between lewd and learned was even more conspicuous on Jenny Seemore's "personal website," where paeans to "Sluthood" are juxtaposed with Jesus's teachings on salvation. The site's creators—presumably Fritz and his wife—were intellectual magpies. They had cherry-picked from the worlds of art, literature, science and religion, spinning their harvest into a theology of sex, power and delusion.

WHEN I MENTIONED the Fritzes' websites to my wife, she suggested I read *The Da Vinci Code.* Jesus and Mary Magdalene's marriage wasn't its only conceit, she recalled. There was also a depiction of spiritually inspired group sex. I found it in the middle of the book. A clandestine society whose past members include Leonardo da Vinci and Sir Isaac Newton keeps the secret of Jesus's marriage alive with a rite called Hieros Gamos, in which masked worshippers stand in a circle and watch an older couple copulate on an altar. The ritual, in which the woman is in the dominant position, is said to sanctify the act of sex, as symbolized by the union of Jesus and Mary Magdalene. "The Hieros Gamos ritual is not a perversion," Robert Langdon, the Harvard professor who is the *Code*'s protagonist, tells the Paris detective. "It's a deeply sacrosanct ceremony." Yet "for the early Church," he explains, "mankind's use of sex to commune directly with God posed a serious threat to the Catholic power base. It left the Church out of the loop, undermining their self-proclaimed status as the *sole* conduit to God. For obvious reasons, they worked hard to demonize sex and recast it as a disgusting and sinful act."

Had *The Da Vinci Code* given the Fritzes another story line for their adventurous sex lives? They had launched their first porn site in April 2003, a month after the book's publication. Perhaps it had fueled some new fantasy of Fritz—whose birthday happens to be December 25—as a Jesus figure, and his "#1 Slut Wife," a latter-day Magdalene. But to what end? Was it to dignify their brand of female-dominant pornography by draping it in the garb of faith? In one online profile, Jenny Seemore listed her title as "American Sex Goddess."

Or was it all some big joke? Walter Fritz, according to his wife's personal Facebook feed, had a regular Christmas—and birthday—ritual: he spent part of the holiday watching the Monty Python film *Life of Brian,* a farce about a man born a stable over from Jesus who, to his great consternation, keeps getting mistaken for the Savior. ("He's not the messiah," Brian of Nazareth's mother wails at a throng of starry-eyed followers in one scene. "He's a very naughty boy.") The movie is a send-up of fanaticism's blindness to readily observed facts.

"Oh does this mean we have to watch it again in December," Fritz's wife asked in the Facebook post, which was dated November 7, 2011. Fritz, it seemed, had long marked one of the holiest days on the Christian calendar by mocking it. Yet three weeks after King tells the collector she wants to publish his papyrus, Fritz's wife asks her husband if they can skip the movie this year. When the Egyptologist Leo Depuydt called the Wife papyrus so overdone it was "ripe for a Monty Python sketch," he might have been righter than even he realized.

Another possibility was that Fritz and his wife drew their own, separate meanings from the papyrus. In 2015, under her real name, his wife self-published a book called *Spiritual Evolution: Universal Truths Volume I.* She called its text "automatic writing," its words channeled, she said, from God and the archangel Michael. "Most do not see or know their higher being, except when they accomplish a great task," she writes. "It is through this spectacular creation, that you can see your higher being and know who your [*sic*] are!" She urges readers to commit their desires "to paper creating a collage of your world; one that you can view like a masterpiece from Heaven."

The dates on the book's diary-like entries, I noticed, overlapped almost perfectly with the collector's email courtship of King. In the penultimate entry, dated just three weeks before King's announcement in Rome, Fritz's wife claimed to channel the following message: "For knowledge as you know, is what brings forth the fortune." It appeared to be an artless rewrite of Jesus's words to Magdalene in King's published translation of the Gospel of Mary: "For where the mind is, there is the treasure."

Could Fritz's wife have convinced herself that a higher being was guiding her husband's hands, too? The Wife papyrus could well be their "spectacular creation," a "collage" of sex and scripture they saw as "a masterpiece" that "brings forth the fortune.

"For all the Bibles and all the churches in the entire world," Fritz's wife continued, "cannot give you what you can give to yourself."

In her landmark book *The Gnostic Gospels*, Elaine Pagels wrote that the Gnostics "considered original creative invention to be the mark of anyone who becomes spiritually alive. Each one, like students of a painter or writer, expected to express his own perceptions"—"their own gnosis"—"by revising and transforming what he was taught... creating new myths, poems, rituals, 'dialogues' with Christ, revelations, and accounts of their visions." Is that what the Fritzes thought they were doing? If a modern believer used ancient writing materials to artistically express a deeply felt spiritual vision, could one even call it a forgery?

Mrs. Fritz's use of the word "collage" was striking. It wasn't just because of scholars' claims that the Wife fragment reshuffled the Gospel of Thomas. It was that Dan Brown himself was one of his era's most successful fusers, or confusers, of fact and fiction. Brown drew—ingeniously in the eyes of some critics, indiscriminately in the eyes of others—from sources as disparate as feminist biblical criticism, tales of the Knights Templar and Stanley Kubrick's *Eyes Wide Shut*. The Gospel of Jesus's Wife might have been a more highbrow pastiche, a postmodern mix and match meant for a single scholar whose subjectivity would blind her to its seams. To turn art into life, all the Fritzes needed was material proof of Jesus's marriage and a real-life Robert Langdon. *The Da Vinci Code*'s Harvard professor, a scholar of "religious symbology," finds the modern descendants of Jesus and Magdalene by deciphering a poem on a scrap of papyrus. Perhaps the Fritzes had found their Langdon in Karen King.

DON'T WANT TO KNOW

I called Walter Fritz on a Monday morning in March 2016. Nearly four months had passed since our strained phone conversation in Florida. Now I had evidence, and I began by walking him through it: the Free University professor who'd identified his photo, the stories of former Egyptology classmates, his registration of the web domain gospelofjesuswife.com.

"So what is it you want to know?" he said.

The truth about how he acquired the papyrus, I said.

"Wait a minute, wait a minute," he interjected. "You assume that I own the papyrus. So how do you get that?"

All the evidence pointed to it, I said.

"Maybe I know the person who owns it," he said. He hinted that the collector was a friend whose identity he was not at liberty to disclose. When I asked whether he'd had any contact with Karen King, he said they never met but that he spoke with her once "just to clarify something."

For someone who wasn't the owner, I said, he seemed to play a fairly central role in "quarterbacking" the papyrus. I chose a deliberately open-ended word, to see how Fritz would interpret it.

"What do you mean by 'quarterback'?" he said. "I don't understand what that means. So you mean by 'quarterback it,' you mean 'forge it'?"

I said that many scholars believed it was a forgery.

"No owner has ever claimed this is real," he replied.

In a sense he was right. In the emails to King, the owner said he didn't have the expertise to make any judgments about the fragment's content, age or authenticity. The owner didn't even request King's opinion on whether it was real. His only questions were whether the translation made sense and whether she had any "ideas" about how to publish it. That's it. It was King who introduced the idea of authenticating it and King who proposed publishing it herself. If the owner knew the papyrus was a fake—or had forged it himself—his emails would be disingenuous. But strictly speaking, they might still be accurate. They had led King to water, but it was she who had decided to drink.

Fritz and I turned to a number of other subjects, but before long he pressed me again on what I'd meant by "quarterback." I said that he had not only studied Egyptology and worked in museums, but proved—in his 1991 article—that he could draw hieroglyphs and pick apart ancient texts. With that background, I said, he must have anticipated questions about his role in a possible hoax—whether he was the owner or not.

"Let's be the devil's advocate and say either Mr. Laukamp or I conspired to forge a papyrus to make a statement," he said. "Well, there is still no scientific evidence at this point that we did it."

But could he have pulled off a near-perfect forgery if he'd wanted to? I asked. "Well, to a certain degree, probably," he said. "But to a degree that it is absolutely undetectable to the newest scientific methods, I don't know." If he was that good, he added, ominously, then he could "probably go around and kill people, and say, 'I commit the perfect murder every single time.'"

I asked him to elaborate.

The legal system convicts murder defendants with "scientific evidence that's not even 5 percent [as rigorous as] what has been done with that little fragment," he said. "Not even 5 percent!" If society was comfortable sending homicide suspects "down the river" on the basis of, say, a hair follicle that is a 90 percent match for one found at a crime scene, then how could it *not* exonerate a papyrus for which there was zero-point-zero scientific evidence of forgery?

From what I'd read of the history of forgery, I knew this was a questionable argument. Lab tests—if carried out by qualified scientists—can expose fakes but can never in themselves authenticate. At best, they can show that the materials an object is made of were around in the era the object supposedly came from, which means only so much if those materials—like blank scraps of ancient papyrus and carbon black ink—are still available today.

"I'm not saying it can't be done," Fritz said, after I'd raised this point. "Everything, apparently, somehow, can be done." Take the West Germans, he said. They had boasted that their ID cards were counterfeit-proof. But after the wall came down, Fritz said, Erich Mielke, the Stasi chief, disclosed that the communists had made look-alike IDs for every West German citizen. "They bought the same printing presses," Fritz said of the East German security services. "They bought the same ink. They bought the same everything, and they were able to forge 'unforgeable' West German ID cards." The trick, he said, "is just using the same manufacturing process."

Was this a roundabout confession? Was he comparing his methods to those of the modern world's most formidable security service? I asked point-blank if he'd forged the Gospel of Jesus's Wife.

His response was unequivocal: "No."

FRITZ COULD HAVE STOPPED THERE. He could have denied everything and hung up. But he didn't. We would have nine more conversations between March and April, totaling some twenty-two hours. He was nearly always obliging. He rarely sought to end calls, even after they'd perdured for hours. He emailed me documents I requested. He let me record certain conversations. Whenever another phone rang during our chats, I could hear him tell the other caller he was busy. I couldn't tell if he was at home or at some office, but I was always the priority, even in the middle of the day. I thought of King's defense of her decision not to identify him: he had said yes to everything she asked. I thought of the credo on his "Call me Wolf" website: submission was the mark of true strength.

After our first couple of interviews, I began to notice a pattern of subtle equivocation. Details, even about his own life, were often qualified as probable, rather than certain, as if to facilitate later revision. A favorite formulation was that one or another turn of events "could have been"—the implication being that it wasn't necessarily so. He was so self-composed during these evasions that I was surprised when he at last lost his cool. It happened when I brought up Jürgen Osing, the former chairman of the Free University's Egyptology Institute.

"Osing?" Fritz said, cutting me off at my first mention of his name. "He was frankly an asshole." Not to male students, Fritz maintained, but to women, whom Osing "found great sexual arousal in humiliating. There was barely a month going by that he didn't have a female student breaking out in tears." (When I later read Osing some of Fritz's remarks, Osing said, "That is very, very low. That is all I will say.")

I told Fritz I'd heard that it wasn't so much female students as himself whom Osing had sidelined. Hadn't the professor seen Fritz as stealing his ideas?

"I might have to tell him he's a goddamn liar," Fritz replied. "The article says, 'This was based on something Professor Osing discussed.' I would have never taken credit for anything he said." Fritz said he had asked Osing whether the eight-page journal article could count as his magister's thesis and Osing had replied that it was far too slight. Magister's theses typically ran eighty to two hundred pages—meaning they were at least ten times the length of Fritz's paper. But Fritz seemed to have hoped for an exception. "Osing is arrogant as fuck," Fritz continued. "Unless you discover a ten-page papyrus and with no mistakes publish it as the first person in the world, . . . it's not quite enough for him. But nothing ever was."

Fritz told me he took a semester of Coptic, which taught him just "a little bit more" than the alphabet. "Nobody is able to read after six months or so." Of the language itself, he said, "I hated it." Still, he denied that Osing influenced his decision to quit Egyptology. He'd left the program, he said, because fields like real estate and business offered faster money and surer job prospects. In any case, he said, Osing couldn't have hurt him if he tried. "I'm not really a pushover—ever—so I never had a problem." (His then wife recalled the matter differently. "There was a change of a leading professor in the Egyptology department," she said, "and that made it very difficult for him.")

In our interviews, Fritz's hostility toward the university—and toward Egyptology more generally—was palpable. He said the institute crawled with bad-mouthers and backstabbers. Egyptology fancied itself a legitimate academic discipline but was in fact a "pseudoscience." Its findings rested less on the evidence for a particular claim than on the renown of the particular professor making it. He pointed to the statue of Queen Hatshepsut at Berlin's Egyptian Museum. Many believed it was a fake. But because a hotshot museum director had paid a fortune for it, no one dared raise questions. "The core was cast of something like granite," Fritz said. "Little things like that make you say, 'Come on, it's real?'

"That's how universities worked in the 1700s and 1800s, and that is still there to this day," he said. "No matter how hard the scientific evidence you may get is, the opinion of the top dog will always supersede—people like Mr. Osing. I'm not saying he's unscientific, but this was a huge turnoff for me." The emperor, in other words, had no clothes. The big names in Egyptology were often such frauds that even students could see through them. Which made Fritz's next claim even more confounding: a major point in the Wife papyrus's favor, he said, were the big names and famous universities behind it. It was appalling, he said, that unaffiliated scholars—the likes of Andrew Bernhard and Christian Askeland—had somehow seized the upper hand in the debate over authenticity. These "county-level manuscript experts" from the "University of Eastern Pee-Pee Land," he said, had the nerve to think that their nitpicking of Coptic handwriting and grammar could ever gainsay "reputable" scientists at places like Columbia and MIT. He likened the critics' expertise to that of a friend of his, a pawnshop owner, who thought he could identify bogus Elvis autographs with nothing more than a loupe.

WHEN ASKED IF HE'D HAD any trouble at the Stasi Museum, Fritz said that the East Germans who hired him were such rubes that as the only West German he had no choice but to "step on toes" to get things done. I said that the complaints I'd heard weren't about his gung-ho leadership or surfeit of expertise. It was the opposite: Drieselmann, the board chairman, told me that Fritz was a lackadaisical manager who knew little about East Germany, failed to maintain records and presided over the museum at a time when objects in his care disappeared.

"I don't remember that," Fritz said. When I shared specific details about the artwork and other items Drieselmann said had gone missing, Fritz said, "Well, you see, this is a big area." He said that so many items had been trashed or plundered by East German activists that entrepreneurs set up flea markets for communist memorabilia in the street outside, which jokingly became known as *Stasi Allee*. "I'm sure stuff disappeared," he said. "It was impossible to secure because [the buildings] had hundreds of offices and there were only a little over a half dozen people" on the museum staff. He denied taking anything besides a copy of Karl Marx's *Das Kapital*, which he said he'd found in a dumpster.

He emailed me a photo of a short but complimentary reference letter that appeared to be signed by Drieselmann. "Mr. Fritz was reliable, motivated and committed in every way," it said. "He always performed the tasks assigned to him punctually and to our perfect satisfaction."

"Of course, I initially hoped it would be a career," Fritz told me of the museum job. But after about three months, "it dawned on me how clueless I really was about all that went on in the East." He felt an *Ossi* would be better suited to the job.

A few days later, however, Fritz confided what he called "the most predominant reason" for his sudden departure: a museum volunteer had found a forty-page Stasi intelligence dossier "that would have put a bunch of high-ranking people in several countries in prison for life." Recognizing its sensitivity, Fritz said he locked it in an office safe. By the next week, he said, the document had mysteriously vanished. A few days later, he said, he was walking home through Volkspark Wilmersdorf, a public green near his Berlin apartment, when a stranger on a bench issued a threat: If any copy of the dossier were to surface, Fritz was a dead man. It was a personal message, the stranger said, from Lieutenant General Gerhard Neiber, head of the Stasi's Department 22, which managed East Germany's secret ties to Carlos the Jackal, the Abu Nidal Organization and other terrorist groups with whom it collaborated to assassinate enemies. When Fritz got home, he said, his then wife told him that someone had called that afternoon saying, "Your husband will be a little late today." The spycraft he observed in his time at the museum, Fritz said, "could probably be used as the basis for a John le Carré novel."

Fritz's then wife told me that no one had ever warned her that Fritz would be home late. But she confirmed that he was in fear. He worried that people were investigating him. When I asked why anyone might be after him, she said, "I don't know, and don't want to know."

IN BERLIN ONE MAY MORNING, I met my German interpreter at the U-Bahn stop at Magdalenenstrasse, or Magdalene Street. When Petra stepped off her train, I said that Magdalene Street seemed like a fitting place for research into the Gospel of Jesus's Wife. She said she never once associated the station with Mary Magdalene. For Berliners like her, Magdalenenstrasse meant just one thing: the Stasi.

We laid eyes on its headquarters after a minute's walk: an eight-story monolith whose recursive right-angled geometries were a totem to totalitarian control. Before the wall fell, writes the former CIA analyst Marian Leighton, "passersby instinctively recoiled at the sight of the building." The East German Ministry for State Security, as the Stasi was formally known, had inserted its tentacles into every crevice of life. No means of surveillance or intrigue—home searches, mail inspection, microphones tucked into church hymnals—was off-limits. The Stasi had an intelligence file on one in every three East Germans, breeding a culture of suspicion and denunciation that turned children against parents, neighbors against neighbors and husbands against wives. The Stasi historian John Schmeidel called it "a system of population surveillance without quantitative parallel in documented history."

JÖRG DRIESELMANN, the Stasi Museum director, was finishing a tour for schoolkids when we caught up with him in the museum lobby. When I showed him Fritz's reference letter, Drieselmann said he had no memory of writing it. If he had, he said, it was only because under German law all employees are entitled to a benign letter, known as an *Arbeitszeugnis*, when they leave a job.

I also asked about Fritz's description of freewheeling back-alley sales of communist memorabilia. Drieselmann gave me an amused look. He said Fritz was deliberately conflating two periods, maybe in hope that as an American I wouldn't know the difference. The "wild times" of dumpster diving and the *Stasi Allee* were in the immediate aftermath of the wall's fall, some two years before Fritz was hired. When Fritz took over, in November 1991, the street vendors were gone and the building behind us—Haus 1—was locked. The missing valuables weren't jetsam strewn about old offices but objects expressly collected for or donated to the museum and then cataloged. "These things were secured," he said. "He was the only one who had this general key" to all the rooms.

PEOPLE AFFILIATED WITH THE museum during Fritz's half year there told me they'd never heard of any secret dossiers or death threats. A major German newspaper, *Die Welt*, had broken the story of the Stasi's ties to international terrorists in a comprehensive four-part series in October 1990, a year before Fritz's hiring. Could a museum volunteer have discovered a stray document nearly two years later that added some new wrinkle? It wasn't impossible, Drieselmann conceded. But none of its content, as Fritz described it, sounded different from what was already publicly known. Drieselmann suspected Fritz's story was "fantasy." Then why did his former wife describe him as fearful and possibly under surveillance? I wondered.

It was now the hour mark, and Drieselmann was looking restless. We were keeping him from his job, and possibly his lunch. He stood up, as though to send us on our way, when a look came over him. There was a volunteer, Drieselmann said, an older East German who had been close to Fritz. His name was Wolfgang Veith, but people called him *Sektoren-Schreck*, or "Spook of the Sectors," a reference to his long Cold War career as a spy for West Germany and the CIA in the postwar "sectors" of a divided Berlin. Veith spoke fluent Russian, had an encyclopedic knowledge of communist history and spent a good deal of time in Fritz's office, according to Drieselmann. "I threw the guy out around the same time I pushed out Fritz," he said, and for the same reason: he didn't trust him.

A year or two later, Drieselmann said, the police showed up at the museum with pornographic photos of young girls. Drieselmann recognized the bath tiles in the background. Veith had taken the pictures in the former private shower of the Stasi chief, Erich Mielke, which was reachable through Mielke's office and now part of the exhibit space. When I asked if Fritz had been implicated, Drieselmann didn't give a direct answer. "This was in Walter Fritz's time at the museum," Drieselmann said. "It's interesting, because maybe these two had some things in common."

According to court files, Veith's two victims—girls aged twelve and fourteen—lived in a nearby orphanage. Heavyset and in his early sixties, Veith appeared to have photographed them from the spring of 1991 to the spring of 1992, meaning he'd begun before Fritz was hired but continued during Fritz's tenure. On August 31, 1995, a Berlin judge convicted Veith of child abuse. The judge rejected Veith's claim that he'd been framed as part of a "Stasi intrigue." The headline in the tabloid *Berliner Kurier*—"Sex Scandal in the Mielke Museum"—covered a third of the front page.

IN A FEBRUARY 1992 museum board meeting, before police discovered the child pornography, Fritz defended Veith against rumors of earlier misconduct—that he stole "large sums of money" from the Checkpoint

Charlie Museum and worked as a double agent for the KGB. Veith was nothing more than an unpaid volunteer, but Fritz said he allowed Veith—and only Veith—a key to a Stasi Museum safe. "He still keeps things there," Fritz told the board. Among the things Veith kept at the museum, according to court files in the child pornography case, were the undeveloped rolls of film he'd taken of the girls.

Veith was in many ways a perfect match for the unnamed "volunteer" who Fritz claimed brought him the sensitive Stasi dossier whose disappearance led to the death threat. If the provenance yarn about Hans-Ulrich Laukamp was any indication, Fritz was a master of anticipatory cover stories. I wondered now whether what Fritz called a dossier was in fact the child pornography. Could Fritz have discovered some of the film, locked it in his own safe while deciding what to do, then been threatened by Veith? An East German novelist who'd spent time in a political prison with Veith called him "the toughest, most ruthless of us all."

A spokesman for the Berlin state prosecutor's office told my interpreter that the case's three-hundred-odd pages of investigative files were destroyed in 2006—the year Veith died. If they held clues to detectives' interest in Fritz, it was now impossible to know. (Fritz did not testify at the trial.) What remained clear was that Fritz showed up in Florida around the time Berlin police appeared at the museum to ask questions about Veith's photos; that Fritz incorporated his photography business, Nefer Art, on September 20, 1995, three weeks after Veith's criminal conviction, when the case was finally settled; and that a few years later he began taking pornographic movies of his own wife and selling them on the web.

Before telling him that I knew about the child pornography case, I asked Fritz for the name of the volunteer who had brought him the explosive dossier.

"A guy named Wolfgang Veith," he replied. When I then asked about Veith's pictures of naked girls and his criminal conviction, Fritz told me he had heard of neither. "What I do recall is someone found jewelry down there—rings—in Mielke's office, and nobody knew what it was." Drieselmann had told me about jewelry, too, but said it was discovered after the detectives showed up with the pornographic photos and searched the museum. They found earrings—the sort of trinkets that teenagers might wear—in Mielke's shower drain.

Could Veith have been behind the alleged death threat? I asked Fritz.

"I doubt it," he said.

FOR A LONG TIME, all I knew about Fritz's move to Florida was what he had told his landlady: he craved a fresh start. His former wife said he chose St. Augustine as a first stop "because of the pilot's school." Florida Aviation Career Training Inc., known by its acronym FACT, had opened in 1990, at the St. Augustine airport. "I thought if you have a pilot's license, you can quickly get from point A to point B," Fritz told me in one of our interviews, but he evaded questions about which points he was hoping to get between.

I asked about the Ringling College of Art & Design, where his landlady's family said he was some kind of high-level student or possibly a professor and where Ringling officials had never heard of him. Fritz said he attended the occasional lecture, but "I never actively studied art at Ringling." What about the collection of paintings and sculpture his landlady's granddaughter reported seeing in his Venice house?

There was a long pause. "I don't recall any of this," he said. "No, I don't recall." He acknowledged meeting Renee Juntunen, his landlady's granddaughter, and he confirmed her account of his giving her grandmother a piece of the Berlin Wall as a gift. But he vociferously disputed the rest of Juntunen's and her husband's recollections. He drew nothing with charcoal, he said. He had no art room, never burned candles in the house and owned no Kollwitz pieces. The closest thing, he said, was a folder of two dozen giclée prints, "which may have been at the house, or not, I don't remember."

WHEN I PHONED HIM AGAIN a few days later, his memory of aspects of his biography appeared to improve. He did collect art and manuscripts, he said. His interest in ancient texts was first piqued by his father, he said, a hunter of game who had brought Coptic, Greek and Arabic papyri home from the Sudan, where he liked to safari. Fritz's fascination with antiquities and adventure deepened as a teenager, he said, after traveling to Rome and reading a nonfiction English-language book his father owned called *The Wanderings of an Elephant Hunter.* "I read it as a child," Fritz told me, "and it was very intriguing."

Fritz named his Florida business Nefer Art because he hoped "to buy and sell manuscripts or get more into art." He even started writing a book, tentatively titled *Wanderings of an Art Collector,* that dealt in part with "certain wealthy individuals [who] use art and archaeology to promote their religious or even political views." He regarded the Green family—the evangelical owners of Hobby Lobby—as some of the most egregious offenders. "They purchase art and ancient artifacts for staggering amounts," Fritz wrote of such collectors, "and employ experts (sic!), to work on these art pieces." (The "sic!" here was his.) Fritz accused them of distorting scholarship by funding quasi-academic jobs in oversubscribed disciplines, an allusion to the role the Green Scholars Initiative plays in biblical studies. "Such a position may make all the difference between a job in the field someone loves, or having to join the ranks of post-graduate cab drivers," Fritz wrote to me. "But what are these researchers going to find out? Probably nothing that isn't in line with the views of the wealthy benefactor."

"Art is political," he added, in a summary of *Wanderings of an Art Collector* that he drafted at my request, after saying he couldn't find his original. From ancient Egypt through the Third Reich, art "was used to send certain messages, or even to manipulate people."

Yet as an aspirant in the art and antiquities world, Fritz said he never made much headway. The paintings, sculptures and manuscripts on his Nefer Art website were mostly stock images, he said, and his boasts of a "substantial" international clientele were part of a fake-it-till-you-make-it campaign. "If you are trying to get more clients," he said, "you have to make yourself [seem] a little bigger than you are."

AT 9:30 IN THE MORNING on March 21, 2016, at the start of our third phone interview that month, Fritz told me to check my email. When I opened his message, I found an image of a typewritten one-page letter bearing his signature. "Dear Mr. Sabar," it began. "I, Walter Fritz, herewith certify that I am the sole owner of a papyrus fragment approximately 3" x 1¼" in size, which was named 'Gospel of Jesus's Wife.'

"I warrant," he added, "that neither I, nor any third parties have forged, altered, or manipulated the fragment and/or its inscription in any way since it was acquired by me. The previous owner gave no indications that the fragment was tampered with either." Nor, "to my knowledge," did Karen King's experts identify signs of forgery. "To guarantee access to qualified scholars at all times, the fragment was placed at Harvard University as a permanent loan at no charge.... I welcome scientific discussion and gladly accept different opinions, but will protect myself against unfounded or sensationalist allegations and suggestions."

A lawyerly parsing of the statement for "non-denial denials" might zero in on the warrant that there was no forgery "since it was acquired by me." Depending on how Fritz defined acquisition and when such acquisition actually occurred, the statement was consistent with Fritz or an accomplice forging it *before* he "acquired" it. Whatever the case, Fritz had come a long way since our first conversation. It was time to hear him out. Over the next four and a half hours, he told me the following story.

He said he first met Hans-Ulrich Laukamp, in the early 1990s, at a lecture by a best-selling Swiss author. The author, Erich von Däniken, was famous for his theory that space aliens—or "ancient astronauts," as he called them—helped build the Egyptian pyramids, Stonehenge and other landmarks that seemed beyond the capabilities of "primitive" man. The talk, he said, was at Urania, an august Berlin scientific society known for its popular public lectures. Fritz said he struck up a conversation with Laukamp afterward—Laukamp bought von Däniken's theories; Fritz didn't—and continued it over beers at a pub across the street. Laukamp liked to sit in on classes at the Free University, Fritz said, and they sometimes lunched on campus together. They did occasionally go to a sauna, but that was after the von Däniken talk.

Fritz said that Laukamp first told him about his papyrus collection, in Berlin, in the mid-1990s. Then, in Florida, in November 1999, Laukamp sold him the half a dozen fragments, for $1,500—the sum whited out in the copy of the contract he gave King. Fritz photographed the papyri, conserved them between Plexiglas and placed them in a safe-deposit box. There they remained, untouched, he said, for a decade.

In 2009, Fritz said, he flew to London to meet a client for an unrelated business deal. When the deal fell through, Fritz thought of Laukamp's papyri. If he could sell them in London, he might at least recover his travel expenses. He visited the shop of an art dealer he knew in the city's elegant Mayfair district, a hub for international art and antiquities trading. Over lunch at a pizza shop, Fritz said, the dealer invited him to email photos of the papyri.

Fritz said he would have been happy to get $5,000 for Laukamp's lot, more than tripling his initial investment. It was no jackpot, but that was fine. Despite the recession, his joblessness and his house going unsold, he denied being in financial straits that year. Three months after the London visit, Fritz said, the dealer called to offer him an eye-popping $50,000 for just one: the papyrus that turned out to be the Gospel of Jesus's Wife. Fritz said he was stunned. "Apparently, he had a client willing to pay a certain amount"—probably twice the $50,000, Fritz guessed.

"Had he said $4,000 or $5,000, I would have sold this in a heartbeat, and the thing would be gone now." But when the dealer came back with $50,000, Fritz decided he needed to know what he had. The last thing he wanted to do was sell himself short. His Coptic was so bad, he told me, that he had scant idea of what any of Laukamp's papyri said. "I had tried myself with little or no success," he said. He thought of asking Osing but had a change of heart. "I just said, 'Well, he's probably just'"—And here Fritz burst into laughter, leaving the sentence midair. "So, I didn't do that."

Osing was "probably just" what? I asked. This was the scholar some former classmates suspected was Fritz's original target. I wanted Fritz to finish the sentence. Why did he change his mind about asking Osing? I asked. Did he think Osing incapable of translating it?

"No, he would have done it, but you know, he can be a butt," Fritz said, without elaboration. "Then, eventually, I couldn't find anybody, so I just emailed Professor King.

"I just knew her," he continued. "I had seen her on TV, I've read her articles, I had read one of her books.... I thought maybe she's somebody that can really shed some light on that. I didn't seek her out for a strategic purpose or something." He was simply well educated, having "probably read hundreds of books about Egyptology, archaeology, ancient Christianity."

I knew he was a former Egyptology student but didn't realize he was versed in early Christianity. What other books on Christian history had he read? "Let me think about it," he said, stammering. "What other books did I read especially about...I mean, I was subscribed to the magazine, *The History of Christianity,* for instance." (There is no such magazine.)

Had he shown the papyrus to any scholars besides King? I asked.

No, he said. She was the only one.

WHEN THE DEALER HEARD that Fritz had approached an expert, Fritz said, "the guy flipped out on me on the phone. He stopped short of calling me a stupid idiot and [was] pretty much like, 'Why did you do this?' I said, 'Well, it would certainly increase the value of the piece, wouldn't it?' He's like, 'No. I'm not interested if it's published.' "

Did the dealer fear that academic scrutiny might expose the papyrus as something other than it was? I asked.

Fritz said he never got an explanation. But he had a theory: the dealer might have shown Laukamp's papyri to a collector like Hobby Lobby's Steve Green, who might have wanted to buy the Wife fragment to keep its controversial message from coming to light. In the tabloid world, the practice is known as catch and kill. Fritz had no proof, he said, but "I can give you names and point out connections."

THE STORY HAD a certain internal logic. But until the point King entered the picture, it was nearly impervious to verification. Laukamp was dead, and Fritz refused to name the London art dealer who'd snubbed him. I decided to contact Urania, the scientific society, the site of the "ancient astronauts" lecture where Fritz said he first met Laukamp. Urania was one of the only named places in Fritz's account. I could certainly imagine Fritz at an Erich von Däniken lecture. The latter's gallimaufry of fact and fiction might well have appealed to Fritz in his university days. So might von Däniken's larger-than-life persona. Soon after his breakthrough 1968 book, *Chariots of the Gods? Unsolved Mysteries of the Past,* was published, Swiss authorities charged him with fraud, forgery and embezzlement in connection with his prior career as a hotelier. According to *The New York Times,* "A court psychiatrist examined von Daniken and found him a prestige-seeker, a liar and an unstable and criminal psychopath with a hysterical character, yet fully accountable for his acts."

There were obvious tactical reasons for Fritz to place Laukamp at a von Däniken talk. It would intimate that Laukamp harbored a secret interest in the ancient world that he kept from relatives, friends and neighbors, along, perhaps, with a secret stash of papyri. Yet to accept Urania as the site of their first meeting would require taking Fritz's word over many of those same friends and relatives, all of whom said that Laukamp had first met Fritz in a gymnasium sauna.

I asked Urania for the dates of von Däniken lectures in the first half of the 1990s, when Fritz said he and Laukamp had met. A press officer wrote back that there weren't any. "I looked through all the programs very thoroughly," she wrote. Von Däniken had lectured at Urania four times between 1984 and 1987—the year of Fritz's arrival in Berlin—but she found no indication of any appearances between 1990 and 1995.

I next combed my notes for inconsistencies between what Fritz told me and what he'd told King. In his emails to her, I noticed, Fritz claimed that "someone in Germany" had translated the Wife fragment in the 1980s and that a Coptic priest had "recently" identified the specific verses contained on his John fragment. I called a number of Coptic churches around Florida, and none of the priests were aware of anyone being approached with Christian papyri. It would have been a wasted effort, they said, because they wouldn't have been able to read it: Coptic seminarians are trained in the late, liturgical dialect of Bohairic, not in ancient Sahidic or Lycopolitan. Fritz's remark about the Coptic priest was a red flag that King, who teaches Coptic, had somehow missed or ignored.

Yet it wasn't only a Coptic priest who had seen the papyri, Fritz had told King in a 2011 email. "I had several people look at some of them in the past couple of years," he wrote. But to me, he said he had shown them to no one besides the dealer and King. How, then, could he have identified the verses on the John fragment? How could he have sent King a decent and nearly complete English translation of the Wife papyrus?

He seemed to almost choke on his words. "That was my own," he said of the translation. "That was my own."

"It's a pretty good translation," I told him. It also flatly contradicted his claims to me—and to King—that he didn't read Coptic and couldn't make out a word of the Wife papyrus. How had he done it?

"I had a Coptic grammar and Coptic dictionary at hand from my university days," he said.

Then why did he lie to King—and me—about having translated the papyrus himself?

"I was probably just a little embarrassed." He said he didn't want to look stupid if his Coptic had grown rusty. "Well, I'm not proud of [lying], but I just, back then, didn't feel like this [translation] was of any value." So he made up the story about someone else translating it. "I didn't want to be the bad guy . . . if the translations turned out to be totally bogus."

If something was wrong with it, you didn't want to be held responsible?

"Kind of, yeah," he said.

I asked Fritz whether anyone alive could vouch for any part of the provenance story—the London art dealer, someone who had known Laukamp to collect papyri, anyone who had seen Fritz with Laukamp at the von Däniken talk or at the Free University. Did he have a single corroborating source to whom he could refer me?

"I don't," he said. "It's very unfortunate."

I CALLED KAREN KING on the afternoon of that same day, a few hours after Fritz confessed to being the fragment's owner. I wanted her perspective on what I'd found out about him and wondered if it would color her view of the papyrus's authenticity. I was also curious how much she already knew.

"I don't see the point of a conversation," King told me. "I haven't engaged the provenance questions at all."

That was partly why I'd called. I'd spent months reporting in Germany and the United States. Didn't she want to know what I'd discovered?

"Not particularly." She said she would read my piece once it was published.

Before she cut the call short, I asked why the papyrus's owner had never supplied originals of his provenance papers—the 1982 Munro letter, the 1999 sales contract, the unsigned note with Fecht's frank interpretation of the Wife papyrus.

"You're in contact with Walt Fritz," she said. "Why not ask him?"

Fair enough, I thought. But why hadn't she at least made her copies public?

"I don't think they're good data," King said. Nothing useful could be gleaned from a scan of a photocopy, which was just "an image of an image." Her unusual phrase, I realized later, was uncannily reminiscent of the Gospel of Thomas's appropriately numbered Saying 22, about the merging of doubles: "Jesus said to them, 'When you make the two into one, ... and when you make male and female into a single one, so that the male will not be male nor the female be female, when you make ... an image in place of an image, then you will enter the kingdom.'" The Coptic word for "an image" also appears on the tiny outcropping at the bottom edge of the Wife papyrus. It is the only word in its eighth and final line, giving it the aspect of a tag or label. I had no idea if the theological dimensions of the con went this deep. On a practical level, however, I did think that images of images, however imperfect, could still be useful.

Experts on forgery had told me that anyone with the technical skill to fake a Coptic papyrus would have no trouble fabricating a trail of modern provenance documents. But after reading a scholarly article on manuscript forgery by the Harvard classicist Christopher Jones, I wondered whether they'd gotten it backward. "Perhaps the hardest thing of all to forge is provenance," Jones wrote. A manuscript is a physical object; to convincingly fake one, all you need are the right tools and materials. Provenance, however, is historical fact: a trail of dates, places, buyers, sellers. To convincingly fake provenance, you need to rewrite history—often recent history.

THE EXISTENCE OF Laukamp's papyrus collection—and even of Laukamp himself—wasn't the only recent history that King had failed to check. She also took for granted that Peter Munro had written the letter Fritz had given her, and that neither Munro nor Fecht would have been interested enough in the Wife papyrus to do anything with it himself. "People interested in Egyptology tend not to be interested in Christianity," she had told me in 2012. Perhaps most Egyptologists. But not Fecht. Marianne Eaton-Krauss, an American Egyptologist long resident in Berlin, served as Fecht's research assistant at the Free University from 1978 to 1983, which covered the year in which Fecht supposedly examined the Wife and John papyri. "He once said to me, 'I'm interested in everything except Egyptology,'" Eaton-Krauss recalled when we met for coffee. In the late 1970s or early 1980s, Fecht had even co-taught a course with Carsten Colpe, the Free University religious historian who was the official sponsor of King's PhD research in Berlin in that very period. The subject of the course—and of a series of articles by Fecht in the 1960s—was the Gospel of Truth, a Gnostic text written in the same rare Coptic dialect as Fritz's Gospel of John fragment. The idea that Fecht might have seen the Wife papyrus—and John's Lycopolitan dialect—and never so much as mentioned them struck Eaton-Krauss and everyone else I spoke to as incredible. "If this had surfaced in the 1980s, it would have been a life-changing event," said a different source close to Fecht's family. Fecht's own fraught history—he served in the German signal corps in World War II despite being at least a quarter Jewish—had made him profoundly attuned to religious history and the complexities of faith. "Anything which is truly scientific about Jesus, not the romantic, not the religious-deluded stuff. The hard scientific stuff—what can you tell from evidence—[he] would have been totally interested."

When I reached Peter Munro's former wife by phone in early 2016, she found the provenance story just as preposterous. In 1982, the year of her former husband's alleged letter to Laukamp, Irmtraut Munro was learning Coptic and studying papyri while pursuing a doctorate in Egyptology. (She is an expert on Books of the Dead.) If her then husband had come across an unusual Coptic papyrus in those years, "he would have told me," she said. My phone call was the first she'd heard of it.

FRITZ'S CONTRACT FOR THE purchase of Laukamp's papyri was dated November 12, 1999. When I asked Fritz where the sale had taken place, he said it was in the kitchen of Laukamp's home in Florida. But Laukamp's stepson and daughter-in-law, the Ernests, had told me that Laukamp was at his dying wife's bedside at that time. Hans-Ulrich had brought Helga back to Germany no later than October 1999, the Ernests said, after a Florida doctor diagnosed her terminal lung cancer. She died that December, and Laukamp had "spent every day at her hospital bed," at Berlin's Heckeshorn Lung Clinic. Fritz said much the same thing in our very first phone interview—possibly forgetting the date of Helga's death or of the purported contract. "I kind of remember this vividly," he told me. Hans-Ulrich booked flights home to Berlin the day after the doctor's diagnosis. "I remember dropping them off at the airport that day. She must have died about three or four or five months later.

"That was one of the main decisions for him to not come here permanently," Fritz added. "He was devastated." Fritz's story—of an anguished, devoted husband who rushed his dying wife home and gave up on America—dovetailed almost perfectly with the Ernests'. At my request, Fritz emailed me a photo of his copy of Munro's 1982 letter to Laukamp, the one in which Munro reports Fecht's identification of the John fragment. I forwarded it to Christian Loeben, the colleague of Munro's. He replied within an hour. "There can be NO doubt... the letter is 100% authentic!" The stationery and the signature looked just right, he said. But when we spoke later that day, after he'd given it a more careful look, Loeben was less sure. A stamp beneath Munro's signature, which bore the Egyptology Institute's address, was the kind that professors used to ink a return address on the outside of an enve-lope. But it was redundant on university stationery like this, on which the address was already printed, and overformal for a letter to a walk-in collector. It was as if someone were trying, perhaps too hard, to impute an official air to a letter that wouldn't have called for one. Also off was the prose. Munro was a stylish writer, even in casual notes, but the writing here was repetitious and stilted—a "stylistic catastrophe," in Loeben's estimation.

Later, thanks to the sharp eyes of a fact-checker at *The Atlantic,* I spotted two errors in the letter's address for Laukamp. Not only were the building number and postal code incorrect, but no such build-ing number existed in that postal code. One of the mistakes could be explained by someone trying to reconstruct Laukamp's 1982 address after postal codes changed following Germany's reunification, in 1990. On the advice of a forensic document examiner, I started gathering as many of Munro's letters from the early 1980s through the mid-1990s as I could find. Scans arrived by email from a former doctoral student; a Dutch Egyptologist who had custody of Munro's archives; a Free University professor; and Christian Loeben—who hastily retreated from his "100% authentic" assessment after reviewing other of Munro's letters.

The problems were endemic. A word that should have been typed with a special German character—a so-called sharp *S,* which Munro used in typewritten correspondence throughout the 1980s and early

1990s—was instead rendered with two ordinary *S*s, a sign that the letter might have been composed on a non-German typewriter or after Germany's 1996 spelling reform, or both. The absence of any words with umlauts reinforced the impression.

By every measure, the "1982" letter didn't look as if it originated in the 1980s at all. Its Courier typeface and information-age date format (with July rendered, with a leading zero, as "07") does not appear in the other Munro correspondence I gathered until the early 1990s—Fritz's final years at the university. The same is true of the letterhead: the school's Egyptology Institute didn't start using it until April 1990. As a student of Munro's during this period, Fritz would have received a signed certificate—on regular institute stationery—that served as the customary proof of course credit. He might also have received a letter of reference. It would not be difficult, the forensic examiner told me, to take an authentic document, lay a sheet of new typewritten text across its middle and make a photocopy. *An image of an image.* This might explain why Munro's typewritten name at the bottom of the letter is parallel with the stationery's design elements, while the rest of the text sits slightly askew. It might also explain why no originals seemed to exist. Later, I noticed that the format of Munro's signature on the "1982" letter was an exact match for the ones on his early 1990s course-credit certificates: just his last name, signed in pen, over a typewritten "Prof. Dr. Peter Munro." At the end of actual letters, by contrast, Munro signed both his first and his last names and didn't type "Prof. Dr. Peter Munro" beneath.

Fritz had also given me a copy of the handwritten note describing Fecht's opinion of the Wife papyrus. A blank sheet that was neither signed nor dated, it offered little inherent basis for evaluation. What was clear, however, was that its handwriting resembled neither Munro's nor Fecht's nor Laukamp's. When I asked the professional document examiner what some of these findings might mean, he said, "Good night, Irene."

WALTER FRITZ HEMMED AND HAWED when I confronted him with these details, but he didn't sound especially rattled. He offered up a scenario of how Laukamp could have signed a sales contract in Florida while at his wife's bedside in Berlin: the contract date might have reflected when Laukamp had given him the papyri, Fritz said, rather than when he signed the contract. When I pointed out that either required Laukamp's presence in Florida, Fritz offered another explanation. He said that Laukamp had returned to America—perhaps even twice—after taking his terminally ill wife back to Germany. "She wasn't dying *quite* at that moment," he said, explaining why a man he'd previously described as "devastated" might have abandoned her on her death-bed. Fritz said he sometimes handled travel arrangements for Laukamp and might even have flight records to send me as proof. I never received any.

When I brought up the 1982 Munro letter, Fritz cut me off. "I can't comment on any issues you have with that letter," he said. "I received a photocopy from somebody, and that's the end of the story." He denied doctoring it. I persisted, going over the evidence point by point. Fritz told me that if the Munro letter was indeed a fake, the forger would have had "no clue" what he was doing. "I've always known where he lived," he said of Laukamp. He claimed no defects in his memory of Berlin's pre-1990 postal codes. All the same, he said he hadn't noticed any of the problems, including the mistakes in Laukamp's address, before I'd pointed them out. He suggested that the letter, whatever its faults, had no bearing on anything.

Then why had he offered it to Karen King? I asked.

"I didn't offer it," he said. "She wanted it."

She wanted proof of provenance, I said, and this was what you gave her as proof.

"No," he said, and I couldn't tell whether he was splitting hairs or hinting at something darker. "I gave it to her because she wanted it. I actually said, 'I wouldn't use it.'"

FRITZ AT FIRST FEIGNED ignorance when I asked about the Jenny See-more websites. He had registered some web domains for a "client in Berlin," he said, but they'd since lost touch. "Of course, I didn't know that most of his sites were pornographic."

"Is that really the story?" I asked. The websites, I said, featured videos of him and his wife. I made clear I didn't judge them; there was no problem with adults wanting to spice up their sex life.

"We dabbled," he said. "We started out as a hobby; then it kind of got big." It was another of his swift backstrokes in the face of facts, a reversal so quick that you almost forgot the audacity of the lie that begot it. He and his wife (whose real name he asked me not to publish) had at one point drawn about a third of their income from the $24.99 monthly memberships to their websites. But he took the websites down—and folded Nefer Art, his murky twenty-year-old Florida business—in 2015. Fritz claimed the timing had nothing to do with intensifying questions about the Wife papyrus and its anonymous owner. The porn business had started to take the fun out of the sex, he said, and in any case they couldn't keep up with better-funded competitors.

He said that he and his wife hadn't read *The Da Vinci Code,* but did see the movie—the only iteration of the story, it turned out, that names Karen King. (The credits list her as a consultant.) But he discounted the idea of a link between his "hotwife" fetish and the Gospel of Jesus's Wife, or between the act of forging religious texts and the "automatic writing" by which his wife channeled divine voices.

"Probably highly coincidental," he said.

His wife told me she was christened in the Roman Catholic Church but rebaptized, as a Baptist, at twenty-one. Now, however, "I embrace all religions." She had been clairvoyant, she said, since she was seventeen. "I'm clear audience," she added, a term for mediums who don't need a go-between to the spiritual world. "I've had that gift, I've been guided, I know things about people. I can just look at someone and I know something about them before I begin a conversation." All the same, she said, she felt no spiritual kinship with the Wife papyrus or *The Da Vinci Code;* "I still don't get it," she said of the movie's plot. Nor were the entries in her book of "universal truths"—entries that neatly overlapped with her husband's wooing of King—specially timed. "The angels asked me to," she said. "I'm here to do God's service. If he wants me to write a book, then I'll write a book."

She couldn't recall when Fritz first showed her his papyri, but said it was sometime between their March 2001 marriage and possibly 2004. "For me it was just like a boy showing his toys," she said. "This was not something I was focused on."

Her blog posts suggest that his manuscripts eventually did become a focus. Under her real name, she had for fifteen years run a home crafts business called Cute Art World. Her signature products were mohair teddy bears and digitally designed collages featuring children, animals and mermaids, which she sold through Etsy, eBay and other online outlets. Yet on August 31, 2009, with their house still on the market and her husband firing off angry letters to the editor about the economy, she advertised an unusual product on her Cute Art World blog:

~My newest Creations~

Pendants of the Virgin Mary holding Jesus in her arms.

On the picture there is IC with a dash over it, which is the Coptic writing for "Jesus."

The little roundel in the lower part of the pendant contains a small, approx. 1/12" long papyrus fragment with the original black ink on it. I glued these fibers in between the picture and the glass. These fragments are really old and come from a larger christian papyrus, dating back to the 2nd Century A.D. The larger papyrus was probably part of a gospel or an early christian text, written in the Sahidic Coptic language. Coptic is is [*sic*] the final stage of the Egyptian language and consists of Egyptian words, written in Greek alphabet. Early Christians used the Coptic language, besides Greek, to write down the Gospels and other early texts about Jesus.

This is no hoax. I can guarantee that the small fragments in the roundel are indeed over 1800 years old. They date back in a time period shortly after Jesus' crucifixion. I got these fragments from a reputable manuscript dealer who was restoring a larger papyrus with a christian gospel on it. The fragments were left over and couldn't be incorporated into the big papyrus any more because they were so small. I have photos of the restoring process.

I am aware that these little fragments don't have any scientific value any more, due to their small size, but I felt I still could get some use out of them by incorporating them into my art. Despite their small size I thought that it may give people a good feeling, having something so old so close to their hearts, because it is something that dates back into a time when Jesus actually lived.

Though the pendants found a buyer or two on eBay, the scenario suggested by the post bordered on the fantastical. The couple were so sure of the papyrus's age that they could "guarantee" its second-century origins—even though no Coptic manuscript has dated before the third, when Coptic surfaced as a written language. Such a papyrus, if authentic, would be a showstopper on two counts: it would remake the history of Coptic, and it would rank as one of the earliest gospel papyri in any language. Every one of its pieces—big or small, loose or intact—would enhance its financial and historical value. Yet somehow this particular "reputable manuscript dealer" was willing to part with multiple pieces bearing "original black ink" at a price—$12.99—low enough to entice online buyers of decorative trinkets.

Key phrases in the blog post, notably "reputable manuscript" and "scientific value," were decidedly those of Walter Fritz, who used both in his early emails to King. Most telling, however, was what the post revealed about the Fritzes' activities in the summer of 2009. They had papyrus they believed was eighteen hundred years old or, at the very least, papyrus they thought could pass as such. They saw papyri from Jesus's time as a source of "good feeling" that could be exploited for profit. And at least one of the Fritzes knew Coptic well enough to print the *iota-sigma*—"the IC with a dash over it"—which was the language's official shorthand for Jesus, its *nomen sacrum*. The same two-letter abbreviation shows up, dead center, in the Gospel of Jesus's Wife. It is the "Jesus," in "Jesus said to them, 'My wife...'"

In late 2011, after Walter Fritz escalated his courtship of King, the bio on his wife's Cute Art World blog abruptly changed. Gone was her longtime professional identity as "Teddy Bear Artist." In its place was "Sending an Angel," a prophetess persona for which I found no precedent. If she had heard divine voices since she was seventeen, it wasn't until her husband's outreach to King three decades later that she advertised it. "When I was given this service," she blogged on October 9, 2011, "it was said to me by God, that I should create higher being angels." She included a link, on Etsy, to one of her first such creations. It was the rakish photo of her husband, with bomber jacket and umbrella, from his Nefer Art website. She had photoshopped white angel's wings onto his back and set the image against a spectral backdrop of the Brandenburg Gate.

As few as three weeks after Fritz's wife adopted this spiritual identity, Karen King pressed the send button on the email that would change everything. She was "able to make some real progress" on the Wife papyrus, King wrote to Fritz, "and would myself be interested in publishing it." Her out-of-the-blue reversal can't but have come as validation of Mrs. Fritz's newly professed powers. Just four months earlier, King had sent Walter Fritz away, saying she couldn't help. Now King was all in. When I'd asked Mrs. Fritz what she could see inside strangers, she told me, "Their heart. I know their heart."

THE NIGHT AFTER FRITZ and I discussed the Jenny Seemore websites, he emailed that there was something he needed me to know. He told me he'd spent part of his childhood in a deeply Catholic town in southern Germany. When he was nine years old, he said, the town priest got him drunk on sacramental wine and raped him in a closet beside the altar.

THE SECRET ROOM

I n the hall of mirrors that was Walter Fritz's life, I sometimes struggled to distinguish the true man from the twisted reflections. Fritz had built walls around each of his past identities, and he didn't like the holes I was drilling through them. The wall that took the longest to breach was the one around his childhood, partly because he deflected virtually all my questions about it.

The few details he disclosed concerned his father, and they were in furtherance of the story of how Fritz encountered his first manuscripts. As an adventurer who brought papyri home from African safaris and owned books like *The Wanderings of an Elephant Hunter* ("my father spoke English"), his father had sparked his childhood interest in history and archaeology, Fritz said. Their closeness was such that his father bequeathed him two personal collections: one of ancient manuscripts, the other of modern German paintings. Like son, Walter Fritz *père* (they shared names, Fritz told me) appeared to be a swashbuckling, globe-trotting hunter-intellectual.

For months, my efforts to confirm this account went nowhere. Then came word from a college classmate who recalled Fritz speaking of a half brother, an actor who played a bit role in early episodes of the TV series *Lindenstrasse,* one of Germany's best-known soap operas. The classmate didn't remember the actor's name, on screen or off, but knew that his surname was something other than Fritz. I used birth dates, hometowns and photos to narrow a list of *Lindenstrasse* actors to half a dozen candidates. I scratched one of them because he had been more than a bit player: Marcus Off had appeared in nearly every season of *Lindenstrasse* since the mid-1980s. In clips of his TV acting on YouTube, it was less Off's looks that put me in mind of Fritz than a certain swagger. "The grim Phil Seegers (Marcus Off) has always been a thorn in the side of the inhabitants of Lindenstrasse," the show's website says of his character. "As a college student, he stood out for his unfriendly, arrogant ways. Later, as a millionaire heir," Seegers turned into "an orchestrator of dark machinations."

I sent Off a message through his personal website. "Yes I am the brother of Walter Fritz," he replied. When we spoke by phone, Off said that he and his older sister, Eva-Maria Off, were the children of a nightclub owner and his wife in the southern German town of Lindau. His dad—a Walter *Off,* not a Walter *Fritz*—had fathered Walter Fritz adulterously. Fritz's mother was one of Walter Off's young waitresses, a single woman sixteen years his junior who couldn't persuade Off to leave his wife or play a role in young Walter's life. As a boy, Fritz had longed for a relationship with his absentee father. But they didn't really get to know each other until 2010, when Walter Off, then in his mid-eighties, was hospitalized with an aneurysm and Fritz, realizing his father's days were numbered, flew to Germany to be by his side. In bouts of consciousness before his death, in 2011, his father opened up to Fritz for the first time, recounting stories of bloodshed, imprisonment and desertion as a teenage soldier in World War II.

Relatives told me that Walter Off didn't speak English, much less read English books on elephant hunting. Nor did he collect German paintings or ancient papyri. "Never," said his eldest daughter, Eva-Maria, a middle school teacher, laughing at the absurdity of the idea. He stalked rabbit and deer in southern Germany in his youth, but later renounced hunting for what he saw as its cruelty. He visited Africa only after his children were grown and never to hunt. "All he shot were photos," said Renate Böhm, Walter Off's decades-long girlfriend, who knew him since the late 1960s. Fritz's tale of his father giving him ancient manuscripts and modern art was nothing more, it seemed now, than a cover story for ancient papyri and modern art he could not otherwise account for. The Hemingway-esque huntsman, collector and sage that Fritz had summoned in our interviews, I realized, wasn't the father he had. It was the one he wanted: a companion and namesake, a higher-being angel who would have fostered his boyhood fascination with history and saved him from wolves dressed like sheep.

TO MANY PEOPLE in the town of Bad Wurzach, Father Matthias Mayer was the stuff of dreams. Affectionate and tireless, he preached to people wherever he found them: in the schools, in the pubs, on the streets. And he listened, showing compassion for every human frailty and digging into his own pockets for families in need. Everyone was welcome at St. Verena Church, a soaring baroque structure, named after an Egyptian saint, whose bell tower could be seen—and heard—from every corner of the town. Father Mayer didn't care whether townspeople were Catholic or Protestant. All could enter, even the Muslim guest workers who toiled in Bad Wurzach's booming glass and plastic factories. The *Stadtpfarrer*—as Germans call a town's senior priest—struck his flock as the picture of Christlike simplicity. He favored a simple black cassock, rather than the business attire worn by many of his generation's clergy. He traveled by foot or bike instead of car. And he confined his living quarters to a single room of the three-story rectory, caring so little about the rest of the building that it fell into woeful disrepair. A newspaper story published on the occasion of his seventieth birthday—and twenty-second year as *Stadtpfarrer*—called him "Matthias with the golden heart."

Walter Fritz told me he was nine when the *Stadtpfarrer* raped him. The rectory was on the same street as the town's elementary school, and Walter passed the building every day on his way home from school. Father Mayer, a slight but energetic man with blue eyes and wispy white hair, was outside one warm afternoon. The year was likely 1974.

"Boy, are you a Catholic?" Walter remembered him calling out.

Walter's father was Protestant. And though his mother's forebears were observant Catholics, she was an atheist whose Social Democrat father—Walter's grandfather—blamed the Church for enabling the Nazis and openly disparaged religion as a pabulum for naïfs. But in the moment, none of that mattered. Father Mayer taught religion at his elementary school, and Walter had sensed his importance. To have his personal attention was electrifying.

"Yeah," Walter replied, not wanting to let him down.

"Good," said Father Mayer, who then began to quiz him. Where had Walter's family moved from? What did his father do? Your father isn't here? Where does he live? What does your mother do? Where are your grandparents?

If the priest was scouting for marks, he could hardly have chosen a more vulnerable boy. Inge Klöck had given birth to Walter on December 25, 1964, but soon gave up on his married, nightclub impresario father. Within a few years, she married an insurance salesman named

Hans-Jürgen Fritz and remade Walter's identity, assigning him her new husband's last name. In 1968, a daughter, Susanne, was born. Inge gave no indication to friends that her children had different fathers. Around the early 1970s, the family moved to a three-bedroom apartment in Bad Waldsee, a quiet town a forty-five-minute drive north of Lindau. Inge charmed her way into the graces of the town's society women, and at a local equestrian club she began an affair with a dashing businessman named Wilhelm Götz. Willi, as he was called, owned a plastics factory in Bad Wurzach that had made him a millionaire. Like Fritz's biological father—and now like Inge herself—Willi was married, with kids.

In the early going, the couple carried out their trysts in the woods around an isolated pilgrimage church, St. Sebastian, on a spruce-covered hill on the outskirts of Bad Wurzach. Willi Götz would send his then fourteen-year-old son, Siegmar, ahead as a scout, to make sure they wouldn't be seen. Then Willi and Inge would ride a pair of his Arabian horses into the woods as Willi's son waited by the church. "I was his spy," Siegmar told me unhappily, in English, at one of his family-owned restaurants in Bad Wurzach. His father, he said, was a self-centered former Waffen SS with an overpowering need to feel idolized by everyone in sight, particularly women. "He wasn't interested in kids," Siegmar said. "He was interested in women. All of them."

In early 1974, Hans-Jürgen Fritz abandoned the family. "He just disappeared," recalled Susanne Fritz, his daughter and Walter's half sister. "He never visited, never called, never paid child support." Willi came to the rescue, giving Inge a job, as his personal secretary, and an apartment in a workers' housing complex he'd recently put up outside the factory gates. No sooner had Inge and her children arrived, however, than Götz exiled her two kids to an apartment across the hall, where they lived alone with Siegmar, the fourteen-year-old son of their mother's lover. Götz, it seemed, wanted Inge for himself in the evenings. The eviction left Walter thrice dispossessed: His biological father didn't want him. The stepfather whose surname he bore, as a fig leaf, had run. And the business tycoon who'd lured his mother to Bad Wurzach had all but kicked him out of her apartment. "Walter was not pleased," Susanne told me, describing their mother as the "most important thing" in Walter's life. "He perceived himself as the man of the house, and [Willi Götz] was an intruder."

At a time when virtually every male authority figure had turned his back on nine-year-old Walter, Father Mayer seemed to think the world of him. He offered Walter a personal tour of St. Verena Church and said he'd make an excellent altar boy. Walter didn't know what an altar boy was, except that it sounded "interesting and prestigious." Inside the church, Fritz said, Mayer taught him how to pour wine into the chalice and talked about transubstantiation—how bread was the body of Christ, and wine, the holy blood. On a second visit, Fritz said, Mayer told him to take off his clothes so he could try on the altar boys' vestment. According to Fritz, Mayer exposed himself, too, and said they should touch each other in certain places. "I did not connect it with sex," Fritz recalled, saying he was too young to understand. "I connected it with some church thing, or something an altar boy had to do." On a third visit, Fritz said, the *Stadtpfarrer* showed him into a closet-like room beside the altar and locked the door. He filled a glass with wine and said that normally only priests drank it, usually in one gulp. Would Walter like to try?

"Now I'm somebody," Fritz remembered thinking. The next thing he recalled, his head was swimming from the wine, and pain shot through his body as the priest bent him over a stool and sodomized him. At some point, Fritz told me, he passed out. The next thing he remembered, the priest was ushering him out of the church.

His mother was still at work when he got home. He said he slunk under his covers and awoke to the wet of blood on his underpants. Ashamed, he shoved the briefs into a waste bin and buried them under the rest of the trash. He felt confused by what had allegedly happened. He kept thinking about transubstantiation. If the wine he had drunk was the blood of Christ, was the blood that now trickled from his body the same sacred effluvium? He wondered whether every altar boy endured the same ordeal.

After the alleged rape, Fritz said he dreaded school, because it meant passing the rectory. He said he feigned illness so his mother would let him stay home. When the priest invited him to the church again one afternoon, Fritz lied, saying his mother needed him home for chores. The priest responded, Fritz said, by gesturing to an ornament above the rectory door—a sculpted eye in a golden triangle flanked by rays of light, a symbol of divine omniscience known as the Eye of Providence. "God knows when you're lying," Fritz remembered Father Mayer saying.

When he returned to the church for the last time, the priest didn't touch him, but warned that God expected everything that happened in the building to stay secret; Fritz was not to tell anyone. When a schoolteacher asked one day whether everything was okay—whether anyone had hurt him—Fritz made a subtle allusion to the *Stadtpfarrer*. "As soon as she realized where this was going, she backed off," Fritz told me. Afterward, "she often ridiculed me in class."

Fritz's sense of isolation—his fears of not being believed—might have been compounded by the talk around town about his mother. His Bad Wurzach schoolmates told me they knew of no other child from that era being raised by a single mother, much less a mother who didn't go to church. Even if she weren't having an affair with a married man, they said, many of the town's righteous would have looked askance at her. Fritz didn't dispute the portrayal. "If you had children in South Germany in the late 60ies and no husband," he wrote to me in one email, "the verdict administered by the Church was clear: Whore!"

But then something astonishing happened. When Inge Fritz and Willi Götz's relationship became more public—when they traded their liaisons in the woods for lunches with their kids at Bauernjörg, one of the town's fancier restaurants—Walter felt transformed from pariah to prince. Teachers began treating him with something near deference. Father Mayer never bothered him again. In fact, Fritz said, the priest strolled up one day outside a popular ice cream shop, mussed his hair avuncularly, and announced to his schoolmates what a good boy he was. "Everybody's attitudes towards me seemed to change," Fritz recalled. It felt like a wonder at the time, but later it nauseated him. He was saved not because his mother had found God or ended the affair; she had done neither. He was saved because the town's respectable classes had learned of his mother's proximity to one of the region's wealthiest men, a tycoon now openly squiring her around town. *That* was what it took to make the powerful respect you. *That* was what struck fear in the hearts of priests. The fact that his mother and Götz were in a "sinful" relationship mattered less to the churchgoing town than Götz's worldly power. Fritz felt he finally understood why Father Mayer had peppered him, at their first meeting, with all those prying questions about his home life. They were aimed at sizing up Fritz's social station—his earthly power—and Fritz made the awful mistake of telling the priest the truth.

———

WALTER FRITZ SAID he kept the alleged abuse secret for decades. He channeled his bottled-up rage and insecurity into arrogance and verbal aggression toward people he viewed as intellectual inferiors. And he worried about his mother, the only constant in his life, who he believed would blame herself were she to find out. "She'd be torn apart," he told me. "Why ruin her last years with this crap? Nobody can undo it."

Then, in late January 2010, the legacy of clergy abuse—a scandal that had already hit the United States and Ireland—exploded into the headlines in Germany. The headmaster of a prestigious Jesuit high school in Berlin announced that seven former students reported being molested by its priests in the 1970s and 1980s. The news rattled the country, prompting hundreds of Germans to tell their own stories. "The wall of silence is coming down," the weekly *Der Spiegel* reported. By March 2010, the media had turned a spotlight on Joseph Ratzinger—Pope Benedict XVI—who as archbishop of Munich in 1980 helped shield an admitted pedophile priest. Other news reports raised questions about Ratzinger's role, as head of the Congregation for the Doctrine of the Faith, in fostering a culture of secrecy and leniency toward accused priests.

Pope Benedict made time in March 2010 to declare priestly celibacy "an expression of the gift of the self to God and to others." But he said nothing about the abuse scandal even as European outrage grew. On April 21, 2010, the pope finally spoke, telling the crowds in St. Peter's Square that he was moved by a meeting with abuse victims. He vowed "the Church's action." Eight days later, Fritz, though dubious of the pope's sincerity, wrote him a letter, reporting the alleged molestation for the first time.

Fritz sent me digital images of prayerful, consoling responses he said he'd received later that year from three high-ranking Vatican officials—letters he found unctuous and patronizing. "The Holy Father's going to pray for me," Fritz told me. "Yeah, fucking great, you know?"

The alleged rape had not only robbed Fritz of his innocence. It had sapped teachers' belief in what he saw as one of his finest traits: his intellect. His grades fell so far that the Bad Wurzach school system deemed him unfit for *Gymnasium*, the high-level track for college-bound students. It took him three years—and a move to a bigger city, after his mother's breakup with Götz—to assemble a strong enough academic record to transfer to *Gymnasium*. But the chip on his shoulder, and the hurt, never went away.

I HATED TO QUESTION anyone's account of abuse. But after everything else I'd learned of Fritz, I didn't know whether to believe him. A few years earlier, I'd written a long magazine article about an alleged victim of clerical sex abuse whose daily protests outside the Vatican embassy in Washington, D.C., made him a hero to the community of survivors. My professional website linked to the article, and I wondered whether Fritz had read it and glimpsed an opening to my sympathies—or even to public sympathy. Fritz had a preternatural gift for turning himself into a mirror of other people's beliefs and desires. "When he was eighteen, he was able to sell a fridge to an Eskimo," Susanne Fritz said when we met for coffee one afternoon in Biberach an der Riss. "He could perfectly adjust in his very young years to the person he was dealing with: he could read that person." As a teenager, he capitalized on the talent by buying old cameras and antiques at Swabian flea markets and reselling them at a handsome profit. It didn't matter whether the person on the other side of the transaction was a farmer or a doctor. Fritz spoke "at eye level," she said. "People would feel totally understood."

This same psychological acuity might well have helped him pinpoint Bad Wurzach's deepest fears. The town held few figures in higher regard than its *Stadtpfarrer.* If Fritz bore a grudge against the town for other, more inchoate reasons—the millionaire who'd jerked his mother around, the teachers who labeled him too dim for the best high school—an abuse charge against the beloved Matthias Mayer was a bullet through the town's heart. And because of the confidentiality afforded alleged victims, he could fire it from behind a veil of anonymity, much as he had the Gospel of Jesus's Wife. It was a tactic right out of one of his favorite books, whose author felled fourteen-thousand-pound bull elephants from behind with a single precision shot to the back of the brain. "To get within hearing distance of these old elephants is comparatively easy," the celebrated Scottish hunter W. D. M. Bell wrote in *The Wanderings of an Elephant Hunter.* "You simply pick up the enormous tracks in the early morning and follow them into their stronghold.... If the shot at the brain is successful the monster falls."

The volume of mail Fritz claimed to receive from high-level

clergy—the replies to his April 29, 2010, letter to the pope—was another reason for caution. "I can't think of a single survivor who has gotten a response from three Vatican officials," David Clohessy, the longtime director of the Survivors Network of those Abused by Priests, said when I reached him by phone. The most common response was silence.

But perhaps Fritz had read the Vatican, too. In our interviews, he more or less admitted just that. He said he wrote his letter to Pope Benedict in German, because German was the pontiff's native language. He didn't ask for monetary compensation, because that would call his motives into question. He paid lip service to pleasant experiences he'd had in church and to the good the Church does in the world, so as not to seem a crank. He wrote that even though Benedict, as Cardinal Joseph Ratzinger, had led the Church in southern Germany, the abuse that took place there wasn't all his fault. "I know what tone to hit when I want to be heard by Catholics—you have to use a certain lingo," Fritz told me at one point. "I didn't want to be too direct in the letter either, because I knew there would never be a response. If you go in there saying, 'Fuck you bastards,' they're not going to reply to you."

Yet from our conversations, it was clear that "fuck you bastards" was closer to how Fritz really felt. The Vatican letters he found patronizing might have sounded so only because of his own less-than-sincere expressions of fealty to the Church. "In the light of your sad story," Prelate Damiano Marzotto, undersecretary for the Congregation for the Doctrine of the Faith, had written to him, "I would like to express my respect and my high esteem that this experience has not been able to obstruct your view on all the good in the Church and the activity of the priests. This is impressively demonstrated in your letter to Pope Benedict XVI."

Was it more important for Fritz to amass written replies from powerful clergy than to tell the Church how he truly felt? For a forger, the official stationery and signatures could be put to any number of uses.

WHEN WALTER WAS A LITTLE BOY, his maternal grandfather gave him a nickname, Bazi, that his mother and half sister still prefer to his actual name. *Bazi* (pronounced *BAH-tsee*) is a Bavarian word meaning "little rascal" or "lovable trickster." As an illustration of how he earned the moniker, his mother, Inge, tells the story of the time an aunt asked him to snip a little rhubarb from her garden for baking—and Walter clear-cut the entire patch.

"But you wanted me to cut the rhubarb," Walter deadpanned at his dumbstruck aunt.

"He liked to play pranks," Inge told my interpreter in a brief phone interview, "but not mean ones. He made you laugh."

The urge to test limits—to needle authority figures—predated the family's move to Bad Wurzach but grew less slapstick and more cerebral once he was there. "It was boring for him to just get a normal reaction," said Siegmar Götz, the son of Inge's lover who lived in the apartment with Walter and Susanne in the mid-1970s. Walter would confront people with "special crazy ideas nobody thought of before" or would "overdo things to provoke, to see people's reactions."

At Wieland Gymnasium, a high school in the larger city of Biberach an der Riss, he devoured books on history, literature and philosophy, on his own time, then used his newfound knowledge to trip teachers up with esoteric questions he knew would leave them sputtering. In subjects where he couldn't outsmart teachers, he asserted himself in other ways. In math one day, he drew a naked woman on the chalkboard, shut its hinged doors, then waited for the unwitting teacher to open them mid-class, to gales of laughter. "He was so bad in math it didn't matter anymore," recalled Marcus Schmid, a high school classmate. Fritz "never swam with the tide," said another schoolmate, Erna Dobler.

Fritz had wanted to be a physician, ostentatiously toting his schoolbooks in a black leather doctor's bag. But his math and science grades made him a poor prospect, and when even the military's medical school rejected him, he applied to be a conscientious objector during a compulsory draft. He would have had no problem faking a religious objection; though Fritz was not a churchgoer, a classmate recalled him as extremely well-read in the Bible and "Church issues." Invoking one's faith was the easiest out, but Fritz "took the much more difficult route of giving political reasons," remembered Hubert Zinngisser, a high school friend. He performed two years of alternative service as an EMT for the local Red Cross, before following his high school girlfriend—and future first wife—to Berlin in 1987 and finding his way to the Free University.

When he sent home word that he was studying Egyptology, his half sister wasn't surprised. "I don't think he would have felt attracted to excavating Neanderthals—that would be primitive," Susanne told me. Egypt's glittering civilization played perfectly to his need to be seen, by merit or by mischief, as exceptional. "He felt destined to deal with a superior culture," she said. Of all the roads his interest in history might have taken, "Egyptology was the most superior historical subject you could pick.

"He was always aiming to be more than he was."

WAS WALTER FRITZ'S STORY of abuse just one more lark? Or had it actually happened? If Fritz had forged the Gospel of Jesus's Wife, the answer went to the heart of motivation. A man who blamed a priest for ruining his life would have plenty of reason to want to undermine Catholic doctrine on Jesus's celibacy. A man obsessed with status— with being seen as the best—would have reveled in the prospect of turning Harvard University into his missile launcher, one capable of inflicting far greater damage on the Church than Osing, the retired, reclusive Egyptologist in Berlin, who hadn't been heard from in years.

Fritz had sent his first email to Karen King on July 9, 2010. That was ten weeks after he reported the alleged abuse to Pope Benedict but before any Church official had replied. It was easy to imagine him doing a slow burn as the days ticked past, piling insult on injury. It was easy to picture him—as Bazi—deciding that if he couldn't get the Vatican's attention the normal way, there was another way that surely would.

MY INTERPRETER AND I drove to Bad Wurzach from the Munich airport on a warm day in May, exiting the autobahn in the southwest German state of Baden-Württemberg and following roads through small villages and rolling farmland.

Fritz's mother was what a friend described as "a migratory bird," a restless and radiant woman who wore her dark hair in a bob and skipped from one town to the next, often, it seemed, on the heels of a new romance. Her four-year stay in Bad Wurzach (population fifty-four hundred)—when her son grew from nine to thirteen—appeared to be one of the longest of Walter's childhood. The stories Fritz told of life here had often left me with the same feeling his papyrus had inspired in its critics: parts of the atmospherics were too *Da Vinci Code*. Fritz told me, for instance, that his family had lived on "God's Mountain Road," steps from a "Holy Blood Chapel up on the hill, the place where the 'real' blood of Christ is stored." *Holy Blood, Holy Grail*, I recalled, was the title of an internationally best-selling 1982 book packed with historical speculation about the marriage and bloodline of Jesus and Mary Magdalene. Its authors, accusing Dan Brown of stealing their theories, sued his publisher. (They lost.) Had Fritz borrowed from both books to turn his hometown into a stage set for a gospel thriller?

He hadn't. Records at the Bad Wurzach town hall and old phone books I found at the U.S. Library of Congress showed that Fritz's family had indeed lived in Bad Wurzach in the years—the mid- to late 1970s—that Fritz said they did. For at least part of that time, they resided in a single-family home on Gottesbergweg, or God's Mountain Road. My interpreter and I found the steep-roofed house, which stood on a slanted street beside the town cemetery. It was a three-minute walk from there to God's Mountain, a hill capped by a Salvatorian monastery with a Holy Blood Chapel. We heaved open its doors and found an ornate gilt-silver cross in a faintly lit alcove to the left of the altar. Inside a glass capsule at the cross's center was a scrap of linen said to be stained with the real blood of Jesus. Every July since 1928, according to a pamphlet I found in the church, hundreds of sashed horsemen in top hats parade the "Holy Blood Reliquary" through town for a *Heilig-Blutfest* that draws thousands of pilgrims from across Europe.

I had emailed the Vatican and the Diocese of Rottenburg-Stuttgart images of the three replies Fritz said he received after reporting his abuse. Church officials confirmed that at least two of the letters—including Marzotto's—were genuine. Both were written in 2010, which meant that if Fritz had invented the molestation story, he had done so more than five years before our first conversation and at least a few months before contacting King.

In the spring of 2016, when Fritz told me of the alleged rape, I had asked him to describe as precisely as possible the setting in which it had taken place. I wanted to see whether the way he told the story differed in any material respects from his tales about the Wife papyrus, which had been shifting and vague, in large part because they were invented. His memories of the alleged abuse, however, were different. He had names, dates and places—concrete details that could be checked against known facts. The location of the alleged rape, for instance, remained vivid. Fritz told me that the altar of St. Verena Church had doors on both sides. The doors were distinguished by a single architectural detail: the one on the left, as you faced the altar, had a lock, Fritz said, while the one on the right didn't. Fritz recalled Father Mayer taking him to the one on the left and securing the door behind him. "It was a small lock," Fritz recalled, but he could still remember its sound; it was like a "dungeon," with "big bolts going down." In his child's eye, he said, the presence of a lock was meaningful. "The left was the secret room, the secret room you had to lock," he said. "That's where the holy stuff, the secret stuff, happened. . . . I don't recall ever being in the other one. I saw the door open, but I never went in there."

What was the room on the left like? I asked.

"Small," he said. Not exactly a closet, but close, and "full of clutter," including a bench or chair.

BAD WURZACH'S CURRENT *Stadtpfarrer,* an upbeat fifty-one-year-old named Stefan Maier, opened the rectory door on a Sunday morning and invited my interpreter and me into a modern conference room. He made a pot of coffee, and I told the story of Fritz's abuse allegations and the Gospel of Jesus's Wife.

Maier said that he grew up elsewhere and hadn't known Father Mayer (no relation), who died in 1980. Still, the late priest remained the best-remembered—and most beloved—*Stadtpfarrer* in living memory. An oil portrait of Mayer, hands clasped over his lap, still hung in the rectory stairwell.

I asked Maier what he would say to Fritz if the charges were true. "I would of course express my feeling that this was horrible," he said, "a horrible experience that he will probably carry all of his life and affect his ability to have relationships and make a happy life. What makes it even more horrible is the fact that priests are the ones who make the love of God real for people." To use one's influence as a priest to sexually abuse a child is "the extreme opposite."

"The Church is my family, so I feel I want to apologize to him," Maier continued. "But at the same time, it's not the Church that did this to him. It's a human being, and some human beings do wrong things, even human beings in the Church."

I had already retraced what Fritz said was his boyhood walk or bike ride home from school. It was a near match for his account: the short distance between the school and the rectory, the downward slope of the sidewalk, a roadside retaining wall, a pair of facing staircases that meet at the rectory door, the Eye of Providence in the door's molding. At my request, Father Maier led me across the street and into the sacristy of St. Verena's. In the back, on long rows of hangers, were the altar boys' long red and white gowns, sorted by size. Another door brought us into an airy sanctuary. I stepped down into the pews and turned around. A wooden door flanked each side of the altar. Both doors had modern cylinder locks. But only one had its heavy, original lock: the one on the left. Maier moved aside a low bench that someone had placed in front of it and slipped a key into the lock. "These doors are never used," he said, but then he corrected himself. "The only ones who use these doors are the altar boys."

The door swung inward onto two concrete steps that led down to a hexagonal floor of about forty-eight by thirty-two inches. To the left of the floor was a cramped nook, too small to stand in, in which were stuffed a wooden lectern, a pair of folded carpets, an extension cord, a vacuum cleaner and a stool. It, too, was a close match for the room Fritz had described. The only discrepancy was that the space wasn't precisely a room. At the other end of the hexagonal floor, it was just five steps up to one of the church's small side exits and another step to a circular staircase, whose spiraling underside formed the space's roof and led to a balcony above the nave. Altar boys used the side doors and staircase to tote an offering bag—a cloth sack on a stick with a bell—to worshippers in the balcony.

Could Fritz have misremembered the space as an enclosed room? Forty years after a traumatizing attack, one could hardly hold a child victim to a perfect description of an alleged crime scene. His account of the setting was accurate in nearly every other respect. In his fear and inebriation, might he have failed to spot the stairs or the side door? Might guilt or shame have suppressed a memory of possible escape routes? Or had the space then had a kind of enclosure? Indeed, against the wall of the low hexagonal floor, I noticed a makeshift wooden partition that might well have suited such a purpose.

When I phoned Fritz after my trip to Bad Wurzach, I told him I had been to the town but not that I had visited the church, much less the locked room to the left of the altar. I wouldn't have lied if he'd asked, but he didn't. I asked him again to describe the room. His account was consistent with his earlier one. I then inquired, casually, how a person might exit the room.

"The door, that's how you get out of the room," he said. Then something seemed to blink in the recesses of memory. "Were there stairs?" he said, more to himself, it seemed, than to me. I hadn't said anything of stairs or any other exit, but here he was, surfacing the one key detail he had failed to mention. I remained silent, wanting to neither lead nor interrupt his reverie. But the memory no sooner came than went. "I don't recall stairs," he said to himself. "Not really."

THE VATICAN HAD FORWARDED Fritz's April 2010 letter to the Diocese of Rottenburg-Stuttgart, which in turn had routed it to Dr. Norbert Reuhs. Reuhs was an investigator with a child sex abuse commission established by the diocese in 2002. He had carried out the initial screen of Fritz's report. When my interpreter called after our visit to Bad Wurzach, Reuhs said he had found Fritz's allegations "plausible." The people and places in Fritz's complaint existed, as described, at the time the abuse was said to have taken place, which wasn't always the case. The diocese knew of no other complaints against Father Matthias Mayer, Reuhs said, but that wasn't especially meaningful. Some priests in the diocese had been credibly accused by multiple victims, others by just one. Many victims never report, a problem Reuhs thought might be more acute in small, insular towns, where the *Stadtpfarrer* often walked on water.

Had he interviewed Fritz? we asked. Put out a call for other possible victims?

He hadn't, he said. Mayer was long dead; there was no way to question him or bring him to justice. More important, because Fritz had taken the unusual step of writing to the pope, rather than the diocese, Reuhs lacked jurisdiction. He sent his preliminary finding back to the Vatican's Congregation for the Doctrine of the Faith. But he said he could take no further action without Vatican orders—orders that hadn't come.

———

ON OUR FINAL MORNING in Bad Wurzach, I returned to St. Verena's and found a woman cutting pink and white flowers in front of the altar. Her name was Maria Schad. She was a grade school religion teacher and church volunteer. She was making bouquets for a girl's baptism later that day. I asked if she'd known Father Matthias Mayer.

"He's not forgotten in this town," she said. "He was always giving the children—the altar boys—chocolates after Mass." She looked up from her clippings. "That was unusual at the time." When I asked why, she said that in those days "children didn't have a good image of church elders." But Mayer made himself so beloved of the town's youth that "all the kids wanted to be altar boys."

Did she know anyone who'd been an altar boy in the 1970s? I asked.

KARL-AUGUST MOHR LIVED just a few blocks from St. Verena's. A winsomely disheveled man in a long-sleeve V-necked T-shirt, he looked only too pleased when we said we wanted to talk about Father Mayer. It was clear that he adored the late *Stadtpfarrer,* a figure he felt was still looking out for the town. "When the sun is out like this," Mohr said, "we still say, even today, 'Thanks, Father Mayer.'"

Mohr, who was born in 1961, three years before Fritz (and didn't know him), said he served as an altar boy from age nine, when he received his first Communion, until he was about seventeen. He and his wife, Brigitte, offered us seats at their dining room table. The more stories they told, the more I saw how much attention Father Mayer had lavished on boys and how much he wanted—or perhaps needed—to feel loved by them. The priest always carried candy in his pockets, Mohr said, and if a nearby street vendor was selling pastries or ice cream, he'd approach children to ask if they'd like him to buy them a treat. "He'd say things like 'Today it's really hot. Do you want to have an ice cream?'"

Later, when he was fourteen, Mohr joined other boys on hiking tours Father Mayer led through the countryside. Fourteen was the legal drinking age, and the *Stadtpfarrer* took pleasure in introducing them to their first sips and smokes. "When we went into a restaurant, he'd say, 'Boys, want anything to drink? Beer? Cigar?'"

Would the priest buy boys alcohol? I asked.

"He did," Mohr said. "It was normal for him."

There was nothing untoward about the behavior, in Mohr's view; Father Mayer was so selfless that all he could do was give. "He didn't have any needs," Mohr said. Nor did he stand on formality. As the town's chief priest, Father Mayer was supposed to sign the certificates awarded children at their first Communion, when most were nine years old. (That was Fritz's age when Mayer allegedly abused him.) But the priest didn't want to be bothered. "He would say, 'Just sign them "Father Mayer,"'" Mohr recalled, breaking into Mayer's hammy, mock-pleading tone. "'Sign! *Please* sign! Please, for me!'" The bemused kids would then forge the priest's signature on their certificates, as instructed, or an older brother would do it for them.

I said that we were writing about a former Bad Wurzach resident who claimed to have been inappropriately touched by the priest. Had Mohr seen or heard anything of that sort?

He furrowed his brows and recoiled. "Not at all, not at all, not at all," he said. "I can't imagine it." He pointed to his many years as an altar boy. "I would have noticed. He was too good of a person."

Was there anything Father Mayer did that might have discomfited some children?

Well, Mohr said, he wasn't sure it counted, but there was something. "If you ran into him in town as a kid, he would take hold of your hand and not let go, kind of dragging you along and peppering you with questions," Mohr recalled. "He would ask, 'Who do you belong to? What family?... How are you? How is school? How are your parents?'"

It was the same barrage of questions, I realized, that Walter Fritz had described to me—the one that compelled him, fatefully, to tell the priest he was the Catholic son of a single mother who'd just moved to town. It was the interrogation that Fritz came to see as a predatory screening. Though Mohr regarded Mayer's questions as well-intentioned, he acknowledged that they were often accompanied by forced physical contact—a grabbing of a child's hand, a dragging along.

I asked Mohr if Father Mayer would have paid special attention to newcomers. "Absolutely, yes," Mohr said. "If a new kid came to town, he would ask, 'Who are you? Where are you from?' He was proactive. If a new kid joined the school, he would approach them. There was no way to get around him." Some kids, not wanting to be accosted, would even cross the street if they saw him coming. "Otherwise you wouldn't get away from him for fifteen minutes." In two out of the three photographs Mohr showed me of the priest in the 1970s, Mayer had one or both of his hands on the shoulders or wrists of children.

Other Bad Wurzach residents who had been Mayer's students or altar boys in the 1970s told me similar stories. They said Mayer drank too much and was not shy about putting his hands on children. He smacked the occasional scalawag. But more often, he hugged or caressed. How close his behavior came to crossing a line was a matter of dispute. Michael Späth, a sculptor and firefighter who had been the priest's elementary school student for five years, saw it as good-natured physical affection. "He used to hug and stroke kids—today this is called sexual molestation," he said dismissively. "Sometimes he kissed you on the forehead or cheek, but nothing sexual."

What was it then? I asked.

"It was enjoying the innocence and friendship of a child," he said. His love of children reflected "his passion for creation."

But Reinhold Kienle, a classmate and childhood friend of Fritz's, had a less sympathetic view. "I didn't like him," Kienle said on the back deck of his home, on a hill outside town. On an overnight field trip to Switzerland that Kienle took as a fourteen-year-old, Father Mayer, clearly drunk, would close in on each boy at the dinner table and sniff their faces, on the pretext of trying to suss out how much beer each had drunk. "We were young and wanted to drink a lot, and Father Mayer comes and smells us, smells our breath," Kienle said, in English. "You didn't like this." The priest's face "was too near. It was a situation where you think, 'Something's wrong here,' you know?"

Like others I spoke with, Kienle hadn't heard of overt sexual contact—either from Fritz, with whom he had lost touch as a teenager, or from anyone else. But he saw Fritz's story as more than plausible. "At the time, no one ever talked about abuse. This was totally swept under the rug. But as a young person, I always had a feeling, 'There is something wrong with [the *Stadtpfarrer*].' You think, 'Stay away.'"

"Had he tried to touch me," Kienle added, "I would have smashed his face."

Another close childhood friend of Fritz's, who asked not to be named, said he'd spoken to a classmate who had a similarly unnerving experience. The classmate, who like Fritz was not a churchgoer, had been riding his bike near the rectory when Mayer approached and suggested they go elsewhere, the friend said. The request so spooked the boy that he sped off.

A couple of Mayer's defenders told me that in 1974—the year of Fritz's alleged abuse—Mayer would have been in his early seventies, too old for libidinal impulses. But a news story published on his seventieth birthday called him "still very robust," and the bizarre behavior Kienle described took place when the priest was in his mid-seventies. The *Stadtpfarrer* was in relatively good health in 1980 when he was struck by a car, and killed, while walking near his house. He'd retired just two years before.

I asked Kienle whether he and Walter Fritz ever talked about religion.

"He just withdrew if something religious came up," Kienle said. "He stopped talking."

When Fritz left Bad Wurzach in 1978, it was a vanishing. His friends had no warning, no goodbye, no idea where he'd gone. "Nobody knew anything," said one of Fritz's close friends, who felt wounded by his unannounced departure. "It shocked me. I never understood why he left without telling me."

THROUGH A CHILD'S EYES in the 1970s, a hard-drinking priest who plied little boys with chocolate, bought them beer at fourteen, and told them to fake his signature on Communion certificates might have seemed like a charming eccentric. Through an adult's eyes in the twenty-first century, the behavior looks much less benign.

Father Mayer appears to have walked right up to the line with many boys. With Fritz, and perhaps only Fritz, he might have felt he could finally cross it. What ultimately happened remains known only to Fritz and Father Mayer, and only one is alive to tell his story. Fritz has a nose for lies just plausible enough to pass for fact. It was one of the reasons his bogus provenance story—starring two Egyptologists at the Free University—had at first struck scholars as eminently reasonable. He also knew how to pitch a story. In his 2010 letter to the pope, he feigned deference to the Church for the express purpose of eliciting a response. "I know what tone to hit," he'd told me. One theory was that Fritz simply wanted Vatican stationery and signatures for some new hijinks. Another was that his life had reached a breaking point and he refused to ever again be ignored. He knew that the Vatican, a prickly institution, was more apt to listen to an abuse victim who had never lost faith than it was to a seething "fuck you bastards" apostate. Fritz, in other words, might have been willing to use deceptive means for what he saw as a righteous end. He lied a little so the Church would hear a larger truth: that the crisis of children abused by priests was real, and that Pope Benedict ignored their cries at his peril.

INVISIBLE HAND

I met Walter Fritz for the first time on a sunny, windswept Saturday on a small island in Sarasota Bay. It was April 9, 2016. After our many phone interviews over the preceding month, he agreed to have lunch, then be photographed for my *Atlantic* article. He recommended we meet on St. Armands Key, a shopping and dining hub separated from downtown Sarasota by the John Ringling Causeway. It was a forty-five-minute drive from Fritz's North Port home.

I was looking over a menu board outside Café L'Europe, where I'd made a reservation, when Fritz broke through a swarm of tank-topped beachgoers. He had tightly cropped dark hair and wore a beige linen suit with a pocket square, tan wing tips and aviator sunglasses. After so many months of chase, it felt odd to take his measure at such close range. I had no doubt he was also taking mine. When I sat opposite him at the small square table, he got up and moved to my left side, so our elbows almost touched.

When the waitress left, Fritz told me that he admired Karen King's tenacity. She had held her ground in the face of relentless attack, at no small risk to her reputation. But he felt she'd made a series of tactical slips that had exposed his papyrus to undue scrutiny and animus. Among her missteps, he said, was her sensational title for it and her "bombastic" decision to announce it beside the Vatican. "If you know you are going into a confrontation, you just don't provide ammunition to the other side," he explained. "She left certain doors open that she should have not left open." Chief among them was her decision to mention the existence of the 1982 Munro letter, which he worried could be found "fishy."

"I wasn't really willing to give this to her," he explained. "I said, 'You cannot base something on a photocopy, because people can say, "Well, it's a forgery, also," and you have no way of invalidating that.'

Yeah, well, she said, 'I need to still have it and see it.' I said, 'Good,' so I gave her everything I had, and then *of course* she mentioned it.... I said, 'It's just not smart.' I also told her, 'You're the boss, who am I?' "

It occurred to me that King, in refusing to publicly release the Munro letter, had adopted Fritz's own, demonstrably false argument: that a photocopy was of no evidentiary value, and therefore no one need see it. It was an argument that King, in her initial dealings with Fritz, had herself rejected. That she later used it to justify withholding the letter raised the question of whether she had developed her own, undisclosed doubts about its authenticity.

I'd asked Fritz to bring the unsigned, undated note that he said came with Laukamp's papyri—the note reporting Gerhard Fecht's belief that the papyrus was "the sole example" of a text in which Jesus speaks of a wife. He pulled a folded photocopy from an inner pocket of his suit jacket. "It's just a little thing," he said. He set it on the table and held his blue pen over the faint, cursive letters, pointing out words he said he couldn't quite read and suggesting that King had perhaps mis-transcribed them. Was this word "*Jude*" (Jew) or "*Jesus*"? he wondered aloud. Was this word "*Ehe*"—German for "marriage"—or something else? That word looked like "Fecht," but the *F* might as easily be an *H* or a *T*. Fritz was effectively saying, *I never read the words this way; King did.* I later showed the note to my German interpreter, who said King had transcribed the handwriting perfectly. It was two short sentences in basic German. Why was Fritz now making this extravagant show of uncertainty? I was reminded again of the Utah forger Mark Hofmann, who liked to highlight problems with the documents he "discovered" so that his targets could feel smart when they brushed aside his amateur-ish doubts. It seemed more than coincidence that Fritz had singled out as unclear precisely those words—"Fecht," "marriage" and "Jesus"—without which the note would be meaningless. If Karen King got it wrong, I asked, how would *he* transcribe or translate it?

He touched the tip of his blue pen to the blank part of the page and began writing:

"Remark:
Proffessor F."

He wrote the two words at a slug's pace, put a period after the *F*, then abruptly stopped and began stammering. "I need to—I—you know what—I really need to send you a better scan. I—I just copied this and then printed it out. It's not good; it's not good." Fritz might have realized that he was about to produce not just a translation but the sort of independently witnessed handwriting sample that a forgery examiner could have a field day with. The two words he'd penned, before thinking better of it, were not without value. They were another sign of how often he struggled with spelling. His emails, websites and public legal records were strewn with errors, many a result of accidental reversals in the order of letters or numbers. This tendency could explain the Coptic letter mix-up that produced the Wife scrap's mangled Line 6 ("Never does man who is wicked always does bring") and the line-sequence gaffe that betrayed the John fragment. In this case, it wasn't just the extra *f* in "Proffessor" that made this latest example interesting. Fritz's capital *P* bore a striking similarity to the capital *P* in the unsigned note.

Some minutes later, Fritz pulled out a copy of the purported November 1999 contract for his purchase of Laukamp's papyri. Unlike the Munro letter or the unsigned note, this was one document he said he would not give me a copy of, citing what he said was his attorney's advice. Fritz suggested, cryptically, that something in it could expose him to charges that the sale never took place. Its date—when Laukamp was at his wife's deathbed in Berlin—had already done that, I thought. Was there something more?

Fritz declined to elaborate. His lawyer warned that "you shouldn't be giving this out because if somebody really wants to hurt you they can use this as a tool [to] do it in the right way," he said. "Somebody could say, 'The guy never bought that.'"

The document, titled "Contract for Sale of Art," was a one-page, fill-in-the-blanks template. I asked if I could copy it by hand. Fritz had no objection. He grew nervous only at the end, when I started to carefully trace Laukamp's signature. "You're gonna see if the signature is, is his?" he stuttered. "It is his signature. It is his signature. I mean, I don't know if there's in the public record any signature like that." There wasn't. In all half a dozen examples in Florida legal records, Laukamp always signed his name, "Hans Ulrich Laukamp," with both given names and a prominent *p*, at the end of his last name, whose distinctive shape called to mind a lasso. In Fritz's contract, the signature is "H. U. Laukam"—with only initials for his first names and an entirely missing final *p*.

But that was only the most obvious problem. A month earlier, when I asked for clarification on when Fritz had lived in Venice, Florida, he'd sent me a photo of the signed rental contract. The lease's start date—April 1, 2000—aligned with listings for Fritz in old Florida phone books and in several sophisticated electronic databases. But a week or so later, apropos of nothing, Fritz sent me a lengthy email telling me to ignore the date on the lease. He said he had actually lived in the Venice rental since perhaps September 1999, but I wouldn't find a record of it, because he paid the landlady in cash for the first few months and she didn't produce a lease until some months later. The difference between September 1999 and April 2000 seemed so trivial that I wondered why he'd bothered to bring it up.

Only later did I understand. The sales contract for the papyri bore Fritz's Venice address. The trouble was that the date written on it was a full four and a half months before other documents said Fritz lived there. The address of a home one didn't rent until April 1, 2000, should not have appeared on a sales contract for papyri dated November 12, 1999. It was this detail that could damn Fritz in court one day and that he'd tried to retract after sending me the lease. This was no "he said, they said" between him and Laukamp's relatives over Laukamp's whereabouts on the day the contract was signed. This was an irreconcilable difference between two legally binding documents, both of which bore Fritz's signature.

FRITZ'S UNEMPLOYMENT STREAK ENDED in August 2013, when he was offered a job with the State of Florida. I filed a public records request for his job application, hoping to learn more about his professional history. He might lie with impunity to a professor or journalist, but prospective employers held his livelihood in their hands. In the records that the State of Florida sent me, Fritz had made some curious claims about his education. To make sure they weren't one-offs, I requested more documents; if Fritz was interested in government work, he'd probably also filed job applications with local cities and counties. Nearly 180 pages arrived from the Sarasota County Schools, where Fritz had applied for positions ranging from cafeteria monitor and janitor to instructional aide and high-level administrator. Among the papers Fritz submitted was a brazen fake: a 1993 magister's diploma in Egyptology from the

Free University—the degree that everyone, including Fritz himself, told me he never obtained. The diploma said that Fritz had passed his Egyptology magister's exam, administered by "Prof. Dr. Munro," with a grade of "*gut*." Also marked "*gut*" was what the diploma listed as his magister's thesis, a manuscript titled "Remarks on the Dating Inscription on the Amarna Tablet KN 27." I recognized the title. It was the eight-page journal article that he published, to Professor Osing's dismay, in 1991, just before he dropped out of the program. He never wrote a magister's thesis, and as Osing told him, nothing a mere eight pages came anywhere close to counting. Most striking were the names and signatures at the bottom of the Egyptology diploma. They belonged to a Professor Dr. Roggemann and a Professor Dr. Seeman. I hadn't remembered any Egyptology faculty by those names. When I inquired of the university, a faculty member wrote back, "Prof. Seeman was an expert on the Russian literature of the Middle Ages, Prof. Roggemann on the law systems of Eastern Europe."

This patent forgery—one that not even Fritz could disown—bore the same modus operandi as the 1982 Munro letter. Someone had taken what was likely an authentic magister's diploma from the Free University's Institute for the Study of Eastern Europe, which the professors Seeman and Roggemann had led. Then the person placed fake text over its center and photocopied it. Like Munro's letter, it was an image of an image. Like the Gospel of Jesus's Wife itself, it was a cut and paste a couple of mistakes short of perfection. Also like the papyrus fragment, it duped people who should have known better, including the staff of an educational consulting firm. At Fritz's request, Educated Choices LLC of Palm Beach Gardens, Florida, examined the magister's degree and wrote a letter certifying it as "the equivalent of a Master's Degree . . . as awarded by a regionally accredited U.S. university." Fritz had included the firm's letter in his job application to the Sarasota County Schools. When I contacted the company to say that Fritz himself acknowledged never obtaining the degree, Eric Sirota, the firm's vice president, said the firm contacts universities to verify documents only in the 15 to 20 percent of cases where student-submitted records arouse suspicion. "Of the thousands of foreign education credentials that we have evaluated over 25 years in business, this is the first such incident about which we have been made aware," Sirota wrote to me. "No system is perfect."

The Egyptology magister's wasn't the only degree Fritz lied about. On multiple applications to state and local governments in Florida he claimed to have attended Berlin's Technical University from 1987 to 1992, and to have earned a 1992 bachelor's degree there in architecture. When I found his first wife, the claim surprised her. It was she who earned an architecture degree at the Technical University in those years while Fritz was studying Egyptology at the Free University. A Technical University spokesperson later confirmed that no one with Walter Fritz's name and anything close to his birth date was ever registered as a student there, much less an alumnus. I showed his former wife a letter of reference, in her name and on her professional stationery, that Fritz had submitted to a Florida agency with which he was seeking a job. "I did not write this letter," she told me.

If Fritz worried about the consequences of submitting fake degrees and reference letters to government agencies, it didn't show. Florida law makes it a first-degree misdemeanor to misrepresent, with intent to defraud, one's "association with, or academic standing or other progress at, any postsecondary educational institution by falsely making, altering, simulating, or forging a document, degree, certificate, diploma, award, record, letter, transcript, form, or other paper." It is also illegal to misstate a material fact on a government job application. On December 10, 2012, moreover, Fritz signed the Sarasota County School Board's antifraud policy, which bars "the submittal of false or fabricated documentation or information."

The Sarasota County Schools didn't end up hiring Fritz. But the State of Florida—to which he'd sent a résumé listing the bogus bachelor's degree—did. In late August 2013, Fritz showed up for work as an information technology specialist in the DeSoto County office of the state Department of Health. A hiring document designated his position "'sensitive' due to the trust and responsibility required."

When I asked him to explain his faked Egyptology diploma and the nonexistent architecture degree he listed on government job applications, Fritz did something he'd never done before: he declined to comment.

IF WALTER FRITZ HAD FORGED the Gospel of Jesus's Wife, how did he do it? I had first asked him about Mike Grondin's online interlinear of

the Gospel of Thomas in 2016, while reporting my *Atlantic* story. Thanks
to the detective work of the independent scholar Andrew Bernhard,
many specialists saw the Michigan computer programmer's eccentric translation—with its alternating Coptic and English lines—as the
source from which a forger cobbled the phrases on the Wife papyrus.
Fritz told me at the time that he knew of Grondin as "somebody that
translated the Gospel of Thomas." But he said he doubted he ever saw
the translation.

Had he consulted Grondin's interlinear in any way while translating the Wife papyrus? I asked.

"No!" he said. "Absolutely not!"

Three years later, while finishing this book, I told him about Bernhard's newer findings. It wasn't just that the handwritten Coptic on the
Wife papyrus reproduced typos—like the missing *mu*—from Grondin's pdf. It was that Fritz's English interlinear of the Wife fragment
showed signs of "extensive" copying from Grondin's of Thomas, down
to bizarre, one-of-a-kind translations like "abdicate."

Then—as if it were the most natural thing in the world—Fritz
pivoted 180 degrees. Yes, he said, it was true. He "owned" Grondin's
interlinear. He had printed it from the internet, had it on his shelf and
used it to decipher the Wife papyrus.

"I took it from Grondin," he said of his English translation. It was
amazing, he marveled, how much a simple Google search could turn up.
"It was just basically patchwork," he said of his translation technique.

"You know what?" he recalled thinking as he perused Grondin's
interlinear. "*That* matches." But his reliance on Grondin's pdf to *translate* the Gospel of Jesus's Wife didn't mean he forged it, he said. "It
doesn't mean I took the *gospel* from Grondin."

This argument required one to believe that Fritz—who stumbled
through a single semester of Coptic—could correctly parse the *scriptio
continua* on the Wife papyrus; identify parts of each line as matches
for haphazard bits of the Gospel of Thomas; then, despite this feat of
linguistic surgery, decide to use an amateur's interlinear of Thomas to
hunt and peck his way toward a translation of the Wife papyrus. Still
more improbably, it required one to accept the matching *Coptic* errors
in both texts as pure happenstance. Lastly, one needed to believe that
Fritz—who had already fabricated and recanted two stories about the
translation—was now telling the truth.

FRITZ HAD LED KING to believe that he'd contacted her because he needed a translation of his papyrus. It was now clear that exactly the opposite had occurred. King had a photograph of his fragment for nearly a year but told him she had managed "no real success." She taught Coptic at Harvard but was not a linguist. A previously untranslated text in *scriptio continua* had apparently strained her capabilities. When she apologized for her failure, Fritz sent King an interlinear that split the unbroken strings of Coptic letters into distinct words and set English ones beneath them. He didn't tell King the interlinear was his, much less that it was a patchwork of Grondin's. ("I was not aware of the direct parallels" to the Gospel of Thomas, he had lied in an October 2011 email to her.) Still, only after she'd seen his translation did she pronounce herself "able to make some real progress." By every indication, she had needed *his* help with the translation—rather than he, hers.

Fritz never imagined it would unfold this way. "I would have expected somebody of that stature to simply take this piece and read it like a newspaper," he said. "I thought it would be a cakewalk; then it turned out it wasn't. That's what prompted me to send her the translation, and I fully expected it to be ridiculed." Yet to his surprise, "she made speedy progress," he said. "It's always easy to take somebody else's [translation] and correct it. But it's very difficult to come up with your own if no one has ever read or translated it."

Unless, apparently, you were Walter Fritz.

WHEN WE FIRST STARTED TALKING, Fritz claimed to have no stake in the extraordinary message his papyrus ushered into the world. Later I saw he cared deeply. He had felt stupid as a boy—"a dumb motherfucker," he said—for failing to grasp the mysteries of the Church. The thing he said happened behind the left altar door at St. Verena Church was the most terrible of those mysteries. But others, like Jesus's virgin birth and transubstantiation, were just as confounding. As a teenager, he thought that the only way to decrypt these puzzles was to become a priest. "If you can't beat them, join them," Fritz told me, darkly, of what he said was his state of mind at the time. "Coupled with some weird, unconscious attraction to the abusers, which was probably the result of an emotional state where I felt vulnerable and was in need of closeness to those who seemed to possess powers which I at that age did not have."

But as he grew older, the quest to understand Catholicism's spiritual truths curdled into revulsion at their bankruptcy. "I thought I didn't understand because I didn't have the ability to understand," he told me. Later, "I said, 'You know what? I didn't understand because there *is* nothing to understand. There's nothing to understand because it's bull crap.'" Among the Church's many dubious claims, Fritz said, was that the Gospels of Matthew, Mark, Luke and John were truer accounts of Jesus's life than the Gnostic gospels. He pointed to the fact that almost no papyri bearing the canonical gospels have been carbon-dated, in part because of the physical damage such tests would inflict on seminal New Testament manuscripts—damage that institutions like the Vatican Library would never countenance. At Columbia University, Fritz noted, the same scientists who identified his fragment's ink as carbon black were developing a nondestructive dating method he believed could upend the accepted chronology of biblical literature. Such tests, Fritz contended, could well show that most of the Gnostic texts were composed *before* the canonical gospels, making them better witnesses to the historical Jesus—a view that virtually no serious scholars share. (Conservative and liberal scholars alike told me that the dates of surviving copies, even when known, are not how they determine the order in which gospels were first composed.)

"All that discussion that the canonical gospels were way before anything else—that's utter bullshit," Fritz told me. "The Gnostic texts that allow women a discipleship and see Jesus more as a spiritual person and not as a demigod—these texts are probably the more relevant ones."

The Roman Catholic Church invented priestly celibacy in the Middle Ages out of nothing holier, Fritz argued, than financial self-interest: popes wanted to safeguard church assets against the inheritance claims of priests' widows and children. But the costs were great. If priests could marry, Fritz told me, "they wouldn't have to abuse kids."

Fritz's spiritual life today was a warp and weft of handwoven fibers. He found a certain kind of inspiration, he said, in the Hindu guru Ramana Maharshi, whose philosophies of self-inquiry as the road to redemption—and of the world as an illusion—paralleled those of the Gnostics. Another strand sprung, it seemed, from texts depicting the transgressive sex lives of the ancients. "Don't forget my favoured prophet, Ho's Ea, the expert on prostitution," Fritz wrote in an online porn forum, making a double entendre of the Hebrew visionary's name. "'I will not punish your daughters when they turn to prostitution, nor your wifes [*sic*] when they commit adultery.' Hosea 4:14." In a seeming dig at the hypocrisy of the holy, Fritz added, "Always remember: To the pure, all things are pure.... Titus 1:15." (Secret Mark, incidentally, quotes the same verse from Titus.)

Another piece of the quilt was Fritz's second wife. She had been prophetic, he said, about everything from people's motivations to imminent traffic accidents. She's normally a terrible speller, he said, but her automatic writing was almost letter-perfect. She even lapsed some-times into a language he suspected was Aramaic, the tongue of Jesus.

When had he first heard her speak this mysterious language?

"During sex," Fritz said.

IT WAS PERHAPS NOTHING MORE than coincidence, but I noticed later that the date of Fritz's first email to King—July 9, 2010—was 114 years, to the day, after German scholars announced their discovery of the Gospel of Mary. The figure 114 is instantly recognizable to experts on the noncanonical gospels. It's the number of Jesus's sayings in the Gos-pel of Thomas, the text from which scholars believe a modern forger harvested the Gospel of Jesus's Wife. Thomas's 114th saying, moreover, happens to contain the most notorious instance of misogyny in early Christian literature: "Simon Peter said to them, 'Let Mary leave us, for women are not worthy of life.' Jesus said, 'I myself shall lead her in order to make her male.'" The email's timing, if deliberate, was a stroke of genius by a man who'd already shown himself a master of minimalism. With a single number that must have been little more than an inside joke, he had linked his fake gospel to the authentic ones with which he'd built it (Thomas) and lured his mark (Mary).

But Fritz spurned all of my theories of motivation. He told me of the alleged rape not because it inspired the Wife papyrus, he said, but because he feared the Vatican might otherwise leak word of it to dis-credit the fragment. To admit motive, of course, was to admit forgery, and Fritz had no plans to confess "to some story of a brilliant genius (me) who forged a manuscript in order to expose the bias and prejudice in the Catholic Church, and the utter ignorance of scholars," he said. "I appreciate your offer to make me look really good and intelligent in this context, but no, thank you!"

AFTER THE WAITRESS CLEARED OUR PLATES, Fritz leaned across the table and told me to shut off my voice recorder. I obliged but continued taking notes. He wanted to keep this next part between the two of us, but I didn't agree, and he continued talking anyway—both then and later in the day, when he returned to the subject after letting me turn my recorder back on. He had a proposition. He had no talent for storytelling, he said, but he possessed the erudition to turn out hundreds of pages of background for a novel he wanted me to write. Instead of doing my own research, which could take years, I would rely on his. "I'd do all the legwork for you, and I wouldn't want anything in return." The book's subject, he said, would be "the Mary Magdalene story," the "suppression of the female element" in the Church, and the primacy of the Gnostic gospels, "maybe accumulating to a thriller story in the present." In three to four months, he said, he could write me the equivalent of *Holy Blood, Holy Grail*, the book of speculative history whose authors unsuccessfully sued Dan Brown's publisher for plagiarism.

"People don't want to read Karen King's book" on Gnosticism or the books of other academics, Fritz went on. They were too dense. "People want something they can take to bed. The facts alone, they don't really matter. What matters is entertainment." The book would be a runaway best seller, he assured me. He leaned across the table and shook his head, as if boggling at the financial possibilities. "It's going to sell like hotcakes, I know it," he said. "If you ever want to do it, I'm so convinced this would be a major success.

"A million copies in the first month or so." A collaboration of the sort he envisioned "could really make a big difference." But one would need to fabricate. "You have to make a lot of stuff up," he said. "You cannot just present facts.

"The truth is not absolute," he added. "The truth depends on perspectives, surroundings."

I let him go on for a while, but I was stupefied. I was investigating a suspected forgery, and the man at its center was asking me to "make a lot of stuff up" for a new project in which he'd be my eager accomplice.

The proposal was so tone-deaf that I wondered whether he was clueless, incorrigible or up to something I couldn't yet discern. I reminded him that I was a journalist, not a novelist. I wrote fact, not fiction. Nor could I relinquish research to or accept services from the subject of a story. But I did have a question. Because the ideas underlying this hypothetical book would be entirely Fritz's, what role would the Walter Fritz character play in the story?

He gave me a quizzical look. "I wouldn't have a role in it," he said. He would be the silent partner, the invisible hand. As I walked back to my car, I realized with something like a shudder that Fritz was trying to draw me into a trap from which my credibility might never recover. I knew enough about his dealings with King and Laukamp to recognize all the signs: the request for secrecy, the strategic self-effacement, the use of other people for his own enigmatic ends.

Fame and fortune would rain down on me, he'd promised. All I had to do was lower my guard and trust him with all the important details.

BACK HOME IN WASHINGTON, I couldn't shake the suspicion that Fritz had turned his mirrors on me. The longer I thought about our lunch conversation, the more I questioned whether he had merely repackaged things he read about me online. In a media interview after a previous book, I talked about a former newspaper editor, a mentor who encouraged storytelling, or "narrative," in journalism. "People don't curl up at night with a great set of facts," I quoted the editor as telling me. The editor's point wasn't to invent facts or renounce research, both of which are firing offenses in journalism. It was to use novelistic technique—plot, character, scene—to tell deeply researched true stories. When Fritz said "people want something they can take to bed" and "the facts alone, they don't really matter," was he coyly enumerating his own philosophy of forgery? Or was he baiting his trap with ideas he thought I already held dear? Was he proposing a kind of *Holy Blood / Da Vinci Code* hybrid because the originals resonated with him, or only because I'd seemed focused on Brown's book as a roadmap to the forgery?

If the truth could be found, I suspected, it was in the footprints the Fritzes had left when their papyri were still an inside joke. Many of the biggest clues so far—Grondin's pdf of the Gospel of Thomas, Fritz's premature registration of www.gospelofjesuswife.com, his wife's porn sites and eBay papyrus pendants—had turned up on the web. I decided to take a deeper look at their online lives.

The Jenny Seemore websites had all come down by 2015. Though web pages and sample videos could still be found in repositories like the Internet Archive, the full library of clips—for paying members only—seemed beyond reach. What I had failed to consider were the site's many former subscribers. I began searching all-purpose, file-sharing websites and noticed that fans had uploaded hundreds of Jenny Seemore videos, possibly her entire oeuvre. I was interested in movies the couple had posted closest to September 18, 2012, the day Karen King announced her discovery. It took a few days, but I eventually found them. The most striking was a six-minute-and-six-second video posted six days after King's announcement. The couple had filmed it in early June but had held it for an anomalously long four months. It was their first upload after King unveiled the papyrus.

Despite its colorful title—"Fucking Jen's Fat Cow-Udders"—the video depicted Fritz and his wife in an uncharacteristically tame sex act. What caught my attention, besides the absence of other men, was the setting: it was filmed inside the couple's home office. The video's focal point was their lovemaking, which unfolded in the center of the frame. But my eye kept drifting to the floor-to-ceiling bookcase behind them. All of the books were upright, except for one, which lay on its side. The video's medium resolution made the title of the sideways book hard to see, but something about the red-and-black typeface on its spine looked familiar. I restarted the clip and noticed that the camera lingered on that corner of the bookshelf for a moment, before panning away. I paused the video, took a screenshot and zoomed in. The book, I could see now, was *Holy Blood, Holy Grail*. The couple's use of this book as a prop—rather than Brown's—was fitting. *The Da Vinci Code* was make-believe. *Holy Blood, Holy Grail*, on the other hand, claimed to be fact. It trafficked in the haze of grays where Fritz felt most at home, a fog in which myth, history and conjecture were so fused that one struggled to tell them apart.

Fritz framed the opening seconds of the movie in such a way that his half-naked wife and the spine of *Holy Blood* formed the base of an invisible triangle. At the top of the triangle—sitting awkwardly on a high shelf—is a photo of Mrs. Fritz in a white dress and Mr. Fritz in a black tuxedo, at what appears to be their wedding. That one or both saw *Holy Blood*'s themes through a personal lens was clear from another book on the same shelf: *The Grail Tarot*, a 2007 volume that, according to its jacket, "relates the quest for the sacred Christian relic to our desire to understand the puzzle of our own lives."

THE GOSPEL OF JESUS'S WIFE, I came to believe, had begun as a joke and ended as an exorcism. It was a settling of scores with all the male authority figures who had robbed Fritz of his potential: his father, Walter Off, who wasn't around to raise him; Father Matthias Mayer, who allegedly raped him; Peter Munro, Gerhard Fecht and Jürgen Osing, the Free University Egyptologists who had seen him as a middling student instead of the prodigy he felt himself to be. Then there was Hans-Ulrich Laukamp. Fritz had first portrayed him to me as a friend, a guileless auto-parts maker whom Fritz rescued from Herzsprung's predations. In later conversations, however, Fritz lashed out at Laukamp, with emotion I hadn't seen before. He accused Laukamp of taking 100,000 euros from ACMB's corporate accounts for Laukamp's grandson's education. Laukamp, who was nearing death, was within his rights to do so, Fritz said, but it hastened ACMB's bankruptcy and left it unable to pay employees, including $5,000 of Fritz's own salary. "I said, 'I don't understand how you can do this to people who were loyal to you for so many years,'" Fritz told me. "He said, 'Well, it's too late now.'... That was pretty much when I got upset and said, 'I'm not doing anything for you anymore.... You're on your own.'"

Each of these betrayers was assigned a role in his provenance story. Fritz turned his deadbeat father into a swaggering hunter of African game and ancient manuscripts who sowed his boyhood interest in antiquities. He cast the Free University as the school whose experts authenticated the papyri. Laukamp was written into the role of simple-minded collector, the rube who sold him the Wife papyrus for a song. Father Mayer was perhaps the only character who played himself. In life, each man had failed Fritz. In death, as ghosts in a tale told by their victim, they would atone.

Fritz had reached a breaking point by 2010. His father was dying, which foregrounded the decades they would never get back. The closest thing Fritz had to a career—a decade-long run as an auto-parts salesman—had sputtered to a close. The Great Recession was taking a toll on his adult websites, and competitors were moving in. He couldn't sell his house, even at a fraction of his original asking price. And his attempts to sell papyri, whatever their source, were hitting a wall. After receiving a cold call and some images from Fritz, Sam Fogg, a prominent London manuscripts dealer, informed him that his collection—ancient tax receipts, business letters and the like—were "run-of-the-mill, boring," and thus of scant market value. "I said, 'Look, this is all great, but the stuff that's really exciting is religious material,'" Fogg recalled. "I must have said, 'Get me some of that, get me the earliest bit of Saint Matthew or something.'" He said he never heard back.

Fritz "was on the ropes for quite a while," said Renate Böhm, his father's live-in girlfriend of many years. Fritz told her "he was writing applications and was very concerned about getting a good job."

"He just felt like he couldn't get a decent job in Florida," a North Port friend, Jennifer Cohen, told me. "They were trying to figure out what they were going to do." The Fritzes talked of restarting their lives in Germany. Their bank balances had fallen far enough that Fritz began hunting deer and boar for meat and taking seasonal work in the warehouse of a neighbor's fireworks company.

Then came the Church pedophilia scandal in Germany, which hit Fritz when he was already down. It might have revived memories of the alleged rape at a moment when Fritz had a panoramic view of the mess it had made of his life. At a time of vulnerability echoing the one in Bad Wurzach four decades earlier, another south German clergyman—Pope Benedict—was failing to understand the toll of abuse on children and on the adults they became.

IF THE PROVENANCE STORY was a reckoning with the men in his life, the papyrus itself was an homage to a woman. I had first thought that its "Mary" was a stand-in for Fritz's own wife. But after my visits to Bad Wurzach, I decided that the more likely inspiration was Fritz's mother. Inge was a self-sufficient, headstrong woman who, like Magdalene, was unfairly seen as a sinner because of the false assumptions people made about her sex life. Fritz told me that his mother "probably had a bad reputation" while dating Willi Götz, the married businessman. But the truth—the one most didn't know—was that she would never be bought. Götz asked her for marriage, which would have left Inge and her children financially secure for life. But she rebuffed him, Fritz said, because Götz refused to swear off other lovers. "My mother is one of very few people I know who persistently has always tried to do the right thing," Fritz told me. "She always took the hard road." Götz "probably thought he had all the rights [to have more affairs] because he was such a good catch. My mother was an absolutely straight flyer: 'No, I'm not going to marry a guy who cheats.'"

Inge went as far as to return a magnificent ring Götz gave her. "Can you imagine?" a friend of hers, Anna Leins, told my interpreter. "So stupid! It was peanuts for him. But she was too proud to keep it." Inge also ditched the Bad Wurzach women's boutique that Götz helped her start. She had given it the English name Lady In, but the lady soon walked out, even though it cost her the friendship of the woman with whom she had founded the store. An acquaintance of Inge's told me, "*Sie hat ihren Mann gestanden*," a German expression meaning "She didn't need a man." A photo from the period captured Inge's fierceness. She is astride one of Götz's Arabian horses, gripping the reins with a look of feral concentration as the animal rears, twists its neck and bares its teeth. Götz had given Inge a horse as a gift early in their courtship. Its name, according to Götz's son, was Al-Qadr, Arabic for "divine destiny." When Inge fled Götz and Bad Wurzach in the late 1970s, she left Al-Qadr, too. If there was such a thing as destiny, it would be of no one's making but her own.

INGE'S FREE SPIRIT was both blessing and curse to her only son. Men came and went from her life, leaving Walter to compete for her affections and fight for his own standing. He begged her, as a teenager, to let him move in with his father, whom he didn't know but came to idolize. "Inge tried to explain that it wasn't a good idea," recalled Lydia Jakubith, a friend of Inge's from Bad Wurzach. "But he wouldn't listen." So Inge enlisted her disciplinarian father—Walter's grandfather—"to explain to Walter what his father was like." That ended the discussion but not Walter's longing. "She always had the upper hand," Jakubith said of Inge. "Even while growing up, Walter couldn't pretend he was the man of the house. She was strong enough to confront him."

It was perhaps no wonder that Fritz's attitude toward women vacillated between deification (his strong-willed mother, his visionary wife, the spouses of Roman emperors) and degradation (his view of women as "holes," his porn sites' fetishization of "slut wives," "whores" and "disgusting FUCKPIGS"). The hotwife fetish—in which he watches, emasculated, as strangers steal the woman he worships—was his first bid to reconcile these warring impulses. His second, more mature effort, I believe, was the Gospel of Jesus's Wife. "You have to tackle your fears and phobias head-on to be able to overcome them," he said of the attitude he cultivated after the alleged abuse. "I was always the kid that actually touched the spider in order to overcome arachnophobia, because I never wanted to allow myself to be afraid of anything."

Karen King thought the fragment's "Mary" was Mary Magdalene but later decided the text was ambiguous. The "Mary," she wrote, could have been either Jesus's mother or his wife, and then only possibly Magdalene. I believe that Fritz saw his mother as the resolution of all three. *Tamaay*—"my mother"—is the only Coptic word on both sides of the papyrus, and in each case it occupies a place of honor, on the first line. "My mother gave me life," reads the front. "My mother," reads the back, where it is followed, on the next line, by a solitary word: "three."

Fritz was never a believing Christian. But the Gnostic gospels gave him the vocabulary to simultaneously skewer the Church for its sins and absolve his mother of hers.

FEELING OF CALM

The Atlantic published my magazine story on its website on the evening of June 15, 2016, and then, in print, across fifteen pages of its July/August 2016 issue. Many readers pinned the blame squarely on the Harvard scholar at its center. "King was [so] blinded by her selfish egotistic wish to rewrite history that she got herself all covered in shame by an animal," wrote one reader.

"I don't think anyone expects infallibility," wrote another, "but she was duped by a nut job faking a text in her academic specialization. Or she knew and she tried to dupe everyone else."

"In her defense," countered another reader, "he does sound like an unusually skilled con-man." One man compared King to the UFO-chasing FBI agent from the TV series *The X-Files*. "I feel sorry for her," he wrote. "Like Fox Mulder, she wanted to believe."

I EMAILED KING A LINK to the story as soon as it posted. "I'm still very interested in your perspectives," I wrote. At 1:44 p.m. the next day, the phone rang. I saw King's name on the caller ID and took a deep breath.

"Who could imagine?" she said of the article. "It's both fascinating and helpful."

Had anything she read changed her view of the papyrus?

"It tips the balance toward forgery," she told me.

King's reaction to the article—after four years of defending the fragment against skeptics—made international news. *The Boston Globe* ran a story atop its front page. Reports appeared in the Associated Press, *The Washington Post* and the website of *The New York Times,* among a raft of news sites around the world.

King told me she had exchanged numerous emails with Fritz, met him at Harvard in December 2011, and had a stack of legal documents he'd signed authorizing tests on the papyrus. But after reading the *Atlantic* article, she said, she realized she barely knew him. Fritz told her he knew a little Coptic but never mentioned his formal training in Egyptology or his years at the Free University, she said. He had presented himself as a "family man" who enjoyed trips to Disney World and whose wife was involved in charity. As for his livelihood, he gave King the impression he was living off wealth from the sale of a former business. (AnneMarie Luijendijk, who also knew his name, later told me that he'd described himself as a car salesman.)

"I had no idea about this guy, obviously," King said. "He lied to me."

FRITZ HAD OFFERED to donate the Wife papyrus to Harvard, which would likely have netted him a tax break. In exchange, he wanted the university to buy his other Coptic, Arabic and Greek papyri. A source had given me the PowerPoint files Fritz put together for his sales pitch to Harvard, with photos of nearly a hundred papyri. Scholars I showed them to said that many of the documentary pieces—ancient letters, receipts and lists—looked genuine. But the small minority that claimed magical or religious content were mostly, if not all, fakes. King said that Fritz identified only two sources for the papyri: half a dozen were Laukamp's; the rest had belonged to his father. Both stories now appeared false.

King, who saw Fritz's offer as generous, shopped his papyri around Harvard. But no one bit. "When I talked to the library people and the lawyers, too, they were like, 'Why should Harvard buy this?'" she recalled.

Fritz then agreed to lend the Wife and John papyri to Harvard for ten years but declined Harvard's pleas that he insure them, even after learning that Harvard itself would not indemnify him against damage or loss. Douglas Gragg, the divinity school librarian, blushed at the recollection. "Of course!" Gragg said when we met in his office one afternoon. "'What would I want to insure junk for?' he was probably thinking. 'What would I insure worthless fragments for?' He wasn't interested in spending any money on it, which I suppose in retrospect could have been a sign." An insurance appraisal was also apt to bring new, outside scrutiny to his collection.

After *The Wall Street Journal* published the May 2014 op-ed about the fishy Gospel of John fragment, King said she urged Fritz to go public. "I told him I was getting a lot of flak for not giving out his name," she said, "and his response was, 'Well, you took this on.'" (Fritz had mentioned this particular request during our lunch in Sarasota, portraying his refusal as a favor to the Harvard scholar. "It's not going to look good," he said of his rationale. "Help from me might not serve you well.")

In interviews with reporters in 2012, King said the owner wanted anonymity because "he doesn't want to be hounded by people who want to buy" the papyrus. Now, four years later, she offered a very different explanation: fear of the press. "When it became clear to him the story would go big," King told me, "he said he didn't want to have a lot of reporters on his front step."

If Fritz insisted she keep reporters at bay, why didn't she conduct her own, independent inquiry into the owner and his provenance story? Why didn't she help scholars willing to discreetly do it for her?

"Your article has helped me see that provenance can be investigated," she told me.

But King had not forsaken all hope. It was theoretically possible, she said, for the Wife papyrus to be authentic even if its backstory was a lie and even if Fritz's John fragment was—as she now believed—"clearly a forgery." Yes, she was now inclined to call the Wife papyrus a fake, too, but only a *probable* one. She would need scientific proof, or a confession, for a final determination. (It wasn't until later, when I began work on this book, that I discovered additional evidence: the forged Egyptology diploma Fritz submitted to the Sarasota County Schools and his admitted ownership—and use—of Grondin's interlinear.)

King said she had no plans to confront Fritz over his lies and what they had cost her. "I see no point," she said. "I'm finding myself not even really angry. I'm mostly just relieved. I think the truth always makes me calm."

AMONG SCHOLARS, opinions about King's conduct covered the waterfront. At one extreme was the Brown University Egyptologist Leo Depuydt, who, two days after my article, told *The Boston Globe,* "I see that King is still at Harvard. Unbelievable." Others expressed sympathy. "Set before Karen seemed an impossible standard to which other academics are not held: You must always be right; you must have handled everything perfectly," said Carly Daniel-Hughes, a Concordia University professor and former student of King's. "Scholars cannot be shielded from the fantastic machinations of a disturbed pseudo-Egyptologist bent on materializing the plot of *The Da Vinci Code*." King's missteps might have ended the career of a junior professor, some said, but they didn't seem to rise to the level of deliberate misconduct. In any case, King was insulated by academic tenure and a long record of respected scholarship.

"The mission of Harvard Divinity School, its faculty, and higher education more generally is to pursue truth through scholarship, investigation, and vigorous debate," the school's dean, David Hempton, said in a statement responding to the *Atlantic* article. "HDS is therefore grateful to the many scholars, scientists, technicians, and journalists who have devoted their expertise to understanding the background and meaning of the papyrus fragment. HDS welcomes these contributions and will continue to treat the questions raised by them with all the seriousness they deserve."

Three years later, at the earliest age permitted under at least one Harvard program, King, at sixty-five, began a phased retirement. Asked about its timing and terms, a divinity school spokesman said, "as a matter of policy, the School does not comment on personnel matters." At a panel at a biblical studies conference in November 2019, King received a standing ovation as she tearfully accepted a book of essays that colleagues—many of them former students—had published in her honor on the occasion of her retirement. She told the audience that its title, *Re-Making the World*, put her in mind of the seven days of creation in Genesis. "I am looking forward to that Sabbath rest, preferably in some quiet cabin far away in the mountains somewhere," she said. "But so far I'm only at the afternoon on Day Six...Lots and lots of work left to be done."

After Fritz's unmasking, many colleagues had been puzzled by King's incuriosity about the fragment's history. Some couldn't decide which was more troubling: her statement that she was "not particularly" interested in seeing my findings before *The Atlantic* published them, or her remark afterward that she didn't realize an object's past could be studied. How could a historian, one at Harvard no less, have failed to see provenance as subject to investigation? Provenance, after all, was nothing more than history—King's own scholarly discipline.

ACT 5

THE DOWNTURNED BOOK OF REVELATIONS

GJW tells us nothing about early Christianity. GJW does, however, tell us something about ourselves—about both our moment in religious history and our moment as an academic field.

—religion scholar Janet Spittler

Histpry, in the traditional view, answers a single question: What happened? It is a dispassionate record of people, places and events, set in the context of a particular time.

But what if some scholars saw history as a kind of fiction? What if they doubted the very possibility of facts? In this view, every historical account—every piece of writing, for that matter—was a kind of stealthy sales pitch, a self-serving tale that promoted the interests of a particular individual or group. The same held for reading. Whether Mary Magdalene was a prostitute or an apostle, for instance, turned less on "what happened" than on which camp—pro-sinner or pro-saint—best publicized its interpretation. The true story of Mary Magdalene, Karen King once wrote, "has little to do with the new evidence from Egypt," like the gospels of Mary and Philip. Rather, the growing ranks of women with jobs and advanced degrees made new interpretations possible, and the advent of mass printing put these rereadings into more hands. Modern readers could thus remake the past for their own times, without fear of contradicting any underlying reality.

As fodder for philosophical discussion and classroom debate, this postmodern school of thought—which gained traction in the 1980s, while King was in graduate school—has had enormous and perhaps rightful influence. But what if a scholar were so steeped in its principles that he or she used them in situations for which they were never quite intended? The question of what a phrase like "Jesus said to them, 'My wife...'" means could well have multiple, equally valid answers for different readers in different eras. But the question of whether the fragment is authentic has only one. Either it was written in antiquity, or it wasn't; either it was part of some larger manuscript, or it wasn't.

The same was true of provenance. Either the fragment had a previous owner named Laukamp who showed it to Munro and Fecht, or it did not. Yet the more I read of King's work, the more I wondered how much of a distinction she made between literary analysis and historical investigation.

"Attractive as the fantasy of pure objectivity...is, and as much as we mortals might desire fixed and unchanging truth(s), history can supply neither," King wrote in one treatise. "History," she wrote elsewhere, "is not about truth but about power relations." In a major theoretical work published the same year as her Mary Magdalene book, King argued that historians' first order of business should be to abandon "the association between truth and chronology." The idea that people closer in time to an event make better witnesses—a bedrock of police work, news reporting and traditional history—was suspect. That certain gospels were composed nearer to Jesus's day, she writes, doesn't in itself make them a clearer window into the views of his earliest followers. "The new physics, from relativity to subatomic particle studies, is in the process of reconceptualizing the Western construction of time," she explained. "This new form of time is discontinuous and unpatterned; it is not serious, real, or true." Which was partly why the history she wrote was less concerned with any objective past than with "enlarging one's imaginative universe" and adding texture to the way people think about religion. If this more enlightened view of history prevailed, she wrote, "then one need never say no to a story, a song, a poem that gives life, heartens, teaches, or consoles, and need never fail to call it true."

It wasn't just that any heartfelt story could be called true. It was that readers could take part in embellishing it, in making it their own. Because so many gospel stories were open-ended, she wrote, they "put pressure" on readers to become "authors and even characters." They invite the reader—a "writer to be"—"to continue the story, tie up loose ends, fill in gaps, or create side paths," which included "adding episodes, filling out the fate of characters [and] wholesale rewriting." She called facts "little tyrants" and accused people who put too much stock in them of "fact fundamentalism."

To understand how young King was when these views took hold, one needed to return to her first year at the University of Montana. King was a twenty-year-old transfer student and newly declared religious studies major when she fell under the spell of Robert W. Funk, a star Montana professor who was equal parts scholar and larger-than-life impresario. Funk was nearly three decades her senior, and King never so much as took a class with him. But the introverted Montana girl and the gregarious religion professor appear to have formed a powerful intellectual bond. Funk, then executive secretary of the Society of Biblical Literature, offered her a student job at his publishing house and tutored her in Greek on van rides to academic conferences. He later wrote her a letter of recommendation for graduate school. "They obviously had a very special relationship," Andrew Scrimgeour, a long-time colleague of Funk's who is working on a biography of him, told me. In June 1981, after King entered the PhD program at Brown, Funk invited her to a small but fateful brainstorming session at his home on Montana's Blackfoot River. Funk wanted to shake up biblical scholarship, to usher its most exciting new findings into the benighted sanctuaries of the traditional church. "He proceeded to fill page after page with fresh ideas," recalled King, who was the only student to attend. "It was exhilarating and transformative. I never looked at our profession the same way again."

King was among ten or so supporters whom Funk persuaded to be start-up investors in Polebridge Press, the for-profit publisher that Funk would use to spread his ideas and those of like-minded scholars, including King. Together the ten contributed about $100,000. "We'll own it so nobody can fire us," Funk told them.

Four years later, on March 21, 1985, King sat with some twenty-nine other religion scholars—all male—as Funk welcomed them to the inaugural meeting of the Jesus Seminar, a project that would become his greatest legacy. For too long, fundamentalists and televangelists had monopolized the imagination of churchgoers, Funk told the group. It was time for accredited scholars to strike back. Their mission would be nothing short of radical: to use the latest historical methods to show that the real Jesus was someone other than the figure of New Testament myth. They would shatter the wall between ivory tower and church by carrying out their work in open meetings where the public and the news media would be warmly welcomed.

"We are about to embark on a momentous enterprise," Funk told the Jesus Seminar's charter members in an after-dinner speech at the faculty club of the University of California, Berkeley. "The religious establishment has not allowed the intelligence of high scholarship to pass through pastors and priests to a hungry laity, and the radio and TV counterparts of educated clergy have traded in platitudes and pieties and played on the ignorance of the uninformed. A rude and rancorous awakening lies ahead.

"What we are about takes courage," he continued. "We are probing what is most sacred to millions, and hence we will constantly border on blasphemy. We must be prepared to forebear [*sic*] the hostility we shall provoke. At the same time, our work, if carefully and thoughtfully wrought, will spell liberty for other millions."

It was less a scholarly lecture than a call to arms. King, who had just begun her first academic job, at Occidental College, would become one of Funk's most committed protégés. Over the ensuing decades, she would travel the country hosting daylong events for the Jesus Seminar and the Westar Institute, the nonprofit that Funk had founded to oversee it. The public paid admission, and the institute videotaped King's talks for resale, calling her a "Westar Star." King was more than just talent. She was a financial investor and longtime board member of Funk's press, which would later publish both her PhD dissertation and her book on the Gospel of Mary. When Funk died in 2005, King was the only colleague quoted in his *New York Times* obituary.

At their public meetings, Jesus Seminar scholars dropped colored beads into a voting box to decide which of Jesus's sayings were genuinely his and which the later inventions of gospel writers. (The colors were red for "That's Jesus!" and black for "There's been some mistake," with pink and gray for points between.) The seminar decided that "eighty-two percent of the words ascribed to Jesus in the gospels were not actually spoken by him." (None of Jesus's sayings in the Gospel of John made the cut. The only part of the Lord's Prayer to survive the knife were the words "Our Father.") The seminar titled its 1993 book *The Five Gospels* because of its daring inclusion of the Gospel of Thomas. Its subtitle—"What Did Jesus Really Say?"—was more provocative still. The book became a best seller.

The Jesus unearthed by the seminar's bead counting was a "secular sage" who slyly needled the powerful and championed the weak but didn't walk on water, rise from the dead or see himself as a messiah. He was a man, not an apocalyptic prophet, and was crucified for being a public nuisance, not because he was the Son of God. Midway through its 1993 book, I discovered, the Jesus Seminar reported a related finding:

"Jesus did not advocate celibacy. A majority of the Fellows doubted, in fact, that Jesus himself was celibate. They regard it as probable that he had a special relationship with at least one woman, Mary of Magdala." A decade before *The Da Vinci Code*—and two decades before the Gospel of Jesus's Wife—a group that counted King as its leading light was publicly broadcasting its view that Jesus was married, possibly to Mary Magdalene.

THE JESUS SEMINAR'S WORK drew precisely the reaction Funk had anticipated. It wound up in TV specials and on the covers of newspapers and magazines. Liberal Protestants embraced its work as spiritually refreshing and invited its members to speak at their churches. But the backlash from scholars and traditional clergy was fierce. Critics accused it of pseudoscience, ideological bias and contempt for Christians who saw the gospels as testaments of faith, not of history. The Emory University scholar Luke Timothy Johnson, one of the seminar's chief detractors, called it "a far better example of media manipulation than of serious scholarship": "Americans love elections: Is Jesus going to win as messiah or not, tune in tomorrow and see how the seminar votes." Though the seminar had no shortage of respected scholars, faculty from Ivy League schools and other strongholds of New Testament research—like Duke and Chicago—were conspicuously absent from its charter membership. One of its most famous fellows was the filmmaker Paul Verhoeven (*RoboCop, Basic Instinct*), who once planned to synthesize the group's findings into a film called *Jesus, the Man*. When Funk described Jesus as a "party animal," "social deviant," or "perhaps the first stand-up Jewish comic," critics saw a scholar who leaned perhaps too heavily on provocation in his quest for what he called "a new narrative of Jesus, a new gospel, if you will."

AT PUBLIC EVENTS, Jesus Seminar colleagues introduced King as royalty. "By the end of the day," promised one emcee, "you will be using our favorite nickname for her: Not Dr. Karen King, but Karen *the* King." Another emcee called her "the Prophet of the Unknowable God." (King's prominent role in the Jesus Seminar went wholly unmentioned in coverage of the Gospel of Jesus's Wife.) Funk, for his part, celebrated

King as "the principal advocate for what she calls 'the radical historicization of Christianity'"—the depiction of its origins as the messy work of human beings rather than an act of God. "She wonders what is left to us now that the transcendent essence of Christianity has evaporated," Funk wrote. "Her answer: We have the history of Christianity itself."

Some observers saw "history" as code for anti-God. "It's only a matter of time before they decide there was no crucifixion and, from there, it's just a short hop to the declaration there was no Jesus at all," complained a reader in a 1995 letter to the *Los Angeles Times*. "Instead of chipping away at the Christian faith, why not just declare the whole thing a hoax and be done with it?"

For King, however, history didn't undermine faith; it enriched it. She wanted other believers to feel the same way. "Christians," she wrote, "will better understand and responsibly engage their own tradition by attending to an accurate historical account of Christian beginnings." And yet for all of King and Funk's talk of the liberatory power of history, it wasn't clear that either of them actually believed in history—not in the way most people did. King wasn't sure that facts or linear time existed, and Funk argued that all history was fabrication. "The Bible, along with all our histories, is a fiction," Funk said in his inaugural 1985 speech to the Jesus Seminar. Like all stories, the Bible was a series of "arbitrary" selections by an author who picked characters and events, then forced them into a causal chain with beginning, middle and end. It was only by exposing the Bible's fictive underpinnings that scholars could conjure a new, better tale. Unaccountably, however, this new tale wouldn't necessarily be any truer than the one it replaced. "What we need is a new fiction," Funk told his colleagues—and only his colleagues. (To my knowledge, Funk did not air this argument in public lectures or media interviews.)

"Not any fiction will do," he went on. "The fiction of the superiority of the Aryan race led to the extermination of six million Jews. The fiction of American superiority prompted the massacre of thousands of Native Americans and the Vietnam War. The fiction of Revelation keeps many common folk in bondage to ignorance and fear. We require a new, liberating fiction, one that squares with the best knowledge we can now accumulate and one that transcends self-serving ideologies." This "new gospel," he said, would place "Jesus differently in the grand scheme, the epic story."

All the same, he added paradoxically, "we need a fiction that we recognize to be fictive." A story whose merits lie not in whether it *is* true but in whether it *feels* true—an asset Funk called "operational effectiveness."

"We must begin to sell a product that has some utilitarian value to someone—or which at least appears to have utilitarian value."

Funk, whose scholarship focused on Jesus's parables, was himself a wizard of wordplay. He no doubt delighted in asking academically trained historians to free the faithful by replacing Christianity's old lies with new, more useful ones. The latter, at least, would be the work of modern scholars, rather than the bloviations of a blinkered Church. Whether the Jesus Seminar would make converts depended on one's point of view. On the upside, Funk told his colleagues, patently fictional stories are "not subject to proof or falsification." Like novels, they succeed only if they feel relevant to people's lives—if they have "operational effectiveness." On the downside, "the majority in our society" didn't see the Bible as fictive. Funk steeled King and his other colleagues for a long and ugly fight. "Satisfactions will come hard," he warned. "But we will set out, in spite of the dangers, because we are professionals and because the issue of Jesus is there to be faced, much as Mt. Everest confronts the team of climbers."

Though King's prose lacks her mentor's grandiloquence, she would spend much of her career building on Funk's disdain for the straitjacket of creed and canon. The "master story" of early Christianity as a time of divinely inspired harmony no doubt soothed some churchgoers, who found in it an escape from the cruelties of a broken world, King wrote. But she cast such believers as victims of delusion, dogma and fear. They "think the church ought to be a safe home in a complex and disturbing world," she wrote in an unpublished 1997 white paper for the Jesus Seminar. They "don't want to think critically or take responsibility for the difficulties of leading a religious life in the (post)modern world." Home, she wrote, quoting from a book of feminist theory, was "an illusion of coherence and safety." Its walls excluded other people and repressed "differences even within oneself." Christians who needed a "canonical home" were deficient not just in politics but in character, she suggested. Canonical homelessness was a test of a person's mettle in the face of "terrors."

"What terrors?" she asked, and here her paper shifted, uncharacteristically, into near stream of consciousness. The terror

that to leave the canonical home means to be overcome by
sin and evil, to [f]all into the seduction and entrapment of
Satan....—that to leave home exposes one to the "threats"
of other religions, other perspectives...—that to leave home
invokes not just the threat, but the reality of excommunication,
of exclusion, of aloneness;—that to take a stand outside the
canonical home means losing the power and prestige that goes
with being a part of the group who owns the truth and wields it
against others outside.

The New Testament canon was an "illusion, full of power to make
one *feel* safe, *feel* superior, *feel* knowing—as long as one doesn't look too
closely or ask too many questions."

Brushes with the abyss were a mainstay of her character. Whether
hiking alone in unfamiliar mountains, biking solo down the West Coast
after college or slipping into communist East Germany to study unpublished transcripts of the Nag Hammadi gospels, "she wanted to see if
she had the toughness and intelligence to walk right up to the edge of
danger and remain in control," her first husband, Barry Chandler, said,
when we met in Montana. "Seeking experiences, even dangerous ones,
was a basic part of her personality."

LIKE THE TITLE CHARACTER in the Gospel of Mary, Karen King had
been spotted early for her intellectual gifts by the charismatic head-
men of a male-dominated field. She was an undergraduate when Bob
Funk recruited her into his charmed circle. She had scarcely earned
her PhD when James Robinson, the California scholar responsible for
English-language translations of the Nag Hammadi gospels, chose her
to organize a name-making conference called "Images of the Feminine
in Gnosticism." Yet much like Mary in her eponymous gospel, King
often found herself fighting for air in rooms full of men. Defending the
Gospel of Mary became a way of defending herself.

The Jesus Seminar, for all its latitudinarian bona fides, didn't take
to the Gospel of Mary. A seminar colleague preparing an anthology
called *The Complete Gospels* "neglected to put the Gospel of Mary in,"
King said in a 2006 speech. "So I did my little feminist thing, being
the only woman there. And they said, 'Fine, if you do it, we'll put it

in. You have three weeks.'" She came to Mary's aid again during the seminar's debates over what the historical Jesus really said and did. Because the seminar discredited the entire Gospel of John—the latest of the four canonical gospels—it effectively nullified Mary's star turn: the novelistic scene, which appears only in that gospel, where the risen Jesus appears first to Mary Magdalene and commands her to tell the apostles of his resurrection. Jesus's words to Mary in the scene "have little or nothing in common with parallel stories connected with the empty tomb and they are not of the nature of memorable utterances that would have been circulated orally before being written down," the seminar concluded in its 1993 book. Indeed, the earliest list of initial witnesses to the resurrected Jesus—Paul's first letter to the Corinthians—makes no mention of Mary Magdalene.

But in 1998, when the seminar published a book on Jesus's deeds— "What did Jesus really do?" it asked—Mary's big scene in John received a promotion. The scholars upgraded the risen Jesus's appearance and words to Mary from a black rating ("largely or entirely fictive") to a gray rating ("possible but unreliable"). In a separate vote, they gave a red rating ("virtually certain"), their highest mark, to a freestanding assertion: "Mary was among the early witnesses to the resurrection of Jesus." The votes not only were at odds with the seminar's earlier book but contradicted one of its chief findings: that Jesus never rose from the dead. The later book, *The Acts of Jesus*, is frank about the pretzel the scholars had to twist themselves into. They voted Mary's scene in John historically possible "after extended debate" and "in a sense, against their better judgment," they said. "The Fellows felt obligated to acknowledge the claim of Mary to have had a vision of the risen Jesus"—even though that vision is of a completely different nature, is not at the empty tomb and occurs in the Gospel of Mary, a text the seminar discounted as fully fictive. And none of that explained the even more incongruous second vote, in which they called Mary's "early witness to the resurrection" almost certain; the phrasing "early witness to the resurrection" implied not a vision but real-life observation of an actual event. At best, a group that set out to tell the public what Jesus really said and did had decided that a vision in a book it called false could be the basis for the reality of Magdalene's witness to a resurrection that never happened. "The votes at the two meetings were not very consistent and not well argued," Lane McGaughy, King's former professor at Montana and a leading Jesus Seminar figure, conceded when I inquired about them.

When I asked another seminar scholar, Kathleen Corley, how the red vote on Mary's witness to the resurrection came about, she said, "That's all Karen King." The scholars wanted to give a "nod" to King's arguments.

But a red rating, I thought, was more than a nod. It was a full endorsement that seemed to come at some expense to the seminar's credibility. How had King brought it off? Her friendship with Bob Funk was part of it, said Corley, a religious studies professor at the University of Wisconsin Oshkosh. But King was also a tactical fighter. At a Jesus Seminar soiree around the time of the final votes, the emcee, a New Testament theologian, announced that he was awarding Corley—a slender, flaxen-haired scholar who wore black heels and a Carolina Herrera cocktail dress—the prize for "blond bombshell of the Jesus Seminar."

"They didn't make fun of her that way," Corley said of King, who didn't tend to dress up for parties. After the awkward moment passed, King walked up to Corley and warned, half jokingly, that the seminar was setting Corley up to take the fall for certain of its votes. "You're going to get the shit for all the feminist stuff," Corley recalled King telling her, even though it was King—not the more conservative Corley—who was its leading Mary Magdalene advocate.

KING'S 2003 BOOK on the Gospel of Mary introduced her work to a mass audience, but it also brought greater scrutiny. Veteran religion journalists who read the book closely spotted a kind of subtle misdirection. In the book's second sentence, King states without qualification—as if settled fact—that Mary was "written early in the second century CE." This date was critical to King's argument that the Gospel of Mary was there at the starting line, that it gave women a voice at the same time as proto-canonical texts, like 1 Timothy, were silencing them. It was only on her book's seventh-to-last page that King gave any hint that her dating defied scholarly consensus. The prevailing view in biblical studies is that Mary dates to the late second century and is a Gnostic critique of the texts that made the canon, rather than their bedfellow.

How, then, did King justify her early date? She couldn't use manuscripts. The oldest copy of the Gospel of Mary dates to the early third century, some hundred years later than the first New Testament papyri. Instead, King took as her premise that every text is a response to another text. Because New Testament writings like 1 Timothy bar women from speaking and teaching, noncanonical texts with the opposite point of view were apt to date to the same period. In one of King's favorite phrases, 1 Timothy and the Gospel of Mary were "in conversation with" each other. "We can now hear the other side of the controversy," as she put it.

The Associated Press correspondent Richard Ostling, a decorated former president of the Religion Newswriters Association, wasn't convinced. "King says the Mary topics 'fit best in an early second century context,'" because of discussions then about "women's roles and the meaning of Jesus' life and teachings," Ostling wrote in a 2003 article. "But those issues were equally pertinent a century later." Indeed, if the existence of animosity toward women were a key criteria for dating the Gospel of Mary, there was scarcely a period in Christian history with which the text *wouldn't* be in conversation.

When King finally discloses the novelty of her dating—at the end of her book—she acknowledges that it relies on "the trickiest of all factors" because of her argument's "circularity." But unless ordinary readers got to the book's final pages, they would have no idea that the cornerstone of King's case was more like a loose floorboard. I was reminded of her Gospel of Jesus's Wife article, in which she waits until the very last sentence to disclose the problem—or "new line of inquiry," as she put it—that the eighth-century radiocarbon date posed for her interpretation. In both cases, King withheld an essential fact until the closing pages, as if it were a curious afterthought rather than a foundational problem with her evidence.

To make the case for the Gospel of Jesus's Wife as second-century literature, King went further—omitting plainly relevant facts in their entirety. Christians had likely composed the text in the second century, she reasoned, because that's when other Christians first asserted the opposite view—that Jesus was celibate. King argued that the theologians Clement of Alexandria and Tertullian, the first known Christians to describe Jesus as unmarried, must have been reacting to texts depicting Jesus as married. Her papyrus discovery was proof—the world's first—that such texts existed, she declared. "We are now able to document a second century controversy over Jesus's marital status." But her argument required one to disregard Clement's and Tertullian's own descriptions of the controversy, which had nothing to do with Jesus's marital status. The question both make clear they are addressing is whether Jesus's celibacy—which they give no indication was in dispute—should be copied by ordinary believers. Their answer is that marriage is fine for the majority, which scarcely suggests a backlash against the prospect of a married Jesus.

Then why should the figure of a plainly celibate Jesus emerge only in the second century, rather than in the first-century gospels themselves? For many historians, the context couldn't be clearer. By the second century, church leaders had lost hope of Jews' accepting Jesus as the messiah. The disciples had left their Jewish homeland—where a sexually active marriage enjoyed biblical sanction—and began to seek converts among Greco-Roman gentiles steeped in Plato's antipathy toward the body. Stoics, Neopythagoreans and other pagan ascetics were growing in number at almost precisely the moment Christian missionaries were entering their lands. Scholars argue that this alchemy of Greek and Christian thought produced a Jesus more avowedly abstemious than the one in the Gospels. "Since Christianity was competing with other salvation cults, the degree of sexual repression in a particular area was somewhat determined by the practice of its leading local rival," observed William Phipps, the foremost authority on the question of Jesus's marital status. "Christians sometimes tried to gain status by outdoing pagans at asceticism." It was probably no accident that the Gnostics, who began writing in the second century, rejected their fleshly bodies and depicted Jesus's as a meaningless shell.

In asserting that Jesus was celibate but that ordinary believers needn't be, Clement and Tertullian weren't reacting to texts that portrayed Jesus as married; they were mediating a dispute between Christians who renounced sex and Christians who refused to forsake physical intimacy—or children—for God. In a Jesus who was celibate but not adamant about it, the former could find a measure of license for their practices, and the latter a sense that the celibacy of the few needn't diminish the matrimony of the many. This view was grounded in historical evidence and the second-century theologians' own words. But King set it aside in favor of her theory that all texts are "in conversation" and that therefore Clement and Tertullian must be reacting to previously unknown accounts of a wedded Jesus.

Even King seemed to know how suspect this line of reasoning was. Speaking to a friendly crowd at Harvard Divinity School in 2006, she allowed that "conversations" between texts might well be of her own imagining. "I put some of these texts in conversation with each other—they may have *never* been in conversation with each other, you know?" she said, with a short laugh. "Nobody in antiquity may have known to put them in conversation. So in some places, we're playing with them. We're creating conversations with these texts, for us to think with." She described her method as "intellectual history in a new key."

KAREN KING HAD PLACED a heavy burden on the Gospel of Mary. It didn't matter that more than half its pages were missing, obscuring its ultimate meaning. It didn't matter that most scholars saw it as too late to compete with the canon. King, who titled her book *The Gospel of Mary of Magdala*, even though the gospel nowhere identifies its "Mary" as Magdalene, wanted the text to say things—and be things—that the available facts didn't always support. In many fields, an incomplete, one-of-a-kind data point might deter a scholar from making sweeping generalizations. But King went in precisely the opposite direction. She not only built "the history of Christianity" atop the discontinuous surviving nine pages of a single text; she called its portrait of the faith's first centuries "in a number of respects more historically accurate than that of the master story."

Yet for all its merits, the Gospel of Mary, like other Gnostic texts, had a tragic flaw that even King saw as unbridgeable: Mary's exaltation came at the expense of her sexuality. It was only by transcending the prison of the flesh—and thus of gender—that the Gnostics believed they could reunite their divine spark with the higher realm. The idea finds its grimmest voice in the 114th and final saying of the Gospel of Thomas, when Jesus says that "every woman who will make herself male will enter the kingdom of heaven." King openly rued this Faustian bargain. "It seems to me that even when the feminine is highly valued, it is often done so at the expense of real sexuality," she wrote in the 1980s. A decade later, she said, "If women exercised legitimate leadership only at the price of their identity as women and the valuing of their own bodies, there would seem to be little here of value for contemporary women except yet another narrative of loss." In an interview a few years after that, she asked, "Do we really want this? Is this just one more argument for giving up the woman's body?"

She was blunter still in a 2006 talk at Harvard Divinity School.

"Her body doesn't count," she said of the Gospel of Mary's protagonist. "What does this erasure of sexuality mean for the appropriation by contemporary feminists?" King's cancer diagnosis made Christianity's broader erasure of the physical body feel even more personal. "It just doesn't strike me that the body is really there," she told the divinity school audience—and anyone who happened to find video of the talk on YouTube. "What will it take for it to be there? Bodies. People's bodies. Our bodies."

As doubts about the Gospel of Jesus's Wife grew, critics portrayed King as a sap for a real-life *Da Vinci Code*. But they'd misread her. King no more regarded Dan Brown's book as a feminist manifesto than she did the Gospel of Mary. For King, the ideological flaw in *The Da Vinci Code* was the inverse of the Gnostics'. Brown's thriller cast Mary Magdalene as Jesus's fertile wife—her uterus the "Holy Grail" for his seed. But it overlooked her spiritual leadership. Brown doesn't make her the prostitute of lore. Still, he "resexualizes" her with "this move to see her as wife and mother," King said during the *Da Vinci* craze. ("She was portrayed basically as a womb...a transmitter of Jesus's genes," AnneMarie Luijendijk, who shares her former professor's view, told an interviewer. "And that makes me, as a feminist scholar, uncomfortable.")

When I set King's critiques of *The Da Vinci Code* and of the Gospel of Mary side by side, I grasped for the first time how ruthlessly precise the forger's aim had been. Put crudely, the *Code*'s Mary was a womb without a brain, while the Gospel of Mary's Mary was a brain without a womb. An astute con artist would need just a few days with King's books, articles and lectures to identify what she saw as the greatest omission in all of Christian literature: an ancient account of Mary Magdalene as both brain and womb—spiritual authority and sexual being, disciple and wife. Anyone who spent $20 for King's 2003 DVD on the Gospel of Mary could have spared themselves the research. At about the hour mark, she tells the conference room that there is no historical proof that Jesus and Mary Magdalene were married. Then, apropos of nothing, she lets people in on something. "If you ask me, 'Well, how would I *like* it to be?'" she says, drawing a circle in the air with her finger and laughing with the California audience. "Then I say, 'Look, I think sex is a good thing.' Why not, okay? I don't have any problems with them, you know, having enjoyed each other. But on the other hand, why is it that whenever we put a man and a woman together, they have to have sex, you know? Can't we do some other things, too, you know, like talk and learn?"

King couldn't have known it then, but she was describing, to a T, the Gospel of Jesus's Wife. A Mary who has sex with Jesus ("Jesus said to them, 'My wife...'") but who also talks and learns ("She is able to be my disciple"). King discovered in the Wife fragment exactly what a forger must have known she would: "robust affirmation," as she put it in her 2014 *Harvard Theological Review* article, "that women who are wives and mothers are worthy and able to be disciples of Jesus."

"So that's where I am on that question, okay?" King said back in 2003, to more audience applause. "Since you asked."

But no one had.

THE NAG HAMMADI "HERESIES" that John Turner passed around in his Gnosticism class at the University of Montana looked for a time like the answer to the wrongness King felt inside her. But in the end, the Gnostics let her down, as they would many other feminists. The tea leaves appeared as soon as King arrived at Occidental College. A *Los Angeles Times* reporter who covered her landmark 1985 conference "Images of the Feminine in Gnosticism" found an atmosphere of deflation. "The general assessment was that the imagery is often too abstract, too difficult to relate to actual social situations and—dismaying to feminists— tends to reflect a male-dominated culture among the seemingly 'liberated' Gnostics," John Dart, the *Times*'s religion correspondent, wrote in a twelve-hundred-word feature. The Duke University scholar Elizabeth Clark said that the takeaway of the conference's twenty-one research papers was that "women scholars could no longer say, 'Look at all these female figures in the texts; it must mean that women were doing all sorts of things in Gnosticism.'" King directed the reporter to one silver lining. Female figures in the Gnostic texts, she said, were never depicted as passive or weak. But later she grew less certain. As much as she celebrated the Gospel of Mary, she hated that its heroine wept when challenged by the male disciples. "I wish she wouldn't do that," she told one audience.

New papyrus discoveries were the only real hope for a more perfect Mary. "Maybe they're sitting in somebody's drawer somewhere," King said in a videotaped 2003 talk in California's wine country. "And they may not even know what they have." In another talk available on DVD, the emcee urged the audience to send King any papyri they might have lying around. King then dangled naming rights. "Once they're published," King said, papyrus owners "can put their name on it, you know. 'The Mary Smith Papyrus,' okay? So if you know anybody like this, encourage them to do that. There is stuff all around."

To a con man in search of a scholar's deepest desires, statements like these must have read like a personal invitation.

IN OUR INTERVIEW after the *Atlantic* piece, King told me she had no idea a papyrus owner's backstory could be so problematic. "Who could imagine?" she said. In truth, trusted colleagues had warned her about the minefield of provenance within days of her Rome announcement. One of the earliest was the acclaimed Coptic papyrologist Malcolm Choat, whose opinion King had personally sought, partly at Bagnall's urging. Choat pleaded for more transparency, not least out of concern for professional ethics. "The situation as it now stands (owner not wishing to be named, acquisition details a bit unclear) is sailing a little bit close to the wind in terms of the American Society of Papyrologists' Resolution Concerning the Illicit Trade in Papyri," Choat wrote in a September 26, 2012, email to King and Luijendijk. The resolution bars the presentation or publication of papyri without a "thorough" exploration of provenance. It also prohibits actions that significantly increase a manuscript's commercial value. "I fear that while the owner remains anonymous these questions will continue to run," Choat wrote.

King's public defense was that she'd promised the owner anonymity. But when Walter Fritz sent me a copy of a permissions form he said he brought to Harvard with his papyri in December 2011, I noticed something surprising: he left everything up to King. "Prof. King," Fritz wrote, "is not obligated to identify the owner by name in connection with the publication of the papyrus fragments, but may do so." When he made an informal request for anonymity five months later, he downplayed its significance. "Just say something like 'private collection' or 'possession of a Florida private collector,'" he suggested in a May 2012 email. "The few that matter in this field do know who I am anyway." The sly, self-contradictory argument was that hiding his identity was a courtesy of no import, because his collection was already known to all the important players in the manuscript world.

The effect of this soft-shoe was to leave King in charge. Fritz's insistence on her autonomy—"You're the boss, who am I?" as he once put it—was a tactic of con men the world over. As the psychologist Maria Konnikova observed of their methods, "The true con artist doesn't force us to do anything; he makes us complicit in our own undoing. He doesn't steal. We give. He doesn't have to threaten us. We supply the story ourselves. We believe because we want to, not because anyone made us. And so we offer up whatever they want—money, reputation, trust, fame, legitimacy, support—and we don't realize what is happening until it is too late."

Con artists, that is, are virtuosos of a sell so soft we don't even realize it's a sell. It's Mark Hofmann saying, "Do you really think it's genuine?" It's Walter Fritz saying, "I'm completely clueless.... Does the Gospel make sense?" It's Fritz writing, as he does in his paperwork for Harvard, that he "gives no guarantee in respect of content, historic background, original provenience, materials, age, or authenticity of the fragments." It's him telling King she "has no obligation to publish." Everything, all of it, is up to her.

THE PRO AND THE CON

Peer reviewers are academia's highway patrol—the officers who pull over speeders before they hurt themselves and others. The *Harvard Theological Review,* like other peer-reviewed journals, sends submitted articles to outside experts before deciding whether to publish. The experts assess an article's validity, quality and originality, then recommend whether to accept the article, reject it, or ask the author for revisions. The goal is to stop bad scholarship from polluting humanity's store of knowledge. To guard against malice or favoritism, peer review is often double-blind: editors withhold the author's identity from peer reviewers, and the reviewers', from the author.

If ever there were an occasion for peer review, the Gospel of Jesus's Wife was it. Since its founding in 1908, the *Review* had published no shortage of penetrating articles. But the journal was rarely the first to announce a new archaeological artifact, much less one as jolting as the Gospel of Jesus's Wife. King's discovery turned not only on theological interpretation—the *Review*'s bread and butter—but on questions of authenticity, archaeological science and scholarly ethics.

The *Review*'s website tells prospective authors to be patient. Even in normal circumstances, it can take three months for the quarterly to accept or reject a piece, and eighteen more months for publication. For a blockbuster article, one imagined a wait of at least that long. King, however, was so certain of a shoo-in that she told me the journal would publish her piece in October 2012, just two months after she'd submitted her first draft. She deemed it so bulletproof that she sent it to the Smithsonian Channel the same day she gave it to the journal. "I'm attaching here the article submitted this morning to Harvard Theological Review," she wrote to the channel's producers on August 10, 2012. "It will go to outside reviewers then get a final edit before publication, but this is a pretty final form."

Was this just self-confidence? Or did King have advance knowledge—or even a measure of control—over the editing and review? Though the *Harvard Theological Review* is published by Cambridge University Press, its editors are Harvard Divinity School faculty. King's status as the Hollis Professor of Divinity would have put the editors in the somewhat awkward position of evaluating a paper by a high-ranking in-house colleague. But that was only the first of the conflicts. On the very day King submitted her article, I discovered, the journal's editors asked the papyrologist Roger Bagnall to peer-review it. Not only had King cited Bagnall in the article as having judged the papyrus authentic; she had asked for his advice on early drafts and served alongside him on the dissertation committee of AnneMarie Luijendijk, the article's contributing author. A few weeks earlier, Bagnall had even sat for the Smithsonian Channel's filmmakers, opining that the fragment dated to the fourth century. Asking Bagnall to anonymously peer-review King's article was like asking an athletic team's co-captain to referee his own game, and to do so, moreover, in disguise.

"Indeed, not only do I know about the papyrus, I've read a draft of the paper and talked about the papyrus in front of a camera, as well as discussed it in person with the authors," Bagnall wrote to Margaret Studier, the managing editor of the *Harvard Theological Review,* after the journal asked him to review King's piece that August 10. "I'd be perfectly happy to read it for HTR, but I wouldn't want there to be any illusion that I'm in any way an outsider in the way that referees typically are."

Four days later, when Bagnall sent Studier some comments on King's draft, he said he saw no need for improvement and "very strongly recommend publication." All the same, he added, "I want to be clear that I wouldn't claim expertise in the non-canonical early Christian literature." Despite Bagnall's warnings about his lack of expertise and independence, the journal used his report as one of its blind peer reviews—giving King cover to claim on the day of her announcement that "in the course of the normal external review process" at least one referee "accepted the fragment."

"They obviously ignored the caveats," Bagnall told me in 2019. (He confirmed he was the favorable reviewer only after I learned of it from other sources.) "Hey, you know, count this as a review! Run it through! Right? I understand that kind of feeling of time pressure, especially because of all the publicity associated with it. But it's not the way I would wish to run a journal."

A co-editor told me the journal simply wanted Bagnall to document why he so favored King's article. Why, then, I wondered, would the editors forward it to King as if it were a customary, double-blind review? If King knew that Bagnall was its author, it raised questions about why she would publicly tout his report as part of the "normal external review process." If she didn't know, her subsequent reliance on Bagnall's opinion of the two unfavorable reviews compounded the conflict; for Bagnall to credit the other reviewers' doubts would be to admit to the journal's editors, who knew his identity, that his own peer review was defective. The journal's decision to send Bagnall's anonymous review to King might have muddied matters further, by giving the public—and perhaps King herself—the false impression that an esteemed expert *besides* Bagnall had judged the fragment authentic.

WITH THE HELP OF SOURCES, I managed to identify the two unfavorable reviewers. Bentley Layton of Yale and Stephen Emmel of Germany's University of Münster were no less than the world's leading all-in-one experts on the Nag Hammadi library, Coptic linguistics and Gnosticism. Layton, a past president of the International Association for Coptic Studies and Yale's Goff Professor of Religious Studies, had literally written the textbook on Coptic. His Coptic grammar is the field's standard reference, and his translations of the Gnostic gospels are among the most definitive. (While a graduate student in Providence, King made pilgrimages to New Haven to study Coptic with him.)

"Something smelled bad," Layton, a Harvard alumnus, told me of his impressions of the photographed papyrus. He said he told the editors that publishing the fragment "would be very embarrassing for the *Harvard Theological Review.*"

The Yale-trained Emmel worked nearly full time in the mid-1970s in the tiled manuscript wing of Cairo's Coptic Museum. He distinguished himself at a youthful age by joining the puzzle-piece-like fragments of the Nag Hammadi gospels for the definitive facsimile—or photographic—edition of the Gnostic texts. Scholars universally described him to me as a giant in the field. When I visited Emmel at his office in Münster in 2017, he gave me a copy of his peer review. I no sooner read it than realized it was the notorious "third review," the critique that had deeply rattled King and the *Harvard Theological Review* in early September 2012. "My first response was shock," King had told me at our dinner that night.

Emmel served on the National Geographic Society panel that judged the Gospel of Judas authentic in 2006 after rigorous scholarly and scientific examination. The Wife papyrus appeared to be something else. "To put it baldly—a fake," he wrote to the *Review*'s editors. The "clumsy and labored" hand looked not like ancient writing but "rather like what any of us [modern scholars] might produce—without practicing a lot." It looked like someone "not very experienced at writing on the surface of papyrus at all." As for the content, "I would say the Gospel of Thomas from Nag Hammadi Codex II was a large part of the forger's source of inspiration." He also labeled it "somewhat suspicious that both Munro and Fecht are fairly recently deceased." Two weeks before King announced her discovery—and in plenty of time to postpone it—one of the field's top scholars had identified nearly every sign of forgery that would surface over the next four years.

When I asked King in 2012 what had so shaken her about the then-anonymous review, she said "part of it was tone." When I read it for myself five years later, the tone—which was nuanced and professional—made less of an impression than did the content. Emmel, without knowing King had written the article, had delicately questioned its author's competence in Coptic. "This short fragment seems to contain four violations of basic Coptic grammar, only one of which was commented upon by the author," Emmel wrote. "I think that the author's knowledge of Coptic (and of Coptic manuscripts) is not deep enough for his/her suspicions to have been aroused as they might have been, and perhaps should have been." He also wondered how the author could call the ugly handwriting "the work of a proficient scribe."

I asked Emmel whether King's revisions had adequately addressed the questions his review had raised. He shook his head. "My impression was she was doing everything she could to rescue this thing as authentic," he said. "She was so interested in having it as a hook for the very interesting work she does on the status of women in Christianity that she was not keen to let it go. My feeling is, You don't need the hook: it's an interesting subject without the papyrus. She could have written the bulk of her article without this text." As for AnneMarie Luijendijk and Roger Bagnall, he said, "I think they all wanted to believe it. I think they found it exciting."

When I visited Luijendijk at Princeton in March 2017, she said that the more genuine-looking script on the papyrus's verso had led her to assume that the entire text was real. "Clearly, I was wrong," she told me. "Now I'm much more careful." In hindsight, she wished that she, King and Bagnall had convened a "colloquium," a larger and more independent group of scholars, before going public.

I called Ariel Shisha-Halevy, the Coptic linguist whom King relied on to excuse the pileup of grammatical errors that had alarmed Emmel. I asked Shisha-Halevy whether—despite his famously permissive views—it was common to have so many linguistic irregularities on so tiny a fragment. He told me it wasn't. Indeed, the "grammatical points of interest"—he dislikes the word "errors"—were so rare that you couldn't even find them all in a single dialect. You had to cherry-pick from at least three, which made their joint appearance in a papyrus scrap with a total of just thirty words, all presumably in the same dialect, "remarkable," he told me. "My answer is, 'No, it is not common.'"

Next I went to Manhattan to see Roger Bagnall.

In 2009, Bagnall had published *Early Christian Books in Egypt*. It was his first book on the papyrology of Christian texts. They weren't his specialty, but he came out swinging. He argued that "problematic assumptions, interests, agendas, and desires"—rather than evidence—were guiding how too many scholars dated Christian papyri. Liberals dated their favorite manuscripts early to show that the orthodox church "betrayed... the original message of the religion it claimed to represent." Conservatives did so to show that the New Testament *was* the original message. Bagnall devoted nearly a whole chapter to a savage takedown of a German scholar who dated a fragment of the Gospel of Matthew, implausibly, to the A.D. 60s. (No surviving gospel manuscripts are thought to date to the first century.) The "gruesome details" of this scholar's "burlesque" stab at paleographic, or handwriting-based, dating left the field with a "horrifying object lesson," Bagnall wrote. "Alertness to agendas, stated and unstated, is essential." Caution was all the more essential with scholars, like the German, who publicized their work through the popular media, Bagnall suggested. It was perhaps more critical still when the texts were in Coptic, whose handwriting is harder than Greek to pin to a particular era and therefore more prone to wishful dating. Because good history relied on accurate dates, papy-rologists "should take care that such datings rest on as strong a founda-tion as possible, a group of parallels as precise as available, and as wide a consensus as possible." Otherwise, their dating risked being—like that of the German scholar he'd pilloried—"just a drive-by shooting."

Two years later, when he took up the Wife papyrus, Bagnall appeared to ignore every one of his own caveats. He worked with a scholar with an acknowledged agenda ("You're talking to someone who's trying to integrate a whole set of 'heretical' literature into the standard history," King told me in our first conversation). He spent a single, drive-by hour examining the fragment firsthand. He used Cop-tic handwriting to date it to A.D. 350 to A.D. 400, a strikingly narrow range for a notoriously imprecise dating method. And he let TV cam-eras into his institute to publicize the discovery in the mass media. His fourth-century date, moreover, was an ideologically resonant gift. It gave King just enough cover to set the fragment in a period *before* Rome drew a hard line between orthodoxy and heresy, before imperial politics scrambled the original message.

A few years later, when it became clear that the handwriting on King's papyrus had no known parallel in any era, I asked Bagnall what group of ancient handwriting samples he'd compared it with in order to arrive so quickly at so certain a date. He told me he couldn't remember, even after checking. "I do not think I could at this point recover with any confidence which ones I happened to look at."

I brought up "An Amorous Triangle," the ostracon that Morton Smith had urged him to publish in the 1970s and that Bagnall finally did in 2010, after deciding the pottery shard wasn't in fact a fake. That recent experience, Bagnall allowed, might have made him more open to accepting the Wife papyrus as genuine. "Having seen something dismissed as a fake when it turned out not to be probably made me feel one ought to be more cautious" before rejecting a strange new text out of hand.

"Scholars have described you as possibly the greatest living papy-rologist," I said, when we met in March 2017 on the campus of Colum-bia University. "Were you wrong about the Gospel of Jesus's Wife?"

"I don't think so," he said, "because I never said it was genuine."

I read him back his own quotations from two years of news articles. To *Smithsonian* magazine, he said that the shabby writing instrument "is one of the things that tells you it's real." To *The New York Times*, he said, "It's hard to construct a scenario that is at all plausible in which somebody fakes something like this," and "I don't know of a single verifiable case of somebody producing a papyrus text that purports to be an ancient text that isn't." To *The Boston Globe*, he said, "I haven't seen any argument that I find at all compelling that would indicate that it's not genuine, it's not ancient." King's article, moreover, expressly noted that Bagnall had seen the fragment and "judged it to be authentic."

When I pressed him on these statements, he permitted himself just one blind spot. "I kept saying, 'How could somebody be so sophisticated and so unsophisticated at the same time?'" he said. "It was a failure of imagination on my part not to have concocted the person of Walter Fritz."

Some of Karen King's supporters contended that she had been unfairly singled out for criticism. She was a historian, not a papyrologist; she had asked for Bagnall's opinion, then relied on it. "Okay, so let them blame me. I'll still wake up in the morning," Bagnall told me. He had warned the Harvard journal about the limits of his independence and expertise. He had advised King to consult a leading specialist on Coptic Christian papyri ahead of her announcement, but she had failed to do so. "The intellectual responsibility for publishing the thing is Karen's," Bagnall said, "and I don't think she would try to duck that by blaming me. What would she have done if I had said, 'No, no, this is surely a fake, don't do it!' I don't know what she would have done."

THE SENSE THAT KING was choosing specialists for reasons other than expertise became clearer as I began looking at the scientists she asked to test the Wife papyrus. Archaeometry, the formal term for archaeological science, is a rarefied, cross-disciplinary field. Whether a practitioner is a chemist, physicist or biologist matters less than her sophistication with the peculiar properties of ancient objects and the way that excavation, transport and conservation affect those properties. The field has its own journals and graduate programs. The best archaeometrists, who often work on interdisciplinary teams, are in high demand. As in any field, there are dabblers—scientists in other specialties "who find a brief fling with the past a break from their usual routine," David Killick of the University of Arizona and Suzanne Young of Harvard write in a survey of the field. But "this is not archaeometry." These dabblers' one-off articles are "bastard offspring," Killick and Young write. "A scientist must have some lasting degree of commitment to archaeology to be called an archaeometrist."

The stakes for the Gospel of Jesus's Wife were great enough—and Harvard's pockets deep enough—to spare little expense on proper testing. After the backlash in Rome, King signaled plans for nothing less. In late September 2012, she told journalists that Harvard's Straus Center for Conservation and Technical Studies would run tests the very next month. The center is a leading lab for the scientific study of art and artifacts. It possesses, according to its website, "a comprehensive range of imaging and analytical techniques [to] identify a wide range of both inorganic and organic materials including pigments, stone, ceramics, paint-binding media, and surface coatings." But October 2012 came and went with no news. Then November and December. Then all of 2013. When I emailed the center's director in 2017 to ask what had become of the planned testing, a senior spokesperson, Lauren Marshall, replied that its staff was too busy with an expansion of the Harvard Art Museums to do the testing. I replied that King's statements to reporters suggested a firm testing date of mid-October 2012. Two weeks later, Marshall revised her response. "There was a date in mid. Oct. for preliminary testing, but it did not occur because of internal concerns about un-framing the object (a tricky process for an object in a glass sandwich), which could threaten its stability." In addition, she wrote, "Our scientist is not an expert in papyrus and we have no papyrus in our collections, for those reasons he referred Prof. King to respected scientists: James Martin of Orion Analytical and John Twilley." In other words, not even the crackerjack staff at Harvard's renowned conservation lab—the oldest of its kind in the United States—felt they had the right expertise for forgery tests on ancient papyri.

The Straus Center's referrals made sense. James Martin led a highly regarded lab that, according to its website, has "investigated art, cultural property, and collectibles spanning more than 4,000 years . . . in more than 1,800 projects for clients in five continents—an accomplishment without precedent in the international art world." The auction house Sotheby's acquired Martin's firm in 2016 and turned it into its global Department of Scientific Research. John Twilley, another prominent expert, was a pioneering scientist at the J. Paul Getty Museum and headed the lab at the Los Angeles County Museum of Art. Martin told me he never tested the Wife papyrus but declined to say more on the record. Twilley said he had never been contacted by King.

When the *Harvard Theological Review* finally published King's article, in its April 2014 issue, it included short reports by the four scientists King had consulted. The scientists whose radiocarbon tests upended King's conclusions by dating Fritz's fragments to the eighth century—Noreen Tuross of Harvard and Gregory Hodgins of the University of Arizona—both had experience with archaeological objects. But the two other scientists, the ones whose tests appeared to validate King, were wholly unknown to the community of art and archaeological scientists. Timothy Swager is a prizewinning chemist at the Massachusetts Institute of Technology and a leading figure in his field. But his field isn't archaeometry: he is best known for inventing a chemical sensor that detects vapors from explosives like TNT. Yet in April 2014, he and two of his MIT graduate students published a report, alongside King's in the *Harvard Theological Review,* titled "Study of Two Papyrus Fragments with Fourier Transform Infrared Microspectroscopy." The acclaimed conservation staff at Harvard's Straus Center had grave concerns about unhousing the papyrus from its Plexiglas sandwich. But in Swager's lab, according to his report, Karen King, a humanities scholar with no professional lab training, uncased the papyri herself, "conducted the transfer of the samples to the microscope," and "carried out all handling of both" the Wife and the John fragments.

Swager's study stupefied actual archaeometrists. The MIT group found that the writing surface was "cellulose," a technical term for plant matter. This was never in dispute; even critics accepted that they were looking at papyrus, rather than, say, parchment or modern paper. Swager's team then found that the material was oxidized, meaning that it had reacted with oxygen. Oxidization can be caused by natural aging, but heat and humidity—well-known forger's tools—can also do the trick. The scientists, however, made no effort to compare the Wife fragment with either unquestionably genuine ancient papyrus or artificially aged papyrus. Unaccountably, they used another of Fritz's papyri, the Gospel of John fragment, as their reference sample; they took its authenticity for granted, even though it belonged to the same collector whose other papyrus many scholars deemed a fake. Discovering no significant difference between the chemistry of Fritz's two papyri, Swager's team concluded that there was nothing to suggest that the

Wife and John fragments had been "fabricated or modified at different times." This finding, I realized, was as consistent with forgery as it was with authenticity. If the papyri had been manipulated or artificially aged at the same time by the same means, of course their chemical makeup would look similar. But Swager didn't portray it that way. "The main thing was to see, did somebody doctor this up?" Swager told *The New York Times*, in an April 2014 article reporting the test results. "And there is absolutely no evidence for that. It would have been extremely difficult, if not impossible."

I wondered for many months why King chose an expert in explosives detection for a crucial scientific study of ancient papyrus. And why a scientist with no experience in archaeological science felt qualified to opine, in the *Times*, on which sorts of papyri were "extremely difficult, if not impossible" to fake and what sorts of test results constituted "absolutely no evidence" of tampering. The sweeping characterization contradicted even Swager's own report, which said, "We found one anomalous feature"—an "orange 'spot' of possible contamination"— "that we were unable to identify."

I found an answer while poring over articles in the small newspaper that covered King's hometown of Sheridan, Montana. In a 1977 news clip announcing King's wedding to her first husband, one of the ushers is listed as "Tim Swager." After a few phone calls around Sheridan, I learned that the Kings had lived next door to the Swagers. Tim's father, the town doctor, and Karen's father, the town pharmacist, were best friends and hunting partners. Tim's mother was the person who persuaded Karen to apply to Western College, which Karen attended for a year before its closure prompted her transfer to the University of Montana. "We've been good friends ever since we moved here in 1959," Carol Lee Swager told me. Her son Tim agreed to test the Gospel of Jesus's Wife, she said, for a simple reason: "[King] asked him to." Tim, Karen and Karen's brother Clifford all lived in Massachusetts now, she said, and they have "a routine where they spend New Year's Eve and Thanksgiving and so forth together. They are very close."

Even if Tim Swager were to have the right expertise—which he didn't—his long-standing personal ties to King posed a sharp conflict of interest. Yet neither he nor King ever disclosed the relationship.

THE LEAD AUTHOR OF KING'S other scientific report would have been equally obscure to experts in archaeological science. James Yardley is a trained chemist, distinguished technology executive, and a professor and senior research scientist in Columbia University's department of electrical engineering. Yet in late 2012, with retirement approaching, Yardley founded a program at Columbia without any obvious ties to his prior experience. He called it the Ancient Ink Laboratory, and he paid for it with a mix of personal, government and corporate research funds. Yardley's team used a laser-based technique called micro-Raman spectroscopy to identify the ink on Fritz's fragments as a simple, carbon-based pigment known as carbon black. Had Yardley's lab found modern, industrial chemicals—like those in, say, a permanent marker—it would have immediately pointed to forgery. The presence of carbon black meant that the fragment couldn't be condemned on the basis of this particular study of ink. But it didn't authenticate the papyrus, either: one can buy carbon black in art supply stores or make it at home with the same simple recipe—soot, water and gum arabic—used by the ancients. Yardley's team glimpsed a possible workaround. With experimental tests on ancient papyri in Columbia's library, they tried to develop a technique for using micro-Raman spectroscopy to estimate the age of carbon-based ink. Ideally, such a test would show whether the carbon black on a papyrus was applied in the recent past or hundreds of years ago. In her *Harvard Theological Review* article, King offered a kind of sneak peek at Yardley's preliminary results, saying that their "implication" was that the Wife fragment's ink was ancient.

When I visited Yardley at Columbia in 2017, he made no effort to conceal the raison d'être of the Ancient Ink Laboratory. On October 2, 2012, just two weeks after King's announcement, he received an email from Roger Bagnall. Did Yardley know of anyone who might be able to test the ink on "the infamous papyrus"? Bagnall wrote.

Yardley was frank about his limitations. "The people within my circle of influence are certainly not experts in characterization of ancient manuscripts," Yardley replied to Bagnall. Not long afterward, however, Yardley decided to take on the project himself. He hired a postdoctoral physicist and enlisted three other scholars: the head conservator at Columbia's libraries; a papyrologist who got his PhD under Bagnall and now worked for him at the Institute for the Study of the Ancient World; and Bagnall himself.

Yardley told me he had no experience with ancient objects or ink identification. "To be truthful, I hadn't the foggiest," he told me. Nor had he used micro-Raman spectroscopy in other areas of science. "I had never ever taken a Raman spectrum in my life." He'd spent most of his career as a high-level research administrator; in the corporate world, his inventions included a fade-resistant carpet fiber and a polymer used to etch circuits onto microchips. "I had not put my fingers myself on an honest-to-God machine and taken honest-to-God data" in thirty to forty years, he said. Moreover, "we didn't know how to analyze the data." But he was a quick study. He had experience with other kinds of spectroscopy, devoured journal articles on ink chemistry and took Monday mornings off to learn his way around a Raman spectrometer.

I puzzled over why a senior research director at an Ivy League school would abruptly found a new program outside his expertise, assemble a team, fund it with his own research money and commit months to learning a new specialty and unfamiliar technology—all because of a request from a papyrologist at another university.

Yardley answered the question within minutes of our 2017 meeting. "It turns out Roger is my brother-in-law," he said. Yardley married Bagnall's younger sister, Anne, a medieval music scholar, in 1975. The couple get together with Roger and his wife socially at least once or twice a month.

Yardley's study at Columbia was a mirror of Swager's at MIT: a scientist with no experience with ancient manuscripts lent the cachet of his elite university to the Wife fragment, without any disclosure by King, Bagnall, the *Harvard Theological Review,* or the scientists themselves of their personal ties to scholars already deeply invested in the fragment's authenticity. Whether these relationships colored the research—whether they influenced the questions the scientists asked or the findings they chose to make public—is difficult to know. But the pressures were obvious. Had Swager or Yardley publicized a finding of forgery in the heat of the media glare, he would have caused serious harm to the professional reputation of a close family friend (King) or relative (Bagnall).

Yardley and Bagnall told me that they saw no reason to publicly disclose their family ties. They viewed them as immaterial to their findings, which, though favorable to Bagnall's public position during the period of intense news coverage, would turn against it as doubts mounted. Bagnall said he chose Yardley not because he wanted a particular result but because he felt no one but family would be willing to take on so seemingly "boring" a lab test. "I couldn't reasonably request it of somebody I didn't have some hold on," Bagnall told me. "So I thought, okay, 'I can get him to do this.'"

Swager did not respond to a detailed list of questions about his undisclosed personal relationship to King, his apparent lack of archaeometry experience, his research methods and the study's cost and funding.

As far as anyone I spoke to knew, no one examined Fritz's papyri with X-ray fluorescence, a nondestructive technique that Harvard's own conservators had advised King to use as a complement to Raman spectroscopy. Neither had anyone compared Fritz's scraps with papyri subjected to so-called humid oven aging, a forger's tool for speedily oxidizing a manuscript. Nor did scientists account for two of the Wife scrap's oddest physical properties: the orange substance visibly splattered across parts of the papyrus and the abnormally low levels of a stable radiocarbon isotope, which could be explained by a forger's effort to artificially lower the carbon 14 date with a petroleum-based substance. To forgo additional tests on a suspicious fragment's two most out-of-place physical features was like ignoring the specks of blood at an otherwise clean crime scene.

Marc Walton, an archaeological scientist, ran a lab at the Getty Conservation Institute before being named co-director of Northwestern University's Center for Scientific Studies in the Arts. He told me that Swager and Yardley are "good scientists" with "really fantastic reputations," but "that does not make them expert in ancient objects. What's really glaringly missing from this is the input from people who are routinely authenticating works of art or objects from antiquity." The science marshaled on behalf of the Wife papyrus struck him as a salvage job, an emergency mission to plug holes in a sinking ship, rather than an exercise in dispassionate research. In a post on Northwestern's website in 2015, he wrote that "the scientific analysis was naïve at best . . . a sleight-of-hand to distract attention from the more vexing problems" identified by experts in handwriting and language. He called it a "laundering" by science that risked giving forgeries a "false legitimacy."

———

ON A SUNDAY EVENING in May 2019, I found Jon Levenson, the co-editor of the *Harvard Theological Review,* outside his house in a Boston suburb. When I told him that the scientists he'd published had close personal ties to King and Bagnall, he said, "Whoa! This is the first I've ever heard of it."

The journal's publisher, Cambridge University Press, requires authors "to declare any potential conflicts of interest... (real or apparent) that could be considered or viewed as exerting an undue influence on his or her duties at any stage during the publication process." Levenson told me that neither the scientists nor the scholars had alerted the *Review*'s editors to any such relationships. If Levenson had known, he said, he would have sought other scientists—ones with prior archaeometric experience and without competing allegiances. "The fact that they are close friends, that certainly is very suspicious and not best practices [or] acceptable practices."

That the journal didn't peer-review the lab studies meant that no outside scientists could assess them before publication. Journalists, meanwhile, were told not to ask. Harvard Divinity School gave exclusives to *The New York Times* and *The Boston Globe* in April 2014 on the condition that the reporters contact no scientists or scholars besides the ones commissioned by King.

CHRISTIAN ASKELAND'S JOB with the Green Scholars Initiative made him an easy target for King's supporters, who sought to discount his findings as evangelically driven. But King, it turned out, had also taken money from affluent culture warriors. In her journal article on the Wife fragment, King thanks someone identified only as Tricia Nichols for "generously" funding the radiocarbon testing. It was a common enough name, but after some false starts I found her. The widow of a medical testing magnate, Nichols is a Southern California philanthropist and abortion-rights activist with no record of having ever before donated to Harvard Divinity School. Her $5,000 gift—which financed the tests King touted as proof of the papyrus's antiquity—coincided with Nichols's public criticism of a hospital that banned elective abortions after affiliating with a Catholic health system. "The Catholic Church's historical position, based on the likes of St. Augustine and Thomas Aquinas, is that women were created to live under the subjugation of men,"

Nichols wrote to her local newspaper in 2013. "This assumption is surpassed only by the sanctimony of the Covenant Health Network. Central to its doctrine is that women are to be denied self-determination
in their healthcare decisions, and male administrators are granted the
audacious right to select which legal reproductive procedures they'll
make available." That the generous funder of a key test had a contemporaneous political stake in a specific test result—one that challenged
"the Catholic Church's historical position"—was never publicly disclosed. I had hoped to ask Nichols how her onetime gift to Harvard
Divinity School related to her foundation's mission, but a representative told me that Nichols didn't want to discuss it.

King did not respond to the questions I sent her about Nichols, the
scientists or the undisclosed conflicts of interest.

IN 2013, WHEN IT FIRST TESTED FRITZ'S PAPYRI, the Ancient Ink Lab
had been in its infancy. But by 2015, Jim Yardley and his colleagues
began refining their methods, increasing sample sizes and strengthen-
ing their statistical models, which they later supplemented with new
examinations of the fragments under a scanning electron microscope.
In November 2016, five months after *The Atlantic* published my investigation, the lab announced the results of new tests that put Fritz's papyri
in a very different light. I was seated in the row directly in front of King
and Luijendijk at the Society of Biblical Literature conference, in San
Antonio, when Yardley and his colleagues projected their revised findings on a screen in front of the packed conference room:

Gospel of John: A forgery
GJW: Evidence is consistent with manuscript as forgery

"The controversy over the Gospel of Jesus's Wife is an excellent
example of the way in which the dueling probabilities of different kinds
of evidence need to be fitted together," David Ratzan, a Bagnall-trained
papyrologist and member of Yardley's research team, told the audience.
"For ultimately the argument against its authenticity rests not on phi-
lology, paleography, or material science alone, but on the consilience
of all three—and in fact, none of these proved as decisive as" the jour-
nalistic investigation of provenance.

I visited Yardley at Columbia University a few months later. He told me he regretted that King used his lab's early, unvalidated results to suggest, in 2014, that the ink on the Wife papyrus was ancient. The informal report from which King took the provisional findings, he said, was "never intended to be a proper scientific presentation of the results." King had cited them in her April 2014 article in the *Harvard Theological Review*, even though Yardley had excluded them from his own report in the same issue. "I would have not allowed it to happen if I had thought about it very much," he said of King's decision. "I intended to give Karen a report of what we saw and what we could conclude, and what we could conclude was pretty minimal." The lab's experimental and "totally unprecedented" dating method turned out to be significantly less reliable than first hoped. At least one type of modern ink produced an ancient date, and some other unknown factor—perhaps having to do with how papyri were stored—was skewing results in unpredictable ways. No outside scientists have managed to replicate the technique. More worrisome still, Yardley's team found that the inks on the John and Wife scraps bore similarities—to one degree or another—to modern soots and charcoals and were too different from those on certifiably genuine papyri for the method to work properly. Yardley said that his team reported its first doubts about the John and Wife papyri at a meeting with King at Columbia on June 13, 2016. There were no press releases from Harvard Divinity School this time.

THE UNDISCLOSED USE OF friends and family to carry out scientific testing went hand in hand with a secret push to purge the April 2014 issue of the Harvard journal of dissenting voices. Three months before publication, Levenson, its co-editor, wrote to Leo Depuydt with some unsettling news. Depuydt was the Brown University Egyptologist who'd argued that the Wife papyrus was so laughable a forgery it was "ripe for a Monty Python sketch." The journal had asked him to write the official rebuttal to King's long-awaited article and had planned to publish them in the same issue. The aim was balance: to give a say to the many scholars who had raised questions about the Gospel of Jesus's Wife.

But King wanted Depuydt out. "The complication," Levenson emailed Depuydt, "is that Karen now tells us that commitments made to the media and to the scientists involved require such strict confidentiality that your response cannot feasibly appear in the same issue but should instead wait until everything (online photos, full lab reports, etc.) has become public. The exact nature, origin and rationale of such commitments I don't know."

The advantages of delaying Depuydt's piece were plain: King and Bagnall's handpicked scientists would have the floor—and the headlines—to themselves when the journal published her article. If Depuydt's critique appeared in the same issue, journalists would be apt to quote from it to balance their stories. If the journal postponed it to the next issue, three months later, few reporters would notice and fewer still would write about it. Levenson told Depuydt that joint publication was "preferable (though not to Karen, obviously), since it would give both the *pro* and the *con* on the issue and not allow the *pro* to monopolize the space of *HTR,* giving the false impression that we are endorsing it."

Levenson seemed to warn, however, that the matter was not entirely in his and his co-editor's hands. Both were tenured professors at Harvard Divinity School—Levenson, a Jewish studies scholar, and Kevin Madigan, a historian of medieval Christianity. But their emails suggested that someone above their heads was calling the shots. Moreover, King was insisting on her conditions, even though she had yet to show the editors the scientific test results she expected the journal to publish. Levenson was unsure whether the journal could "shake free" from King's "constraints," he wrote. He and his co-editor very much wanted to send Depuydt copies of King's article and scientific reports, so Depuydt would have time to respond, "but cannot, alas, now promise that we shall succeed."

Depuydt was livid. The *Review,* he wrote to Levenson, had agreed "on more than one occasion" to publish his rebuttal in the same issue as King's paper. If the journal reneged at the eleventh hour, at King's urging, Depuydt said he would go public with what "will with certainty be interpreted by quite a few as an effort at suppression." The idea that unexplained "commitments to the media and to the scientists" barred contemporaneous scholarly critique was unfathomable, Depuydt wrote. "We are, after all, in the truth business."

"Kevin and I are in total agreement with your conditions and principles," Levenson replied. But whether they would prevail did not appear to depend on them. "We are trying to have others farther up the chain of command than we to help with this."

Later, when I asked Levenson who those others were, he said he couldn't recall what he meant by his phrasing but warned against reading anything into it. "There was no pressure from anybody," he maintained. "Our editorial autonomy was completely respected by the dean and everybody else."

ON A TUESDAY IN APRIL 2017, I called David Brakke, a distinguished historian of early Christianity at Ohio State University. Brakke, who holds degrees from Harvard and Yale, is friendly with Karen King and close to other important figures at Harvard Divinity School. Toward the end of a long interview about the Gospel of Jesus's Wife, I asked whether the divinity school faced any unusual pressures in 2010 and 2011. I was curious about what was going on in the background while Walter Fritz was trying to stoke Karen King's interest in his papyri.

Brakke told me the school was in a state of transition. Its long-time dean, William Graham, announced in September 2011 that he was stepping down. As the search got under way for a successor, a long-simmering debate over the place of religious studies at Harvard returned to the fore. "There was talk about how to kind of present the divinity school and its relevance and usefulness to the world," Brakke told me. But not just to the public. To the university, too; to the university, perhaps most. "There are people with strong voices at Harvard who are like, 'Why do we have a divinity school?'—who are opposed to the whole thing."

This was news to me. It certainly hadn't come up during coverage of the Wife papyrus. When I asked Brakke which "strong voices" at Harvard had questioned the existence of its divinity school, he said that if I was really interested in the issue, I needed to begin a lot earlier.

IN OCTOBER 2006, a task force charged with overhauling Harvard's undergraduate curriculum proposed a new track called Reason and Faith in which every student would be required to take a course. "Reason and Faith is a category unlike any that Harvard has included in its general education curriculum," the task force wrote. The classes would treat religion academically, covering topics like church versus state, the history of religion, gender and worship, the Vatican as an institution. The subject was important, the task force said, because 94 percent of Harvard's incoming students report that they discuss religion "frequently" or "occasionally" and because religion is *"realpolitik,"* a force in the world that has inspired everything from war and terrorism to public debates over school prayer and same-sex marriage. "Harvard is no longer an institution with a religious mission, but religion is a fact that Harvard's graduates will confront in their lives both in and after college." Harvard's status as an educational bellwether landed the recommendation in headlines from New York to New Delhi.

The requirement was all but doomed, however, when an influential Harvard psychology professor assailed it as wholly out of place at a secular university. "The juxtaposition of the two words makes it sound like 'faith' and 'reason' are parallel and equivalent ways of knowing, and we have to help students navigate between them," the professor, Steven Pinker, wrote in a blistering opinion piece in *The Harvard Crimson*. "But universities are about reason, pure and simple," he continued. "Faith—believing something without good reasons to do so—has no place in anything but a religious institution, and our society has no shortage of these. Imagine if we had a requirement for 'Astronomy and Astrology' or 'Psychology and Parapsychology.'" He warned of the example Harvard was setting and questioned why religion should be elevated above other, perhaps more important historical forces, like nationalism, markets, class or globalization. "For us to magnify the significance of religion as a topic equivalent in scope to all of science, all of culture, or all of world history and current affairs, is to give it far too much prominence. It is an American anachronism, I think, in an era in which the rest of the West is moving beyond it."

"If I was designing a university from scratch, I wouldn't give it a divinity school," Pinker said when I reached him by phone. He had no objection to secular courses on the world's religions, "but a school of divinity presupposes there is such a thing as a divinity, and I'm not sure universities should be taking a stance." Though many Harvard faculty have a certain celebrity, Pinker—a best-selling author and public intellectual instantly recognizable for his sudsy mane of white curls—was a force to be reckoned with. Within six weeks, the Reason and Faith proposal was dead. At a meeting of the Faculty of Arts and Sciences, where the proposal quietly perished, its lone defender was a theologian at Harvard Divinity School, whose faculty expected to design and teach some of the courses. The Reverend Peter Gomes, a professor of Christian morals and the minister at Harvard's Memorial Church, accused his "learned and articulate colleagues" of caving to "fears of Jesuits under beds and priests in every corner."

"I hope you will have the courage of your original convictions," Gomes went on. "I hope the committee will recover its nerve."

It didn't. The proposal's collapse was an indignity for the divinity school, but it was hardly the first. Harvard had held its nose from the day the school was built two centuries earlier.

THE PURITAN FAMILIES whose boats came ashore in Massachusetts Bay Colony in 1630 had a common purpose: to rid the Church of England of its Roman Catholic taint. The spare furnishings and "congregational" self-rule of their newly built prayer houses were rebukes to papist pomp and hierarchy. But the Puritans' "City upon a Hill" was a fragile experiment. As its English-born clergy died off, they feared their New Jerusalem would lose its way. So in 1636, "dreading to leave an illiterate Ministry to the Churches, when our present Ministers shall lie in the Dust," Puritan lawmakers established a "colledge" amid the cow yards of Cambridge. Every student, one group of Puritans reported, would be "plainly instructed" that "the maine end of his life and studies is, *to know God and Jesus Christ,* ... the only foundation of all sound knowledge and Learning." The Latin word on its seal, "Veritas," referred not to secular facts but to sacred knowledge. The college was christened Harvard after an obscure thirty-one-year-old minister who willed the school some books and money before dying of tuberculosis in a nearby town. But many colonists called it "the School of the Prophets."

Not until 1816, nearly two centuries later, did America's oldest university decide to wash its hands of religion. It did so by founding a divinity school. Observation, measurement and experiment—the calling cards of the Enlightenment—had sidelined God as a guarantor of *veritas*. Not coincidentally, Divinity Hall became the first Harvard building erected outside the Yard, the enclave of greens, dormitories and classrooms that still anchors the campus. The divinity school's remote location, in what was then a "rustic woodlands," was, in the acid words of one early dean, "the curious consequence of a movement... to remove the troublesome subject of theology from among the responsibilities of the University."

As Harvard molted from Congregational seminary to secular university, its leaders' faith changed with it. In the early nineteenth century, after a bitter struggle, Harvard awarded both its presidency and the Hollis Professorship of Divinity—the post now held by King—to Unitarians, ending the stranglehold of the college's orthodox Calvinist founders. Unitarians drew spiritual meaning not from revelation, but from reason, experience and independent inquiry. They saw Jesus as a man, not a divine being, and rejected the trinitarian godhead and the idea of original sin. Their searching, liberal theology suited a college whose *Veritas* of faith was giving way to a *veritas* of reason. "Unitarianism," wrote Samuel Eliot Morison, a historian of Harvard, was "a halfway house to the rationalistic and scientific point of view, yet a house built so reverentially that the academic wayfarer could seldom forget that he had sojourned in a House of God." The rest of Harvard soon moved out of the halfway house, doffing its parochial past and embracing the Enlightenment. But the divinity school made the halfway house its home. Its boosters saw no conflict in its mission: "the serious, impartial and unbiased investigation of Christian truth."

In a renowned address at the divinity school in 1838, the Reverend Ralph Waldo Emerson urged seniors to free the faith from its "noxious" obsession with the person of Jesus. "The soul knows no persons," Emerson said, fusing Christianity and transcendentalism. "It invites every man to expand to the full circle of the universe." Half a century later, a professor named Francis Peabody would pioneer the Social Gospel, a liberal Protestant movement that drew on social science to confront alcoholism, environmental pollution and inequality. In 1980, the divinity school's Helmut Koester shook the field of biblical studies again, arguing that five of the noncanonical gospels were at least as old and "valuable" as the New Testament as guides to Jesus's earliest teachings. Three years later, the groundbreaking feminist theologian Elisabeth Schüssler Fiorenza published *In Memory of Her,* the first of several books urging scholars to "write women back into early Christian history" by filling the silences in patriarchal scripture.

Whenever some nabob tried to argue that the study of faith had no place at Harvard, the divinity school always found a way to remind the university of its roots. "It would be false to all our traditions," the school's benefactors remonstrated in the 1850s, when Harvard's president petitioned the courts for a permanent divorce from the school, "if in a college named for a Puritan minister, fostered by a Puritan clergy, intended to be, and often called a 'School of the Prophets,' bearing on its corporate seal the motto of 'Christ and the Church,' religion should be the only subject deliberately excluded."

The 1850s crisis subsided, but not Harvard's suspicion of its divinity faculty. Unlike many other schools—and most of its elite peers—Harvard has no academic department of religious studies. That gives the divinity school outsize influence over how students learn about religion—influence that Harvard administrators have long sought to bridle. Though the divinity school houses the better number of specialists and courses in religion, for instance, it lacks the ability to independently admit students to the doctoral program or to the undergraduate major in religion. Nor does it control what courses such students take. Those rights reside on the Yard, in something called the Committee on the Study of Religion; a rotating panel appointed by the dean of the Faculty of Arts and Sciences, it includes roughly equal numbers of FAS and divinity scholars. The only admissions the divinity school oversees are those for its far less prestigious master's programs, whose applicants are bound for ministry, social service and other nonacademic jobs. The master's students hail from some thirty faith traditions, range in age from their twenties to their sixties and come from prior jobs as disparate as navy officer, bartender and banker. The largest single group are Catholic women, King had told me, "because their people don't take them." On top of the thicket of red tape were the ways—sometimes subtle, sometimes not—that professors on Harvard's main campus looked down on the school. The long-standing prejudice, fair or not, was that most divinity faculty, however accomplished, lacked the high distinction of professors on the Yard and would never have been offered jobs there.

One of the divinity school's most powerful detractors was Lawrence Summers, the former U.S. Treasury secretary, who became Harvard's president in 2001. "He considered the place a hotbed for students more interested in activism than academia," the journalist Richard Bradley wrote in a 2005 book on the Summers era. When Summers named William Graham dean in 2002, some divinity faculty feared an ulterior motive. Graham was a professor in Harvard's Department of Near Eastern Languages and Civilizations; that is, he came from the *Yard*—a laurel he rarely failed to lord over his new charges. He was also a historian of Islam in what had always been a Christian divinity school. Moreover, Bradley reported, Graham was the first dean not to be an ordained minister or priest, "fueling the theory that Summers wanted to make the divinity school less of a training ground for ministers and more a center for scholars of religion." Graham had little desire to preside over a school with "a lackluster endowment, a fractious faculty, and a politicized student body." But when other promotions failed to materialize, a colleague of Graham's said, "Bill probably figured that he had the opportunity to turn the divinity school into a truly secular, intellectual institution."

By all appearances, Graham tried. Breaking with the school's nearly two centuries as an unofficially Unitarian institution, he filled posts with specialists in Buddhism, Hinduism, Judaism and Islam. The goal, at least in part, was to bring the school into the modern era of religious studies and put it on stronger footing with the Yard. The Reason and Faith debacle in 2006—and Steven Pinker's ongoing broadsides—were the first sign that Graham had perhaps underestimated the steepness of his hill. Worse news arrived a few months later, when two leading divinity school professors took parting shots as they abruptly left for other universities. "The Divinity School is very much interested in taking over the study of religion, which would really be a disaster," Robert Orsi, a highly regarded scholar of American religious history who defected for Northwestern, told *The Harvard Crimson*. Because of its focus on training ministers, he suggested, the school was ill-equipped to treat religious studies disinterestedly, as an evidence-based discipline. "Although the Divinity School claims that undergraduates take their courses, they don't," he said. "We really believe religious studies needs to have a presence [on the Yard] that is separate and distinct from the Divinity School." Thomas Lewis, a philosopher of religion, voiced similar misgivings as he left for Brown. That the scholars held leadership posts on the Committee on the Study of Religion—Orsi, as chair, and Lewis, as director of undergraduate studies—lent their critiques extra sting.

When Lawrence Summers resigned, in turmoil, in 2006, divinity faculty glimpsed opportunity in his successor. Drew Faust, who would become Harvard's first female president, was a major Civil War historian who seemed poised to understand the divinity school's aims. Her soon-to-be-published book, *This Republic of Suffering,* touched on the role of Christian faith in helping survivors of America's deadliest war reckon with its carnage. Still, Faust was a creature of the Yard. Whether she shared its suspicion of the school was unknown. Divinity scholars wasted no time courting her. "Not only do we have a woman president, but we have a humanist," the scholar Ann Braude enthused at a Harvard Divinity School gathering in Faust's honor in March 2007, while Faust was still president-elect.

Important figures at the divinity school were soon doubling down on its distinctive approach to scholarship. In a new mission statement that raised eyebrows among recently hired faculty, the school proclaimed that theology and religious studies "depend on and reinforce each other." That is, the ancient way of studying faith—through investigations of the nature of God and of the logic of scripture, often by devout believers—went hand in glove with the modern methods of secular social scientists and historians. In a journal paper responding to the Reason and Faith controversy, the Harvard divinity scholar Amy Hollywood suggested that the methods of the Enlightenment were perhaps overrated. Because faith explains the universe to believers and every believer experiences religion in his or her own way, maybe "reason" wasn't the best way for scholars to study it, she argued. You might be able to separate "fact" from "meaning" and "value" in a physics class, but "in the study of religion it is impossible." If religion professors require students to wrestle with texts, lectures and rituals in purely "rational terms," Hollywood wondered, "what do we lose—in understanding, in pleasure, or in the pursuit of whatever we conceive the good to be"?

"Rather than attempt to mime scientific methods," Hollywood concluded, scholars of religion needed "other ways of understanding." As King herself had once written, "One need never say no to a story, a song, a poem that gives life, heartens, teaches, or consoles, and need never fail to call it true."

A nonchalance among some divinity faculty toward empirical facts—a wariness about their very possibility—distressed even some of the master's students. A graduate named Matt Bieber praised the school as a "refuge" from the "nastiness" much of the world directs at religion. "But there's something missing—a concern for truth," Bieber, who had majored in philosophy at Princeton, wrote on his blog.

> Now, for anyone educated in higher education's dominant
> paradigms over the last half a century, that word alone
> can bring snickers. (I once heard an HDS professor invoke
> Harvard's motto—*Veritas*—only to chortle and move on
> without explaining himself. In that lecture hall, he knew he
> didn't need to.)
> But that word is still above Harvard's gates, as it should be.

TENSIONS BOILED OVER in February 2010, when *Newsweek* published a feature story headlined "Harvard's Crisis of Faith."

"The Harvard faculty cannot cope with religion," *Newsweek*'s religion editor, Lisa Miller, wrote, calling the study of religion at Harvard "uniquely dysfunctional." "It cannot agree on who should teach it, how it should be taught, and how much value to give it.... Harvard likes to regard itself as the best of the best. Yet even public universities—the University of Texas, Arizona State and Indiana University, for example—generate more excitement around the subject of religion than Harvard does." The point was hard to miss: Harvard's religion program was so sleepy of late that it was getting beaten by state universities in flyover country.

Walter Fritz's first email to King—about a discovery sure to return Harvard to the front ranks of exciting religion scholarship—arrived less than five months later.

FAUSTIAN BARGAIN

As Harvard president, Drew Faust had an entire university to run. Brush fires at the divinity school didn't normally rate her time. But the exodus of prominent faculty—and the public lashings they'd given the school on their way out—had gotten her attention. Particularly concerning was news that two recent recruits from Princeton were already on their way out. When Harvard Divinity School hired Marie Griffith and her husband, Leigh Schmidt, in 2009, it hailed the pair as "two of the very best mid-career historians of American religion active in the academy today." Faust summoned them to her office in Massachusetts Hall a year or so later to ask why they were unhappy.

Their complaints—about the second-string status of divinity faculty and the blurred lines between scholarship and ministry—echoed those of other prominent faculty who'd recently left. The couple told me that Faust gave every indication that she took their grievances seriously. "Her concern was genuine," Griffith said of their meeting. "I think she really recognized [the problem] and wanted to do something." But they had no idea how long it might take, and in March 2011 they quit, accepting offers from a new Center on Religion and Politics at Washington University in St. Louis. Another prominent new hire, Mark Jordan, who was particularly beloved of students, soon followed them out the door, telling *The Harvard Crimson* that he blamed "the present configuration of this complex institution."

In September, William Graham announced his resignation as Harvard Divinity School's dean.

THE NEXT MONTH, divinity faculty opened their in-boxes to find a disquieting message from the university's president. "I write to make you aware that I have asked a group of distinguished scholars and academic leaders from outside the University to offer me their advice on how we can strengthen the study of religion at Harvard," Faust wrote. The six-member panel she assembled included the president of Bryn Mawr College, the chancellor of the Jewish Theological Seminary, a former dean of the University of Chicago Divinity School and highly esteemed religion professors at Berkeley, Penn and Princeton. Faust charged them with a top-to-bottom review.

"This is an important moment for the study of religion, and I believe that Harvard can do more," Faust wrote. Among the questions she was asking the committee to investigate was "the Divinity School's academic and professional effectiveness."

The letter raised immediate alarm. "The Harvard Divinity School was very upset," said one of the advisory panel's members, who like the other members I interviewed asked for anonymity to speak freely about a sensitive subject. "They simply did not see any way in which anything we recommended didn't threaten their control over the study of religion."

At an organizational meeting in early November, at the Harvard Club in Manhattan, Faust advised committee members to pull no punches. "We have a real problem," she said, according to a person who was there. "The sky's the limit; you recommend what you think is necessary, no matter how radical."

"It's an issue when you have your stars leaving," a second committee member told me, referring to Faust's concern about the faculty departures. "There was a kind of crisis."

Faust's resolve was underscored by her choice of committee chair. Caroline Bynum, an eminent medieval historian and Harvard alumna, had played bad cop for Faust before: she chaired a panel, in 2000, that softened the ground for Faust's job as the first dean of the Radcliffe Institute for Advanced Study, which rose from the ashes of Radcliffe College, the 120-year-old women's institution that Harvard had dissolved, amid controversy, the year before. Bynum's panel was "my cover," Faust told the *Harvard Gazette*. "I think there were 30,000 Radcliffe alums, and 20,000 of them were irate, but none of them could blame me. I was like an innocent who marched in and said let's move to the future."

In naming Bynum chair of the External Advisory Committee on

the Study of Religion at Harvard, Faust signaled that another blood-letting might be in the offing. Faust took to calling 2011–2012 her "year of religion." From November 2011 to January 2012, her blue-ribbon com-mittee made multiple visits to campus and carried out meetings and interviews with dozens of deans, professors and students. Some divin-ity professors feared that the ultimate aim was to pave the way for a department of religious studies on the Yard, a move that would dim the divinity school's candle still further by drawing a bright line between professors who did serious scholarship and those who trained min-isters. A stand-alone department, that is, would dismantle the divin-ity school's central conceit: that theology and religious studies—faith and reason—depended on and reinforced each other. "If they ceded religious studies as a discipline over to the Yard, the struggle for intel-lectual respectability would be that much harder," a former divinity professor told me.

The strongest objections came from a group of feminist faculty. "These very articulate and gifted women had arrived at a situation at the divinity school where their politics and their scholarship were finally taken seriously," a committee member told me, "and if there was any move toward anything in the Yard, they [feared they] would lose those gains." Laura Nasrallah, a professor who obtained her PhD under King, read aloud a letter she said had been approved by the entire divinity faculty; it accused the committee of failing to adequately con-sult the school as it went about its work.

The panel met with many divinity professors. But the more it investigated, the more its members saw a department on the Yard as the surest path to respectability for religious studies at Harvard—and to excitement from undergraduates. "Harvard, with its rich legacy and immense resources in the field of religious studies, has the opportunity to create a model for the study of religion," the committee wrote in its final report. "Yet our committee sensed from the president, deans, and others we consulted that, increasingly," Harvard seemed "underpow-ered for this task.... The absence of a religious studies department in the Faculty of Arts and Sciences at Harvard is, in our view, a troubling omission for a university of such comprehensive distinction across a broad range of the humanities and social sciences."

The panel's recommendation was the divinity school's "worst nightmare," a committee member told me. "They would be forever a divinity school; they would not be a religious studies department." Nor would they be the kind of hybrid they saw as their trademark but that critics—particularly new hires—deemed a "recipe for disaster."

"They had a mission and [felt that] our committee booby-trapped it," this person recalled. "They were furious. Even personally, my friends at HDS said, 'How could you?'"

BUT THEN SOMETHING CHANGED. In January 2012, with the committee's work only half done, Faust's assistant began sending it signals to back off. "We started getting real pressure not to recommend what we wanted to recommend," a member of the panel told me. "I mean real pressure."

Just how much Faust's initial impulses had shifted became clear that March, when she named a new divinity school dean. Her search for Graham's successor had narrowed to two finalists. One was David Hempton, a mild-mannered Harvard Divinity School professor who had served, with Karen King, on the search committee that had recommended his own candidacy to Faust. The other was a scholar at another university who would have brought fresh eyes to the study of religion at Harvard—precisely what many saw as Faust's priority. On March 30, 2012, however, Faust showed up at a hastily arranged gathering at the divinity school and made an unexpected announcement: she was giving the job to Hempton.

Following Faust to the lectern, Hempton, a historian of European evangelicalism, heaped praise on the very feature of the school that Leigh Schmidt, Robert Orsi and other high-profile defectors saw as its greatest weakness: its hybrid mission to mint both pastors and PhDs. "Bringing together religious and theological studies," Hempton said, in the brogue of his native Northern Ireland, was one of the things about the school that "I love." Unlike Graham, who'd come from the Yard, Hempton was a divinity school insider in the mainstream Protestant mold of many who had come before him. His appointment was a revanchist triumph, a vote of confidence in the school's ability to save itself. Faust credited "the respect and the admiration that the faculty have for David [Hempton]." There was "electricity" in the room, she said, "because of the love that the divinity school felt for [him] and I think the relief and gratitude" that he accepted the appointment.

"Relief" was an odd choice of words, but in retrospect its meaning seemed plain. What had begun as a plan by the Harvard president to bring aggressive outside reform to the study of religion had turned into an effort to placate rank-and-file divinity scholars who didn't see the need. "As if having a separate divinity school for those who believe (in something) and a religion department (where religions are taught-about) would improve anyone's deep grasp of religion," the Harvard theologian Francis X. Clooney, a Jesuit priest, had written a couple of years earlier. "Such a split might be functionally useful, but deeply dull. Harvard will do better by adhering patiently to its current difficult mix, even if it sets the university on edge."

In their remarks at the announcement ceremony, I noticed, both Faust and Hempton made unbidden references to the post held by Karen King. "The oldest professorship at the University, as we know because the cow won't let us forget it, is the Hollis Professor of Divinity, established in 1721," Faust said, referring to the traditional right of Hollis appointees to graze a cow on the Yard. "I was just remembering the cow as I walked over here today." When Hempton took the microphone, he, too, invoked the Hollis chair, but in a more sardonic vein. Faust's entanglement with the cow, he said, with an arch look, made it easy for him to wring concessions from her. "I do have a wonderful blackmail photograph of the president tethering a cow out there," he quipped, "which I think is against the Cambridge bylaws." (Hempton declined to speak with me for this book. His spokesperson did not dispute that Hempton opposed a religious studies department on the Yard and that he made his views known to Faust.)

When the advisory panel gave Faust its final report, in June 2012, its members were greeted by deafening silence. Some feared their report would never see daylight. Faust waited three months to release it—with a cover letter spiking its chief recommendation. "The deans and I believe that the advancement of the study of religion at Harvard will be best accomplished through a careful crafting of a partnership of FAS [the Faculty of Arts and Sciences] and HDS, beyond what exists today," she wrote, "and that the establishment of a new department in FAS alone would undermine rather than advance that creative interdependence and would divert resources and attention from the intellectual and substantive foundation of our teaching and research."

To some members of Faust's outside committee, it was an almost inexplicable capitulation to the status quo. Someone, or something, had changed Faust's mind. Faust declined my request for an interview. "She feels that others are in a better position to discuss this with you," her assistant wrote to me.

AFTER LEARNING ABOUT THESE threats to the school's future, I returned to my notes to look over some dates.

On June 25, 2011, after ignoring Walter Fritz for nearly a year, Karen King rebuffed his requests and sent him away. "I made some initial attempts at the material you sent, but without real success," she wrote to him. "Perhaps you have found someone who can offer more help." As she elaborated to a Harvard press officer, "I didn't believe it was authentic and told him I wasn't interested."

The next day, June 26, Fritz went for broke. He told her that a European manuscript dealer had "right now" offered him a sum "almost too good to be true." If King didn't move fast, he suggested, his papyrus might vanish into a "private collection for good." He said he'd already shown it to "several people." The hard sell forced him to break character. Gone was the casually naive collector who didn't read Coptic and wasn't sure what he had. In its place was a slick pitchman. His email was a textbook appeal to scarcity and urgency—*Hurry while supplies last!*

King could have replied with something as noncommittal as "Can you give me a few weeks?" But she said nothing. It was as clear a sign as any that she wasn't falling for it; she wasn't interested in the papyrus, now or ever. She was a tenured senior professor at Harvard, with nothing to gain and everything to lose. "This is not a career maker," King told *The Boston Globe* shortly before the announcement in Rome. "If it's a forgery, it's a career breaker."

Then—four months after rejecting Fritz and before so much as showing photos of the papyrus to AnneMarie Luijendijk or Roger Bagnall—King inexplicably wrote Fritz back. On October 15, 2011, in a startling reversal, she outlined for Fritz a nearly complete plan to publish the papyrus herself; "arrange to have a papyrological specialist authenticate and date the fragment"; and find a home for it in the Harvard University Library, where it would "join one of the ancient fragments of The Gospel of Thomas among other important works." King even adopted the collector's term for the papyrus, calling it a "gospel fragment," even though its literary genre was anything but clear.

"I look forward to hearing from you," she wrote.

This was no longer Fritz selling King. This was King selling Fritz.

FOR ALMOST EVERY REPORTING PROJECT, I make a timeline. It's usually just a text file with a chronological list of dates and corresponding events. I thicken the chronology as I come across new material, tucking new items between those already in the list. It's the easiest way, I find, to illuminate the forces that propel people from one chess square in their lives to the next. A move that seems puzzling in isolation can make sense when one discovers what comes right before or after it.

In the spring of 2017, I supplemented my timeline with dates tied to the controversy over the study of religion at Harvard. The dates spanned from the proposed Reason and Faith requirement in 2006 to Drew Faust's rejection of her advisory panel's key recommendation in 2012. An appendix of the panel's report contained not just the text of Faust's letter announcing the panel's formation but also the date she sent it: October 13, 2011. I put it into my timeline:

10/13/2011: *Harvard President Drew Faust sends a "Dear Colleagues" letter informing faculty that she is bringing in outside scholars to assess the study of religion at Harvard.*

When I glanced at the entry directly beneath it, it felt as though a blindfold were lifted.

10/15/2011: *King bites.*

Two days after Faust announced an outside investigation that threatened the future of Harvard Divinity School, King told Fritz that she wanted his papyri after all.

MY TIMELINE SOON POINTED UP other alignments between Faust's investigation and King's activity around the Gospel of Jesus's Wife. On Wednesday, December 14, 2011, members of Faust's review panel were at Harvard Divinity School, spending long days interviewing faculty. But they weren't the only visitors. Walter Fritz was there, too. December 14 was the day Fritz handed King his papyri and signed a release permitting them to be "published in any manner Prof. King and/or her associates see fit." It was a haunting tableau: a con man invited into the divinity school on the same day as members of a blue-ribbon panel charged with determining the school's "academic and professional effectiveness."

"I tremendously enjoyed my meeting with her," Fritz recalled of the visit. That King might have sensed some risk in his presence became clear when I found Russell Pollard, who was then the interim head of the Andover-Harvard Theological Library, which adjoins the divinity school. Instead of meeting Fritz in her own office, King asked Pollard if they could borrow his. "There had been a request that this be very private, and Karen thought my office was a good private space," recalled Pollard, who stayed for the meeting. A decision was made— perhaps at King's behest, he said—to store the papyri in the empty bottom drawer of a file cabinet in his office. It was less a high-security arrangement than a stealthy one. "We kept it quiet," Pollard said. "Part of the idea was that no one would suspect it was there."

CALENDARS LINED UP AGAIN on September 19, 2012, the day the Gospel of Jesus's Wife debuted on the front pages of *The New York Times* and *The Boston Globe.* Every dean, professor and student who glanced at the newspapers that day would see that Harvard Divinity School was as potent a force in the study of religion as any institution in the land. So would anyone who saw the encampment of news trucks outside 45 Francis Avenue, the school's Gothic headquarters. And anyone who visited Harvard University's website, where the discovery—complete with a photo of King and the papyrus—spanned the top of its home page, with links to a Harvard-produced news feature and a YouTube publicity clip. That same day, though no one seemed to notice the coincidence, Drew Faust made a quiet announcement: she was rejecting her own panel's advice that a department of religious studies be created on the Yard. She was sparing Harvard Divinity School a potentially humiliating fate. The panel had given Faust its final report in early June. But she waited until September 19—a day of triumphant headlines for the study of religion at Harvard—to simultaneously release and neuter it.

Did a forgery help save Harvard Divinity School?

A few weeks before King announced her discovery, the divinity school's small public relations staff, unprepared for so big a story, approached the Yard for help. Harvard's central Public Affairs and Communications office took charge, photographing the papyrus, interviewing King for in-house publications and inviting *The New York Times* and *The Boston Globe* to campus for advance interviews. It was the office's job to inform Faust in advance of major news stories concerning Harvard; King's discovery—a sensational Christian text headed for the front pages of major newspapers—would have been no exception, according to two sources close to the office. Faust was unusually attuned that month to the power of the media to shine a light on scholars' work. A Ric Burns documentary, based on Faust's book *This Republic of Suffering*, premiered on PBS the same day as King's announcement of the Wife papyrus in Rome. Faust had spent the preceding week promoting the Civil War documentary in talks and media interviews. When a *Boston Globe* reporter asked whether there was any overlap between running a major university and having one's scholarship enter popular culture, Faust said, "The key question is, What is meaningful to people, and how do you make them understand the world in which they live?"

Emails read to me by members of Faust's religion advisory committee showed forethought to the timing of her public release of their report. At 9:00 a.m. on Monday, September 17, 2012, according to the emails, Faust called her panel's chair and said she was releasing the report—and announcing her opposition—in exactly two days.

I asked Faust about the timing of her announcement, her foreknowledge of the Wife papyrus and the extent of her communications with Hempton or King. "She is not available to comment on this," Faust's assistant replied.

KAREN KING WAS NOT among the divinity professors who felt the need to make her voice heard at every faculty meeting. She showed little interest in the gladiatorial battles of ego that are a fixture of Harvard culture. But people were wrong to ascribe her reserve to meekness. King's stomach for risk was as strong as anyone's. Yet where others brawled, King maneuvered. On the rare occasions she entered the fray, she had a plan that was already several steps ahead of the opposition. It was how she persuaded the childhood church she'd rejected to sponsor her senior-year trip to Norway. It was how she used a West German government scholarship to fund research in communist East Germany. It was how, as a professor, she made the leap from second-tier California college to the world's most illustrious university with just one book to her name: her dissertation, published twelve years after graduation and in the nick of time, by a press in which she was a board member and investor. And it was how she conducted herself at Harvard, including her bid to eject Depuydt's rebuttal from the *Harvard Theological Review* on the basis of unspecified "commitments" to scientists whose conflicts of interest she failed to disclose.

"She didn't show her cards openly, like a lot of other people did," Emily Neill, the former PhD candidate, said of King's approach to department politics. "She kind of showed up in important moments and tipped the balance in certain ways."

The Gospel of Jesus's Wife, I came to believe, was King's boldest intervention, a daring play for survival in a time of uncertainty. King had earned her degrees in traditional departments of religious studies, at the University of Montana and Brown; they were the sorts that Faust's panel had held up as models for a secular institution as eminent as Harvard. But for King, Harvard Divinity School had become a more congenial home. The school was a kind of Ivy-fringed Jesus Seminar, peopled by no small number of scholars for whom reason and faith were mutually reinforcing. "For me the study of religion, whether as a historian or as a literary critic, [is] all about deepening one's understanding and deepening one's faith," King told a television interviewer who asked how she separated her personal religious beliefs from her scholarship. The degree to which she saw the practice of faith as what her work was "all about" was striking. The aim wasn't so much knowledge for its own sake, or even for history's sake. Historians like her, she wrote in one book, produced "resources" that religious communities could use to "engage in constructive critique and reformation of their own traditions." The goal, she said elsewhere, was to make "tradition uncomfortable, which is always a good thing." She was restoring lost works to the Bible not for the sake of more choices to mix and match from, but to open believers to an entirely new model of the faith. It's not about "one more perspective, one more voice," she told colleagues. "It's about what happens when these are included in the story." For King, what happened was nothing short of an act of creation. To treat noncanonical texts as the equal of Matthew, Mark, Luke and John was to reinvent ancient Christianity. It was "to forge the world," as she put it in a 2019 speech, using a word whose multiple meanings—to shape, to create, to fake—can't have been lost on her. In 2012, when I asked if she saw her scholarship as opening Christianity to a larger, more inclusive group of believers, she demurred. "I'm less interested in proselytizing or a bigger tent for its own sake than I am in issues of human flourishing," she told me. "It's more the How do we get along? ... What does it mean for living now? ... So yeah, if health and wellbeing and all kinds of things were improved, I don't really care how big the tent is.'"

The rejection by her Sunday school teacher, the woman who scoffed at King's childhood conversion, might have planted the seeds of this rebellion. But Bob Funk cultivated it to maturity. "Our work," he told the charter members of the Jesus Seminar in 1985, "will spell liberty" for millions. In 1996, he appointed King head of two special Jesus Seminar panels, charged with remaking the Christian canon and creeds. "The goal of the Canon Seminar is going to be to produce a new New Testament by the end of 1999," King told the Religion News Service.

> She noted that the legitimacy of the canon has "clearly been undermined by historical criticism over the last couple of centuries." Similarly, King said, the Creed Seminar will examine how the Christian church's early statements of belief, known as creeds, were formed. First on the Seminar's agenda is the Nicene Creed.... In addition to studying the origin and evolution of the statement, King said, the scholars intend to "... write counter-creeds, if you will" that will consider "other possibilities that could have come into being."

The effort was dropped, but a decade and a half later Hal Taussig, a fellow charter member of the Jesus Seminar and one of King's closest confidants (she dedicated her Gospel of Mary book to him), decided to try again. Taussig, a progressive Methodist pastor and theologian, impaneled his canon-making "council" with scholars he said met two key criteria. One was that they "explicitly saw their work as theological and spiritual as well as academic." The other, which he deemed "centrally important," was "national experience in telling large numbers of the American public what they might read for their spiritual welfare." King was one of the first scholars Taussig invited, and one of the first to accept.

King no sooner joined the project than prevailed on Taussig to set up a small "sub-council" first. This allowed her and a few others to preemptively narrow the field, culling more than half of the forty-three sacred texts that Taussig saw as candidates for his "New New Testament" before the full council could consider them. The sub-council's meeting was in late October 2011, two weeks after King told Fritz she wanted to publish his papyrus. Then she pressed Taussig to do something he wasn't comfortable with. To be included in *A New New Testament*, as the book would be called, Taussig had decided that an early Christian text had to be composed before A.D. 175, the outside date by which all scripture in the traditional New Testament was thought to have been written. King, however, asked that a special exception be made for one of her favorite texts, the Diary of Perpetua, even though its early third-century origins "violated our date boundaries," Taussig wrote. "King argued that the real possibility that the Diary of Perpetua was the first early Christian document to be written by a woman and was a gripping firsthand account of a Christian martyr were important enough factors for *A New New Testament* to be opened to it.... I opposed its inclusion on the basis that it was too late (beyond 175 CE) to be considered a contemporary writing of the traditional New Testament."

It was an almost surreal dispute. Taussig, the pastor, was insisting on historical defensibility, while King, the historian, was treating dates as adjustable furniture. King persuaded the sub-council to include the Diary of Perpetua in the preapproved choices forwarded to the full council, thereby overruling Taussig, the book's author. King then persuaded the full council to extend the cutoff to A.D. 205, to give cover to Perpetua's anachronistic inclusion. After Taussig pointed out that this later date would require consideration of works by anti-Gnostic theologians like Tertullian and Irenaeus, the council retreated, dropping Perpetua and allowing the original cutoff of A.D. 175 to stand.

Nearly a year later, in early September 2012, I briefly mentioned the Jesus Seminar to King during our dinner interview for my *Smithsonian* article. King became visibly irritated. The Jesus Seminar no longer asked questions that interested her, she told me, but she didn't want to talk about it. Her reaction surprised me: all the old news clips I'd read portrayed her as one of the seminar's leading lights.

Now I had a clearer view. The seminar's founder, her mentor Bob Funk, had died in 2005, leaving her longtime intellectual home—and theological battering ram—adrift. A few years later, the "New New Testament"—a project of the seminar colleague who'd been her closest confidant—rejected her methods as unsound. Harvard Divinity School was her last stand.

IN JUNE 2011, King had deemed Fritz's papyrus a forgery and walked away. But in October 2011—two days after Faust put Harvard Divinity School in her crosshairs—King changed her mind. If the university created a department of religious studies on the Yard, the divinity school would have seen its star fade, and King's with it. King was not among the minority of divinity professors with a joint appointment on Harvard's Faculty of Arts and Sciences. If she nonetheless got one of the new posts on the Yard, her approach to history could feel decidedly out of place. ("Steve Pinker is just the tip of the iceberg," a member of Faust's panel told me, referring to the depth of Yard hostility toward divinity scholarship.)

Before the historian Leigh Schmidt left in 2011, he had spoken with King about his frustrations. King advised him against pressing for change. She counseled that he keep his head down, stay out of campus politics and focus on the research he could do in a place where people left you alone. "She had come around to seeing the wisdom of the current structures and also just that 'these are battles you don't need to fight,'" Schmidt told me. "She said, 'You're letting this bother you way too much. It bothered me once, and then I learned I can go up to my very nice office and get my work done. You should do that, too.'"

Whether or not there was active coordination between King, the divinity school and the president's office, the timing of Faust's rebuff of her own panel raises the question of whether she saw King's history-making discovery as at least partial proof that the school could right itself. If Harvard Divinity School could produce scholarship worthy of the front page of *The New York Times,* it could do anything. Never in the newspaper's 161-year history had Harvard Divinity School research been the main subject of a front-page story. This possible secondary motive—survival, her own, her school's—could explain King's sudden interest in a papyrus she'd already spurned, as well as her baffling rush to announce in the face of two ominous peer reviews, ones that in any other circumstance might have slowed a scholar down. It could explain other things, too: the refusal to name Fritz or release his provenance documents, even though she was free to do so; the desire to publish in a Harvard journal whose editors she could keep an eye on; the decision to forgo scientific testing ahead of her announcement; the absence of photos at her presentation in Rome; the choice afterward of scientists whose chief qualifications were their undisclosed personal allegiances; the bid to sideline Depuydt and block journalists' access to outside voices as a condition for exclusives; the failure to release images of Fritz's Gospel of John fragment, images that surfaced a full year and a half after Rome, by accident, in an ink chemistry report; the struggle of the *Harvard Theological Review*'s editors to control publication in their own journal.

Somewhere in her heart, it seemed, King knew that the Gospel of Jesus's Wife was dead the moment anyone outside her influence looked too closely at it. Rome made clear just how limited that influence was, how limited anyone's would have been in the same circumstances. But by then it was too late. The papyrus had grown so freighted with cargo—personal, institutional, ideological—that no one on board had the courage, or strength, to pull the emergency brake.

EPILOGUE

Services

It is for such objects that we may reserve Plato's conception of the "simulacrum," the identical copy for which no original has ever existed.

—cultural theorist Fredric Jameson

For five years, a scholar and a con man walked shoulder to shoulder, one in darkness, the other in light, evangelists for a lie. It would be wrong to say they had nothing in common. Both were loners from small towns. Both savored risk and resented authority. Both believed in the salvific power of their own intelligence and saw head-to-head conflict as less effective than tactical surprise. But none of these explained it. The key to their improbable union, rather, was an idea on which they'd both found purchase: that truth is in the eye of the beholder. For a confidence man, the idea's appeal is obvious. A con depends for his livelihood on the propensity of people to see what they want to see. But for a scholar, a professional truth seeker, the calculus is more complex.

Not so long ago, Karen King believed in—or at least paid lip service to—the time-tested bellwethers of historical truth: the credibility of one's sources, and the strength of one's evidence. In a 2004 talk at a Times Square hotel, King asked the audience to imagine that a policeman had accused her of an "evil deed" and that her alibi was that she was at the store buying milk at the time of the alleged incident. Whose side would the audience take? she asked. "A major issue for us [historians] in making these kinds of decisions is our confidence in the character of the source, right?" she said. "If you knew me to be a habitual liar, you would probably doubt everything I said. If you were confident about my character and know me well, you might even stand up against the police [to defend me]."

Next came evidence. "You want to interview the clerk at the grocery store," King continued. "You want to see if I've got a receipt with a time stamped on it; you want to see if there's milk in my refrigerator, those kinds of things. And of course eyewitnesses are really terrific."

"So historians are like this," she continued. "We always want our evidence."

Yet when it came to the story Walter Fritz told about the Gospel of Jesus's Wife, King probed neither source nor evidence. She had no eyewitnesses, no confirmed receipts. She didn't check Fritz's refrigerator for milk, and stood in the way of journalists and scholars who offered to check for her. She claimed afterward that she didn't know provenance could be investigated, but her 2004 talk showed that she, like any educated person, had all the basic tools. If "historians are like this"—if they were uncompromising in their quest for truth—then it was fair to ask whether King, in championing the Wife papyrus, was acting as a historian or as something else.

King's rallying cry in news interviews and public talks was that "good history" made believers "accountable" for the way they practiced their faith. But King's scholarship suggested the opposite: Her ideological commitments were choreographing her practice of history. The story came first; the dates managed after. The narrative before the evidence; the news conference before the scientific analysis; the interpretation before the authentication. Her rich sense of what Christianity might be—if only people had the right information—too often preceded the facts. Nowhere in her 2012 article on the Wife papyrus did she mention the well-known scriptural trope of the Church as Jesus's bride, an omission that made her case for a human wife seem more straightforward than it actually was. When a scientific test dated the papyrus to the eighth century, she buried its historical significance in the final sentence of an "Afterword," treating a major challenge to her thesis as a trivial aside. When a bid for historical accuracy threatened to exclude one of her favorite texts from *A New New Testament,* King sought to move the goalposts for just that text. For the Gospel of Mary, she marshaled a different tactic. When scholars said it was too recent to have been written alongside texts that made the New Testament, King relied on a circular logic to make Mary their contemporary—without disclosing her methods until her book's final pages. As backup, she urged scholars to abandon "the association between truth and chronology" and renounce the term "Gnostic," which she argued was just a modern euphemism for "heretical."

"There was and is no such thing as Gnosticism," she declared on the first page of her 2003 book *What Is Gnosticism?* This position was at odds with scholars no less acclaimed, or liberal, than April DeConick, Marvin Meyer and Bart Ehrman, who continue to see it as a useful category. Ancient Christians used the term *gnostikoi* to mean people who have gnosis, or sacred knowledge. And most of the writings that scholars call Gnostic share a broadly similar worldview, regard gnosis as the path to salvation and feature a recurring cast of distinctive characters.

The problem, for King, wasn't that the texts had nothing in common. A decade earlier she herself had published articles identifying "the Gnostics" as a particular social group, and "Gnosticism" as a "common attitude of mind" with a "common goal of ethics" and a shared idea of "gnosis." Libraries, she noted in her book, were "replete" with books describing Gnosticism's beliefs, origins and history. The problem, rather, was that Christianity would be better off if scholars stopped calling attention to what distinguished such texts, as a group, from the books of the New Testament. King proposed no substitute for "Gnosticism" that better reflected their shared history or content. She just wanted people to stop categorizing. "My purpose is preeminently ethical," she reveals in a "Note on Methodology" in *What Is Gnosticism?*'s final pages, a familiar location in King's work for what are often vital disclosures. Her "goal" was to "relativize" scientific objectivity—"to shift the criteria for the adequacy of truth claims away from objectivity to ethics." In other words, a thing was true *not* if it was real; it was true if—in King's estimation—it was a moral good.

This was a perfectly sound stance for a theologian, ethicist or minister. But King called herself a historian. She cloaked what were primarily ethical positions in the guise of empirical history. To make the point that the noncanonical gospels were the equals of those in the New Testament, for instance, King chose to argue that Gnosticism never existed and that, in any case, historical time was just a "Western construction" that was "not serious, real, or true." The Gnosticism scholar

Dylan Burns called King's work part of a "crypto-theological" project to normalize the use of texts like the gospels of Mary and Thomas in church. If a member of your Bible reading group says, "'Well, that's just Gnostic garbage,'" he told me, "you can walk in and say, 'There's no such thing as Gnosticism. This is just a Christian text.'"

Her justification for the title "The Gospel of Jesus's Wife" was so strained that her footnotes included an extensive disclaimer. "The use of the term 'gospel' here," she wrote, "regards the probable genre to which this fragment belonged and makes absolutely no claim to canonical status nor to the historical accuracy of the content as such. This invented reference in no way means to imply that this was the title in antiquity, or that 'Jesus's wife' is the 'author' of this work, is a major character in it, or is even a significant topic of discussion." If her title needed so much qualification, people wondered, why hadn't she just chosen a more accurate one?

I eventually learned the reason. A batch of emails Walter Fritz gave me showed that King and AnneMarie Luijendijk had originally called the papyrus "The Mary Fragment." A title of that ilk—short, restricted to the facts—would have tempered overreaction and misunderstanding, comporting perfectly with the sober approach to publicity that King claimed was a priority. But two months before Rome, King wrote to Fritz that she and Luijendijk were dropping "The Mary Fragment" because "for the publication we need to decide on something that will stick."

"AnneMarie and I have renamed [it] The Gospel of Jesus's Wife," King wrote a couple of weeks later. "What do you think!?"

When Fritz replied that "'Jesus's Wife' bears substantial potential for controversy," King countered that it was rather "The Mary Fragment" that risked confusion. "The term 'Fragment' would not be clear to a general audience," she wrote. "Fragment of what? they might well ask."

The exchange solved one of the saga's most vexing riddles. The title "The Gospel of Jesus's Wife" was a product not of scholarship but of market analysis—a hunt for words that would "stick" with a "general audience."

"Fragment of what?"—it turned out—would have been the smartest question a general audience could have asked. It would have required King to be exactly what she asked of believers: accountable.

LIBERATING FAITH FROM THE GRIP of insular elites was a worthy cause. But King's approach to it looked scarcely more like history than the work of theologians at the Vatican or Moody Bible Institute who cherry-picked other ancient texts as "historical proof" for the righteousness of their beliefs. Secular historians don't lead creed and canon councils. They don't craft new New Testaments. The idea that churchgoers need "good history" to "think with" in order to be "responsible believers" is not a fact; it's a judgment. The orthodox, of course, have their own definition of responsible belief—adherence to a set of texts and rules they see as delimited by God. When they gathered to pray, did they need to forgo—or at least wink at—their idea of God-givenness to pass King's test? The non-orthodox possessed other alternatives to King's "good history" model of faith. Some believers find spiritual truth—and ethical guidance—in myth, fantasy and nature. Some find it in silent meditation and esotericism, others in channeling what they hear as the voices of angels. Still others see houses of worship as refuge, a place to contemplate a more perfect future, not salvage an imperfect past. Did that make their belief any less responsible?

King had kept her scholarly dissecting tools away from The Thunder, Perfect Mind for a simple reason: the text moved her, and she didn't want to stick pins in whatever it was that made it so personally transcendent. "I've never been able to write about it," she told a divinity school audience, "because I always just wanted to say, 'Wasn't that great?'" If other people took the same hands-off approach to their favorite spiritual texts—or to the New Testament as a whole—could King blame them?

"Who gets to say what the right religion is?" King once asked. From her writings it was clear she saw herself as one such decider. The story of Christianity "serves us better if it has all the loose ends" and "the things that don't add up," she asserted. "We need complexity for the complexity of our lives." Her use of blanket pronouns like "we," "us," and "our" left little room for believers who might experience their faith in a different way. It drew a line between an "us" of responsible believers and a "them" of irresponsible ones—a practice nearly as old as the faith itself, even if King's adaptation inverted the traditional boundaries.

FOR KING, THE PHRASE "Jesus said to them, 'My wife'"—like any other bit of scripture—wasn't objective truth or history. Whether written in A.D. 28, when Jesus was said to be alive, or a century later, as King had suspected, it never could be. Like any story, it was written by someone with a personal or ideological stake in portraying Jesus as married. (King was correct on that score, though her date was off by some nineteen hundred years.) For postmodernists in King's mold, the historical Jesus's actual marital status was *a priori* unknowable and in some ways beside the point. "Truth" (a word postmodern thinkers nearly always set between quotation marks) was just a language game, won by the player who told—and sold—the best story.

Yet in public, King presented herself as a just-the-facts historian. She spoke of wanting "historical information," "all evidence possible," "an accurate view of history," "the full data set." Her use of scientific-sounding words like "data" simultaneously cast her scholarship as evenhanded and dispassionate while tarring that of parochial institutions as hopelessly ideological. "One criterion for good history," she said, "is accounting for all the evidence and not marginalizing the parts one doesn't like or promoting unfairly the parts one does like." How, then, did King explain her failure to investigate provenance amid multiple warnings from colleagues? Why didn't she do a single scientific test before launching a publicity blitz for the papyrus? Why didn't she consult a senior Coptic papyrologist, as Roger Bagnall suggested, after the peer reviewer questioned the fragment's handwriting? Why did she soft-pedal the implausible eighth-century date, seek to sidetrack Depuydt's rebuttal, refuse to release provenance documents, and bar reporters from contacting other scientists? If this wasn't "marginalizing the parts one doesn't like," what was?

Authenticity, I grew to believe, was never central for King, because "authenticity" was a construct that relied on "bare facts," which she argued had no meaning outside "storied worlds." What fired her intellect was the papyrus's text, its *story*—a narrative that amplified her long-standing views about women's wrongful exclusion from the Church, a lullaby that filled a long-lamented lacuna. Whether or not the Gospel of Jesus's Wife was authentic, it had what King's mentor, Bob Funk, called "operational effectiveness." It *felt* true to many people's experiences today. It was an entrée—a business card, in both size and function—to authentic but longer and more complicated texts, like the Gospel of Mary and the Diary of Perpetua, with which King earnestly wanted believers to engage. It was a parable with the power to improve lives. "What difference does it make if the story says Jesus was married or not?" King told *Harvard Magazine* in July 2017, more than a year after saying the Wife papyrus was a probable fake. "Well, it makes a big difference. It touches everything from people's most intimate sense about their lives and their own sexuality to large institutional structures. It affects who gets to be in charge, who gets to preach and teach, who can be pure and holy. Should people be married or not? Can you be divorced or not? Is sexuality sinful, by definition? All of this depends on what kind of story you tell."

But for a historian, didn't the story need to be true—or at least part of the actual past—before you could tell it?

A FEW MONTHS AFTER MY *Atlantic* article and her change of mind about the papyrus's authenticity, King complained to *The Harvard Crimson* that a "hot story of scandal" was detracting from the very real themes addressed by the papyrus's text. "Focus on whether it's a forgery or not is taking attention off the things that really matter," she said, "which are the issues about authority, women's roles, sexuality, and everything attached to them." (In comments beneath the piece, a reader going by "righteousreverenddynamite" offered a pointed summary of King's new view of the Gospel of Jesus's Wife: "Fake but accurate.")

A part of King saw the Wife papyrus—and perhaps had always seen it—much as she had *The Da Vinci Code:* it was a fiction that advanced a truth. A lie that got people thinking about "the things that really matter." A tall tale that could be called "true" because its heart was in the right place. In her 2004 interview on MSNBC, King had rhapsodized about "the services" *The Da Vinci Code* provided. The fictitious thriller showed people "the enormous diversity of early Christianity." It got people to ask questions about issues—from women's roles to the basis of church authority—"all being hotly debated in the early church." Which made me wonder how tolerant King might be of other fakes offering similar "services," whether by enlarging the audience for her ideas or by raising the profile of Harvard Divinity School—aims not wholly unconnected.

I remembered something King said during my visit to her office before the announcement in 2012: the papyrus was in many ways more means than end. "It will start a conversation," she told me. It would get people talking about questions of sex, marriage and women's religious leadership that still touched, and troubled, the faithful in the profoundest of ways. That, she said, would be "the longest real impact."

FOR KING, I CAME TO BELIEVE, the value of the Wife fragment never depended on authenticity, not exclusively. Two weeks after her Rome announcement, *The Chronicle of Higher Education* reported that King had been chastened by the backlash. She regretted her name for the papyrus and was asking around for something less "inflammatory." Until the scientific tests came back, the watchword was caution. She had been "dinged by some for jumping the gun," the newspaper reported. "Now she, like everyone else, is waiting for the [scientific] results."

The ensuing evidence suggested otherwise. With the scrap's authenticity in doubt and lab tests still pending, King took a semester's leave from Harvard for a lecture tour on her discovery's sweeping implications for history. The speeches, about one a month over the first half of 2013, were so beneath radar that only local news outlets and the websites of sponsoring venues covered them. King claimed to worry about how readily people could mistake her papyrus for biographical proof of a married Jesus. Yet she titled most of the talks "Was Jesus Married?"—a hook as incongruous with her professed aims as the coinage "The Gospel of Jesus's Wife." (Despite telling the *Chronicle* that she was searching for a "new, less exciting" name for the fragment, she would never change it.)

"Everybody thought I said that Jesus was married; the people who hate me and the people who love me both think I said something I didn't say," she declared—at a Las Vegas event titled "Does It Matter if Jesus Was Married?"

"A lot of the controversy is based on a misunderstanding," she complained to a Kalamazoo, Michigan, newspaper before an April 2013 speech there—a speech she titled "Was Jesus Married?" That King's lectures left even her own audiences confused raised questions about who precisely was to blame for the misunderstanding.

But King could do only so many "Was Jesus Married?" talks before the scientists finished their work. If the results pointed to forgery, her discovery—and the implications she'd heralded in countless media interviews and lectures—would go down as just one more chapter in the annals of mortifying hoaxes. So King came up with a contingency plan.

ON FEBRUARY 19, 2013, with the Wife papyrus still undergoing testing, King submitted an article to *New Testament Studies,* a premier journal that competed with the *Harvard Theological Review* for important papers on early Christian literature. The article announced a major discovery: King had found an ancient gospel that "portrays the incarnate Jesus as actually married (to Mary Magdalene)." This history-making papyrus wasn't the Gospel of Jesus's Wife, which King nowhere mentioned in the article. It was the Gospel of Philip, one of the texts found at Nag Hammadi in 1945. It was the one that called Mary Magdalene Jesus's *koinonos,* or companion, and that featured Jesus kissing Mary Magdalene on a part of her body that was unknown because of the hole in the papyrus where the part was named. King knew Philip backward and forward. She'd often spoken and written about it. But never before had she detected anything carnal. Indeed, for years, King, like her colleagues, was adamant that the gospel, like other early Christian writings, showed only a spiritual kinship. "There's nothing particularly in these texts that would advocate a sexual relationship between Jesus and Mary," King told an audience in 2003. "If anything, the opposite: that their relationship was one of a disciple to a teacher. Okay? Always in that kind of way." Now she realized how wrong she'd been, how wrong all scholars had been. A text depicting a married Jesus, it turned out, had been hiding in plain sight for decades.

What the editor of *New Testament Studies* (*NTS*) didn't know was that King's article wasn't completely original. In fact, it was in large measure a cut-and-paste of the draft *Harvard Theological Review* (*HTR*) paper King published on a Harvard website the day of the Rome announcement—the paper, that is, that *HTR* had provisionally accepted but wasn't publishing until the science came back. When I set the articles side by side, I noticed that King had taken nearly nine pages from the *HTR* article that dealt with the Gospel of Philip. Then, with minimal reworking, she dropped them into her new piece for *NTS*. The submission appeared to conflict with both journals' posted editorial policies, which bar consideration of articles that have been submitted elsewhere. John Barclay, a British theologian who was *NTS*'s editor, told me he was unaware of the article's origins or its substantial overlap with King's publicly posted Gospel of Jesus's Wife draft until I mentioned them in a November 2016 email. King never told him, despite a Cambridge University Press ethics policy requiring authors to "acknowledge and cite" parts of submitted articles that "overlap" with articles submitted or published elsewhere and "to provide the editor with a copy of any submitted manuscript that might contain overlapping or closely related content." A 2019 update of the policy calls the practice "self-plagiarism." King did not respond to my questions about the submissions.

When I took a finer-grained look at the two articles, I noticed telling word changes in some of the duplicate sentences. In the *HTR* draft she published online in 2012, King voiced a note of caution. The Greek and Coptic words for "companion" in Philip "could," as one possibility, imply marriage and sex. Five months later, for *NTS*, she said those same words "often do" imply those things. In less than half a year, an ancient word's sexual connotation had gone from a possibility to a frequent occurrence. But that wasn't all. In her draft for *HTR*, she wrote, "It is therefore plausible to read this passage as a reference by Jesus to Mary Magdalene as 'his lover.'" Five months later, for *NTS*, she wrote, "It is therefore plausible to read this passage as a reference by Jesus to Mary Magdalene as 'his spouse.'" The reason for the switch from "lover" to "spouse" is unclear, because the footnotes, which exclusively cite the translation "lover," are identical in both articles.

No one knew it at the time, but King submitted the article to *NTS* shortly after receiving another jolt of disturbing news about the Wife papyrus. The month before, Malcolm Choat—the distinguished Australian papyrologist whom King had privately consulted—sent her and *HTR* a report that cast serious doubt on Bagnall's dating of the handwriting. After spending two days examining the papyrus firsthand— far longer than Bagnall and Luijendijk combined—Choat found no basis for their conclusion that the handwriting dated to the fourth century. In fact, he wrote, the hand bore no similarity to literary (including biblical) papyri "of any period." Nor did it resemble the hands of fourth-century documentary manuscripts, or those of informal, magical or school manuscripts of any era—an extraordinarily diverse set of styles spanning multiple centuries. Choat, who was one of the world's foremost Coptic papyrologists, stopped short of calling the hand alone proof of forgery. But in diplomatic prose, he had blown a hole through the main supports for the fourth-century date. When Luijendijk, too, failed to come up with a good match for the script, King dropped her author credit from the *HTR* article. "I think she was hoping I would find a better handwriting parallel," Luijendijk said when we met at Princeton in 2017. "I did a lot of work trying to find a good parallel and I never found it."

The timing of King's epiphany about the Gospel of Philip seemed more than coincidence: if she reversed her long-standing view on Philip before scientists exposed the Wife fragment as a fake, the story she wanted to tell about the "alternative tradition" of a married Jesus would have other legs to stand on. *NTS* published "The Place of the *Gospel of Philip* in the Context of Early Christian Claims About Jesus' Marital Status" in its October 2013 issue. Six months later, King's *HTR* piece would footnote it no fewer than five times, using it to casually state—as a matter of unqualified, established record—that Philip depicts Jesus's "marriage with Mary Magdalene."

King did more than produce a fallback, or understudy, for the Wife fragment, should lab tests or other new evidence unmask it as a fraud. She hastily reversed years of her own scholarship to create a new historical context for belief in its authenticity. *The Gospel of Jesus's Wife, it turns out, isn't the first ancient text to depict a wedded Jesus,* she was now saying. *The Gospel of Philip is.* This reversal was all the more remarkable because the Wife fragment's chief selling point—the one that vaulted it into the headlines in 2012—was King's claim that "no extant early Christian writing other than *GosJesWife* unequivocally represents Jesus as married."

Over months of reporting, I asked a wide range of Gnosticism experts whether any serious scholar saw the Gospel of Philip as portraying Jesus and Mary Magdalene as actual husband and wife. The question was usually met with a pained look or an awkward silence, even among admirers of King's other work. "It was mentioned in *The Da Vinci Code*," one told me. Like several other scholars, he sheepishly pointed to Dan Brown's novel as the closest parallel. "That's the argument there. So, in popular literature."

IF FACTS AND FAITH were the same for King, the implications for both scholarship and religious belief were significant. Either the best kind of faith belonged to the people with the most accurate data, the fact finders for whom the universe's mysteries were less fuel for the contemplation of God than a complex problem that science would eventually solve. Or the best facts were no different from faith, a set of collectively agreed-upon illusions with no more basis in the observable world than belief in an unseen God. If fact and faith were the same, that is, then either faith didn't exist, or facts didn't. Not in the way most people thought, anyway. But King wanted it both ways: she sought to expose the Church's "facts" as positions while promoting her own positions as facts. She needed a double standard—one that permitted stories she judged virtuous to pass as true, regardless of the underlying evidence, while denying the same to narratives she found unethical or "operationally ineffective." The criteria that guided these case-by-case decisions were a mystery. King had never "put in writing [a] self-conscious assessment" of how her religious beliefs—her "own Christian subjectivity"—shaped her judgments about truth, according to one close colleague. The colleague called it a major omission—a "significant epistemological lacuna"—particularly for a scholar who saw all facts as self-serving points of view.

The scholarly outcry over the Wife papyrus showed that evidence-based history and science still held sway in much of the world, no matter how out of vogue they were among the theorists on King's bookshelves. Her audience now wasn't a graduate seminar but millions of people around the world and the professional journalists who helped make sense of the day's news. King's comeback, a year and a half after her announcement in Rome, was classically postmodern. In the eyes of critics, it wasn't so much science that she returned with as a likeness, or simulacrum, of science, a spectacle of important-looking graphs and statistical measures, adorned with photos of expensive laboratory instruments.

"For most people 'True' still means historically true," the biblical scholar Stephen Patterson told colleagues in the aftermath of *The Da Vinci Code.* "That is why, when ideology goes in search of ultimate validation, it is not enough to reach for religion only. It needs history, too. And so the artist supplies it: bowdlerized, filched, fudged or just plain made-up—in the murky *nether* world of historical fiction the distinction between the history and the fiction is easily lost. It matters not. The sympathetic reader knows how it really went down. Can't prove it. Don't need to. Wink.

"All of this has taken historians of the Bible a little by surprise," Patterson added. "While [the academic fashion for] postmodern doubt seems well advised in moderate doses, if *The Da Vinci Code* passes for 'meticulously researched' history today, perhaps we could set aside our theoretical misgivings for a moment and do what history we can."

In the early 1990s, King's Harvard colleague, the pioneering theologian Elisabeth Schüssler Fiorenza, warned of the bind postmodernism posed for feminists. "The paradox," Schüssler Fiorenza wrote, quoting another scholar, is that " 'while we regard patriarchal discourses as fiction, we nevertheless proceed as if our position, based on a belief in the oppression of women, were somewhat closer to the truth.' " She urged scholars to trade the "scientific-positivist" approach for a "rhetorical-political" one. To transform from fact finder to ethicist would free feminists from Western notions of objectivity, which in Schüssler Fiorenza's view were indivisible from male power. As the writer and activist Audre Lorde once put it, "The master's tools will never dismantle the master's house." It was perhaps no surprise that Schüssler Fiorenza, though she cared about history, called herself a theologian. She couldn't be more explicit about the politics underpinning her work. Her method was "hermeneutics"—a system of interpretation that encouraged women to claim their rightful place in scripture through against-the-grain readings and imagination. King's predicament was that she called herself a historian. She demanded that people be "accountable" to facts and history, though she herself believed in neither.

IN THE FALL OF 2016, I was forwarded a notice about a lecture King was giving at a church on New York's Upper East Side. The talk was one in a series of special Harvard Divinity School events for alumni and donors in honor of the school's two hundredth birthday. The talk's title was "The Rhetoric of Forgery," and the announcement said that "birthday cake" would follow.

It was five months after my *Atlantic* magazine story, and five months after King's response—that Fritz had duped her—became international news. I had recently returned from an overseas conference on biblical forgeries, where scholars picked over the wreckage of the papyrus that rooked Harvard and of the fake Dead Sea Scrolls that tricked Hobby Lobby's Green family. I left with at least one impression: Modern forgers didn't care whether their marks were liberal Episcopalian women or conservative evangelical men. They sought out people with prestige (the aptly named King), money (the fittingly named Greens), and an unshakable confidence in their own beliefs.

I wondered whether King's New York speech would be a reckoning. I was curious what sense she made of it all, now that the hubbub had died down. Her insights, however painfully acquired, would be a service to a field all too prone to counterfeiters and mountebanks. All the same, it was peculiar that Harvard Divinity School would use one of the most embarrassing episodes in its history—and a still-fresh one—to celebrate its bicentennial.

A little after nightfall on November 7, 2016, I turned onto Fifth Avenue and looked up at the limestone arches of the Episcopal Church of the Heavenly Rest, a marriage of Gothic and Art Deco styles overlooking Central Park. Inside, a woman with a divinity school badge led visitors to a chamber called the Chapel of the Beloved Disciple. Chandeliers dangled from trusses on the vaulted ceiling, and the walls were stenciled with golden fleurs-de-lis.

I straightened when King said she had worked on her talk for weeks. But my hopes were misplaced. King didn't want to talk about forgery. She wanted to rise above that and talk instead about the way people *talked* when they *talked* about forgery. And not necessarily the way they spoke about recent ones, like the Gospel of Jesus's Wife, but the way the Church Fathers cried "fake" whenever they encountered an ancient text they didn't happen to like. King had recently reread the works of heresy hunters like Irenaeus, and she found in their narratives a reliable trio of stock characters. The first was "'*the critic*,' who is always the hero, the one who exposes," she said. Then came "*the forger*" and "*the audience*."

The "'critic,'" King explained, "thinks his own character and motives are pure and righteous, and those of the 'forger' as lying, cheating, and often maybe sexually promiscuous or otherwise immoral. The 'audience' is also of two kinds: those who believe in the forgers are dupes, ... whereas those who believe the critic are smart, they're in the know, and they're also of course righteous and pure."

I began to wonder about the sincerity of King's statement, earlier that year, that she'd finally changed her mind about the papyrus's authenticity. Part of her, it seemed, could only see it through the looking glass of theory. The fragment, in this view, wasn't an actual fake from a self-identified "hotwife" pornographer in twenty-first-century Florida whose unmaskers had won real-world praise for their sleuthing. The problem was that a *rhetoric* of forgery as old as Christianity—featuring dupe, critic and sexually promiscuous forger—had won out over her narrative of an extraordinary new gospel about a married Jesus. Forget facts, she seemed to be saying; the battle between orthodoxy and heresy was as much a language game now as it was eighteen hundred years earlier.

King didn't once mention the Wife papyrus during the lecture, though there was no larger elephant in the room. In the question-and-answer session, when it became clear that no one in the pews had the nerve to ask about it, King broke the tension. "When I was working on this, I obviously had something like the Gospel of Jesus's Wife in mind," she said. "I was very interested in the way that charges about forgery could distract and keep one from looking at the things that were at stake really."

Yet if King didn't want a forgery to distract, why had she spent four years defending one? Why do it, when each passing month put the issues she cared about in deeper and deeper jeopardy? In the face of menacing peer reviews and warnings from every corner of her field, she doubled down again and again rather than head for the exits. At fault for the fiasco, she decided, were neither the facts she got wrong nor the provenance she failed to investigate. At fault weren't the conflicted scientists she commissioned or the devious con man who fooled her. To blame, rather, were tricks of language as old as the Bible. Modern incarnations of Irenaeus were still using an ancient "rhetoric of forgery" to attack the kind of Christianity that King wanted for the faithful and that she was fairly certain at least some of Jesus's earliest followers did, too.

Before joining divinity school alumni for red wine and birthday cake, King handed out color copies of Harvard's earliest seal, which dated to 1643. Inside a hand-drawn shield, the word *Veritas* unfurled across three open books. In later centuries, all three of the books faced up, as they still do today, on countless Harvard buildings, T-shirts and gift-shop souvenirs. But in the college's early years, when the training of ministers was its sole mission, the third book was face down. Scholars believe that the overturned volume symbolized either the limits of reason or the mysteries God had yet to reveal.

King now added to these possibilities a third: that the face-down book represented ignorance. What better reason for truth seeking could there be than honesty about how little we really knew?

"Knowledge that appears too solid can [cause] harm in many ways, in part by shutting down other ways of thinking and living, shutting down curiosity and discovery," she said. "So on the occasion of this bicentennial, I suggest we look to the Harvard seal, affirming *Veritas* against every lie. But also turning at least one of the books facedown again, . . . to teach the extent of our ignorance, insofar as we can comprehend it, as a very important truth."

ACKNOWLEDGMENTS

I have many people to thank for making this book possible. In the summer of 2012, the editors Terry Monmaney and Michael Caruso of *Smithsonian* magazine took a chance on a relatively new freelancer, dispatching me to Harvard and Rome for the first story on the Wife papyrus, then deftly editing a complicated, feature-length article under tight deadline. The opportunity to take up the story again, in the fall of 2015, owes entirely to Denise Wills, then a senior editor at *The Atlantic* and now its deputy editor. Denise is one of the most gifted narrative editors I know and a person of uncommon decency, bringing out the best in her writers and saving them from their worst. I owe many thanks, too, to Scott Stossel, then the magazine's editor, who believed in the piece even when it was still half-formed, and to then associate editor Billy Brennan, an up-and-comer whose fact-checking of my eleven-thousand-word *Atlantic* article was as meticulous as a forensic audit.

Overseas investigative reporting depends in large measure on the skill of local fixers, multitalented interpreters whose ability to open doors, read tricky situations and get sources talking can make or break a journalist's efforts. In Germany, I was fortunate to work with two of the country's very best: Petra Krischok and Claudia Himmelreich. Their intelligence, charm and instincts delivered again and again under the most trying of circumstances. I cannot thank them enough for their reporting breakthroughs, pleasant company and patience over months of tedious toil and travel. In Voss, Norway, the retired local journalist Arne Hofseth went above and beyond to track down people who remembered Karen King. In Oslo, Tina Aasen pitched in on short notice. Almut Schoenfeld helped with additional interviews in Germany, and the persistent Gabriella Savio wrung responses from sources at the Vatican.

At the U.S. Library of Congress, where I spent many days, the wonderful staff helped me find obscure academic treatises, hard-to-locate articles and paper copies of international phonebooks going back fifty years. I am thankful, too, to the resourceful archivists and librarians of Brown University; Columbia University; Drew University; Free University, Berlin; Harvard University and Harvard Divinity School; International Christian Youth Exchange, at Church of the Brethren headquarters, in Elgin, Illinois; Occidental College; Sheridan High School; Technical University of Berlin; University of Michigan Papyrology Collection; University of Montana; and the Venice Museum & Archives in Florida. I'm indebted to David Royle, Charles Poe and Joanna Brahim of the Smithsonian Channel, and the filmmakers Hannah Veale and Andy Webb, for talking to me about the origins of their documentary. In Florida, the staff of *The North Port Sun* sent me a photo of Walter Fritz at a critical time and graciously answered questions about the city. At *The Chronicle of Higher Education,* Ginnie Titterton combed through years of classified ads to find the official 1995 and 1996 postings for the faculty job King would fill at Harvard Divinity School. The scholars Candida Moss and Joel Baden, who wrote a book on the Museum of the Bible, also gave helpful guidance.

In Germany, the Egyptologists Christian Loeben and Karl Jansen-Winkeln were patient with my many questions and of immeasurable help at key moments in the reporting. In the United States, my appreciation goes to two other Egyptologists: Jacco Dieleman helped me understand various points of linguistics, and Miriam Müller translated scholarly papers from the German. In the Netherlands, another Egyptologist, André Veldmeijer, came through at a crucial juncture. I am grateful to Jan Tonnemacher for his hospitality in Berlin, and to Sam Loewenberg for the introduction.

I also need to thank AnneMarie Luijendijk, Roger Bagnall and James Yardley; though aspects of the Gospel of Jesus's Wife affair did not always put them in the most flattering light, they spoke openly with me for the book, out of what I believe was a sincere desire for other scholars and scientists to learn something from the ups and downs of their experience.

My agent, Andrew Blauner, has been a steadfast advocate. At Doubleday, my attentive editor and publisher, Bill Thomas, was an invaluable sounding board and a master of story form. Daniel Novack, senior counsel at Penguin Random House, fielded numerous legal questions with encouragement, precision, and wisdom. Thanks, too, to Doubleday's Maria Massey, and to Margo Shickmanter, Nora Grubb and Khari Dawkins.

Lou Bayard, Billy Brennan, Clara Germani, Jonathan Rockoff, Joe

Stephens, Denise Wills, Diana Yap, and my wife, Meg, offered invaluable critiques of various drafts, for which I remain ever thankful. All remaining faults and errors are my own. Meg, and our children, Seth and Phoebe, endured my many absences with patience and understanding; I thank them for their counsel and support.

Finally, many sources trusted me with sensitive information. I won't forget their faith in the project or their willingness to risk something in the name of truth.

NOTE ON SOURCES AND METHODS

This book is a work of investigative journalism, presented in the form of narrative nonfiction. To speak with sources and gather research material, I traveled to twelve American states and to Austria, Germany, Israel, Italy, Norway and Switzerland. I visited Germany three times—in 2016, 2017 and 2018—for a total of about forty-five days of on-the-ground reporting. More than 450 people were interviewed for this book: some 350 by me alone; some 50 with a foreign-language interpreter at my side; and the rest by the interpreters alone—experienced journalists and fixers who posed my questions to non-English-speaking sources. I observed at least two turning points in the story firsthand: I was the only journalist in the room in Rome when King presented her discovery to colleagues on September 18, 2012, and, to my knowledge, the only reporter present when the Ancient Ink Lab publicly raised suspicions about the papyri before a packed room of scholars at a conference in San Antonio on November 21, 2016.

I examined thousands of documents, including internal emails, business reports, government records, personal letters, educational transcripts, meeting minutes, web domain registrations, land records, police files, marriage and divorce records, travel documents and receipts, web-group membership records, unpublished scholarly dissertations, employment files, immigration papers, the personal papers of scholars and university administrators, and European government records of residents' address changes going back nearly half a century. I obtained some of these materials directly from interviewees; much of the rest came from archives or through public records requests in the United States and Europe. Sources not clearly identified in the narrative are found at the end of the book, in notes ordered by page number and keyed to exact wording in the text. There is also a selected bibliography.

I interviewed Karen King six times, for a total of more than six hours, in connection with my 2012 articles for *Smithsonian* magazine and with my 2016 article and subsequent online story for *The Atlantic*. In October 2016, I informed King that I was beginning work on a book and expressed hope that we might speak from time to time as I pursued my reporting. Between then and September 2019, I made multiple interview requests by email; certified letters to her home and office; and phone messages at her work, home and cell numbers. I offered King multiple opportunities to comment on, add context to or dispute my reporting. She did not respond to any of my requests.

I interviewed Walter Fritz thirteen times between November 2015 and April 2019, for a total of some twenty-seven hours. Because of his tendency to dissemble, I took pains to vet nearly everything he said and to point out, in the book, the many times his assertions did not align with external evidence. Material for the second part of "Rome"—this book's prologue—comes from my phone interviews with Fritz; scans of Delta Air Lines boarding passes for his December 14, 2011, visit to Harvard; emails he sent to King; and photographs of the Rabinowitz Room at the Andover-Harvard Theological Library. According to Harvard, the room's stained-glass window panels date as early as the fifteenth century and were collected from family chapels across Europe after World War I.

King and Fritz provided me with the text of various of their email exchanges. The emails King gave me spanned from 2010 to 2011, and the ones from Fritz, from 2012 to 2016. AnneMarie Luijendijk provided copies of other Fritz emails to King—emails that King had forwarded to her. I was able to corroborate aspects of these emails and their sent dates through other reporting, but did not have direct access to King's or Fritz's email servers and do not know the full extent of their communications. Fritz redacted parts of the emails he sent me, parts that might well have raised additional questions.

I either observed quoted dialogue firsthand or based it on the firm recollection of one or, as often as possible, both participants in a conversation. Some material in this book appeared previously in the magazine articles I wrote for *Smithsonian* and *The Atlantic*. But most is the product of new reporting that has never before been published.

NOTES

vii   "We search after truth": Thomas Hollis to Benjamin Colman (member of the Harvard College Corporation and Overseers), August 1, 1720. Quoted in Josiah Quincy, *The History of Harvard University* (Cambridge, Mass.: John Owen, 1840), 1:234. Hollis, a Baptist, was a London hardware merchant and philanthropist. He endowed the Hollis Professorship of Divinity in 1721 with what he termed "an honorable stipend," in hopes of making the Congregationalist-run Harvard more ecumenical.

PROLOGUE: ROME
  xi   "I dubbed it": Author's firsthand observation and recording of King's presentation at the Tenth International Congress of Coptic Studies, Rome, Italy, September 18, 2012.

SOLICITATIONS
  3   "incredibly inclusive": King, "Thinking About Women and Heresy."
  3   "the master story": King, *Gospel of Mary of Magdala*, 190.
  4   "In a quiet voice": Benjamin H. Dunning and Laura S. Nasrallah, "Introduction," in Petrey, *Re-Making the World*, 15.
  4   "Some woman offered me": King, phone interview by author, August 28, 2012.
  4   "Poison": Bonar, "High Stakes Marriage."
  4   "Repent," people had urged: Bruce Buursma, "Jesus' Quotes Put to Scholarly Test," *Chicago Tribune*, October 6, 1986.
  4   "kooky": King, phone interview by author, August 28, 2012.
  5   "an unknown Gospel": Text of emails sent to the author by King in September 2012, after she deleted the collector's name, email address, and other identifying details, in order to honor his request for anonymity. "0-11" and "02-11" appeared to be personal catalog numbers, assigned by the collector.
  6   "*peje Iēsous nau ta-hime*": Scientific English transliteration of Coptic based on guidance from Hany Takla (email to author, February 1, 2019) and Stephen Emmel (email to author, February 8, 2019). An informal guide to the line's pronunciation would be "*peh-jeh yay-SOUS NOW ta-HEE-meh*."
  6   completeness of the Church's "data": See, for example, Gibson, "Bits the Bible Left Out," 42.

STRANGE TEACHINGS
  7   "I saw the way": Paul Strathern, *Napoleon in Egypt* (New York: Bantam Books, 2009), 6.
  8   "an archaeological El Dorado": Hélène Cuvigny, "The Finds of Papyri: The Archaeology of Papyrology," in Bagnall, *Oxford Handbook of Papyrology*, 31.
  8   Warnings about price gouging: Donald Malcolm Reid, *Whose Pharaohs? Archaeology, Museums, and Egyptian National Identity from Napoleon to World War I* (Berkeley: University of California Press, 2002), 77.
  8   On a January day in 1896: Schmidt, "Ein vorirenaeisches," 839.
  8   "of uncommon refinement": Ibid.

8 "The Gospel according to Mary": The title's three-line format is visible in image of papyrus, in King, *Gospel of Mary of Magdala*, 27.

8 "preach the good news": This and other quotations from the Gospel of Mary are from King's translation, in ibid., chap. 2.

10 The Gnostics were "deluded people": Scholars differ on whether "the Gnostics" were an out-in-the-open community of believers, a secret sect, or just a slur invented by the Church Fathers for Christians seeking their own meanings in Jesus's life and teachings.

10 "We are thus for the first time": Harnack postscript to Schmidt, "Ein vorirenaeisches," 846.

11 In a previous edition: *The Nag Hammadi Library in English,* edited by James M. Robinson (Leiden: E. J. Brill, 1977), 471.

11 "head-on" attack: King, "Gospel of Mary," in *Nag Hammadi Library* (1988), 524.

11 "the Lord Jesus chose men": *Catechism of the Catholic Church*, para. 1577.

11 "presents a radical interpretation": King, *Gospel of Mary of Magdala*, 3–4.

12 "until now": Ibid., 155.

12 "She was someone who loved": Berchman, phone interview by author, November 2, 2016.

12 "I was raised to think": King, *Karen L. King: The Gospel of Mary*.

12 "a very cowboy ethic": King, "Thinking About Women and Heresy."

13 "Words of Christ, Lost 1,300 Years": Photograph of newspaper page, in Nongbri, *God's Library*, 3.

13 There was no single "type": Nongbri, email to author, December 18, 2018.

14 *Lex Youtie:* Paul Schubert, "Editing a Papyrus," in Bagnall, *Oxford Handbook of Papyrology*, 207.

15 "represents every person who is not at home": King, *Revelation of the Unknowable God*, 54.

15 "The metaphor that probably comes closer": King, *Forbidden Scriptures*.

15 nearly a quarter of the Jewish women: Tal Ilan, "Notes on the Distribution of Jewish Women's Names in Palestine in the Second Temple and Mishnaic Periods," *Journal of Jewish Studies* 40 (1989): 191. Of the 247 names Ilan collected from various sources, 58 were Mariamme or its shorter version, Maria.

16 No fewer than three: The Gospel of Thomas, the Gospel of Mary, and the Gospel of Philip. Though the gospels of Mary and Thomas do not specify that their Mary is Magdalene, most scholars accept the identification.

16 "These missing leaves": King, *Karen L. King: The Gospel of Mary*.

16 She made up her mind: King, phone interview by author, August 28, 2012, among other sources.

THE HARVARD IMPRIMATUR

17 No doubt some pretenders: Though most scholars attribute pastoral letters like 3 Corinthians and 2 Thessalonians to writers other than Paul, whether to call them "forgeries" or the more euphemistic "pseudepigrapha" is hotly debated. For a provocative take, see Bart D. Ehrman, *Forged: Writing in the Name of God—Why the Bible's Authors Are Not Who We Think They Are* (New York: HarperCollins, 2011).

17 "at the dictation" of: Quoted in Tommy Wasserman, "Simonides' New Testament Papyri: Their Production and Purported Provenance," Marginalia, *Los Angeles Review of Books,* July 6, 2018, marginalia.lareviewofbooks.org.

18 "WORLD EXCLUSIVE!": Cover, *Biblical Archaeology Review,* November/December 2002, www.biblicalarchaeology.org.

18 "Okay, Jesus married?": King, phone interview by author, August 28, 2012.

18 "Just the *idea* of it": King, interview by author, Somerville, Mass., September 4, 2012.

18 "The name of Harvard University": Webb/Veale interview transcripts.

18 "I was highly suspicious": King, phone interview by author, August 28, 2012.

18 Three weeks later, in late July: Program of the 65th General Meeting of the Studiorum Novi Testamenti Societas, held at Humboldt University; and official photograph of conference attendees.

18 The presidential address: The address, provided to author by Collins, closely follows the subsequent article: Adela Yarbro Collins, "The Female Body as Social Space in 1 Timothy," *New Testament Studies* 57, no. 2 (April 2011): 155–75.

18 The apostle Paul's First Epistle: Many modern historians date 1 Timothy to the second century and argue that it was written by Paul's followers rather than by Paul himself.

18 to both marry and lead: "Although again the fragmentary nature of [the Wife papyrus] makes it difficult to speculate on the nature of this controversy," King wrote in the public September 2012 draft of her *Harvard Theological Review* article, "comparative data offer (at least) three possibilities: women's leadership roles, the interpretation of Jesus's teachings, and Christian teaching on sexuality and marriage. These are not mutually exclusive."

18 on the very day of Collins's lecture: The date of the address was July 28, 2010, according to the official minutes of the 65th General Meeting of the Studiorum Novi Testamenti Societas. The date and content of the collector's message appear in the compilation of anonymized emails provided to author by King in 2012.

19 "I didn't believe it was authentic": Colen, "HDS Scholar Announces Existence of a New Early Christian Gospel from Egypt."

20 on which we "perform" our identities: King, "Response," 145.

20 "revolutionized my thinking": Ibid., 145–46.

20 "no longer made any sense": King, "Thinking About Women and Heresy."

21 "Kill us, torture us, condemn us": Tertullian, *Apologeticum,* chap. 50.

21 "There were other [early] Christians": Gibson, "Bits the Bible Left Out," 45.

21 notices in mainstream news stories: See, for instance, Sarah Sentilles, "My Take: Five Women in Religion to Watch," CNN, *Belief Blog,* March 5, 2012, religion.blogs.cnn.com, which notes that King "is at work on a book about 'martyrdom and its discontents.'"

22 "I'm a very visual person": Nick Ellis, "Department of Style," *Daily Princetonian,* September 2012, www.dailyprincetonian.com.

22 "opened up worlds": Luijendijk, interview by author, Princeton University, April 23, 2019.

22 "She just stood up": Luijendijk, phone interview by author, August 31, 2012; Luijendijk, in-person interview by author, Princeton University, March 3, 2017.

23 Three days earlier: The date of King's email to the collector—October 15, 2011—was provided to the author by King. The date of King's first email to Luijendijk about the papyrus—October 18, 2011—was provided to the author by Luijendijk.

23 "If you were a forger": Luijendijk, phone interview by author, August 31, 2012.

24 Her master's thesis: AnneMarie Luijendijk, *The Reconstruction of Oxyrhynchus Papyrus 654: A Greek Fragment of the Gospel of Thomas* (master's thesis, Vrije University, August 1996).

24 "That is exactly the look": Webb/Veale interview transcripts.

24 "garbological" lens of her latest scholarship: AnneMarie Luijendijk, "Sacred Scriptures as Trash: Biblical Papyri from Oxyrhynchus," *Vigiliae Christianae* 64, no. 3 (January 2010): 228.

24 "It would be impossible": Goodstein, "Faded Piece of Papyrus."

24 When Roger Shaler Bagnall: Bagnall, interview by author, Manhattan, March 21, 2017; the date the meetings with the Stanford professor began—August 1960—is listed in his undergraduate application to Harvard, folder "RSB—College Admissions," box 1, Bagnall Papers.

25 The sight of costumed men: Bagnall, interview by author, Manhattan, March 21, 2017.

25 "was impressive as far as it went": Loose-leaf pages titled "Eastern Trip 1963," July 3 entry, folder "RSB—College Admissions," box 1, Bagnall Papers.

25 "the narrowest of specialists": Samuel Noah Kramer, *History Begins at Sumer: Thirty-Nine Firsts in Recorded History,* 3rd ed. (Philadelphia: University of Pennsylvania Press, 1981), xix. The book was originally published in 1956.

25 first in his high school class: Class rank written in pen by high school counselor on loose-leaf pages titled "Academic Record," in folder "RSB—College Admissions," box 1, Bagnall Papers. According to author's interview with Bagnall, there was technically a three-way tie for first place.

26 "This papyrus contains": Roger S. Bagnall, "An Order for Nails," *Bulletin of the American Society of Papyrologists* 5, no. 2–3 (October 1968): 99.

26 "The excitement aroused by the text": Peter van Minnen, "The Century of Papyrology (1892–1992)," *Bulletin of the American Society of Papyrologists* 30, no. ½ (1993): 7.

26 "an obscure verbose": Domenico Comparetti, quoted in David Sider, *The Library of the Villa dei Papiri at Herculaneum* (Los Angeles: Getty, 2005), 63.

26 "Outside Italy": Carel Gabriël Cobet, quoted in Peter van Minnen, "A Dutch Opinion of Amedeo Peyron," *Aegyptus* 76, no. ½ (January–December 1996): 158.

26 A new classics chairman: The chairman, a Greek intellectual historian named Eric Havelock, came to Yale in 1963, after sixteen years at Harvard. He stayed until his retirement in 1971.

26 the literature of great writers: John G. Brim, "Classics: Disputes, Resignations, Suspicion," *Yale Daily News,* March 4, 1966; Bagnall, phone interview by author, April 30, 2019.

26 The chairman soon came after: Bagnall, phone interview by author, April 30, 2019.

27 "Charging that the classics": Robert Kilpatrick, "How Yalies Rate Their Courses and Their Teachers," *New Haven Register,* April 14, 1968, 18.

27 That the target of his ire: Bagnall told me he had "an underdeveloped sense of fear and a big mouth" (phone interview, April 30, 2019).

27 If they wanted to liberate the field: Bagnall, *Reading Papyri,* 114, 116.

27 The Andrew W. Mellon Foundation: Columbia University, "Roger Bagnall Selected for $1.5 Million Mellon Foundation Award," Columbia News, December 18, 2003, www.columbia.edu.

28 "small and perpetually vulnerable": Bagnall to Nicholas Dirks, April 20, 2005, folder "Columbia University, Correspondence and Memoranda, 1981–2005," box 28, Bagnall Papers.

28 painful reminder of how easily: The extent to which memories of his Yale days rankled years later can be seen in Bagnall's letter to Yale's president, A. Bartlett Giamatti, February 14, 1979, folder "Miscellaneous A–K," box 44, Bagnall Papers.

28 "I often pray": Luijendijk to Bagnall, June 12, 2001, folder "Luijendijk, AnneMarie," box 40, Bagnall Papers. Luijendijk typed the greeting in Greek.

28 "Your expertise in Egyptian papyrus": King to Bagnall, July 23, 2001, folder "Luijendijk, AnneMarie," box 40, Bagnall Papers.

28 "my 'papyrological hero'": Luijendijk to Bagnall, postcard, May 1, 2005, folder "Luijendijk, AnneMarie," box 40, Bagnall Papers.

29 "As Justice Stewart said": Bagnall, phone interview by author, August 30, 2012.

29 "I have little to no respect": Baer Charlton, web post, The Picture Framers Grumble, July 12, 2004, thegrumble.com.

29 Between 1994 and 2009: Anderson Cooper, "$80 Million Con," *60 Minutes,* CBS, May 22, 2016; Colin Moynihan, "Dealer in Art Scheme Avoids Prison Term," *New York Times,* February 1, 2017.

29 "I don't know of": Goodstein, "Fresh Doubts."

30 "We all sort of stared": Farrior, "Divorcing Mrs. Jesus."

30 "The handwriting is not nice": Wangsness, "Hint of a Married Jesus."

30 the letters varied in height: King, "'Jesus Said to Them, "My Wife...,"'" *Harvard Theological Review* 107, no. 2 (April 2014): 136.

30 "The flow of ink": Bagnall, phone interview by author, August 30, 2012.

30 "It really looks incompetent": *The Gospel of Jesus's Wife* (TV documentary), History Channel cut.

31 "That is one of the things": Bagnall, phone interview by author, August 30, 2012.

31 "You'd have to be really": Ibid.

31 "Somebody was having a bad pen day": *Gospel of Jesus's Wife* (TV documentary), History Channel cut.

31 Bagnall set aside an hour: Though King would later describe the firsthand examination as lasting several hours, both Luijendijk and Bagnall told me it was a single hour. The meeting began at 2:30 p.m. Bagnall's next meeting was at 4:00 p.m.

32 *amicitia papyrologorum*: International Association of Papyrologists, "Amicitia Papyrologorum," website, Internet Archive Wayback Machine, February 10, 2017, capture, http://web.archive.org/web/20170210045828/http://www.ulb.ac.be/assoc/aip/amicitia.htm.

32 "The world," he thought: Goodstein, "Faded Piece of Papyrus."

33 "a new understanding of worship": Smith, *Secret Gospel, 5.*

33 "ready for a rest": Ibid., 8.

34 "completion of the spiritual union": Ibid., 107.

34 a theologian browsing: Robert M. Price, "Second Thoughts on the Secret Gospel," *Bulletin for Biblical Research* 14, no. 1 (2004): 131.

34 sensational Greek manuscript: In *The Mystery of Mar Saba,* a fragment of parchment called "The Shred of Nicodemus" appears to disprove the idea that Jesus was resurrected. Its namesake, a Pharisee, writes that he and Joseph of Arimathea removed Jesus's body from the tomb, leaving only his linen cloths, and "buried Him in the sepulchre near the garden." Hunter, *Mystery of Mar Saba,* 283.

34 "The other two": Ibid., 282.

35 with more than a dozen printings: Ian Hunter, "The (Continuing) Mystery of Mar Saba," *National Post* (Canada), June 30, 2005.

35 "the most outrageously successful": Jeffery, *Secret Gospel of Mark Unveiled,* 236.

35 "On sober reflection": Umberto Eco, *The Name of the Rose* (Orlando: Harcourt, 1983), 4.

35 Smith, who died in 1991: Tony Burke, ed., *Ancient Gospel or Modern Forgery? The "Secret Gospel of Mark" in Debate* (Eugene, Ore.: Cascade Books, 2013), 95.

36 "One fake is not published": Roger S. Bagnall, *The Florida Ostraka: Documents from the Roman Army in Upper Egypt* (Durham, N.C.: Duke University, 1976), 1.

36 "I wish you'd published the fake": Smith to Bagnall, April 17, 1977 (rendered "17 / IV / 77" by Smith), folder "Smith, Morton," box 23, Bagnall Papers.

36 "Would anything in the writing": Smith to Bagnall, May 21, 1977 (rendered "21 / V / 77" by Smith), folder "Smith, Morton," box 23, Bagnall Papers.

36 But it looked very much: Smith might also have been sizing up the chances that Secret Mark would one day be exposed. It is also possible that he had an entirely innocent interest in forgeries.

36 Writing in the journal *Chronique:* Bagnall and Cribiore, "O. Florida," 213–14.

37 "the crowns": Ibid., 214.

37 "He purported to be acting": Bagnall, email to Katie McCormick (FSU librarian), February 7, 2018, obtained through author's public records request. The Dutch papyrologist was Pieter Sijpesteijn. McCormick contacted Bagnall after I made inquiries about the provenance of the FSU collection.

37 "a complete cover story": When I asked Bagnall about the ostraca's provenance in an April 30, 2019, interview, he conceded that the dealer's tale of selling them on behalf of a Dutch woman—an account Bagnall had published in 1976 without qualification—was probably "just a complete cover story." Bagnall suspected that the dealer, Pieter Sijpesteijn, had acquired the ostraca in Egypt "in the very recent past." It was Sijpesteijn who had first labeled the fragment "fake?"

37 "the disappointment factor": King, phone interview by author, August 28, 2012. "We were totally being cool and collected scholars who could barely contain ourselves," King said of herself and Luijendijk. "I had to not really let myself feel much excitement because of the disappointment factor—if it turns out to be a hoax or something."

38 "The fragment gets a cab": Luijendijk, interview by author, Princeton University, March 3, 2017.

38 "Certainly in the six figures": *The Gospel of Jesus's Wife* (documentary), Smithsonian Channel cut.

38 "Some evangelical nut": Webb/Veale interview transcripts.

38 "Let's stop": Wangsness, "Hint of a Married Jesus."

BURNING QUESTIONS

39 She was the girl: "Loss Is Felt," *Passamari,* March 26, 1971, 1.

39 "Is the best method": Karen King, "Up-Grade Assemblies," *Passamari,* April 16, 1971, 2.

39 kids picked on her: King, interview by author, Somerville, Mass., September 4, 2012.

39 "brown eyed beauty": Edie Martinell, "Meet Marie King," *Passamari,* December 15, 1970, 7.

39 The one person Karen craved: Minnetta King and school friends of Karen King's, interviews by author.

39 "Two can live as cheap": Warren Swager, interview by author, Sheridan, Mont., April 23, 2017.

39 Before turning twelve, Karen: Mary Tilton, "Sheridan: Finish Safety Course," *Dillon (Mont.) Tribune-Examiner,* November 26, 1965, 3.

40 "No hens," he said: Karin Dworkin (former student of King's), phone interview by author, January 4, 2017.

40 either you were part of the group: "If you didn't fit in," King told me, "you didn't fit into the world." (Somerville, Mass., September 4, 2012.)

40 She rode the family horse: Karen King, Minnetta King, and various childhood friends of Karen King's, interviews by author.

40 "an opportunity to spend time": Wangsness, "Harvard Divinity Professor."

40 In an act of rebellion: The Reverend Janis Hansen, interview by author, Sheridan, Mont., April 23, 2017.

40 "a little bit stuffier": Max Steiner (King classmate), phone interview by author, February 15, 2017.

40 Its pastor, the Reverend John Vickers: *Progressive Years: Madison County* (Sheridan, Mont.: Madison County History Association, 1983), 2:57.

40 Vickers raised eyebrows at Sheridan: Gloria Barnosky (King classmate), phone interview by author, February 17, 2017.

40 Karen was the only minor: Wangsness, "Harvard Divinity Professor."

40 But there was another reason: Kathleen Wuelfing, phone interview by author, February 22, 2017.

40 even her parents didn't know: Minnetta King, interviews by author.

40 "an evangelical conversion": Wangsness, "Harvard Divinity Professor." Wangsness describes only the conversion, not what happened after King came back.

41 "That was a very difficult thing": Wuelfing, phone interview by author, February 22, 2017.

41 "Who gets to say": King, *Karen L. King: The Gospel of Mary.*

41 a Christian exchange program: The International Christian Youth Exchange, a pacifist, ecumenical program founded by the Church of the Brethren in the wake of World War II.

41 "to stress the idea": "Youth Reports," *Dillon (Mont.) Daily Tribune-Examiner,* November 12, 1970, 4.

41 "I almost was afraid": Minnetta King, phone interview by author, April 5, 2017.

41 a housewife: This is the word Karen King uses in "Candidate's Application."

41 local adviser to the Future Homemakers of America: Sharon Dudden, "Sheridan: Hold Style Show," *Dillon (Mont.) Tribune-Examiner,* May 5, 1966, 7. The article identified her as "Mrs. George King." Before Karen was born, her mother, Minnetta, was a U.S. government agricultural extension agent who taught rural Montanans everything from sewing and furniture repair to the law. After Karen went off to college, Minnetta ran a bed-and-breakfast and had a long career raising Arabian horses.

41 "I was raised United Methodist": King, "Candidate's Application."

42 "No, it was the romance": King, interview by author, Somerville, Mass., September 4, 2012.

42 "We came back to school": Gilman, phone interview by author, February 15, 2017.

42 a thirteenth-century church: The Vangskyrkja, a landmark in the center of Voss.

42 "She wanted people to hear": Tjelle, interview by author, Skånevik, Norway, September 13, 2016.

42 the fall of 1973: King had spent her freshman year (1972–1973) at Western College, in Ohio, before transferring to the University of Montana.

43 "the responsibility of white youth": Alan Higbee, "White Youth Should Fight for Socialism, Carmichael Says," *Montana Kaimin,* October 10, 1973, 1.

43 "the truth of their freedom": The Second Treatise of the Great Seth.

45 "evil interpreters": Irenaeus, *Against Heresies,* bk. 1, preface.

45 "Never before has a single": Jonas, *Gnostic Religion,* xxix.

46 "The overriding appeal": Stokan, phone interview by author, May 4, 2017.

46 "Mind trips": Elliott Hewitt, phone interview by author, December 9, 2016.

46 "Norman Rockwell": Max Steiner, phone interview by author, February 15, 2017.

46 "pretty much Mayberry": Vicki Selvidge, phone interview by author, February 20, 2017.

46 "There was no crime": Gloria Barnosky, phone interview by author, February 17, 2017.

47 "every person who is not": King, *Revelation of the Unknowable God*, 54.

47 a warning stamped: Turner, interview by author, San Antonio, November 20, 2016; Pagels, *Gnostic Gospels*.

47 "I felt a very intense": King, "Thinking About Women and Heresy."

47 "I definitely chose the university": King, interview by author, Somerville, Mass., September 4, 2012.

47 that she would never write about: King, "Thinking About Women and Heresy."

48 "This is my favorite text": Ibid.

48 "in any kind of synchronization": Turner, interview by author, San Antonio, November 20, 2016.

48 "She's always had some sort": McGaughy, interview by author, Salem, Ore., December 13, 2016.

48 "she was working like two levels": Kelson, phone interview by author, May 2, 2017.

49 Manhattan was her first big-city experience: Gibson, "Bits the Bible Left Out," 43.

49 "Apparently," recalled Trillin: Trillin, email to author, November 6, 2016.

49 proposed to her Montana boyfriend: Chandler, phone interview by author, December 1, 2016.

49 "double ring ceremony": Helen Fenton, "Sheridan News," *Dillion (Mont.) Tribune-Examiner,* September 2, 1977, 5.

49 officiated by an Episcopal priest: Certificate of Holy Matrimony, August 7, 1977, in State of Rhode Island divorce records.

49 In Providence, King persuaded: Chandler, phone interview by author, December 1, 2016. The church was Saint Stephen's in Providence.

49 They divorced in 1982: State of Rhode Island court records. King filed for divorce in November 1981, citing irreconcilable differences. A judge granted it in May 1982.

49 "running battle": "Portrait of an Author."

49 "ethically unacceptable fantasy": King, "Body and Society in Philo."

49 To his chagrin: "Portrait of an Author."

49 "I sincerely feel more at home": King to Chandler, April 28, 1976.

50 "DAAD scholarships could be used": Grothus, emails to author, December 20, 2017. He sent a 1982 English-language brochure as confirmation.

50 Some days, they detained her: "Portrait of an Author."

50 once they strip-searched her: Wangsness, "Harvard Professor Relishes Adventure."

51 "It was very dirty work": Hans-Gebhard Bethge, phone and in-person interviews by author's interpreter, Berlin, March 1 and 8, 2017.

51 every Tuesday for more than a year: In interviews and a few autobiographical squibs about her time in Berlin, I noticed, King never spoke of these Tuesday meetings. She recounted "once-a-week" border crossings, on Fridays, to study with Hans-Martin Schenke, the eminent Nag Hammadi scholar who lived in East Berlin proper, where King's visa was valid.

51 she took up cigarettes: Minnetta King, interview by author, Sheridan, Mont., April 24, 2017.

51 Yet Karl-Wolfgang Tröger: Tröger, phone interviews by author's interpreter, February 19, 2018.

51 A binder some two hundred pages thick: Bethge, phone interview by author's interpreter, January 8, 2019.

52 prized inspirational teaching: Axel Steuer (former Occidental College religious studies chair), phone interview by author, February 14, 2017.

52 "Are the decisions that were made": Rich Barlow, "Spiritual Life: Another View of Christian Scripture," *Boston Globe,* July 19, 2003.

52 "What happens if": King, *Gospel of Mary of Magdala,* 158.

52 Questions were the lure: Bernadette Brooten, phone interview by author, May 3, 2017. "She puts forth all kinds of questions," Brooten said, "and that invites people."

52 "It's like the wink and nod": Emily Neill, phone interview by author, December 6, 2016.

52 "a wild ovation": Karin Dworkin, phone interview by author, January 4, 2017.

52 "this big mind": Cynthia Wells, phone interview by author, January 5, 2017.

52 "To those who walk in": Karen King, "Loftsgordon Address" (speech, Occidental College Senior Convocation, May 31, 1989), transcript in Occidental College Library Special Collections and College Archives.

53 "Excellent, important, eminently reasonable": Slaughter to Roger Boesche, Memo, "Establishing a Women's Center," May 14, 1990, Occidental College Library Special Collections and College Archives.

53 "Well-meaning male colleagues": King, "Thinking About Women and Heresy."

53 aloof solipsists fixated: See Pagels, Gnostic Gospels (Kindle edition, loc. 2397), for instance, or Jonas, Gnostic Religion, 270, 271, and 281. Jonas speaks of a "gnostic libertinism," "indifference," "immoralism," and "profound moral helplessness."

53 "illegitimate domination": King, "Who Are the Gnostics?," 16.

53 "life experiences": King, "Translating History," 270.

54 "a sharp and biting critique": King, "Ridicule and Rape," 15.

54 "sharp critique of illegitimate power": King, Gospel of Mary of Magdala, 3.

54 "the mystery": King, Secret Revelation of John, 66.

54 "To my knowledge": King, "Reading Sex," 532.

54 "as people who don't belong": King, "Who Are the Gnostics?," 15.

54 Some women faculty asked her: King, interview by author, Somerville, Mass., September 4, 2012.

55 Moreover, she had placed: Karen King, "Kingdom in the Gospel of Thomas," Foundations and Facets Forum 3, no. 1 (March 1987): 48–97.

55 start-up investor: Lane McGaughy (executive director of the Westar Institute), interview by author, Salem, Ore., December 13, 2016.

55 board member: Karen King, Curriculum Vitae, September 2014, hds.harvard.edu.

55 "It never occurred to me": King, interview by author, Somerville, Mass., September 4, 2012.

55 There had been an impasse: Author's interviews with sources close to the hiring process.

55 "It was a very embattled place": Neill, phone interview by author, December 6, 2016.

55 "A lot of people went": Lewis, interviews by author, Kristiansand, Norway, September 15–16, 2016.

55 "If I can think of any mistakes": Ibid.

56 "What history can do": King, interview by author, Somerville, Mass., September 4, 2012.

56 "Some people call this": King, Gospel of Mary of Magdala: Westar Stars, DVD.

56 As a student, during a break: Karin Dworkin, phone interview by author, January 4, 2017.

56 the sense she gave colleagues: Harvey Cox, phone interview by author, February 17, 2017. "She's an enormously hard worker," Cox, a renowned theologian who was her predecessor as Hollis Professor of Divinity, said. "One time I asked, 'What are you doing in your spare time?' She said, 'In my spare time, I work.'"

THE COMPLICATION OF MARY

59 The version of Mark: James Tabor, "The 'Strange' Ending of the Gospel of Mark and Why It Makes All the Difference," Bible History Daily, Biblical Archaeology Society, April 1, 2018, www.biblicalarchaeology.org.

60 In a single opening volley: Scholars disagree on whether the author of Mark 16:9 borrows from later gospels or is an "independent witness." For a technical discussion, see James A. Kelhoffer, Miracle and Mission: The Authentication of Missionaries and Their Message in the Longer Ending of Mark (Tübingen: Mohr Siebeck, 2000), 132–33, 137.

60 "What did these seven devils": Haskins, Mary Magdalen, 93.

60 "became a model for women": King, "Canonization and Marginalization," 31.

60 "In the Middle Ages": Diane Winston, "The Female Apostle," Washington Post, March 20, 1994.

61 "feminine counterpart": Haskins, Mary Magdalen, 386.

61 missing word is "mouth": The scholar credited with filling the hole was Hans-Martin Schenke, an esteemed East German translator of Philip who happened to be Karen King's mentor during her graduate research year in East Berlin. Schenke came to believe that the only word short enough to fit was the two-letter Coptic word for "mouth." Most scholars went along with the restoration, though other authorities noted that the words for "cheek," "forehead," and "feet" would also fit. "He called it 'the famous hole,'" his former wife, Gesine Schenke Robinson, a Coptic scholar, told me when we met for lunch near her Southern California home in 2017. She said that her late husband's strict upbringing in communist Germany had made sex an uncomfortable topic. Philip's hole was, for him, a kind of playful release valve. "He made dirty jokes, very dirty jokes about it," she said. "The dirtier, the better." She recalled him saying, "That's the most curious hole in the world."

61 In early Christianity, kisses were exchanged: Mount Holyoke College, "On Kissing: A Q&A with Michael Penn," News & Events web page, June 13, 2006, www.mtholyoke .edu.

61 As for *koinonos*: Jane Schaberg, *The Resurrection of Mary Magdalene: Legends, Apocrypha, and the Christian Testament* (New York: Continuum, 2004), 152.

62 "You're saying the Christian Church": Brown, *Da Vinci Code*, 268.

62 carried out voluminous research: Brown, "First Witness Statement."

62 "It says nothing of marriage": Brown, *Da Vinci Code*, 266.

63 That the language is Coptic: Technically, *koinonos* is a Greek loanword to Coptic, though that fact brings the language no closer to Aramaic.

63 "Dr. King said she wants nothing": Goodstein, "Faded Piece of Papyrus."

63 "just coincidental": Char Matejovsky (Polebridge Press managing editor), phone interview by author, March 29, 2017.

63 "a national source for background": Polebridge Press, "Mary of Magdala," website, Internet Archive Wayback Machine, June 20, 2010, capture, https://web.archive.org /web/20100620062127/http://www.maryofmagdala.com/.

63 King's book was reviewed: Dinitia Smith, "Books of the Times: Discovering Magdalene the Apostle, Not the Fallen Woman," *New York Times*, October 25, 2003.

63 sold more than ten thousand copies: Polebridge Press, "Mary of Magdala," website, Internet Archive Wayback Machine, January 3, 2004, capture, https://web.archive.org /web/20040103030808/http://www.maryofmagdala.com:80/.

63 another sixty-five thousand: Lane McGaughy (Polebridge editor), email to the author, January 13, 2017, listing 75,281 copies sold as of that date.

63 some featured interviews: See, for instance, ABC News Presents, *Jesus, Mary, and Da Vinci*, November 3, 2003.

64 "a year and a half": King, interview by author, Somerville, Mass., September 4, 2012.

64 "I see just a huge hunger": Juli Cragg Hilliard, "The Peril and the Promise," *Publishers Weekly*, November 15, 2004.

64 "As a professor of ecclesiastical history": *Deborah Norville Tonight*, April 29, 2004.

65 "touching so many people": Beth Barrett, "Deciphering the Code," *Los Angeles Daily News*, February 1, 2004.

65 "King deals with": C. E. Jampel, "Ruffling Religious Feathers," *Harvard Crimson*, February 12, 2004.

66 "If anyone knows": Veale, phone interview by author, March 30, 2017.

66 "Well, it's interesting": Ibid.

67 "It doesn't get much more senior": Webb, Skype interview by author, December 11, 2017.

67 "Do you have a few minutes": David Royle and Charles Poe (Smithsonian Channel executives), phone interview by author, November 30, 2016; and written timeline, with quoted email text, provided to author by Smithsonian Channel, March 20, 2017.

67 a new slogan: Jacqueline Trescott, "Smithsonian Aims to Change Its Brand," *Washington Post*, December 16, 2011.

67 "was a shiny new object": Royle and Poe, phone interview by author, November 30, 2016.

68 "even from among people": Ibid.

68 "if Karen had consulted": Author's interview with source close to Harvard's press office, who requested anonymity to discuss a sensitive subject.

69 "Well," King replied: Webb, Skype interview by author, December 11, 2017.

69 "In talking to the press": Author's contemporaneous reporting notes from King's impromptu press conference at the Institutum Patristicum Augustinianum, Rome, September 19, 2012.

71 "it puts into greater question": King, phone interview by author, August 28, 2012.

71 "a new word": Webb/Veale interview transcripts.

A BRILLIANT JEWEL

72 around A.D. 206: Peter Brown, *The Body and Society: Men, Women, and Sexual Renunciation in Early Christianity* (New York: Columbia University Press, 2008), 168.

72 "gave the highest proof": Eusebius, *Church History,* bk. 6, chap. 8.

73 "It would be absurd": Birger A. Pearson, "Did Jesus Marry?," *Bible Review* 21, no. 2 (Spring 2005).

74 "who say outright that marriage": Clement of Alexandria, *Stromateis,* bk. 3, chap. 6, line 49.

75 "restless" sexual maturity: Augustine, *Confessions,* trans. E. B. Pusey (Oxford: John Parker and Rivingtons, 1876), 21–22.

75 "I was in the habit": Augustine, *Confessions,* trans. Sarah Ruden (New York: Modern Library, 2017), 52.

75 "Shortly thereafter": Stephen Greenblatt, "The Invention of Sex," *New Yorker,* June 19, 2017.

76 In a clever stroke of logic: Augustine viewed the Virgin Mary as free from personal sin but did not address whether she was guilty of original sin. Catholics established the doctrine of her "Immaculate Conception" later.

76 "it is still Eve": Augustine, Epistle 243.

76 "loves his enemy": Augustine, *Our Lord's Sermon on the Mount,* chap. 15.

77 "only men with a tonsure": Peter De Rosa, *Vicars of Christ: The Dark Side of the Papacy* (New York: Crown, 1988), 413.

77 "Our Lord decreed": English translation from Latin of "De concubinis sacerdotum," in James A. Brundage, *Law, Sex, and Christian Society in Medieval Europe* (Chicago: University of Chicago Press, 1987), 402.

77 "On our side we have Scripture": Quoted in Phipps, *Clerical Celibacy,* 153.

77 "The thought of those young priests": Quoted in ibid., 172.

78 "For some of them": Quoted in Kimba Allie Tichenor, *Religious Crisis and Civic Transformation* (Waltham, Mass.: Brandeis University Press, 2016), 36.

78 "Our intention," he said: Quoted in Phipps, *Clerical Celibacy,* 176.

78 "modern stirrings of opinion": Pope Paul VI, *Sacerdotalis caelibatus* (Encyclical, Rome, June 24, 1967), w2.vatican.va.

78 "a revolutionary mentality": Alfred Friendly Jr., "More Priests Ask for Right to Wed," *New York Times,* July 3, 1969; Pope Paul VI's general audience, July 2, 1969, w2.vatican.va.

78 "the Jewish mentality": Šeper, *"Inter Insigniores."*

79 "Anyone who substitutes his own": Friendly, "More Priests Ask for Right to Wed," 12; Pope Paul VI's general audience, July 2, 1969.

81 "My Dean" appeared to refer to David Hempton: In a May 23, 2019, email to the author, a Harvard Divinity School spokesperson said, "Dean Hempton had no objection with Prof. King exploring the possibility of Harvard purchasing Fritz's papyrus collection, but he indicated that it would be up to the University to decide whether it wanted to evaluate the collection's worth and whether or not it wished to pursue a purchase of it."

81 "Would you like to see the fragment?": Royle and Poe, phone interview by author, November 30, 2016.

82 "If it's a forgery": Wangsness, "Hint of a Married Jesus."

82 "Given the worries": Madigan and Levenson, email to King, September 4, 2012, provided to the author by Bagnall. (King had forwarded it to Bagnall.)

83 Rather than being: This was not a unanimous view. Some scholars argued that the National Geographic team mistranslated and misinterpreted the Coptic text.

83 To help make the case: For an overview, see Joseph G. Barabe et al., "Examination of the Gospel of Judas Using an Integrated Approach to Ink Characterization," *Microscopy Today* 14, no. 4 (July 2006): 6–15.

83 "not usually done": King, phone interview by author, August 28, 2012.

84 Founders' Tower: Harvard Divinity School, "Saluting Andover Hall at 100 Years," web article, May 9, 2012, hds.harvard.edu.

84 "Deeply in need of your advice": King, email to Bagnall, September 5, 2012, provided to the author by Bagnall.

84 Bagnall replied, with characteristic speed: King's email was time-stamped 12:12 p.m., Bagnall's reply, 12:40 p.m., according to copies of the emails forwarded to the author by Roger Bagnall, May 1, 2019.

AUGUSTINIANUM

86 "It caught like a raging fire": Grech, phone interview by author, July 13, 2017.

88 the minute King announced: Under what is known as a news embargo, *Smithsonian*—along with *The New York Times* and *The Boston Globe,* the two other publications granted early access to King—agreed to King's request that nothing be published before then. I interviewed King at Harvard a week before the *Times* and the *Globe* and was the only journalist in the room in Rome when King announced the discovery to colleagues.

89 Looking out over some three dozen: Author's contemporaneous reporting notes and author's digital voice recording of King's presentation, Rome, September 18, 2012.

90 in part because of a stray letter: In Coptic, negations like "not" appear at the ends of sentences. The character at the end of the line was the first letter either of the negation or of some other, undiscernible word.

90 The New Testament describes: Author's research.

91 "highly likely that this Mary": King, " 'Jesus Said to Them, "My Wife…" ' " (September 18, 2012, public draft).

92 "correct sexual relations": Ibid.

92 In her talk, King had sought: As part of this complex argument, King said that the Wife papyrus made her wonder whether the Gospel of Philip—which depicts Jesus kissing Mary and refers to an enigmatic ritual called the "Bridal Chamber"—might also allude to a wedding between Jesus and Mary Magdalene.

93 "means 'wife' not 'woman' ": F. L. Griffith, "The Old Coptic Horoscope of the Stobart Collection," *Zeitschrift für Ägyptische Sprache und Altertumskunde* 38 (1900): 80.

93 When Coptic scribes translated: Author's analysis, from electronic searches of biblical databases and interviews with scholars.

93 Found nowhere in any known text: I wondered whether marriage contracts and other ancient legal documents might have an instance of *ta-hime.* But when I asked the German Egyptologist Tonio Sebastian Richter, the foremost expert on the linguistics of Coptic legal papyri, he checked and turned up nothing. "I couldn't find a single attestation of possessive pronoun plus hime," he wrote to me. Richter, email to author, April 4, 2018.

93 *peje Iēsous nau ta-hime:* Scientific English transliteration of Coptic based on guidance from Hany Takla (email to author, February 1, 2019) and Stephen Emmel (email to author, February 8, 2019). An informal guide to the line's pronunciation would be *peh-jeh yay-SOUS NOW ta-HEE-meh.*

94 "all things": Valentinus, frag. 3, *Lost Writings of Valentinus.*

94 "We don't have any evidence": The Finnish scholar speaking is Ismo Dunderberg.

95 In view of that history: The first person to foreground these points, as far as I can tell, was the journalist Eleanor Barkhorn, who published "The Bible Refers to Jesus' Wife, Too," on the *Atlantic* website, www.theatlantic.com, within hours of King's announcement on September 18, 2012.

96 AnneMarie Luijendijk, who was in the room: Luijendijk, interview by author, April 23, 2019.

98 "Being married myself": Online comment beneath Goodstein, "Papyrus Referring to Jesus' Wife." The online reader comments in this section were selected, for represen-

tativeness, from a variety of articles, some written in the immediate aftermath of the discovery, others later.

99 "the biggest fan group": "Ancient Papyrus—Does It Matter if Jesus Was Married?"

99 "We all thought it was weird": Lewis, interview by author, Kristiansand, Norway, September 16, 2016.

100 "looked like twenty-first-century handwriting": Alin Suciu, Skype interview by author, November 8, 2016.

100 The trouble, historically: Willy Clarysse, "Egyptian Scribes Writing Greek," *Chronique d'Égypte* 68, no. 135–36 (1993): 193.

100 "grammatical monstrosity": Depuydt, "Alleged *Gospel of Jesus's Wife*," 186.

101 "belongs to the genre of Gnostic": International Association for Coptic Studies, "Minutes of the Tenth Business Meetings of the IACS, Rome, 22 September 2012 (at the End of the Tenth International Congress of Coptic Studies), Anne Boud'hors Presiding," Newsletter 57 (October 2012), electronic edition, 13–14.

103 The *Times,* the *Globe,* and *Smithsonian:* Goodstein, "Coptic Scholars Doubt"; Wangsness, "Scholars Begin to Weigh In"; Sabar, "Gospel According to King."

104 "inept forgery": Giovanni Maria Vian, "In Any Case a Fake," *L'Osservatore Romano,* October 3, 2012, English edition, 11. The Italian edition of the newspaper was published on September 28, 2012.

104 "What is the rule on wedding gifts?": Stephen Colbert, "Wife of Jesus," *The Colbert Report,* September 19, 2012, www.cc.com.

104 "Jesus was married?": Jon Stewart, "The God Wife," *The Daily Show with Jon Stewart,* September 20, 2012, www.cc.com.

104 She was scheduled to give: When I asked her about it five years later, Luijendijk told me she had been seven months pregnant with twins and feared giving birth prematurely in a city not her home.

105 "When you call it 'The Gospel of Jesus's Wife'": Pagels, phone interview by author, September 24, 2012.

105 "quite satisfied": Author's contemporaneous reporting notes and digital voice recording of King's presentation in Rome, September 18, 2012.

105 "colossal double blunder": Depuydt, email to editors of the *Harvard Theological Review,* September 19, 2012, provided to the author by Depuydt on October 31, 2016.

105 "Using bold letters": Depuydt, "Alleged *Gospel of Jesus's Wife*," 174.

106 "It's really about as clear": Webb/Veale interview transcripts.

106 "bats on the ceiling": Robin Lane Fox, "Batson Comes out of the Belfry: The History Books May Not Have to Be Rewritten ...," *Financial Times,* May 25, 1991.

107 "How's that for sincere masochism": King to Barry Chandler, April 28, 1976.

107 "Scholars are by nature": Wangsness, "Scholars Begin to Weigh In."

ACT 2: DOUBT

109 "Proof," I said: Raymond Chandler, *Farewell, My Lovely* (New York: Vintage Crime/ Black Lizard, 1992), 280.

EPSILON AND IOTA

111 That Andrew Bernhard had eclectic: The sections on Bernhard are based largely on three days of interviews with him in Portland, Oregon, December 14–16, 2016, as well as numerous phone calls, documents, and emails.

114 selectively deleting words: Bernhard was working in Coptic. What follows are approximate English equivalents that preserve some of the peculiarities of Coptic syntax. Deleted words from Thomas are formatted as strike-through text, and the words in the Wife papyrus are in bold.

114 "grammatical monstrosity": Depuydt, "Alleged *Gospel of Jesus's Wife*," 186.

114 "horrendous syntactic mash": Email to colleagues from senior Coptic scholar, October 2012, provided by source requesting anonymity.

114 "Frankenstein": Christian Askeland, interview by author, Oklahoma City, January 26, 2017.

114 such a disaster: The line's subject was clearly "man," in the sense of "mankind." But then the line goes haywire. Under the rules of Coptic grammar, the words should read

"man *when* wicked," not "man *who* is wicked." But that was just the first problem. The self-negating double conjugation of the verb "to bring" was as gruesome in Coptic as it was in English. In Bernhard's view, it threw a wrench into Watson's theory.

114 "I am truly embarrassed": King, email to Bagnall, September 5, 2012, provided to the author by Bagnall.

115 "interesting features" and an "as-yet only:": King, " 'Jesus Said to Them, "My Wife…" ' " (September 18, 2012, public draft).

116 Three days later, a pair of European scholars: Alin Suciu and Hugo Lundhaug, "A Peculiar Dialectal Feature in the Gospel of Jesus's Wife, Line 6," *Alin Suciu* (blog), September 27, 2012, alinsuciu.com.

THE KINGDOM OF GOD PUZZLE

118 "I thought, 'Wait a minute' ": Quotations and other material in this section are drawn from Grondin, interviews by author, Macomb, Mich., January 12–13, 2017, as well as follow-up phone calls, emails, documents, and other supplemental materials.

119 "I look forward": Stevan L. Davies, *The Gospel of Thomas and Christian Wisdom* (New York: Seabury Press, 1983), 155.

119 The book had thirty lessons: Thomas O. Lambdin, *Introduction to Sahidic Coptic* (Macon, Ga.: Mercer University Press, 1983).

122 well-known saying: Gospel of Thomas saying 45; Matthew 12:35; Luke 6:45.

124 He was adding and deleting spaces: Grondin, phone interview by author, November 21, 2018.

124 "Just when you might have thought": Mark Goodacre, "Jesus' Wife Fragment: Further Evidence of Modern Forgery," *NT Blog,* October 11, 2012, ntweblog.blogspot.com.

124 The British newspaper *The Guardian:* Andrew Brown, "The Gospel of Jesus's Wife: A Very Modern Fake," *Guardian,* October 16, 2012, www.theguardian.com.

125 "I've never learned to use": Karen King, in "To Speak or Not to Speak: When Should Professors Speak Out?," panel discussion at Harvard Divinity School, YouTube, filmed September 9, 2014, uploaded to YouTube by Harvard Divinity School on September 15, 2014, www.youtube.com.

126 "ugly and unprintable": Bartlett, "Lessons of Jesus' Wife."

126 a cautionary tale: Ibid.

126 panic button: Bonar, "High Stakes Marriage."

126 Security measures for the fragment: William Stoneman (curator of early books and manuscripts, Houghton Library, Harvard), interview by author, March 15, 2017. The collector's Gospel of Jesus's Wife and Gospel of John fragments were the only holdings for which a librarian had to sit beside researchers examining them.

126 "there was a period": Nicola Denzey Lewis, interview by author, September 16, 2016.

126 "Harvard is like riding a tiger": Christopher Jones (Harvard classicist), phone interview by author, October 24, 2016.

RIDING A TIGER

127 there was talk of displaying: "I can remember calling over to the Freer | Sackler [Museum], and there was quite a lot of enthusiasm about displaying it," David Royle, the Smithsonian Channel's executive vice president, said. Phone interview by author, November 30, 2016.

128 "dispel all rumors of forgery": Theodore R. Delwiche, "Divinity School Report Finds Fragmentary Artifact of 'Gospel of Jesus's Wife' Authentic," *Harvard Crimson,* April 11, 2014.

128 "big disappointment": Goodstein, "Papyrus Referring to Jesus' Wife."

130 "In my judgment": King, " 'Jesus Said to Them, "My Wife…," ' " *Harvard Theological Review* 107, no. 2 (April 2014): 158.

130 "just about as strong": WGBH News, "Greater Boston Video." The chyron on the screen during the interview read, "Was Jesus Married? Ancient Text Authenticated."

ACT 3: PROOFS

131 "The forger confronts a chessboard": Anthony Grafton, *Forgers and Critics: Creativity and Duplicity in Western Scholarship* (Princeton, N.J.: Princeton University Press, 1990), 59.

133 "the absolute authority": The Museum of the Bible Inc., Schedule O, U.S. Internal Revenue Service Form 990, 2010.

134 "He's the only evangelical": Burns, Skype interview by author, August 31, 2016.

136 since that November: November 13, 2012, according to King, "'Jesus Said to Them, "My Wife...,"'" *Harvard Theological Review* 107, no. 2 (April 2014): 154.

136 in the extended Columbia ink study: Yardley and Hagadorn, "Report: Ink Study" (full version). Photos of the John fragment appear on pp. 6 and 7. The scientists included the images, beneath a grid, to pinpoint the locations of tested ink, having no idea of the sensation they would cause among scholars who recognized the layout of the Coptic text.

136 There are roughly two hundred known copies: Hans Förster (a scholar at the University of Vienna), email to author, November 29, 2018. "Old" is used here to mean all the dialects besides Bohairic. Of those roughly two hundred copies, twenty-seven are on papyri, according to Matthias Schulz, also of the University of Vienna (December 4, 2018, email).

136 But just two are in Lycopolitan: Askeland, *John's Gospel,* 141–43.

136 quickly acquired the manuscript: Askeland obtained his PhD in 2011. De Gruyter published his book in 2012.

137 But the other Lycopolitan John: Ibid., 142.

137 A British archaeologist had found it: Thompson, *Gospel of St. John,* ix. The archaeologist was Guy Brunton.

138 Had the gospel survived in its entirety: Emmel, "Codicology of the New Coptic (Lycopolitan) Gospel of John Fragment."

139 a modern typesetting feature: Askeland, "Lycopolitan Forgery," 331. See Askeland's paper for the full range of problems with Harvard John.

139 Hook told me: Hook, email to the author, January 22, 2017.

140 "If you want to say": Steve Green, "The Hobby Lobby Story" (speech, March 2013), Council for National Policy, Internet Archive Wayback Machine, September 7, 2019, capture, http://web.archive.org/web/20190907070057/https://cfnp.org/wp-content/uploads/2018/05/March-2013-Green.pdf.

140 "We are storytellers first": Sandra Hindman, "We Are Storytellers First," *Fine Books & Collections* 11, no. 4 (Autumn 2013): 32. The Gospel of Judas codex was one of the artifacts the Greens were offered but ultimately declined to buy. "[Steve] Green said, 'Anything not in the Bible we wouldn't want,'" David Trobisch, who directed the Museum of the Bible's collections from 2014 to 2018, told me. (Interview, Washington, D.C., October 20, 2017.)

140 Hobby Lobby would eventually: U.S. Attorney's Office for the Eastern District of New York, "United States Files Civil Action to Forfeit Thousands of Ancient Iraqi Artifacts Imported by Hobby Lobby," press release, July 5, 2017, www.justice.gov.

140 Israeli authorities, meanwhile: Daniel Estrin, "Israeli Authorities Arrest Antiquities Dealers in Connection with Hobby Lobby Scandal," NPR, July 31, 2017, www.npr.org; Amanda Borschel-Dan, "Arrest of Jerusalem Antiquities Dealers Opens a Smuggling Pandora's Box," *Times of Israel,* August 1, 2017, www.timesofisrael.com.

140 Before long, humanities scholars: Daniel Burke, "Bible Museum Says Five of Its Dead Sea Scrolls Are Fake," CNN, October 23, 2018, www.cnn.com.

140 The Museum of the Bible next accused: Candida Moss, "Did Oxford Scholar Secretly Sell Bible Fragment to Hobby Lobby Family?," *Daily Beast,* June 24, 2019, www.thedaily beast.com. For an insider account, see Jerry Pattengale, "The 'First-Century Mark' Saga from Inside the Room," *Christianity Today,* June 28, 2019, www.christianitytoday .com. The Oxford scholar Dirk Obbink, a MacArthur "genius" grant recipient, had previously denied the allegations.

141 "sort of a reversal": Williams, phone interview by author, April 4, 2018.

141 "The use of an ugly woman": Eva Mroczek, "Gospel of Jesus' Wife Less Durable than Sexism Surrounding It," *Religion Dispatches,* May 6, 2014, religiondispatches.org.

141 women make up: April DeConick (Rice University scholar who chaired SBL's Status of Women in the Professions panel in 2016), phone interview by author, March 1, 2017.

142 "hyping a fragment": Christian Askeland, "Was Mrs. Jesus Pimped?," *Evangelical Textual Criticism* (blog), September 27, 2012, evangelicaltextualcriticism.blogspot.com.

142 "Jesus Had a Sister-in-Law": Christian Askeland, "Jesus Had a Sister-in-Law," *Evangelical Textual Criticism* (blog), April 24, 2014, evangelicaltextualcriticism.blogspot.com.

142 "The stance seems to be": Charlotte Allen, "'Jesus' Wife' Papyrus a Forgery? You're a Sexist!," *Los Angeles Times,* May 16, 2014, www.latimes.com.

142 "Where is the Gospel of Mary?": Bernhard, interviews by author, Portland, Ore., December 2016.

143 "It's never a good sign": Joel S. Baden and Candida R. Moss, "New Clues Cast Doubt on 'Gospel of Jesus' Wife,'" CNN, *Belief Blog,* April 29, 2014, religion.blogs.cnn.com.

143 published an op-ed: Jerry Pattengale, "How the 'Jesus' Wife' Hoax Fell Apart," *Wall Street Journal,* May 1, 2014, www.wsj.com.

143 "scientific results": Smithsonian Channel, "Smithsonian Channel Exclusive Home to Story Behind Discovery of the Gospel of Jesus's Wife: Premieres Monday, May 5 at 8pm ET/PT," press release, April 23, 2014. Internet Archive Wayback Machine, June 13, 2017, capture, https://web.archive.org/web/20170613031436/http://static.smithsonian channel.com/sc_assets/pdf/press/2014_Gospel_Wife.pdf

143 *The New York Times* published its own story: Goodstein, "Fresh Doubts."

144 "Forgeries corrupt": Francis Watson (unsigned), "Editorial," *New Testament Studies* 61, no. 3 (July 2015): 290.

144 Among them were back-to-back articles: Askeland, "Lycopolitan Forgery"; Bernhard, *"Gospel of Jesus' Wife."*

145 "Among the real scholars": Nina Burleigh, *Unholy Business: A True Tale of Faith, Greed, and Forgery in the Holy Land* (New York: Smithsonian Books/Collins, 2008), 33.

145 but a reply to a question: Karen King, "Karen King, Hollis Professor of Divinity at Harvard University, Responds," *Biblical Archaeology Review,* September/October 2015, 8–9.

145 The rabbi's family had wondered: Rabbi Avram Israel Reisner, "Another Explanation—Not a Forgery," *Biblical Archaeology Review,* September/October 2015, 8; and Reisner, email to author, March 26, 2018.

145 Though the rabbi wasn't either: Reisner, email to author, March 26, 2018. Reisner said he did not know King. "I never did follow up on Dr. King's kind offer to share other thoughts, because I had no relevant ones."

146 "theologically distinctive": King, "'Jesus Said to Them, "My Wife...,"'" *Harvard Theological Review* 107, no. 2 (April 2014): 157. Other scholars disputed this argument. The problem with the Wife papyrus, they contended, wasn't that its narrative resembled those in other gospels. It was that the copyist appeared to snip from different parts of the Gospel of Thomas, then jam the disjointed phrases together to say something new.

146 a few "rare" examples: Ibid., 140, 142, 155.

146 "proof that the statements": Ibid., 156.

146 Why King refused to release: At least a few scholars began to wonder whether "the owner" and his "papers" even existed.

146 The owner, I wrote: Sabar, "Inside Story."

147 "You need to figure out": Beckwith, phone interview by author, March 2, 2018.

148 It was that nearly every error: Bernhard seemed to correctly guess the reasons for line 6's monstrous Coptic grammar: the owner's translation began, as he had suspected, with the English words "No man who is wicked," rather than "Never does man who is wicked." For a full analysis of the owner's translation, see Bernhard's article "Postscript: A Final Note."

148 "Where I got it from": Grondin, email to author, May 7, 2016.

149 Three years later, his curiosity piqued: Choat, interview by author, San Antonio, November 18, 2016.

149 some ten times longer: AnneMarie Luijendijk and Roger Bagnall told me that the March 2012 meeting in Bagnall's office lasted about an hour.

149 This time Choat spotted traces: Some of these problems had been noticed in an examination a couple of months earlier by the University of Texas papyrologist Geoffrey S. Smith, who had been a student of King's at Harvard and Luijendijk's at Princeton. Andrew Bernhard was at last able to examine the fragment firsthand in December 2015, once it had left the divinity school's custody and was moved to Houghton Library.

150 "For now": Wangsness, "Case of the Gospel."

CROSSROADS

154 "Somehow, with that meditation": Solana, interview by author, Migdal, Israel, June 19, 2015.

155 "our sincerest thanks": King, "'Jesus Said to Them, "My Wife..."'" (September 18, 2012, public draft). "We wish to offer here our sincerest thanks to the owner, who wishes to remain anonymous, for permission to publish this papyrus fragment," she wrote.

156 The very next year, Egypt: Also in 1983, President Ronald Reagan made the United States a signatory to a United Nations convention sharply restricting international trade in antiquities.

157 "at once an invitation": King, *Revelation of the Unknowable God,* 54.

157 "I just sort of googled them": King, phone interview by author, August 28, 2012.

158 "Well, um, the current owner": King, interview by author, Somerville, Mass., September 4, 2012.

158 A week after my Harvard visit: Author, email to King, September 12, 2012.

158 King responded: King sent the author four emails on September 13, 2012, but none addressed the question of Laukamp's full name.

158 Ten days after that: Author, email to King, September 28, 2012.

158 "I didn't think I had it": King, email to author, September 28, 2012.

158 "The lack of information": King, "'Jesus Said to Them, "My Wife...,"'" *Harvard Theological Review* 107, no. 2 (April 2014): 157.

158 "We're very intrigued": WGBH News, "Greater Boston Video."

159 King sent me the emails: King emailed the messages to me on September 13, 2012, in the form of a Word file into which she'd pasted the dates and body of the messages. She did not include email headers, thus excluding the collector's name, email address and other identifying details. In the bodies of the messages, she replaced his name with "(OWNER)" and his current location with "(PLACE)."

159 He committed to a specific year: The 1997 date was mentioned in the owner's July 9, 2010, email to King. King didn't receive—or perhaps even ask for—a sales contract until October 2, 2012, after her announcement in Rome, when the owner emailed her a copy.

160 I used a commercial website: The cost of the search was $3.

160 "They were nice": Lehmann, phone interview by author, December 10, 2015.

160 "*Nein*": Stremlow, interview by author, Berlin, January 23, 2016.

161 "holiday home": Dümke, interview by author, Berlin, January 23, 2016.

161 he and his brother won a small contract: Author's interviews with Laukamp's relatives and associates.

162 In Berlin, the initials: Axel Herzsprung, interview by author, January 25, 2016.

163 "What are we going to do next year": City of North Port, "Commission Budget Workshop," June 24, 2009, online video, http://cityofnorthport.granicus.com/mediaplayer .php?clip_id=50&view_id=9. Fritz's testimony begins at 0:37:30.

163 In 1991, someone named Walter Fritz: Fritz, "Bemerkungen zum Datierungsvermerk auf der Amarnatafel Kn 27."

163 Could the article's author: German phone books had listings for hundreds of Walter Fritzes; Florida phone books had at least half a dozen.

164 It turned up even: Rita E. Freed, Yvonne J. Markowitz, and Sue H. D'Auria, eds., *Pharaohs of the Sun: Akhenaten, Nefertiti, Tutankhamen* (Boston: Museum of Fine Arts in association with Bulfinch Press/Little, Brown, 1999), 95n4 and 295.

164 Deep Hole: Jennifer Earl, "Dozens of Alligators Flock to 134-Foot-Deep Sinkhole in Florida," CBS News, March 10, 2017, www.cbsnews.com.

164 "to raise horses, kennel dogs": David Hackett, "Residents Happy to Keep Lifestyle," *Sarasota Herald-Tribune,* November 27, 2003, www.heraldtribune.com.

165 "World War III": Christi Womack, "State May Rethink Bullets in the Backyard," *Sarasota Herald-Tribune,* March 14, 2015, www.heraldtribune.com.

167 "Sometimes the odor": Quoted in photo caption, in Susan E. Hoffman, "Noise from Construction Equipment Annoys Residents," *North Port Sun,* January 4, 2006.

168 His elderly landlady: Her name was Elli Kunkewitz, a Berlin native who had immigrated to the United States after World War II. "In Memory of Elli Erika Kunkewitz,

November 8, 1926–October 15, 2011," Dignity Memorial (website), chattanooga-north-chapel.tributes.com.

168 But her granddaughter, Renee Juntunen: Juntunen, phone interviews by author, February and March 2016 and May 2019, and in-person interview by author, Venice, Fla., April 7, 2019.

168 In the summer of 2000: John Juntunen, phone interview by author, May 1, 2019.

169 "Neither our registrar": Stephanie Lederer (editorial and PR manager at Ringling College of Art & Design), email to author, February 19, 2016.

169 According to its internet site: The Nefer Art website, now gone, is preserved in partial form on the Internet Archive Wayback Machine. A September 25, 2013, capture: http://web.archive.org/web/20130925080333/http://nefer-art.com:80/main.html.

169 "Our customer database is substantial": Google cache of the page "Nefer Art—Antiquities | Rare Prints | Photographs | Web Desing [sic] for Art Collectors," emailed to the author by the journalist Owen Jarus on February 3, 2017. Jarus wrote a couple of stories about Laukamp for the online news site Live Science in 2014 and 2015, raising important questions about Laukamp's role in the provenance story. He told me he had independently developed suspicions about this Walter Fritz but couldn't pin them down. He didn't write about this Fritz until after my 2016 piece in *The Atlantic*.

170 "Brooklyn Museum 16.580.31": Page Glimpse (website), www.pageglimpse.com/nefer-art.com#webresults.

170 Another described an ancient Egyptian headrest: Compare the snippet of Nefer Art's website visible at www.siteglimpse.com/nefer-art.com with the British Museum's Explore pages, now hosted by the Google Cultural Institute, artsandculture.google.com/asset/hematite-headrest-amulet/pQGDN-fADsmHkg.

170 Nefer Art's "About" page: About Page, Nefer Art, website, Internet Archive Wayback machine, September 25, 2013, capture, http://web.archive.org/web/20130925080323/http://nefer-art.com:80/about.html.

171 Two experts in ancient Arabic: Simon Hopkins (Hebrew University of Jerusalem), email to intermediary that was forwarded to author, December 16, 2015; Hazem Hussein Abbas Ali (Beni-Suef University, Egypt), email to author, December 20, 2015.

171 Well-connected people: Elyse Brady (executive director of the St. Augustine Art Association), email to author, April 26, 2018; Jan Miller (president of the Art Galleries of St. Augustine, an umbrella group for local galleries), and Bill Green (artist and owner of the St. Augustine Gallery), phone interviews by author, February 17, 2016.

171 Neither had the national and international dealers: Author's phone or email interviews with the dealers Sue McGovern-Huffman, October 17, 2016; Gabriel Vandervort, October 17, 2016; Lee Biondi, December 6, 2016; Scott Carroll, July 17, 2017; Bron Lipkin, April 27, 2018; and, in Florida, Richard Brockway (late 2015/early 2016). Much later, in fall 2019, I found one dealer, Sam Fogg, who said a Walter Fritz he hadn't previously known once called him cold. That phone call is described later in the book.

THE LITTLE DARLING AND THE STASI

172 News of Laukamp's: René Ernest appears to have learned of the news from Owen Jarus, a reporter for the website Live Science who conducted a brief email interview with him in German in 2014. "Ernest was astonished to hear that Laukamp's name had been linked to this papyrus," Jarus reported. "'Gospel of Jesus's Wife': Doubts Raised About Ancient Text," Live Science, April 22, 2014.

172 "special plight": Head of the Federal Emergency Admission (immigration) Procedure, Berlin, "Immigration Committee Residence Permit" for "Mr. Laukamp, Hans-Ulrich," October 19, 1961, provided to author by his stepson, René Ernest, and Ernest's wife, Gabriele, on May 24, 2016.

172 He came ashore: Axel Herzsprung, interview by author, Berlin, January 25, 2016.

174 "He was an eel": Biberger, interview by author, Berlin, February 1, 2016.

174 Walter Fritz struck classmates: Details about his Free University years—1987 to 1992—are from author's interviews with numerous former classmates, professors and other associates.

174 stock German villains: Kim Ryholt, Skype interview by author, November 16, 2016; Ryholt quotation in Karen Sofie Egebo, "Svindler opfandt Jesu hustru," *Kristeligt Dagblad* (Danish newspaper), June 29, 2016, www.kristeligt-dagblad.dk.

174 "a harmless country boy": Ulrike Dubiel, interview by author, Free University, Berlin, May 24, 2017.

175 "a coward": Voss, interview by author, Hannover, Germany, May 22, 2017.

175 "He never explained the change": Binkowski, interview by author, Hannover, Germany, May 22, 2017.

175 "exalted": Ralf Bossier, interview by author and interpreter, Berlin, February 1, 2016.

175 "He acted like a real snob": Jedamski, interview by author and interpreter, Berlin, February 1, 2016.

176 "He had ties to a research center": Fritz's former wife, interview by author, May 16, 2017. A North Port Police Department file on a December 2006 burglary of Fritz's home lists one of the stolen items as a wood-inlay chessboard "purchased in Egypt in 1988," suggesting 1988 as a possible year for at least one of Fritz's Egypt visits.

176 "a fresh and energetic student": Rößler-Köhler, phone interview by author's interpreter, September 22, 2016.

176 He told classmates that two adjoining letters: Christian Loeben, email to author, February 1, 2016.

176 "terrible mistake": Loeben, interview by author, Hannover, Germany, January 29, 2016.

177 "Fritz was quite eager": Jansen-Winkeln, interview by author, Berlin, January 28, 2016.

177 A 1991 reference letter: Contained in the Sarasota County Schools' response to author's public records request, June 2017.

177 Loeben told me he saw: According to Loeben, Fritz was in the company of Rolf Krauss, a staff researcher at the museum who helped Fritz with his 1991 journal article. Colleagues described Krauss as deeply embittered over his own disappointed ambitions in Egyptology. Despite numerous interview requests, Krauss declined to speak to me.

177 The work there happened: This process was described to me by, among others, Myriam Krutzsch, the chief papyrus conservator at Berlin's Egyptian Museum, during a June 2018 visit to the museum.

177 had roughly twenty-one thousand fragments: Verena Lepper (curator for Egyptian and Oriental Papyri at the Egyptian Museum, which is located in the former West Berlin), emails to author, April 28, 2016.

178 "Nobody watched me": Hedrick, phone interview by author, January 2, 2018.

178 "24/7" access to the papyri: Mirecki, phone interview by author, February 17, 2017.

178 "unlisted and unidentified fragments": Schenke Robinson, "How a Papyrus Fragment Became a Sensation," 393.

178 "It is possible": Wildung, email to author, July 4, 2017.

178 On Mondays, when the building: Christian Loeben, interview by author, Hannover, Germany, May 22, 2017.

179 Foppish and gregarious: Biographical details about Munro are drawn from interviews with multiple colleagues and former students, in particular Christian Loeben, who was put in charge of Munro's papers and wrote his official obituary.

179 He had earned the lowest passing mark: Author's interviews with German Egyptologists.

180 "Walter would say": Dubiel, interview by author, Free University, Berlin, May 24, 2017.

180 "We can wait until Christmas": Susanne Voss, interview by author, Hannover, Germany, May 22, 2017.

180 "You're like the remains of chalk": Binkowski, interview by author, Hannover, Germany, May 22, 2017.

181 "We all knew about the article": Ryholt, Skype interview by author, November 16, 2016.

182 One remembered seeing: Email to author from Christian Loeben, relaying the memory of Andrea Binkowski, February 1, 2016. Confirmed by author in later interview with Binkowski.

182 "Walter Fritz, 27, antiquities scholar": "Menschen," *Stern,* February 27, 1992, 15.

183 "Nobody from the group knew him": Drieselmann, phone interviews by author's German interpreter, February 5 and March 14, 2016.

183 "Egypt and dead kings": Suárez, phone interview by author's interpreter, October 9, 2017.

183 "I think I may have said": Kilz, interview by author, Bautzen, Germany, June 24, 2018.

184 according to a transcript: ASTAK, "Protokoll 16/2."

184 Fritz failed to appear: Drieselmann, phone interviews by author's interpreter, February 5 and March 14, 2016.

184 "That was someone": Juntunen, interview by author, Venice, Fla., April 7, 2019, and phone interview by author, May 2, 2019.

184 "They met in a sauna": Herzsprung, interview by author, Berlin, January 25, 2016.

185 In the end, he said: I could find no evidence of any court cases besides ACMB's bankruptcy, whose records are closed to the public.

186 "A new machine would have cost": Author's interview with APG's owner, Berlin, February 1, 2016.

186 On July 8, 2010: Walt Fritz, "Cut Top Salaries by 35 Percent," letter to the editor, *North Port Sun,* July 8, 2010.

187 "I must say, it looks exactly": Hensel, phone interview by author's interpreter, November 30, 2016.

HOTWIFE

189 "America's #1 Slut Wife": Come Depot, website, home page, Internet Archive Wayback Machine, September 8, 2012, capture.

189 The couple advertised the dates: These notices were posted in various Yahoo groups and other web forums, mostly between 2004 and 2010. Fritz used the name "Walt" or one of various aliases, including "Jenshubby," "Wolf Wilson" and "hookerwifes hubby1." The couple required men to bring photo ID proving they were twenty-one or older.

189 "about 2 hours away from Disney": "Swinger Jenshubby (Couple)" profile, The Adult Hub, website.

189 There was no charge: "MEET & INVITE JENNY (a 'How-To' Guide)," Come Depot, website, Internet Archive Wayback Machine, July 3, 2010, capture.

189 "I just wanted to thank you": Comment from Doug, dated July 30, 2002, quoted on Fan Mail page, Come Depot, website, Internet Archive Wayback Machine, July 1, 2014, capture.

189 "When I met Walt": "Jenny Interviewed," *Hot Wife Blog,* May 15, 2005.

189 "Because you know everyone wants": Jenshubby, forum post, Slut Wives website, August 23, 2006.

190 "over 40 HOURS": Home page, Come Depot, website, Internet Archive Wayback Machine, December 24, 2014, capture.

190 In an interview on one of their German-language: Mike Hammer interview, "Fragen— Interview mit Jenny," Gangbang Jenny, website, Internet Archive Wayback Machine, November 24, 2005, capture. A reference to the interview on their English-language Come Depot website says it was conducted on August 30, 2004.

190 Couples can get to know one another: Author's interviews with people in the scene.

190 "the lifestyle: the insatiable wives": Vice staff, "Mandingo!," *Vice,* August 24, 2011, www.vice.com.

190 "The basic rule of swing": Hammer, phone interview by author, June 13, 2017.

190 The Florida Mandingos: www.thefloridamandingosclub.com.

191 two months before their wedding: Fritz and his wife were married in Venice, Florida, on March 29, 2001, according to the marriage certificate filed with the Sarasota County Clerk.

191 "My group has become the biggest": femalebarebackgangbangextreme, Yahoo Group, Internet Archive Wayback Machine, December 3, 2003, capture.

191 "this incredible, extreme, married": "Top 20 Hotwives 5-2, Ranked 5: Jenny Seemore," *Hot Wife Blog,* March 15, 2010.

191 On September 25, 2012: Domain name registration records, retrieved by the author through Reverse Whois searches on the website DomainTools.com. Fritz changed the street addresses, for four of their websites, between September 25 and November 9,

2012. On November 29, 2012, he changed a fifth website—one devoted to his porn persona "Wolf"—to private registration, masking its ownership.

191 Then, in 2015: Domain registration histories from DomainTools.com; page captures, dating back to the launch of their first websites in 2003, from the Internet Archive Wayback Machine.

192 "Call me Wolf": Bio page, Wolf's Straight Bareback Extreme List, website, Internet Archive Wayback Machine, October 19, 2012, capture.

192 "scholarly country bumpkin": Lindsey, "Dealer in Mormon Fraud."

192 "Usually he just leaned back": Charles Hamilton, *Great Forgers and Famous Fakes: The Manuscript Forgers of America and How They Duped the Experts,* 2nd ed. (Lakewood, Colo.: Glenbridge, 1996), 270.

192 "sweet, unobtrusive": Lindsey, "Dealer in Mormon Fraud."

193 "I won't go so far": Steven Naifeh and Gregory White Smith, *The Mormon Murders: A True Story of Greed, Forgery, Deceit, and Death* (New York: St. Martin's Paperbacks, 2005), 529.

193 "The owner supplied": Wangsness, "Case of the Gospel."

193 The "About" page: "About Jenny Seemore," Jenny Seemore's Personal Website, Internet Archive Wayback Machine, October 22, 2012, capture.

195 "The Hieros Gamos ritual": Brown, *Da Vinci Code,* 335–36.

196 "American Sex Goddess": Jenny Seemore profile, Fat Forums, website.

196 "ripe for a Monty Python sketch": Depuydt, "Alleged *Gospel of Jesus's Wife,*" 174.

197 "considered original creative invention": Pagels, *Gnostic Gospels,* Kindle edition, loc. 782.

DON'T WANT TO KNOW

200 the communists had made look-alike IDs: Fritz exaggerated the number of West German IDs—actually passports—that the Stasi had forged, but German news reports and our own interviews corroborate the thrust of the anecdote. "We made the entire IDs ourselves," Günter Pelzl, a former Stasi chemist who once led the department that forged the passports, told my interpreter in January 2019. "The inks we reproduced after thoroughly analyzing those used."

201 Magister's theses typically ran: Karl Jansen-Winkeln, interview by author, Berlin, January 28, 2016.

203 head of the Stasi's Department 22: Neiber's position and portfolio are described in Leighton, "Strange Bedfellows," 652–58.

203 "passersby instinctively recoiled": Ibid., 647.

204 "a system of population surveillance": John C. Schmeidel, *Stasi: Shield and Sword of the Party* (London: Routledge, 2008), 26.

204 A major German newspaper: Leighton, "Strange Bedfellows," 665n36.

205 and the CIA: He is identified as a CIA agent in a book by a pair of former Stasi officers: Herbert Kierstein and Gotthold Schramm, *Freischützen des Rechtsstaats: Wem nützen Stasiunterlagen und Gedenkstätten?* (Berlin: Ost, 2009), 171. In response to my Freedom of Information Act request, the CIA declined to confirm or deny the existence of records concerning Veith.

205 According to court files: Final Judgment, Criminal case against Wolfgang Erich Veith on charges of sexually abusing children, State Prosecutor of the State Court of Berlin, Tiergarten, August 31, 1995.

205 a Berlin judge convicted: Veith was convicted in the case of the twelve-year-old girl. The other girl was fourteen, which was the age of consent in Germany.

205 "Stasi intrigue": Anne Losensky, "9000 Mark Strafe: Porno-Fotos in Mielkes Dusche," *BZ,* September 1, 1995. A female friend of Veith's, confusing his rolls of film for hers, had taken them to a photo shop, where employees developed them and, seeing the child pornography, called the police.

205 "Sex Scandal in the Mielke Museum": "Sex-Skandal," *Berliner Kurier,* September 1, 1995. The scandal was also covered in at least four other German newspapers, all on September 1, 1995: *Berliner Morgenpost, Berliner Zeitung, Bild,* and *BZ.*

205 In a February 1992 museum: ASTAK, "Protokoll 16/2." A transcript of the tape-recorded meeting was given to the author by a former board member.

206 Fritz said he allowed Veith: According to the February 1992 meeting transcript, Fritz told the board, "On the first or second day of my presence here, I took control of the keys of all the safes, except for one, where Mr. Veith was keeping things."

206 Among the things Veith kept: The judge's ruling says Veith kept the undeveloped film in a "*Kasten*," which generally translates as "box." It doesn't specify where in the museum the *Kasten* was.

206 "the toughest, most ruthless": Erich Loest, "Die gemordete Zeit," *Die Zeit* (online), June 4, 2009, www.zeit.de.

206 A spokesman for the Berlin: Stefan Stöhr, phone interview by author's interpreter, July 31, 2017.

206 Drieselmann had told me about jewelry: It was unclear whether Fritz and Drieselmann were referring to the same discovery.

207 "which may have been at the house": Fritz, email to author, June 30, 2019. He also said he never spoke to the granddaughter, Renee Juntunen, about Kollwitz; never showed her how to draw with charcoal; hung no pictures of any kind on the wall; and "never painted in my life." He called anything to the contrary "utter BS." Juntunen shared her recollections in a face-to-face interview with me at her home in 2019 and repeated the story in a phone interview she let me voice-record. Her husband shared most of his memories by phone. She did not have photos of the house's interior during Fritz's roughly yearlong stay there, but her detailed memories of other of her grandmother's tenants corresponded with what I discovered about those tenants in public records and police reports. The first quotations in this paragraph—"I don't recall"—were from a 2016 phone interview with Fritz, after I'd interviewed Juntunen by phone but before I'd met her and her husband in person in Florida in 2019 and heard their recollections at greater length.

208 *The Wanderings:* Bell, *Wanderings of an Elephant Hunter.*

208 "Dear Mr. Sabar": The letter, which appeared to be photographed with a phone camera, bore the dateline "Sarasota, March 20, 2016."

209 "permanent loan at no charge": According to various sources, the loan was for a ten-year period, renewable by mutual consent and subject to cancellation by either party at any time.

211 "I can give you names": Fritz never did. People associated with the Greens' papyrus collection told me they knew nothing about the Wife fragment before Karen King's announcement in Rome.

211 "A court psychiatrist": Richard R. Lingeman, "Erich von Daniken's Genesis," *New York Times,* March 31, 1974, www.nytimes.com.

212 "I looked through all the programs": Sophie Charlotte Erichsen, email to author, March 23, 2016.

213 "I don't see the point": King, phone interview by author, March 21, 2016.

214 "Perhaps the hardest thing": Christopher Jones, "The Jesus' Wife Papyrus in the History of Forgery," *New Testament Studies* 61, no. 3 (July 2015): 374.

214 "He once said to me": Eaton-Krauss, interview by author, Berlin, January 30, 2016.

214 Fecht had even co-taught: Regine Christiane Schulz (Egyptologist and museum director who had been a research assistant at the Free University Egyptology Institute in those years), Skype interview by author, January 14, 2016.

215 John's Lycopolitan dialect: "It would be like, 'Wow, that's not only remarkable for being such an early copy of John; it's also remarkable that we can identify a dialect like Lycopolitan,'" Jacco Dieleman, an eminent scholar of Egyptian language, told me. (Phone interview, October 21, 2015.)

215 "If this had surfaced": Author's phone interviews with source close to Fecht's family, 2017 and 2018.

215 "he would have told me": Irmtraut Munro, phone interview by author, January 26, 2016.

216 Not only were the building number: Laukamp's longtime address—as well as his specific use of it in 1982—was confirmed by multiple sources: official Berlin phone books; pre- and post-unification postal code maps of Berlin consulted by the author at the Library of Congress; interviews with longtime neighbors; and public documents filed by the Laukamps in connection with their Florida home. Credit for identifying the

error in the postal code belongs to William Brennan, then an associate editor at *The Atlantic.*

217 The same is true of the letterhead: Author's information from multiple sources: copies of department letterhead from the 1980s and 1990s; interviews with a longtime Free University Egyptologist, who reviewed internal departmental documents at author's request; author's personal examination of professors' 1980s and 1990s letters in the secretarial office of the Egyptology Institute, May 25, 2017.

217 It would not be difficult: A forger wouldn't even need a matching typewriter. Commercially available software can clone fonts from scans of old documents.

219 folded Nefer Art: The State of Florida dissolved the company on September 25, 2015, after it failed to file that year's annual report, according to online records of the state's Division of Corporations.

219 "I embrace all religions": Walter Fritz's wife, phone interview by author, April 12, 2016.

219 entries that neatly overlapped: Though Fritz's wife claimed to channel angels since she was seventeen and her book was self-published in June 2015, when she was in her early fifties, the entries span only February 26, 2011, to August 29, 2012. That is, they are entirely contained within the period between Fritz's first email to King (July 9, 2010) and King's announcement in Rome (September 18, 2012).

220 "~My newest Creations~": Cute Art World Blogspot, "Christian Glass Pendants," August 31, 2009, Internet Archive Wayback Machine, May 24, 2010, capture, https://web.archive.org/web/20100524203354/http://cuteartworld.blogspot.com/2009/08/christian-glass-pendants.html. The scholar Christian Askeland brought this web page to author's attention.

221 And at least one of the Fritzes: In a brief email exchange in September 2019, Walter Fritz's wife claimed that her husband wrote the blog post, made the pendants, and sold them on eBay through her Cute Art World store.

221 "Sending an Angel": The last capture of an "About Me" section calling her a Teddy Bear Artist was on August 17, 2011, web.archive.org/web/20110817150305/http://cuteartworld.blogspot.com/. To judge by later page captures, the Sending an Angel persona replaced it no later than September 25, 2011.

THE SECRET ROOM

223 Marcus Off had appeared: Off is also an acclaimed voice actor. He dubbed Johnny Depp's lines for German releases of the *Pirates of the Caribbean* movies.

223 "The grim Phil Seegers": "Lindenstrasse: Marcus Off spielte Phil Seegers," Westdeutscher Rundfunk Köln, www1.wdr.de.

224 "Yes I am the brother": Marcus Off, email to author, April 11, 2016.

224 "Never," said his eldest daughter: Eva-Maria Off, interview by author, southern Germany, May 14, 2017.

224 "All he shot were photos": Böhm, phone interview by author's interpreter, May 19, 2017.

225 "Matthias with the golden heart": "Bad Wurzachs Stadtpfarrer wird 70 Jahr alt," *Schwäbische Zeitung*, February 13, 1971.

225 And though his mother's forebears: Walter Fritz, phone interview by author, March 29, 2016; his mother's designation as "RK," or Roman Catholic, on a 1974 address registration filed with the City of Bad Waldsee, Germany.

225 she was an atheist: Author's 2018 interviews with various friends and relatives of Fritz's mother. Walter's maternal grandfather, Narziss Klöck, was a butcher whose first name reflected his sense of superiority, people said. Narziss is German for Narcissus.

225 Father Mayer taught religion: Fritz told me he wasn't in Mayer's class, which was taught to a younger grade, but often saw the black-robed priest around the school.

225 Inge Klöck had given birth: Official documents list Walter Fritz's birthplace as the southern German town of Sigmaringen.

226 Inge gave no indication to friends: Author's 2018 interviews with friends and acquaintances of Fritz's mother.

226 Inge charmed her way: Author's 2018 interviews with friends and acquaintances of Fritz's mother. Affair confirmed by children of Inge Fritz and son of Wilhelm Götz. Inge declined interview requests from author and his interpreter.

226 Willi was married: Siegmar Götz (Götz's son), interviews by author, Bad Wurzach, June 21–22, 2018.

226 "I was his spy": Ibid.

226 In early 1974: German address registries show that Hans-Jürgen Fritz left Bad Waldsee for another town in January 1974 and that Inge left, for Bad Wurzach, the next month.

226 "He just disappeared": Susanne Fritz, interview by author, Biberach an der Riss, June 18, 2018.

226 No sooner had Inge and her children: Siegmar Götz, interviews by author, Bad Wurzach, June 21–22, 2018; Walter Fritz, phone interview by author, April 4, 2019.

226 "Walter was not pleased": Susanne Fritz, phone interview by author's interpreter, February 4, 2018; Susanne Fritz, interview by author, Biberach an der Riss, June 18, 2018.

228 They were aimed at sizing up: "Had I said my dad was a police officer," Fritz told me, "of course he wouldn't have done anything."

229 "The wall of silence": "Inside Germany's Catholic Sexual Abuse Scandal," *Spiegel Online*, February 8, 2010, Internet Archive Wayback Machine, February 11, 2010, capture, https://web.archive.org/web/20100211142230/http://www.spiegel.de/international/germany/0,1518,676497,00.html.

229 By March 2010, the media: Dietmar Hipp et al., "Did Archbishop Ratzinger Help Shield Perpetrator from Prosecution?," *Spiegel Online*, March 22, 2010, www.spiegel.de.

229 "an expression of the gift": "Solid Priestly Identity Essential as Secularism Grows, Pope Tells Priests," *Catholic News Agency*, March 12, 2010, www.catholicnewsagency.com.

229 "the Church's action": Pope Benedict XVI, General Audience, St. Peter's Square, April 21, 2010, w2.vatican.va.

229 Eight days later: The date of Fritz's letter—April 29, 2010—is mentioned in the replies sent to him by Church officials. Fritz said he didn't have a copy of the letter he sent.

229 Fritz sent me digital images: The images showed a letter to Fritz from Monsignor Peter B. Wells, then assessor of the Holy See's Secretariat of State, dated August 12, 2010; a letter from Prelate Damiano Marzotto, undersecretary for the Congregation for the Doctrine of the Faith, dated October 25, 2010; and a letter from Gebhard Fürst, bishop of Rottenburg-Stuttgart, the diocese that oversees the parish of Bad Wurzach, dated December 17, 2010.

230 "To get within hearing distance": Bell, *Wanderings of an Elephant Hunter*, 2, 4.

231 "I can't think of a single": Clohessy, phone interview by author, April 15, 2016.

231 The most common response: Barbara Dorris (SNAP official), phone interview by author, April 15, 2016.

232 "But you wanted me to cut": Inge Fritz, phone interview by author's interpreter, February 5, 2018. She declined further interview requests after speaking with her son.

232 The urge to test limits: Anna Leins (Bad Waldsee neighbor), phone interview by author's interpreter, August 13, 2018.

232 to trip teachers up: Susanne Fritz, interview by author, June 18, 2018, and Marcus Schmid (classmate), interview by author, June 19, 2018, both in Biberach an der Riss, Germany.

232 "He was so bad in math": Schmid, interview by author, Biberach an der Riss, Germany, June 19, 2018.

232 "never swam with the tide": Dobler, phone interview by author's interpreter, June 2017.

232 when even the military's medical school: Susanne Fritz, interview by author, Biberach an der Riss, June 18, 2018.

232 "took the much more difficult route": Zinngisser, phone interview by author's interpreter, July 26, 2017.

234 *Holy Blood, Holy Grail:* Baigent, *Holy Blood, Holy Grail.*

234 sued his publisher: The defendant was Random House Group Limited, a U.K. affiliate of what is now Penguin Random House LLC, whose imprints published both *The Da Vinci Code* and *Holy Blood, Holy Grail*, as well as (full disclosure) the present book.

234 Records at the Bad Wurzach town hall: Address registration record for Ingeborg Fritz, emailed to author's interpreter by Stadtverwaltung Bad Wurzach (Bad Wurzach City Administration) on May 22, 2017.

234 old phone books: National and municipal 1970s phone books for Bad Wurzach and vicinity, viewed by the author at the Library of Congress, Washington, D.C.

234 Church officials confirmed: A Vatican official confirmed the authenticity of the letter from Prelate Damiano Marzotto, undersecretary for the Congregation for the Doctrine of the Faith; a spokesperson for the Diocese of Rottenburg-Stuttgart did the same for the letter from Bishop Gebhard Fürst. Officials at the Vatican's Secretariat of State said they couldn't validate the third letter, from Monsignor Peter Wells, but the terse, one-line reply didn't specify whether they were questioning its authenticity or had simply failed to find a record of it.

235 "I would of course express": Maier, interview by author, Bad Wurzach, May 18, 2017.

236 Both doors had modern cylinder locks: Church officials could not remember when the modern locks were installed, but said it was the 1960s or 1970s at the earliest and 1999, when the church was last renovated, at the latest.

237 Fritz's allegations "plausible": Reuhs, phone interview by author's interpreter, September 13, 2017.

238 "He's not forgotten in this town": Schad, interview by author, Bad Wurzach, May 20, 2017.

238 "When the sun is out": Mohr, interview by author, Bad Wurzach, May 20, 2017.

240 "He used to hug and stroke": Späth, interview by author, Bad Wurzach, June 18, 2018.

240 "I didn't like him": Kienle, interview by author, Bad Wurzach, June 20, 2018.

240 Mayer approached and suggested: Phone interview by author's interpreter with close elementary school friend of Walter Fritz's, August 22, 2018.

241 "Nobody knew anything": Author's interview with close elementary school friend of Fritz's, Bad Wurzach, June 23, 2018.

INVISIBLE HAND

246 Nearly 180 pages: The applications were submitted between November 2012 and June 2013, a period in which the prospects of the Wife papyrus being taken for authentic grew dimmer and dimmer.

247 "the equivalent of a Master's Degree": David R. Sirota, Educated Choices LLC, "Re/ Education Equivalency Evaluation of Walter Fritz" (one-page letter "To Whom It May Concern"), January 31, 2013, contained in the response of the Sarasota County Schools to the author's 2017 public records request.

247 "Of the thousands of foreign": Eric Sirota, email to author, July 12, 2017.

248 no one with Walter Fritz's name: Susanne Cholodnicki (Technical University press officer), email to author, June 11, 2018.

248 "association with, or academic standing": Florida Statute 817.566.

248 It is also illegal: Florida Statute 110.1127(d)1.

248 When I asked him to explain: Fritz, phone interview by author, April 4, 2019.

249 "extensive" copying: Bernhard, "Postscript: A Final Note".

250 "able to make some real progress": King, email to Fritz, October 15, 2011. AnneMarie Luijendijk confirmed the impression; she told me that when King emailed her an image of the papyrus three days later, King hadn't yet translated it herself. Luijendijk, interview by author, Princeton University, March 3, 2017.

252 "Don't forget": Jenny's Hubby (Site Administrator), "Ezekiel quote...," forum index, Come Depot, Internet Archive Wayback Machine, January 11, 2009, capture. Jenny's Hubby is one of Fritz's porn aliases.

252 114 years, to the day: Carl Schmidt's report on the discovery was presented to the Prussian Academy of Sciences on July 9, 1896 (Schmidt, "Ein vorirenaeisches," 839).

256 "relates the quest": John Matthews, The Grail Tarot: A Templar Vision (New York: St. Martin's Press, 2007), back cover.

257 "run-of-the-mill, boring": Fogg, phone interview by author, September 26, 2019. In a follow-up email, Fogg said that his files record the date of Fritz's first call as March 24, 2011. "He called my assistant on that day asking if we wanted to buy manuscripts and then called a second time and spoke to me." Fritz mentioned Fogg to King in a May 7, 2012, email, four months before her announcement in Rome. It was by way of persuading her that she needn't disclose his identity because important people already knew who he was. "The few that matter in this field do know who I am anyway," he

wrote to her. Fogg may have been yet another sacrificial lamb in Fritz's phony provenance story—the unnamed "art dealer" in London's Mayfair district who Fritz told
me offered $50,000 for the Wife papyrus then angrily cut off negotiations after Fritz
contacted King. In his May 2012 email to King, which I obtained as I was finishing
this book, Fritz said that Fogg "got really mad" because publication would ruin the
price. When I reached Fogg by phone in 2019, he told me that Fritz never showed
or mentioned the Wife papyrus and that he never got mad at him about anything.
"None of that is true," Fogg said. He said King never contacted him to check the
veracity of the story Fritz told about him. Fritz did not respond to my request for
comment.

257 Fritz "was on the ropes": Böhm, phone interview by author's interpreter, May 19, 2017.

257 "He just felt like": Cohen, phone interview by author, July 11, 2017.

257 hunting deer and boar: Ibid. A neighbor thought the deer and boar were for the Fritzes'
dog, rather than for themselves.

257 taking seasonal work: Henry Jakimer (neighbor), phone interview by author, December 11, 2018.

258 "Can you imagine?": Leins, phone interview by author's interpreter, August 10, 2018.

258 She had given it the English name: Agnes Eisele, interview by author, Bad Waldsee,
June 19, 2018; 1970s phone books for Bad Wurzach in the U.S. Library of Congress.

258 *"Sie hat ihren Mann"*: Monika Grohse, interview by author, Ummendorf, Germany,
May 19, 2017.

258 "Inge tried to explain": Jakubith, interviews by author, Bad Wurzach, June 16 and 19,
2018.

259 his porn sites' fetishization: Come Depot, Gangbang Jenny, Jenny Seemore's Personal
Website, Strap-On Slut Wife, Welfare Queens, Wolf's Straight Bareback Extreme List.

FEELING OF CALM

260 in print, across fifteen pages: Sabar, "Unbelievable Tale of Jesus's Wife," 64–78. The
magazine story took six months to research and write. The present book incorporates
two additional years of investigation.

260 "King was [so] blinded": This and the other comments were posted by readers beneath
ibid. (web).

261 "Of course!": Gragg, phone interview by author, Cambridge, Mass., March 16, 2017.

262 "he doesn't want to be hounded": Goodstein, "Faded Piece of Papyrus." The same
explanation appears in Wangsness, "Hint of a Married Jesus," and "New Gospel
Revealed," *Harvard Magazine.*

262 "When it became clear to him": King, interview by author, June 16, 2016. Her revised
explanation appears to be the accurate one: it dovetailed with July 2012 emails that
Fritz showed me in which he told King he wanted the papyrus "on your back, and you
can fight off reporters."

262 "I see that King": Wangsness, "'Jesus's Wife' Scholar Now Says."

262 "Set before Karen": Carly Daniel-Hughes, "Mary Magdalene and the Fantasy Echo,"
in Petrey, *Re-Making the World,* 151.

263 "The mission of Harvard Divinity School": Harvard Divinity School, "Statement from
HDS Dean David N. Hempton on the 'Gospel of Jesus' Wife,'" June 20, 2016, Internet Archive Wayback Machine, June 26, 2016, capture, https://web.archive.org/web
/20160626203420/http://gospelofjesuswife.hds.harvard.edu/introduction.

263 Three years later, at the earliest age: A tribute to King's scholarship published in fall
2019 wishes her well "as she begins her retirement" and "the next phase of her career."
(Petrey, Preface, *Re-Making the World*). Sources told me that her retirement is phased,
which at Harvard typically means half-time work for two to four years before departure. A divinity school spokesman, Michael Naughton, declined to say whether King
was partaking in a Harvard program for tenured professors sixty-five or older with at
least a decade at the university, or whether her arrangement was different (emails to
author, September 2019).

263 "I am looking forward": King, "Honoring the Scholarship of Karen L. King" (panel presentation), Society of Biblical Literature annual conference, San Diego, November 24,
2019.

ACT 5: THE DOWNTURNED BOOK OF REVELATIONS

265 "GJW tells us nothing": Janet E. Spittler, "Responses to Mark Goodacre, James McGrath, and Caroline Schroeder on the *Gospel of Jesus' Wife*," in *Fakes, Forgeries, and Fictions: Writing Ancient and Modern Christian Apocrypha*, ed. Tony Burke (Eugene, Ore.: Cascade Books, 2017), 373.

OPERATIONAL EFFECTIVENESS

267 "has little to do": Karen King, "Back to the Future: Jesus and Heresy," in Jesus Seminar, *Once and Future Jesus*, 97.

268 "Attractive as the fantasy": King, "Factions, Variety, Diversity, Multiplicity," 230.

268 "History," she wrote elsewhere, "is not about truth": King, *What Is Gnosticism?*, 235.

268 "the association between truth and chronology": Ibid., 228.

268 That certain Gospels were composed: Ibid., 228–29.

268 "The new physics": Ibid., 234.

268 "This new form of time": Ibid., 235.

268 "enlarging one's imaginative universe": King, "Factions, Variety, Diversity, Multiplicity," 230.

268 "then one need never say": Ibid., 235.

268 "put pressure": Karen L. King, "Endings: The *Gospel of Mark* and the *Gospel of Judas*," in *Early Christian and Jewish Narrative: The Role of Religion in Shaping Narrative Forms*, ed. Ilaria Ramelli and Judith Perkins (Tübingen, Germany: Mohr Siebeck, 2015), 64–65.

268 "little tyrants": King, "Christianity Without a Canon."

268 "fact fundamentalism": King, "Back to the Future," 86.

269 offered her a student job: King, "Remembering Robert Funk," 3.

269 "They obviously had a very special": Scrimgeour, phone interview by author, November 11, 2016.

269 "He proceeded to fill": King, "Remembering Robert Funk," 3.

269 King was among ten: Lane McGaughy (executive director of the Westar Institute), interview by author, Salem, Ore., December 13, 2016.

269 Together the ten contributed: Lane C. McGaughy, "Robert W. Funk—a Profile," *Fourth R* 19, no. 2 (March–April 2006): 6.

269 "We'll own it": McGaughy, interview by author, Salem, Ore., December 13, 2016.

269 "We are about to embark": Funk, "Jesus Seminar Opening Remarks."

269 after-dinner speech at the faculty club: Lane McGaughy, email to author, June 22, 2018, with pdf of inaugural March 1985 program.

270 his *New York Times* obituary: Laurie Goodstein, "R. W. Funk, 79, Creator of Jesus Seminar, Dies," *New York Times*, September 10, 2005.

270 "That's Jesus!": Funk, Hoover, and the Jesus Seminar, *Five Gospels*, 37. This was the seminar's informal description of the four bead colors.

270 "eighty-two percent of the words": Ibid., 5.

270 "Our Father": Ibid., 148.

271 "Jesus did not advocate celibacy": Ibid., 220–21.

271 "a far better example": Luke Timothy Johnson, *The Real Jesus: The Misguided Quest for the Historical Jesus and the Truth of the Traditional Gospels* (New York: HarperSanFrancisco, 1996), 1.

271 "Americans love elections": Johnson, quoted in Goodstein, "R. W. Funk."

271 who once planned to synthesize: Stephen Goode, "Taking the Words out of his Mouth," *Insight Magazine*, October 3, 1994.

271 "party animal": Tom McNichol, "The Gospel Truth: Rejecting the Miracles as They Embrace the Message, Scholars Seek the Historic Jesus," *Los Angeles Times*, December 13, 1992.

271 "social deviant": Funk and the Jesus Seminar, *Acts of Jesus*, 33.

271 "perhaps the first stand-up Jewish comic": Jeffery L. Sheler, Mike Tharp, and Jill Jordan Seider, "In Search of Jesus," *U.S. News & World Report*, April 8, 1996.

271 "a new narrative of Jesus": Funk, "Jesus Seminar Opening Remarks."

271 "By the end of the day": Christine Shea, in King, *Forbidden Scriptures*.

271 "the Prophet of the Unknowable": Perry Kea, in King, *Karen L. King: The Gospel of Mary*.

271 King's prominent role: I became fully aware of it only while researching this book.

272 "the principal advocate": Robert W. Funk, "The Once and Future Jesus: The End of the Old, the Advent of the New," in Jesus Seminar, *Once and Future Jesus,* 9.

272 "It's only a matter of time": Ferde Rombola, letter to the editor, *Los Angeles Times,* March 22, 1995, articles.latimes.com.

272 "Christians," she wrote, "will better understand": King, "Letting Mary Magdalene Speak."

272 "What we need is a new fiction": Funk, "Jesus Seminar Opening Remarks."

273 "think the church ought": King, "Gospel of Mary" (Canon Seminar, 1997).

274 "she wanted to see": Chandler, interview by author, Proctor, Mont., April 28, 2017.

274 "Seeking experiences": Chandler, email to author, May 4, 2017.

274 chose her to organize: King, *Images of the Feminine in Gnosticism,* xviii.

274 "neglected to put the Gospel": King, "Thinking About Women and Heresy."

275 "have little or nothing in common": Funk, Hoover, and the Jesus Seminar, *Five Gospels,* 466.

275 But in 1998: Funk and the Jesus Seminar, *Acts of Jesus,* 478.

275 In a separate vote: Ibid., 479.

275 "after extended debate": Ibid., 478.

275 discounted as fully fictive: King, *Karen L. King: The Gospel of Mary.* "When the Jesus Seminar voted on the Gospel of Mary, they voted everything black," King told the California audience. "I was a little annoyed."

275 "The votes at the two meetings": McGaughy, email to author, August 7, 2018.

276 "That's all Karen King": Corley, phone interview by author, December 4, 2018.

276 "written early in the second century": King, *Gospel of Mary of Magdala,* 3.

276 This date was critical: "Her argument is that both were produced about the same time, 125 CE, and taken together reflect a raging gender war in the early church," Kenneth Woodward, *Newsweek*'s religion writer, wrote in 2003 (Woodward, "Quite Contrary Mary"). "But she does this by taking certain liberties with the dating of these two texts. No one knows when either was written, but some scholars put Timothy in the 90s CE, and some scholars put the Gospel of Mary in the late—not early—second century. King maximizes the dates of both, like bookends with nothing in between, for her purposes."

277 "We can now hear": King, "Difference and Diversity," 141.

277 "King says the Mary topics": Richard N. Ostling, "Harvard Professor Joins the Buzz About Mary Magdalene," Associated Press, December 30, 2003.

278 "Since Christianity was competing": Phipps, *Clerical Celibacy,* 86.

279 "I put some of these texts": King, "Thinking About Women and Heresy." In her April 2014 article for the *Harvard Theological Review,* King beat a sharp retreat from her public claims in 2012 about the text's being evidence for "a second century controversy over Jesus's marital status" (King, "'Jesus Said to Them, "My Wife…"'", September 18, 2012, public draft).

279 "the history of Christianity": "The History of Christianity" is the title of the longest chapter in King, *Gospel of Mary of Magdala,* 155.

279 "in a number of respects": Ibid., 190.

279 "It seems to me": King, *Images of the Feminine,* xvii.

279 "If women exercised legitimate": King, "Prophetic Power and Women's Authority," 32.

279 "Do we really want this?": Jeff Sharlet, "Battle Lines in the Jesus Wars," *Chronicle of Higher Education,* May 11, 2001.

280 "Her body doesn't count": King, "Thinking About Women and Heresy."

280 Still, he "resexualizes" her: King, *Gospel of Mary of Magdala: Westar Stars,* DVD.

280 "this move to see her": Jonathan Darman, "An Inconvenient Woman," with Anne Underwood, *Newsweek,* May 29, 2006.

280 "She was portrayed basically": Webb/Veale interview transcripts.

280 "If you ask me": King, *Karen L. King: The Gospel of Mary.*

281 "The general assessment": John Dart, "Sessions on Gnostic Texts Cool Feminist Scholars' Enthusiasm," *Los Angeles Times,* November 30, 1985.

281 "I wish she wouldn't do that": King, *Karen L. King: The Gospel of Mary.*

281 "Maybe they're sitting in somebody's drawer": Ibid.

282 "Once they're published": King, *Forbidden Scriptures.*

282 "The situation as it now stands": Choat, email to King and Luijendijk, September 26, 2012, provided to author by Choat.

282 "Prof. King": Pdf of one-page document titled "Permission to Reproduce and Publish," signed by "Walt Fritz," with a line above the signature stating, "Cambridge, MA, dated this 14th day of December 2011." Emailed to the author by Fritz on March 13, 2017. In our first interview (phone, August 28, 2012), King told me that Fritz did bring his own forms to Harvard, though in the end Harvard drew up its own.

283 "The true con artist": Maria Konnikova, *The Confidence Game: Why We Fall for It . . . Every Time* (New York: Viking, 2016), 6.

THE PRO AND THE CON

284 she told me the journal: King, interview by author, Somerville, Mass., September 4, 2012.

284 "I'm attaching here": David Royle and Charles Poe (Smithsonian Channel executives), phone interview by author, November 30, 2016; timeline given to the author by the Smithsonian Channel.

285 "Indeed, not only do I know": Bagnall, email to Studier, August 10, 2012, provided to the author by Bagnall.

285 "very strongly recommend": Bagnall, email to Studier, August 14, 2012, provided to author by Bagnall.

285 "in the course of the normal": King, "'Jesus Said to Them, "My Wife . . .'"" (September 18, 2012, public draft).

285 "They obviously ignored": Bagnall, phone interview by author, April 30, 2019.

286 A co-editor told me: Jon Levenson, interview by author, Newtonville, Mass., May 5, 2019.

286 If King knew that Bagnall: King didn't answer my question about whether she knew Bagnall was the one favorable reviewer (author's email and postal letter to King, September 4, 2019).

286 "Something smelled bad": Layton, phone interview by author, September 6, 2016.

288 "Clearly, I was wrong": Luijendijk, interview by author, Princeton University, March 3, 2017.

288 cherry-pick from at least three: Shisha-Halevy, email to author, February 19, 2017. He identified the dialects as Lycopolitan, Sahidic, and Nitrian Bohairic, with a fourth grammatical irregularity having "unclear distribution."

288 "remarkable," he told me: Shisha-Halevy, phone interview by author, February 17, 2017.

288 "problematic assumptions, interests, agendas": Bagnall, *Early Christian Books*, 1.

288 "betrayed . . . the original message": Ibid., 2–3.

288 "gruesome details": Ibid., 26.

288 "burlesque": Ibid., 48.

288 "horrifying object lesson": Ibid., 26.

288 Coptic, whose handwriting: In his book *Egypt in Late Antiquity,* Bagnall notes that Coptic handwriting experts, when confronted with new evidence, have been forced to revise the proposed dates of some papyri by two centuries or more (256).

289 "should take care that such datings": Bagnall, *Early Christian Books,* 49.

289 "just a drive-by shooting": Ibid., 31.

289 "You're talking to someone": Sabar, "Inside Story."

289 A.D. 350 to A.D. 400: "I'd be perfectly comfortable dating this between 350 and 400," Bagnall told the Smithsonian Channel's filmmakers in the summer of 2012. In an August 30, 2012, phone interview with this book's author, he cast A.D. 400 as a hard upper limit, saying, "Nobody could say this was part of the fifth century."

289 And he let TV cameras: Bagnall sat for a lengthy interview with the Smithsonian Channel, in the summer of 2012, at the Institute for the Study of the Ancient World.

289 Rome drew a hard line: The Edict of Thessalonica, issued by three Roman emperors in A.D. 380, made Nicene Christianity the law of the land. It established an official, enforceable line between "Catholic" Christians whose views aligned with the state's and the "foolish madmen" and "heretics" whose views did not.

289 "I do not think I could": Bagnall, email to author, August 2, 2017.

289 "I don't think so": Bagnall, interview by author, Columbia University, March 21, 2017.

290 "is one of the things": Sabar, "Gospel According to King."

290 "It's hard to construct a scenario": Goodstein, "Faded Piece of Papyrus."

290 "I don't know of": Goodstein, "Fresh Doubts."

290 "I haven't seen any argument": Wangsness, "Finding Adds to 'Jesus's Wife' Thesis."

290 "judged it to be authentic": King, "'Jesus Said to Them, "My Wife..."'" (September 18, 2012, public draft).

290 He had advised King to consult: "I wonder if it would be worth bringing someone like Malcolm Choat into this to help; I know the Coptic documentary material from this period tolerably well, but not so much the literary," Bagnall emailed King and Luijendijk on September 5, 2012, in response to King's plea for help after the unfavorable peer reviews. "Of course it's possible that the presentation at the congress in Rome will bring a lot of information out of the woodwork, but I suppose it would be nice to have a firmer view to present in advance of that."

290 "who find a brief fling": David Killick and Suzanne M. M. Young, "Archaeology and Archaeometry: From Casual Dating to a Meaningful Relationship?," *Antiquity* 71, no. 273 (September 1997): 520.

291 "There was a date": Lauren M. Marshall, email to author, April 4, 2017.

292 The scientists whose radiocarbon tests: Tuross and Hodgins published separate reports—each titled "Accelerated Mass Spectrometry Radiocarbon Determination of Papyrus Samples"—in the April 2014 issue of the *Harvard Theological Review*.

293 "The main thing was to see": Goodstein, "Papyrus Referring to Jesus' Wife."

293 "We found one anomalous": Joseph M. Azzarelli, John B. Goods, and Timothy M. Swager, "Study of Two Papyrus Fragments with Fourier Transform Infrared Microspectroscopy," *Harvard Theological Review* 107, no. 2 (April 2014): 165.

293 "orange 'spot' of possible contamination": Azzarelli, Goods, and Swager, "Study of Two" (full version): 19.

293 "Tim Swager": Helen Fenton, "Sheridan News," *Dillon (Mont.) Tribune-Examiner,* September 2, 1977, 5.

293 Tim's father, the town doctor: Warren and Carol Lee Swager (Tim's parents), phone interview by author, April 5, 2017.

294 "the infamous papyrus": Bagnall, email to Yardley, October 2, 2012. This and Yardley's reply, sent October 4, were provided to the author by Yardley.

295 "To be truthful": Yardley, interview by author, Columbia University, March 20, 2017.

296 "boring" a lab test: Bagnall, phone interview by author, April 30, 2019.

296 Swager did not respond: I emailed the questions to Swager and the two graduate students who worked on the study. I also sent them to Swager at his MIT lab by certified mail and at his home by first-class mail (May 2019). I received no responses.

296 X-ray fluorescence: Unlike the Raman technique, which identifies molecules, XRF detects atomic elements, which could potentially distinguish store-bought from homemade carbon blacks and make other fine-grained distinctions. Ira Rabin and Mary Kate Donais (archaeological scientists), emails to author, May 2019.

296 the orange substance: King, "'Jesus Said to Them, "My Wife...,"'" *Harvard Theological Review* 107, no. 2 (April 2014): 134. In a one-sentence footnote, King briskly states that the scientific instruments used to study the ink and papyrus failed to identify the mystery substance. Whether those instruments—and the scientists who used them—were right for such tests is unmentioned. Nor is the reason she sought no further testing.

296 isotope, which could be explained: Gregory Hodgins (University of Arizona scientist), phone interview by author, January 9, 2017. The levels of this isotope, carbon 13, a relative of carbon 14, were lower in the Wife papyrus than they were in every one of the more than forty papyri from different collections that Hodgins consulted.

296 "good scientists": Walton, phone interview by author, February 22, 2017.

296 "the scientific analysis was naïve": Marc Walton, "Pitfalls of Using Science to Authenticate Archaeological Artifacts," Northwestern University website, May 2, 2015, science forart.northwestern.edu.

297 "to declare any potential conflicts": Cambridge University Press, "Cambridge Journals Ethical Standards," Internet Archive Wayback Machine, May 24, 2013, capture, https://web.archive.org/web/20130524171154/http://journals.cambridge.org/action/stream?pageId=6728&level=2.

297   on the condition: The condition—that the reporters "contact no outside sources for comment beforehand" (Wangsness, "Finding Adds to 'Jesus's Wife' Thesis")—appeared to govern only the *Times* and *Globe* reporters' first stories about the testing, though neither publication later delved into any questions about the scientists or the science.

297   Her $5,000 gift: The Cirila Fund, U.S. Internal Revenue Service, Form 990-PF, Return of Private Foundation, 2012 (for tax year beginning July 1, 2012, and ending June 30, 2013).

297   "The Catholic Church's historical position": Tricia Nichols, "Attitudes Toward Women Antiquated," Mailbag, *Daily Pilot,* July 9, 2013, articles.dailypilot.com.

298   never publicly disclosed: In her *Harvard Theological Review* article, King identifies the funder only as Tricia Nichols, a common name. There is no mention of her location, her foundation (which gave the money), or any details that would allow readers to easily discern her identity, much less the political fight in which she was then engaged.

298   a representative told me: Marilyn Blank, phone interview by author, June 2, 2017.

298   questions about Nichols, the scientists: Author's emails and postal letter to King, September 4, 2019.

298   "The controversy over the Gospel": David Ratzan, "Dating Ancient Egyptian Papyri Through Raman Spectroscopy: Concept and Application to Fragments of the Gospel of Jesus's Wife and the Gospel of John" (paper presented with co-authors Sarah Goler and James T. Yardley at the annual conference of the Society of Biblical Literature, San Antonio, November 21, 2016).

299   "never intended to be a proper scientific": Yardley, interview by author, Columbia University, March 20, 2017.

299   King had cited them: King, "'Jesus Said to Them, "My Wife…,"'" *Harvard Theological Review* 107, no. 2 (April 2014): 135. She wrote that the "implication" of Yardley's study was the fragment "belongs" among ancient papyri.

299   even though Yardley had excluded them: James T. Yardley and Alexis Hagadorn, "Characterization of the Chemical Nature of the Black Ink in the Manuscript of the Gospel of Jesus's Wife Through Micro-Raman Spectroscopy," *Harvard Theological Review* 107, no. 2 (April 2014): 162–64.

299   on June 13, 2016: Meeting agenda and parts of presentation emailed to author by Yardley.

299   "The complication": Emails between Levenson and Depuydt, January 13, 2014, here and below, provided to the author by Depuydt.

301   In October 2006: The task force was conducting the first major review of Harvard's undergraduate curriculum since 1978. Its focus was general education—the set of classes, outside a major, that students must complete to earn a Harvard degree.

301   "Reason and Faith is a category": Harvard University Faculty of Arts and Sciences, *Preliminary Report: Task Force on General Education,* October 3, 2006, 18–21.

302   New York to New Delhi: Lois E. Beckett, "Gen Ed Draft Awaits Grade," *Harvard Crimson,* October 27, 2006.

302   "The juxtaposition of the two words": Steven Pinker, "Less Faith, More Reason," *Harvard Crimson,* October 27, 2006, www.thecrimson.com.

302   "If I was designing": Pinker, phone interview by author, June 10, 2019. Pinker said that like other faculty on the main campus he had "not a whole lot of knowledge of what's actually done at the divinity school."

303   "learned and articulate colleagues": Lois E. Beckett and Evan H. Jacobs, "'Reason and Faith' Requirement Scrapped," *Harvard Crimson,* December 12, 2006.

303   "dreading to leave an illiterate Ministery": *New England's First Fruits* (London: Henry Overton, 1643), 23–32.

303   "the School of the Prophets": Morison, *Three Centuries of Harvard,* 24.

303   "rustic woodlands": Ibid., 243.

304   "the curious consequence": Francis Greenwood Peabody, quoted in Williams and Petersen, *Divinings,* 2:42.

304   "a half-way house": Morison, *Three Centuries of Harvard,* 191.

304   "the serious, impartial and unbiased": *Foundations for a Learned Ministry: Catalogue of an Exhibition on the Occasion of the One Hundred Seventh-Fifth Anniversary of the Divinity*

School, Harvard University (Cambridge, Mass.: President and Fellows of Harvard College, 1992), 43.

304 "The soul knows no persons": Emerson was a visiting speaker. The address was regarded as a scandal, both outside and inside Harvard.

304 as old and "valuable": Helmut Koester, "Apocryphal and Canonical Gospels," *Harvard Theological Review* 73, no. 1–2 (April 1980): 130.

304 "write women back": Elisabeth Schüssler Fiorenza, *In Memory of Her: A Feminist Theological Reconstruction of Christian Origins* (New York: Crossroad, 1983), xvi.

305 "It would be false": Quoted in "The History of the Divinity School," *Harvard Alumni Bulletin,* November 9, 1916, 116.

305 Those rights reside: Only since 2014 or 2015 has the divinity school dean had more than a consulting role in the appointment of divinity faculty to the committee. (Email to author from former divinity school dean William Graham, September 19, 2019.)

305 "He considered the place": Bradley, *Harvard Rules,* 259.

306 a laurel he rarely: Author's phone interview with a former divinity school professor.

306 "fueling the theory that Summers": Bradley, *Harvard Rules,* 263–64. Graham told me that he had no plans to shrink or sideline the ministerial training program but did want to strengthen religious studies (phone interview, May 8, 2019). Other sources suggest Graham was the second dean, rather than the first, who wasn't clergy.

306 "The Divinity School is very much interested": Angela A. Sun, "Religion to Lose Two Top Profs," *Harvard Crimson,* May 3, 2007.

307 "Not only do we have": Harvard Divinity School, "A Conversation with Drew Gilpin Faust," YouTube, filmed on March 8, 2007, posted by Harvard Divinity School on May 30, 2014, www.youtube.com.

307 "depend on and reinforce": History and Mission, Harvard Divinity School website, Internet Archive Wayback Machine, August 11, 2011, capture, https://web.archive.org /web/20110811213357/https://hds.harvard.edu/about/history-and-mission. "Religious and theological studies depend on and reinforce each other" was the first of the new mission statement's "Guiding Principles." The school adopted the statement, in 2008, "to express the purpose of the School and the community's aspirations for the twenty-first century."

307 "in the study of religion": Amy Hollywood, "On Understanding Everything: General Education, Liberal Education, and the Study of Religion," *PMLA* 126, no. 2 (March 2011): 460–66.

307 "One need never say no": King, "Factions, Variety, Diversity, Multiplicity," 235.

307 "refuge" from the "nastiness": Matt Bieber, "The Perils of Lazy Pluralism (Should Harvard Divinity School Still Exist?)," *Matt Bieber* (blog), January 24, 2015, Internet Archive Wayback Machine, February 15, 2015, capture, https://web.archive.org /web/20150215094102/http://www.mattbieber.net:80/perils-lazy-pluralism-harvard -divinity-school-still-exist. The post drew angry, dissenting replies from some classmates.

308 "The Harvard faculty cannot cope": Lisa Miller, "Harvard's Crisis of Faith," *Newsweek,* February 22, 2010. Miller noted that just 33 undergrads decided to major in religion the previous year, compared with 704 in economics, 217 in history, and 45 in classics. "History and Literature," another boutique major without an official department, had 155 majors. The twenty-six-hundred-word article barely mentioned Harvard Divinity School, as if its role in the academic study of religion at the university were almost beneath notice.

FAUSTIAN BARGAIN

309 "two of the very best": Harvard Divinity School, "Two Scholars of American Religious History Appointed to HDS Faculty," news release, May 20, 2009, hds.harvard.edu.

309 "Her concern was genuine": Griffith, phone interview by author, June 22, 2017.

309 "the present configuration": Matthew M. Beck, "Divinity School Professor to Leave Harvard," *Harvard Crimson,* March 23, 2012. Jordan returned to Harvard in 2014, after deciding that conditions had improved.

309 In September, William Graham announced: Graham claimed not to be rattled by the faculty departures, which he described as routine for any academic institution, or by the bad press about the state of religious studies at Harvard. He told me he stepped down for a number of reasons: he wanted to return to writing and teaching; felt that a decade of big changes under sometimes trying circumstances was a "long and strenuous" enough tenure for a dean; and believed that a new dean should be in place ahead of a major new fundraising campaign. (Phone interview by author, May 8, 2019; and email to author, September 17, 2019.)

310 The six-member panel: The committee members were Carolyn Bynum (chair), Arnold Eisen, Jane McAuliffe, Richard Rosengarten, Barbara Savage, and Robert Sharf.

310 "my cover": Colleen Walsh, "'What the Hell—Why Don't I Just Go to Harvard and Turn My Life Upside Down?,'" *Harvard Gazette,* May 3, 2018.

311 "year of religion": Harvard Divinity School, "A Conversation with President Drew Faust and Dean David Hempton."

311 read aloud a letter: Author's phone interview with a panel member, who, like two other members interviewed, asked not to be named in order to discuss sensitive issues. Asked by author for a copy of the letter, Nasrallah said she "may have lost data in a laptop transfer" and didn't remember the letter. Nasrallah, email to author, May 13, 2019.

311 "Harvard, with its rich legacy": President's External Advisory Committee, *Report,* 3.

311 "The absence of a religious studies department": Ibid., 12. The panel weighed half measures—like a department run jointly by the Yard and the divinity school—but decided that would only inflame tensions. The best option, they wrote, was for the Faculty of Arts and Sciences to have sole control over the new department. FAS could hire new faculty or recruit from the divinity school, but the choice would be FAS's.

312 One was David Hempton: In a May 23, 2019, email to the author, a divinity school spokesperson said that Hempton recused himself from the committee once his name came up as a possibility for the deanship.

312 "Bringing together religious": Harvard Divinity School, "Harvard President Drew Faust Introduces David Hempton as New HDS Dean."

312 His appointment was a revanchist: Faust put Hempton in charge of convening an internal committee of Yard and divinity faculty "to develop a plan for potential ways forward." Faust, "Statement on the Report on the Study of Religion at Harvard."

312 "the respect and the admiration": Harvard Divinity School, "Conversation with President Drew Faust and Dean David Hempton."

313 What had begun as a plan: Author's interviews with members of Faust's external committee. At a divinity school event in April 2013, Faust said of the committee, "I thought it would be helpful if I had some outside eyes, who had not taken all Harvard's assumptions for granted, to just look at what was happening and give me some advice." Harvard Divinity School, "Conversation with President Drew Faust and Dean David Hempton."

313 "As if having": Francis X. Clooney, "A Harvard Catholic Perspective on 'Harvard's Crisis of Faith,'" *America,* February 20, 2010, www.americamagazine.org.

313 "The oldest professorship": Harvard Divinity School, "Harvard President Drew Faust Introduces David Hempton as New HDS Dean."

313 Hempton declined to speak with me: Harvard Divinity School spokespeople, emails to author, May 2019.

313 "The deans and I": Faust, "Statement on the Report on the Study of Religion at Harvard." Faust supported smaller reforms aimed at bringing more of the divinity school's offerings to undergraduates and to other of Harvard's professional schools.

314 "She feels that others": Katie Tiger (Faust's executive assistant), email to author, June 3, 2019. In a May 20, 2019, email to Tiger, I had written, "I'd love to chat with [Faust] about her decision-making on the committee's report, and about her own vision, at the time, for the future of religious studies at Harvard. Because some of the scholars I interviewed described personal meetings with Dr. Faust, I also wanted to fact-check their accounts with her for accuracy and context."

314 "I didn't believe it was authentic": Colen, "HDS Scholar Announces Existence of a New Early Christian Gospel from Egypt."

314 "This is not a career maker": Wangsness, "Hint of a Married Jesus."

314 On October 15, 2011: President's External Advisory Committee, *Report,* Appendix A: Religion Committee Announcement, 18–19.

316 "There had been a request": Pollard, phone interview by author, April 14, 2017.

316 And anyone who visited: Home page of the Harvard University website, Internet Archive Wayback Machine, September 19, 2012, capture, https://web.archive.org/web/20120919094131/http://www.harvard.edu/.

316 That same day: Faust, "Statement on the Report."

316 A few weeks before: Author's phone interview with source close to Harvard's Public Affairs and Communications office. A divinity school spokesman did not dispute the account.

317 It was the office's job: The sources requested anonymity to speak about a sensitive subject.

317 "The key question is": Joseph Kahn, "Work of Harvard's Faust Gets the PBS Treatment," *Boston Globe,* September 11, 2012.

317 "She is not available to comment on this": Katie Tiger (Faust's executive assistant), email to author, September 5, 2019. In emails to Tiger and Faust and in a certified letter to Faust, I had asked, among other things, whether Faust saw September 19, 2012—at the time a propitious and exciting day for the study of religion at Harvard—as in part a fitting moment for her own announcement of confidence in current leadership to advance the study of religion at Harvard.

318 "She didn't show her cards": Neill, phone interview by author, December 6, 2016.

318 "For me the study of religion": "Untold Stories of Christianity with Karen King," *Story in the Public Square,* Rhode Island PBS, February 5–10, 2019.

318 "engage in constructive critique": King, *What Is Gnosticism?,* 246–47.

318 "tradition uncomfortable": Kristin Ahlforth Winter, "Leap of Faith: Bible Scholar Examines the Growth of the Jesus Tradition," *Occidental Magazine* 17, no. 3 (Summer 1994): 28.

318 "one more perspective": King, "Honoring the Scholarship of Karen L. King" (panel presentation), Society of Biblical Literature annual conference, San Diego, November 24, 2019.

318 "To forge the world": Ibid. King's full quote: "Inclusion [of such diverse texts], then, is about working together, critically and constructively, to forge the world, in its becoming, making and remaking."

319 "I'm less interested": King, interview by author, Somerville, Mass., September 4, 2012.

319 "Our work": Funk, "Jesus Seminar Opening Remarks."

319 "The goal of the Canon Seminar": Jorge Aquino, "Jesus Seminar Next Takes Aim at New Testament," Religion News Service, *Salt Lake Tribune,* October 26, 1996.

319 "explicitly saw their work": Taussig, "New New Testament."

319 King was one of the first: Taussig, *New New Testament,* 513.

320 King no sooner joined: Ibid.

320 culling more than half: Ibid., 514–15.

320 "violated our date boundaries": Ibid., 516.

320 King then persuaded the full council: Taussig, "New New Testament."

320 After Taussig pointed out: Ibid. According to Taussig's *New New Testament* and the author's interview with the council member Celene Lillie (April 3, 2019), some scholars objected to Perpetua's late date and others to its violent content. Taussig did not respond to multiple interview requests.

320 King became visibly irritated: Though I briefly asked King about the Jesus Seminar in 2012, my *Smithsonian* magazine story focused on the papyrus discovery and did not mention the seminar.

320 leaving her longtime intellectual home: In the March–April 2006 issue of the Westar Institute publication *The Fourth R* (vol. 19, no. 2), Lane McGaughy, King's former University of Montana professor, who would become executive director of the Westar Institute, reflects on the Jesus Seminar's uncertain prospects after Funk's death.

321 "Steve Pinker is just the tip": Pinker told me he was unaware of Faust's advisory committee, which had not interviewed him.

321 "She had come around": Schmidt, phone interview by author, June 21, 2017.

321 Whether or not there was active coordination: Faust declined to answer my questions about her announcement's timing, the papyrus and the extent of any communications with Hempton or King.

321 Never in the newspaper's: Author's search of ProQuest database of *New York Times* stories from 1851 to 2012. The last time Harvard Divinity School had been the chief subject of any front-page *Times* story was a January 1954 article on a $1 million donation to the school by John D. Rockefeller Jr. The first front-page *Times* story to mention the school was an 1885 piece about the jail-cell suicide of a swindler who won admission to the school by forging recommendation letters. "A Book Thief's Death," *New York Times*, October 31, 1885.

EPILOGUE: SERVICES

323 "It is for such objects": Fredric Jameson, *Postmodernism, or, The Cultural Logic of Late Capitalism* (Durham, N.C.: Duke University Press, 2003), 18.

323 "evil deed": King, *Gospel of Mary of Magdala: Westar Stars*, DVD.

325 "the association between truth and chronology": King, *What Is Gnosticism?*, 228.

325 renounce the term "Gnostic": Ibid., 218–19. "The function of this discourse has remained unchanged: to represent the other," she writes. "In the end, I think the term 'Gnosticism' will most likely be abandoned."

325 "There was and is no such thing": Ibid., 1–2.

325 share a broadly similar worldview: Though she finds fault with their work, King details earlier scholars' taxonomies of this worldview. (See ibid., 62–63, 115–37.) She concedes that the term "gnosis" "was used broadly in antiquity" and that the term "Gnostic" was used by Clement of Alexandria, Irenaeus, Tertullian, and Plotinus.

325 identifying "the Gnostics": King, "Who Are the Gnostics?" and "What Is Gnosticism?"

325 Libraries, she noted: King, *What Is Gnosticism?*, 2.

325 "My purpose is preeminently ethical": Ibid., 245–46.

325 "Western construction": Ibid., 234–35.

326 a "crypto-theological" project: Burns, Skype interview by author, August 31, 2016.

327 "I've never been able to write": King, "Thinking About Women and Heresy."

327 "Who gets to say": King, *Karen L. King: The Gospel of Mary*.

327 "We need complexity": Gibson, "Bits the Bible Left Out," 42.

328 "historical information": Zipp, "Harvard Divinity Professor Karen King to Give Talk."

328 "all evidence possible": King, *Gospel of Mary of Magdala: Westar Stars*, DVD.

328 "an accurate view of history": King, "Letting Mary Magdalene Speak."

328 "the full data set": Gibson, "Bits the Bible Left Out," 42.

328 "One criterion for good history": King, "Letting Mary Magdalene Speak."

328 "bare facts": Gibson, "Bits the Bible Left Out," 40.

329 "What difference does it make": Ibid. The date of the interview comes from Gibson (email to author, January 28, 2019).

329 "Focus on whether it's a forgery": Bonnie K. Bennett, "'Gospel of Jesus' Wife' Researcher Says Frenzy Distracts from Larger Issues," *Harvard Crimson*, November 11, 2016.

329 "Fake but accurate": righteousreverenddynamite, online commenter, beneath ibid., www.thecrimson.com.

330 "Everybody thought I said": "Ancient Papyrus—Does It Matter if Jesus Was Married?"

330 "A lot of the controversy": Zipp, "Harvard Divinity Professor Karen King to Give Talk."

330 left even her own audiences confused: See, for instance, Jenna Neumann, "Harvard Professor Challenges Jesus' Celibacy," *College Fix*, April 12, 2013, www.thecollegefix.com.

331 "portrays the incarnate": King, "Place of the *Gospel of Philip*," 565–66.

331 "There's nothing particularly": King, *Karen L. King: The Gospel of Mary*.

331 the draft *Harvard Theological Review*: King, "'Jesus Said to Them, "My Wife..."'" (September 18, 2012, public draft).

331 The submission appeared to conflict: "Prospective Authors," *Harvard Theological Review* page on Harvard Divinity School website, Internet Archive Wayback Machine, March 18, 2013, capture, https://web.archive.org/web/20130318191858/http://www.hds.harvard.edu/faculty-research/research-publications/harvard-theological-review/prospective-authors; "Instructions for Contributors," *New Testament Studies* online, Internet Archive Wayback Machine, December 14, 2010, capture, https://web.archive.org/web/20101214141758/http://assets.cambridge.org:80/NTS/NTS_ifc.pdf. It wasn't until three months after she submitted the article to *NTS*—and only after it was peer-reviewed, revised, and accepted—that she informed *HTR* that it contained the Gospel of Philip material originally in her *HTR* article, according to dates supplied to the author by *NTS* editor John Barclay and by *HTR* co-editor Jon Levenson.

332 King never told him: "As far as I can remember," Barclay told me in a November 2, 2016, email, "she made no reference to the Gospel of Jesus' Wife either in the NTS article or in correspondence with me about it."

332 Cambridge University Press ethics policy: Cambridge University Press, "Cambridge Journals Ethical Standards," Internet Archive Wayback Machine, May 24, 2013, capture, https://web.archive.org/web/20130524171154/http://journals.cambridge.org/action/stream?pageId=6728&level=2. The press publishes both *HTR* and *NTS*.

332 "self-plagiarism": Cambridge University Press, *Publishing Ethics: Academic Research*, Version 2.0 (May 2019 update), Internet Archive Wayback Machine, July 2, 2019, capture, https://web.archive.org/web/20190702022203/https://www.cambridge.org/core/services/aop-file-manager/file/5b44807ace5b3fca09545 31e/CUP-Research-Publishing-Ethics-Guidelines-2019.pdf.

332 King did not respond: Author's emails and postal letter to King, September 4, 2019.

332 words for "companion" in Philip "could": King, "'Jesus Said to Them, "My Wife..."'" (September 18, 2012, public draft), 38.

332 "often do". King, "Place of the *Gospel of Philip*," 577.

332 "'his spouse'": Ibid.

332 because the footnotes, which exclusively cite: Ibid., n61; King, "'Jesus Said to Them, "My Wife..."'" (September 18, 2012, public draft), 38n91. In both articles, the footnote says, "Bart D. Ehrman translates the term *koinônos* as 'lover' in *Lost Scriptures: Books That Did Not Make It into the New Testament* (Oxford: Oxford University, 2003) 41."

332 The month before, Malcolm Choat: Choat emailed King and *HTR* his analysis of the Wife fragment's handwriting on January 3, 2013 (Choat email to author, March 23, 2018). King submitted her Gospel of Philip article to *NTS* on February 19, 2013 (John Barclay, email to author, November 1, 2016).

332 "of any period": Malcolm Choat, "*The Gospel of Jesus's Wife:* A Preliminary Paleographical Assessment," *Harvard Theological Review* 107, no. 2 (April 2014): 160–62. In papyrology, the term "literary" includes poems, narratives, plays, and scripture, among other texts produced for artistic or formal spiritual purposes. "Documentary" papyri include letters, business records, petitions, tax receipts, and the like.

333 "I think she was hoping": Luijendijk, interview by author, Princeton University, March 3, 2017. Of King's decision to strike her as a contributor, Luijendijk added, "I was okay with it.... We are still very good friends."

333 "marriage with Mary Magdalene": King, "'Jesus Said to Them, "My Wife..."'" *Harvard Theological Review* 107, no. 2 (April 2014): 150.

333 "no extant early Christian writing": King, "'Jesus Said to Them, "My Wife..."'" (September 18, 2012, public draft), 33.

333 "It was mentioned in *The Da Vinci Code*": Hugo Lundhaug, phone interview by author, October 31, 2016.

334 "put in writing": Hal Taussig, "The End of Christian Origins? Where to Turn at the Intersection of Subjectivity and Historical Craft," *Review of Biblical Literature* 13 (2011): 36. In this probing survey of the field of early Christian studies, Taussig, then a visiting professor at Union Theological Seminary in New York, diagnoses a broader crisis. "The Christian origins stage is littered with bombast, self-righteousness, and sleight of hand," he writes, alluding to scholarship across the ideological spectrum. "The epistemological challenges are so substantive and the resolve for advanced study fragile

enough that one wonders whether there is enough energy for much actual movement beyond the current blockage" (43–45). Taussig appears to have written the article before the meetings of his "New New Testament" council, meaning that his critique of King—a longtime friend he regards here as one of the field's "major role models"— predated their contretemps over the Diary of Perpetua and King's announcement of the Gospel of Jesus's Wife.

334 "For most people": Stephen J. Patterson, "Rome Is Burning," *SBL Forum* 3, no. 1 (January 2005): online, www.sbl-site.org.

335 "The paradox": Elisabeth Schüssler Fiorenza, *But She Said: Feminist Practices of Biblical Interpretation* (Boston: Beacon Press, 1992), 91, quoting the cinema studies scholar Barbara Creed.

335 "scientific-positivist": Elisabeth Schüssler Fiorenza, *The Book of Revelation: Justice and Judgment*, 2nd ed. (Minneapolis: Fortress Press, 1998), 205.

335 "The master's tools": Audre Lorde, *Sister Outsider: Essays and Speeches,* rev. ed. (Berkeley, Calif.: Crossing Press, 2007), 112.

335 overseas conference on biblical forgeries: The conference—"Fragments of an Unbelievable Past? Constructions of Provenance, Narratives of Forgery"—was held at the University of Agder, in Kristiansand, Norway, September 14–16, 2016.

337 Harvard's earliest seal: For a recent look at the history of the seal, see Corydon Ireland, "Seal of Approval," *The Harvard Gazette,* May 14, 2015, https://news.harvard.edu /gazette/.

SELECTED BIBLIOGRAPHY

Note: Many additional sources will be found only in the notes.

"Ancient Papyrus—Does It Matter if Jesus Was Married?" YouTube video of January 23, 2014, panel discussion with Bart Ehrman, Mark Jordan, and Karen King at the University of Nevada, Las Vegas. www.youtube.com.

Antistalinistische Aktion Berlin-Normannenstrasse. e.V. (ASTAK). "Protokoll 16/2." Typewritten minutes and transcript, dated February 15, 1992, of the February 12, 1992, meeting of the ASTAK board ("ASTAK-Vorstand"). Provided to the author in Berlin in June 2018 by former ASTAK board member, secretary and founder Heinz Meier.

Askeland, Christian. *John's Gospel: The Coptic Translations of Its Greek Text.* Berlin: De Gruyter, 2012.

———. "A Lycopolitan Forgery of John's Gospel." *New Testament Studies* 61, no. 3 (July 2015): 314–34.

Azzarelli, Joseph M., John B. Goods, and Timothy M. Swager. "Study of Two Papyrus Fragments with Fourier Transform Infrared Microspectroscopy." Full version of shortened *Harvard Theological Review* report, posted to Harvard's Gospel of Jesus's Wife website, April 2014. Internet Archive Wayback Machine, March 28, 2018, capture. https://web.archive.org/web/20180328233839/https://projects.iq.harvard.edu/files/gojw/files/swagergjwftirfinalreport.pdf.

Bagnall, Roger S. *Early Christian Books in Egypt.* Princeton, N.J.: Princeton University Press, 2009.

———. *Egypt in Late Antiquity.* Princeton, N.J.: Princeton University Press, 1993.

———. Papers, 1967–2001. Rare Book and Manuscript Library, Columbia University, New York.

———. *Reading Papyri, Writing Ancient History.* New York: Routledge, 1995.

———, ed. *The Oxford Handbook of Papyrology.* New York: Oxford University Press, 2009.

Bagnall, Roger S., and Raffaella Cribiore. "O. Florida inv. 21: An Amorous Triangle." *Chronique d'Égypte* 85, no. 169–70 (2010): 213–23.

Baigent, Michael, Richard Leigh, and Henry Lincoln. *Holy Blood, Holy Grail.* New York: Delacorte Press, 1982.

Bartlett, Tom. "The Lessons of Jesus' Wife." *Percolator* (blog). *Chronicle of Higher Education,* October 1, 2012. www.chronicle.com.

Bell, W. D. M. *The Wanderings of an Elephant Hunter.* London: "Country Life," 1923.

Berliner Kurier. "Sex-Skandal im Mielke-Museum: Pornofotos auf dem Sofa und in der Dusche." September 1, 1995. www.berliner-kurier.de.

Bernhard, Andrew. "The *Gospel of Jesus' Wife:* Textual Evidence of Modern Forgery." *New Testament Studies* 61, no. 3 (July 2015): 335–55.

———. "Postscript: A Final Note About the Origin of the *Gospel of Jesus' Wife.*" *New Testament Studies* 63, no. 2 (April 2017): 305–17.

Bonar, Samantha B. "High Stakes Marriage." Occidental College, online news, February 8, 2013. www.oxy.edu.

Bradley, Richard. *Harvard Rules: The Struggle for the Soul of the World's Most Powerful University.* New York: HarperCollins, 2005.

Brown, Dan. *The Da Vinci Code.* New York: Doubleday, 2003.

———. "First Witness Statement of Dan Brown." *Michael Baigent and Richard Leigh v. The Random House Group Ltd., HC04C03092.* High Court of Justice Chancery Division, Royal Courts of Justice, London, 2006.

Colen, B. D. "HDS Scholar Announces Existence of a New Early Christian Gospel from Egypt." Harvard News Office press release, September 18, 2012. Internet Archive Wayback Machine, September 20, 2012, capture. https://web.archive.org/web /20120920235247/http://www.hds.harvard.edu:80/news-events/articles/2012/09/16/hds -scholar-announces-existence-of-new-early-christian-gospel-from-egypt.

Depuydt, Leo. "The Alleged *Gospel of Jesus's Wife*: Assessment and Evaluation of Authenticity." *Harvard Theological Review* 107, no. 2 (April 2014): 172–89.

Emmel, Stephen. "The Codicology of the New Coptic (Lycopolitan) Gospel of John Fragment (and Its Relevance for Assessing the Genuineness of the Recently Published Coptic 'Gospel of Jesus' Wife' Fragment)." *Alin Suciu: Patristics, Apocrypha, Coptic Literature, and Manuscripts* (blog), initial publication, June 22, 2014. Revised, March 26, 2015. Internet Archive Wayback Machine, November 15, 2017, capture. https://web.archive .org/web/20171115171604/http://www.uni-muenster.de/imperia/md/content/iaek/_v /emmel-codicologyharvardjohn-2015-03-26.pdf.

Farrior, Mary-Evelyn. "Divorcing Mrs. Jesus." *College Hill Independent* (Providence, R.I.), October 5, 2012.

Faust, Drew Gilpin. "Statement on the Report on the Study of Religion at Harvard," September 19, 2012, Harvard University website, www.harvard.edu.

Fritz, Walter. "Bemerkungen zum Datierungsvermerk auf der Amarnatafel Kn 27." *Studien zur Altägyptischen Kultur* 18 (1991): 207–14.

Funk, Robert W. "Jesus Seminar Opening Remarks." Speech, Berkeley, Calif., March 21, 1985. Westar Institute. www.westarinstitute.org.

Funk, Robert W., Roy W. Hoover, and the Jesus Seminar. *The Five Gospels: What Did Jesus Really Say? The Search for the Authentic Words of Jesus.* 1993. San Francisco: HarperSanFrancisco, 1997.

Funk, Robert W., and the Jesus Seminar. *The Acts of Jesus: The Search for the Authentic Deeds of Jesus.* San Francisco: HarperSanFrancisco, 1998.

Gibson, Lydialyle. "The Bits the Bible Left Out: Karen King, Studying Early Texts, Plumbs Christianity's Origins." *Harvard Magazine,* November–December 2018.

Goodstein, Laurie. "Coptic Scholars Doubt and Hail a Reference to Jesus' Wife." *New York Times,* September 21, 2012, A14.

———. "A Faded Piece of Papyrus Refers to Jesus' Wife." *New York Times,* September 19, 2012, A1.

———. "Fresh Doubts Raised About Papyrus Scrap Known as 'Gospel of Jesus' Wife.'" *New York Times,* May 5, 2014, A17.

———. "Papyrus Referring to Jesus' Wife Is More Likely Ancient than Fake, Scientists Say." *New York Times,* April 10, 2014, A12.

The Gospel of Jesus's Wife (TV documentary). Directed by Andy Webb. London: A Blink Films / Treasures Investigations production in association with Smithsonian Channel, Shaw Media, Discovery Networks Europe, SBS-TV Australia, and Historia. The documentary was part of a series called—depending on the market—*Treasures Decoded* or *Secrets.* Premiered on the Smithsonian Channel, in the United States, on May 5, 2014; and on History Channel Canada on August 30, 2013. The cuts for the two channels are slightly different.

Harvard Divinity School. "A Conversation with President Drew Faust and Dean David Hempton." YouTube, filmed on April 5, 2013, posted to YouTube on May 6, 2013, www .youtube.com.

———. "Harvard President Drew Faust Introduces David Hempton as New HDS Dean." YouTube, filmed on March 30, 2012, posted to YouTube on April 24, 2014, www.you tube.com.

Harvard Magazine. "A New Gospel Revealed." September 18, 2012. harvardmagazine.com.

Haskins, Susan. *Mary Magdalen: Myth and Metaphor.* New York: Riverhead Books, 1995.

Hunter, James H. *The Mystery of Mar Saba.* Grand Rapids, Mich.: Zondervan, 1940.

Jeffery, Peter. *The Secret Gospel of Mark Unveiled: Imagined Rituals of Sex, Death, and Madness in a Biblical Forgery.* New Haven, Conn.: Yale University Press, 2007.

Jesus Seminar. *The Once and Future Jesus.* Santa Rosa, Calif.: Polebridge Press, 2000.

Jonas, Hans. *The Gnostic Religion: The Message of the Alien God and the Beginnings of Christianity.* 3rd ed. Boston: Beacon Press, 2001.

King, Karen L. "Beyond Orthodoxy and Heresy: Christian History in Light of Discoveries from the Egyptian Desert." Introductory essay for a never-published book called *A Reader's Guide to the Nag Hammadi Library,* presented at a spring 1996 Jesus Seminar/ Westar Institute meeting.

———. "The Body and Society in Philo and the Apocryphon of John." In *The School of Moses: Studies in Philo and Hellenistic Religion: In Memory of Horst R. Moehring.* Edited by John Kenney. Atlanta: Scholars Press, 1995.

———. "Candidate's Application." International Christian Youth Exchange, December 9, 1970. Series 13, box, 4, International Christian Youth Exchange/Volunteers Exchange International, Brethren Historical Library and Archives, Church of the Brethren, Elgin, Ill.

———. "Canonization and Marginalization: Mary of Magdala." In *Women's Sacred Scriptures.* Edited by Kwok Pui-lan and Elisabeth Schüssler Fiorenza. London: SCM Press, 1998.

———. "Christianity Without a Canon." Unpublished paper for the Jesus Seminar, New Orleans, November 23, 1996.

———. "Difference and Diversity: Writing the History of Ancient Christianity." In *Complexity: Interdisciplinary Communications,* 2006/2007. Edited by Willy Østreng, Oslo: Centre for Advanced Study at the Norwegian Academy of Science and Letters, 2008.

———. "Factions, Variety, Diversity, Multiplicity: Representing Early Christian Differences for the 21st Century." *Method and Theory in the Study of Religion* 23, no. 3–4 (2011): 216–37.

———. *Forbidden Scriptures: Early Christianity and the Nag Hammadi Texts.* DVD. Sonoma, Calif.: Polebridge Press, 1996.

———. "The Gospel of Mary." In *The Nag Hammadi Library in English.* 3rd ed. Edited by James M. Robinson. San Francisco: Harper & Row, 1988.

———. "The Gospel of Mary." Unpublished paper for the Canon Seminar of the Jesus Seminar, Santa Rosa, Calif., March 1997.

———. "The Gospel of Mary of Magdala." *Fourth R* 16, no. 5 (September–October 2003): 3–8.

———. *The Gospel of Mary of Magdala: Jesus and the First Woman Apostle.* Salem, Ore.: Polebridge Press, 2003.

———. *The Gospel of Mary of Magdala: Westar Stars on Broadway.* DVD. Santa Rosa, Calif.: Polebridge Press, 2004.

———. "'Jesus Said to Them, "My Wife …"'": A New Coptic Papyrus Fragment." *Harvard Theological Review* 107, no. 2 (April 2014): 131–59.

———. *Karen L. King: The Gospel of Mary.* DVD. Santa Rosa, Calif.: Westar Institute, 2003.

———. "Letting Mary Magdalene Speak." *Beliefnet* (2003). www.beliefnet.com.

———. "The Place of the *Gospel of Philip* in the Context of Early Christian Claims About Jesus' Marital Status." *New Testament Studies* 59, no. 4 (October 2013): 565–87.

———. "Prophetic Power and Women's Authority: The Case of the Gospel of Mary (Magdalene)." In *Women Preachers and Prophets Through Two Millennia of Christianity.* Edited by Beverly Mayne Kienzle and Pamela J. Walker. Berkeley: University of California Press, 1998.

———. "Reading Sex and Gender in the Secret Revelation of John." *Journal of Early Christian Studies* 19, no. 4 (Winter 2011): 519–38.

———. "Remembering Robert Funk." *Fourth R* 19, no. 2 (March–April 2006): 3, 20.

———. "Response." *Journal of Feminist Studies in Religion* 22, no. 2 (Fall 2006): 145–47.

———. "Response to Leo Depuydt, 'The Alleged *Gospel of Jesus's Wife:* Assessment and Evaluation of Authenticity.'" *Harvard Theological Review* 107, no. 2 (April 2014): 190–93.

———. *Revelation of the Unknowable God: with Text, Translation, and Notes to NHC XI, 3, Allogenes.* Santa Rosa, Calif.: Polebridge Press, 1996.

————. "Ridicule and Rape, Rule and Rebellion: The Hypostasis of the Archons." In *Gnosticism & the Early Christian World: In Honor of James M. Robinson.* Edited by James E. Goehring et al. Sonoma, Calif.: Polebridge Press, 1990.

————. *The Secret Revelation of John.* Cambridge, Mass.: Harvard University Press, 2006.

————. "Thinking About Women and Heresy." YouTube. Filmed on May 1, 2006, posted by Harvard Divinity School on June 2, 2014. www.youtube.com.

————. "Translating History: Reframing Gnosticism in Postmodernity." In *Tradition und Translation: Zum Problem der interkulturellen Übersetzbarkeit religiöser Phänomene: Festschrift für Carsten Colpe zum 65. Geburtstag.* Edited by Christoph Elsas. Berlin: De Gruyter, 1994.

————. *What Is Gnosticism?* Cambridge, Mass.: Belknap Press of Harvard University Press, 2003.

————. "What Is Gnosticism?" *Fourth R* 4, no. 3 (May 1991): 1–6.

————. "Who Are the Gnostics?" *Fourth R* 4, no. 4 (July 1991): 14–16.

————, ed. *Images of the Feminine in Gnosticism.* Harrisburg, Pa.: Trinity Press International, 2000. First published in 1988, by Fortress Press.

King, Karen L., with contributions by AnneMarie Luijendijk. "'Jesus Said to Them, "My Wife…"': A New Coptic Gospel Papyrus."
——August 10, 2012, draft, the first submitted to *Harvard Theological Review,* provided to author by a source, forty pages.
——August 23, 2012, draft, provided to author by King, forty pages.
——September 13, 2012, draft, provided to author by King, and, evidently, to reporters for *The New York Times* and *The Boston Globe,* fifty-two pages.
——September 18, 2012, public draft, posted to the news pages of Harvard Divinity School website the day King announced the papyrus, fifty-two pages. Internet Archive Wayback Machine, September 21, 2012, capture. https://web.archive.org/web/20120921154949/http://news.hds.harvard.edu/files/King_JesusSaidTo Them_draft_0917.pdf. The article's footer says "Forthcoming Harvard Theological Review 106:1, January 2013," but the journal delayed publication until April 2014. For nineteen months, the September 2012 draft constituted the only published—or electronically published—version of the article.

Leighton, Marian K. "Strange Bedfellows: The *Stasi* and the Terrorists." *International Journal of Intelligence and CounterIntelligence* 27, no. 4 (2014): 647–65.

Lewis, Nicola Denzey. *Introduction to "Gnosticism": Ancient Voices, Christian Worlds.* Oxford: Oxford University Press, 2013.

Lindsey, Robert. "Dealer in Mormon Fraud Called a Master Forger." *New York Times,* February 11, 1987.

Morison, Samuel Eliot. *Three Centuries of Harvard, 1636–1936.* Cambridge, Mass.: Harvard University Press, 1936.

Moss, Candida R., and Joel S. Baden. *Bible Nation: The United States of Hobby Lobby.* Princeton, N.J.: Princeton University Press, 2017.

Murphy, Cullen. *The Word According to Eve: Women and the Bible in Ancient Times and Our Own.* Boston: Houghton Mifflin, 1998.

Nongbri, Brent. *God's Library: The Archaeology of the Earliest Christian Manuscripts.* New Haven, Conn.: Yale University Press, 2018.

Pagels, Elaine. *The Gnostic Gospels.* New York: Random House, 1979.

Petrey, Taylor G., ed. *Re-Making the World: Christianity and Categories: Essays in Honor of Karen L. King.* Tübingen: Mohr Siebeck, 2019.

Phipps, William E. *Clerical Celibacy: The Heritage.* New York: Continuum, 2004.

"Portrait of an Author: Karen L. King." *Fourth R* 4, no. 4 (July 1991).

President's External Advisory Committee on the Study of Religion at Harvard. *Report of the President's External Advisory Committee.* Submitted by the committee in June 2012, released by Harvard's president, Drew Faust, on September 19, 2012. Harvard University website. Internet Archive Wayback Machine, January 2, 2013, capture. https://web.archive.org/web/20130102175850/http://www.harvard.edu/sites/default/files/content/Statement_on_Religion_Report_09192012.pdf.

Sabar, Ariel. "The Gospel According to King." *Smithsonian* (print and web), November 2012. The story's web headline was "UPDATE: The Reaction to Karen King's Gospel Discovery." www.smithsonianmag.com.

———. "The Inside Story of a Controversial New Text About Jesus." *Smithsonian* (web only), September 18, 2012. www.smithsonianmag.com.

———. "Karen King Responds to 'The Unbelievable Tale of Jesus's Wife.'" *The Atlantic* (web only), June 16, 2016. www.theatlantic.com.

———. "The Unbelievable Tale of Jesus's Wife." *The Atlantic,* on the web June 15, 2016, in print in the July/August 2016 issue. www.theatlantic.com.

Schenke Robinson, Gesine. "How a Papyrus Fragment Became a Sensation." *New Testament Studies* 61, no. 3 (July 2015): 379–94.

Schmidt, Carl. "Ein vorirenaeisches gnostisches Originalwerk in koptischer Sprache." In *Sitzungsberichte der Königlich Preussischen Akademie der Wissenschaften zu Berlin.* Berlin: Verlag der Königlichen Akademie der Wissenschaften, 1896.

Šeper, Franjo. "*Inter Insigniores:* On the Question of Admission of Women to the Ministerial Priesthood." Declaration, presented to and approved by Pope Paul VI, Rome, October 15, 1976. www.vatican.va.

Smith, Morton. *The Secret Gospel: The Discovery and Interpretation of the Secret Gospel According to Mark.* 1973. Middletown, Calif.: Dawn Horse Press, 2005.

Taussig, Hal. *A New New Testament: A Bible for the 21st Century Combining Traditional and Newly Discovered Texts.* New York: Houghton Mifflin Harcourt, 2013.

Taussig, Hal, interviewee. "A New New Testament: A Bible for the 21st Century Combining Traditional and Newly Discovered Texts." *Fourth R* 26, no. 5 (September–October 2013). www.westarinstitute.org.

Thompson, Herbert, ed. and trans. *The Gospel of St. John According to the Earliest Coptic Manuscript.* London: British School of Archaeology in Egypt and Bernard Quaritch, 1924.

Wangsness, Lisa. "The Case of the Gospel of Jesus's Wife Still Isn't Closed." *Boston Globe,* November 29, 2015.

———. "Finding Adds to 'Jesus's Wife' Thesis: Papyrus Tests Detect No Modern Forgery." *Boston Globe,* April 10, 2014.

———. "Harvard Divinity Professor Relishes Adventure: Jesus Finding Put Scholar in Spotlight." *Boston Globe,* November 11, 2012.

———. "Hint of a Married Jesus: Harvard Historian's Finding May Bear on Modern Christianity." *Boston Globe,* September 19, 2012.

———. "'Jesus's Wife' Scholar Now Says Papyrus Is Likely Fake." *Boston Globe,* June 18, 2016.

———. "Scholars Begin to Weigh In on 'Gospel of Jesus's Wife.'" *Boston Globe,* September 27, 2012.

Webb, Andy, and Hannah Veale. Complete, unpublished transcripts of filmed summer 2012 interviews with Karen King, AnneMarie Luijendijk, and Roger Bagnall, for Blink Films / Smithsonian Channel documentary on the Gospel of Jesus's Wife. Provided to the author by Webb.

WGBH News. "Greater Boston Video: Harvard Scholar Researching Ancient Reference to Jesus's Wife." YouTube, April 16, 2014. www.youtube.com.

Williams, George Huntston, ed. *The Harvard Divinity School: Its Place in Harvard University and in American Culture.* Boston: Beacon Press, 1954.

Williams, George Huntston, and Rodney L. Petersen. *Divinings: Religion at Harvard: From Its Origins in New England Ecclesiastical History to the 175th Anniversary of the Harvard Divinity School, 1636–1992.* Vols. 1–3. 2nd rev. ed. Göttingen: Vandenhoeck & Ruprecht, 2014.

Woodward, Kenneth. "A Quite Contrary Mary." *Beliefnet* (2003). www.beliefnet.com.

Yardley, James T., and Alexis Hagadorn. "Report: Ink Study of Two Ancient Fragments Through Micro-Raman Spectroscopy." Full version of shortened *Harvard Theological Review* report. Posted to Harvard's Gospel of Jesus's Wife website, April 2014. Internet Archive Wayback Machine, March 28, 2018, capture, https://web.archive.org/web/20180328233154/http://projects.iq.harvard.edu/files/gojw/files/yardleyharvardfragmentreportrev07.pdf.

Zipp, Yvonne. "Harvard Divinity Professor Karen King to Give Talk, 'Was Jesus Married?' at Kalamazoo College in April." *Kalamazoo Gazette,* April 4, 2013.

INDEX

ILLUSTRATION CREDITS

Page 1   MS Coptic 11, Houghton Library, Harvard University
Page 2   (top) Bill Greene/*Boston Globe*/Getty; (bottom) Caren Huygelen fotografie + film
Page 3   (top) Redux; (bottom) AP/Gregorio Borgia
Page 4   (top) Hadnagy Photography; (bottom) Courtesy of Occidental College Library
          Special Collections and College Archives
Page 5   (top) Sarah La Du Photography; (bottom) Ariel Sabar
Page 6   (top) Ariel Sabar; (bottom) MS Coptic 12, Houghton Library, Harvard University
Page 7   (top) Walter Fritz; (bottom) Courtesy of Christian E. Loeben
Page 8   (top) Courtesy of Christian E. Loeben; (bottom) Ariel Sabar
Page 9   (top) Courtesy of Siegmar Götz; (bottom) Ulrike Dubiel
Page 10   Courtesy of Christian E. Loeben
Page 11   (top) Courtesy of Kim Ryholt; (bottom) *Stern*
Page 12   Lisette Poole

A NOTE ABOUT THE AUTHOR

ARIEL SABAR is an award-winning journalist whose work has appeared in *The Atlantic, The New York Times, Harper's Magazine, The Washington Post,* and many other publications. He is the author of *My Father's Paradise: A Son's Search for His Jewish Past in Kurdish Iraq,* which won the National Book Critics Circle Award.